COAST TO COAST RAVES FOR
THE SEARING, BEHIND-THE-SCENES
STORY OF TV'S MOST CONTROVER-
SIAL JOURNALIST!

"He is true to his John Wayne-of-the-news persona..."

—SACRAMENTO BEE

"Brisk, informative, bound to win many readers."

—PUBLISHERS WEEKLY

"Highly recommended!"

—LIBRARY JOURNAL

"Hot."

—Liz Smith, NEW YORK DAILY NEWS

CLOSE ENCOUNTERS

**Mike Wallace &
Gary Paul Gates**

BERKLEY BOOKS, NEW YORK

CLOSE ENCOUNTERS

A Berkley Book / published by arrangement with
William Morrow & Company, Inc.

PRINTING HISTORY
William Morrow edition published 1984
Berkley edition / October 1985

ISBN: 0-425-08269-5

A BERKLEY BOOK ® TM 757,375
Berkley Books are published by The Berkley Publishing Group,
200 Madison Avenue, New York, New York 10016.
The name "BERKLEY" and the stylized "B" with design are
trademarks belonging to Berkley Publishing Corporation.
PRINTED IN THE UNITED STATES OF AMERICA

FOREWORD

It was half a dozen years ago that the notion of doing this book first took root. And in that time I've changed my mind half a dozen times about whether—and how—to put it together. Simply writing it, of course, would have been the most obvious way. That is, writing it myself. But at the beginning, because I wasn't sure I'd have time for the task, I worked with a young ghost writer named Neil Offen. We had long conversations, taping sessions, followed by months of waiting for the product of those encounters. Neil and I became good friends, but somewhere along the way we agreed that it wasn't going to work out.

So the following summer I settled down to have a go at it myself, and by the time I quit I had put fifty thousand words to paper. But then I had to go back to work on *60 Minutes,* and the fact is that the rigors of doing twenty-five or thirty film pieces a year for that broadcast soaked up just about all available psychic energy and made it impossible (at least for me) to work up the requisite ardor that such an additional undertaking required. At that point, I felt I had no choice but to abandon the project, or at least put it off until a time when the ticking stopwatch of *60 Minutes* was no longer serving as the insistent alarm clock that governs most of my working life.

But my agent, Bill Adler, who must bear the responsibility for inducing me to do this book, was determined to keep the venture alive, and when Bill has his mind set on something he is a very persuasive fellow. This warm and resourceful man has been a close friend of mine since the middle 1950s, when we worked together at Channel 5 in New York. In later years, after he turned his attention to the vagaries of publishing, Adler helped to nurture books out of Dan Rather, Howard Cosell, and Phil Donahue (as well as others), and he promised to get me the help I needed to see this book through to completion. He suggested that I try teaming up with another writer, Gary Paul Gates.

That prospect appealed to me, mainly because of Gary's credentials. He had worked as a writer at CBS News in the early 1970s, and so he knew the territory and many in the cast of characters. Moreover, he had collaborated with Dan Rather on *The Palace Guard,* a book about the Nixon White House, and he went on from there to write *Air Time,* a first-rate, behind-the-scenes account of the growth and evolution of television journalism at CBS. Bill and I were able to persuade Gates to throw in his lot with us, and not long after we began working together, we came up with a plan to give the book a rather unorthodox, two-voice structure. What has finally emerged three years later are the alternating chapters of those two voices: Gates's third-person history and reporting, juxtaposed with my first-person recollections and gut reactions to the events and experiences I've encountered across the years.

We had valuable help along the way. From start to finish, Gary and I were assisted by the solid research of my former *60 Minutes* associate, Mignette Hollyman. Then, as the manuscript began to take shape, we greatly benefited from the guidance and skill of our editor, Bruce Lee, and our copy editor, Sonia Greenbaum.

What you are about to embark on is the story of one mostly lucky man's encounters with growing up professionally. As you'll discover, I've gotten into some scrapes, and I've learned something about myself and others. I've met a few of the mighty and nearly mighty and many of the not so mighty along the way and have had a mostly satisfying if occasionally unsettling time doing it. And I have come to understand, in the process of getting all this down on paper, that a reporter's life is probably as stimulating and arguably as useful as any professional life I can imagine. But, of course, that is just one man's opinion. You'll have to judge for yourself.

—MIKE WALLACE

May 1984

CONTENTS

CHAPTER

ONE

IN THE FALL OF 1985, Mike Wallace observed his seventeenth anniversary as a correspondent on *60 Minutes*, the most successful news program in the history of television. Moreover, he has the distinction of being the only correspondent who had appeared on that showcase broadcast, year in and year out, since its inception. But in 1968, when he embarked on the long-running adventure of *60 Minutes*, Wallace had already established an enviable reputation. At that time, he was primarily known as the man who, more than a decade earlier, had pioneered what was to become his special trademark: the candid and penetrating television interview. In other words, it didn't start with *60 Minutes*, even though there now exists an entire generation of viewers who have seen Wallace in action only during this latter phase of his career. They have no memory of an earlier television era, the 1950s, when Mike Wallace first unveiled his singular brand of browbeating charm.

That is their misfortune. For the tone and style that Wallace introduced back then, in the Ike Age, broke new ground in television and became the enduring model for so much that has followed. The characteristics of that style—thorough preparation, quick, hard intelligence and insistent probing to get at the face behind the mask, the elusive truth behind the nervous evasion—are, of course, most clearly manifest in the later work of Wallace himself on *60 Minutes*. But that is hardly the extent of it. For each time a Ted Koppel or a Barbara Walters or a

Phil Donahue (to name some others who have been extolled for their skills as television interviewers) zeroes in with the kind of question that, when the chemistry is right, can transform a mere interview into a compelling and revealing psychodrama—on those occasions, it is easy to recognize the strong stamp of the Wallace influence. Even those who have adopted a less combative, more cerebral approach—such as Bill Moyers and William F. Buckley—have reason to be indebted to Wallace who, when the mood suits him, can be just as effective with the velvet glove as he is with the iron fist.

The Wallace technique was born on a program called *Night Beat*, a modest little show that was seen only by viewers in New York City and its environs. It was on *Night Beat* that Mike Wallace found his métier and, to a great extent, his public identity. Discovering that identity had not been easy, for Wallace was not exactly a youngster when *Night Beat* made its debut in the fall of 1956. At the time, he was thirty-eight years old and had seventeen years of broadcasting experience behind him. What's more, there was almost nothing in that background that could be cited as an omen or early-warning signal of the explosion that Wallace set off with his face-to-face interviews—close encounters of a new and special kind—on *Night Beat*.

The long road of *Night Beat* began in the Boston suburb of Brookline. The son of Russian-Jewish immigrants, Myron Leon Wallace was born and raised in a community that seems, in retrospect, to have been a hotbed for overachievers. In addition to Wallace himself, Brookline spawned such contemporaries as the once and future prince, John F. Kennedy, Leonard Bernstein, David Susskind, Arlene Francis and—a few years later— Barbara Walters. (*Many* years later, when Wallace did a *60 Minutes* profile on Leonard Bernstein, one of his producers suggested, not altogether in jest, that the piece should have been titled "Two Boys from Brookline.")

The sole blight on an otherwise happy childhood and adolescence was a severe case of acne that first hit him when he was in high school. The disfigurement and the painful sensitivity that came with it persisted well into his early manhood, leaving scars that, in later years, would inspire TV critics to observe that Wallace's "pockmarked, prizefighter's face" served to enhance the abrasive tone of his interviews.

From Brookline, Mike went to the University of Michigan where his early intention was to major in English and pursue a career in teaching or, perhaps, the law. But one day, midway through his sophomore year, he wandered into Morris Hall, the university's broadcast center. Like Yossarian's response to the chaplain in Joseph Heller's *Catch-22*, it was love at first sight. The major in English was quickly scrapped in favor of Speech and Broadcasting. The guiding force behind Morris Hall was an austere, patrician professor named Waldo Abbot, who became Wallace's first mentor in what was to become his life's work. (And the studio engineer, incidentally, was Jerome Wiesner, who would go on to become the president of MIT.) Professor Abbot not only tutored Mike in the fundamentals of broadcasting, but he also helped him land an announcer's job, at a small station in Grand Rapids, following his graduation in 1939.

The world of professional broadcasting that Wallace entered in the summer of 1939 was as far removed from the power and glamour of a big network production like *60 Minutes* as the old propeller airplane was from the spaceships that later transported men to the moon. In the first place, all the action was confined to the older medium—radio. Television was then nothing more than a primitive experiment, and there were many who believed that it could never succeed as a commercial venture. After all, went the argument, the folks at home could listen to the radio while they were cleaning the house or getting ready to leave for work, but how could they be induced to sit still for hours at a time and watch things happen on television?

Even more to the point, the tradition of broadcast journalism had not yet been clearly established. The networks and local stations did offer newscasts at various intervals, but they were largely "rip-and-read" operations. (That is, the announcers would "rip" copy off the wire-service machines and "read" the news items, usually verbatim, that had been prepared by rewrite men from the United Press and the Associated Press.) Very few stations in those days employed full-time reporters who went out into the street to cover stories themselves. The big breakthrough in that area was then just starting to take shape in Europe, where Edward R. Murrow was recruiting a talented corps of young wire-service reporters—such as Eric Sevareid, Charles Collingwood and Howard K. Smith—who, along with Murrow himself, would transmit vivid, on-the-scene accounts of critical events in World War II to the CBS radio stations back home. But that great pioneering effort, a milestone in the history of broadcasting, had little impact or influence on a young man like Wallace who, fresh out of college, was starting his career at a small station in a placid city in the heart of the Midwest, a region then still rooted in the isolationist view that the impending war in Europe would not impinge on the security of Fortress America.

Although the station in Grand Rapids, WOOD, hired Mike as an announcer, he was soon given a chance to try his hand at other on-air assignments: news, community affairs, quiz shows and, needless to say, commercials. In fact, that was the start of a jack-of-all-trades pattern that would characterize his work over the next decade and a half.

After just nine months in Grand Rapids, Wallace moved on to a far more ambitious station in a larger city—WXYZ in Detroit—and it was from there that his voice was first heard by a national audience. At the time, WXYZ was a fairly big deal in network radio. Some of the most popular programs of that era were broadcast coast-to-coast from the Detroit station, including such legendary serials as *The Green Hornet* and *The Lone Ranger*. Wallace soon found himself involved in all of them in some capacity or other: announcer, narrator and sometimes actor. (". . . the thundering hoofbeats of the great horse, Silver, the Lone Ranger rides again!")

He also broadcast the news at WXYZ, an assignment that entitled him to be designated a "Cunningham News Ace." Cunningham, a local drugstore chain, sponsored five-minute newscasts which began with the recorded sound of a fighter plane at full throttle—"Rrrrrrr . . ."—blaring over the air waves, after which the announcer would proclaim in appropriately stentorian tones: "The Cunningham News Ace is on the air!" At which point, if he happened to be the Ace on duty for that particular segment, Wallace would read the news items that had been furnished by the wire services.

One of Mike's co-workers at WXYZ—a fellow News Ace—was a young southerner named Douglas Edwards. For both Edwards and Wallace, Detroit was merely a way station en route to the big time. Each of them would go on to become a major correspondent at CBS News. In fact, within two years after their paths crossed at WXYZ, Edwards was working for the CBS network in New York; and by that time, Wallace also was cultivating greener pastures—in Chicago.

Mike made the jump to Chicago in 1941 and for the next decade that was his home base, save for a two-year hitch as a naval officer in the Pacific during World War II. (Trained as a communications officer, he served on a submarine tender on the west coast of Australia and later in the Philippines.) In Chicago, both before and after his stint in the Navy, Wallace bounced around a great deal, from station to station and one job to another. He was still exploring all avenues of radio programming, from news and public affairs to soap operas and panel shows. But his best work, in terms of establishing a beginner's credentials in journalism, was on a program called *The Air Edition of the Chicago Sun*. Until then he had been nothing more than a reader of newscasts, a voice transmitting copy that had been assembled and written by others. But in his job on *Air Edition*, he came under the guidance of a first-rate editor, Clifton Utley, who encouraged Mike to develop his own reporting and writing skills.

It was also during his years in Chicago that Wallace discovered how much he enjoyed the parry and riposte of interviewing. He began to sense, with growing confidence, that he had an aptitude for that kind of spontaneous, on-the-spot reporting. His first big opportunity to demonstrate that skill on a regular basis came in 1946 shortly after his discharge from the Navy. Walgreen's, the drugstore company, had decided to sponsor an interview program called *Famous Names* on WGN, one of Chicago's most powerful stations, and Mike was hired to do the interviewing. *Famous Names*, which was broadcast live five afternoons a week out of the Balinese Room of the Blackstone Hotel, was basically a frivolous enterprise, a puff-and-patter exchange with show-business celebrities who were in Chicago to plug their latest play or movie or nightclub act.

As such, it bore little resemblance to the hard-hitting interviews that would make Wallace's own name famous in years to come. But it was a start, and there was one particular interview on *Famous Names* that brought Mike to a crossroad in both his personal and professional life.

Before leaving Detroit, Mike had married Norma Kaphan, whom he had met and courted when they were students together at the University of Michigan. They had two children, Peter and Christopher. But by 1947 the marriage was on the rocks, and it was at that vulnerable point in his life that an attractive actress, Buff Cobb, walked into the Balinese Room to be interviewed on *Famous Names*.

Buff Cobb, the granddaughter of humorist Irvin S. Cobb, had come to town in the Noël Coward play *Private Lives*. What aroused Mike's curiosity, however, was not that theatrical venture so much as her *own* private life. In preparing for the interview, he read that Miss Cobb had married Hollywood attorney Greg Bautzer when she was seventeen and, at twenty-one, had divorced him to marry an actor, William Eythe. Mike couldn't wait to ask her about all *that*. Of course, he had no way of knowing then that he was destined to become husband number three. In other words, that interview eventually led to marriage, which, in turn, led to their working together on the air as an interview team.

That last wrinkle was Mike's idea and he was able to sell it to WMAQ, the local NBC station, even though Buff had no experience in radio and had never interviewed anyone in any medium. Mike and Buff were hired to co-host a new nightly interview program, *The Chez Show,* so called because it was broadcast live from the lounge of the Chez Paree, Chicago's most popular nightclub in those days. Determined to make the new show a success, Mike subjected Buff to a rigorous crash course in the art of the interview. He would offer a few general suggestions and then suddenly snap at her: "I'm Betty Grable, ask me ten questions!" Or "I'm Jack Benny, ask me ten questions!" Buff would then ponder and squirm and grope to come up with suitable queries, while Mike sat and glared, ready to pounce on her at her first lapse into banality or irrelevance.

But the Draconian tactics paid off, for Buff was a quick study, and by the time *The Chez Show* went on the air she had what it took to measure up to her husband's exacting standards. As a result, the program was a hit, and in the months ahead it steadily grew in popularity. By the spring of 1951 *The Chez Show* was doing so well that it attracted the attention of CBS executives in New York, who were looking for fresh talent for their rapidly expanding television network. CBS sent its scouts to Chicago to look Mike and Buff over and soon thereafter, the couple was invited to New York to star in their own show on network television, an afternoon diversion which would be called *Mike and Buff*.

Husband-and-wife shows were very much in vogue then, on both radio and television. There were Tex McCrary and Jinx Falkenburg, Faye Emerson and Skitch Henderson, Dorothy Kilgallen and Dick Kohlmar, Peter Lind Hayes, and Mary Healy—and now, in 1951, CBS wanted to launch Mike Wallace and Buff Cobb into the swim.

But Wallace had reservations about making the move. The prospect of television certainly did not disconcert him, for he had gone through his baptism in that medium. His assorted free-lance chores in Chicago had included several stints on the tube. He had done a little acting, playing the lead role in a private-eye series. He hosted a panel show and emceed an unintentionally hilarious weekly beauty contest, sponsored by a local beer, Tavern Pale. Thanks to some heartless wags who made a habit of stuffing the ballot boxes with the names of unlikely contestants, the show often featured fat ladies and the kind of faces that come to mind when one thinks of Cinderella's stepsisters. Trivial stuff, to be sure, but in truth, he had little to choose from. Television was then struggling through its infancy, and quality programs of any kind were so rare as to be almost nonexistent.

For Wallace, the chief value of those early romps on television was the discovery he made about himself vis-à-vis the new medium. Many of his radio colleagues were frankly terrified of "that damn picture box" (as an apprehensive Eric Sevareid once described it), and some of them were unable to make the transition; when television replaced radio as the dominant force in broadcasting, their careers languished. But Mike soon learned that, unlike them, he was not camera-shy, and he managed to convey a compelling visual presence to go along with his expressive voice, which had been one of his natural strengths on radio.

So it was not television *qua* television that gave Wallace qualms about the New York offer. It was, rather, the high-stakes, high-powered world of the radio and television networks that were centered in that metropolis. By 1951 Wallace had become a solid fixture in Chicago media circles. He could write his own ticket at almost any radio or television station in town. Having conquered that turf and built a reputation there, he was reluctant to abandon the security of Chicago for the uncertainty of New York. Yet at the same time, he was stimulated by the challenge and knew he would never forgive himself if he let the chance slip by.

So at the age of thirty-three, Mike Wallace moved to New York, and there he has remained. From that day to this, New York has been his home, his professional base, the city where his life and career would reach peaks of fulfillment that could scarcely have been envisioned—even in his headiest fantasies—when he left Chicago in the summer of 1951.

The transition from a late-night radio show in Chicago to a daily program on national television proved to be a smooth one. *Mike and Buff* enjoyed a three-year run on CBS, and as talk shows go, it was better than most, certainly a cut or two above the fare being offered by other husband-and-wife teams. Unlike their counterparts, who were content simply to natter away at each other about this and that, Mike and Buff structured their program around specific themes. Sometimes the themes were light and frivolous, but at other times they were quite serious, frequently controversial, and on those occasions *Mike and Buff* generated the kind of lively give and take that many years later would attract viewers to Phil Donahue's morning show.

The success of their talk show enabled Mike and Buff to find their niche in the glittering, celebrity-conscious world of Manhattan. Nor was that the extent of Wallace's work for CBS during his first few years in New York. As had been his wont in Detroit and Chicago, he continued to divide his time between news and entertainment programs. That in itself was not unusual, for the lines of distinction between those two spheres were not as clearly drawn then as they would later become, and working both sides of the street was a fairly common occurrence. To cite an example, for a few months in 1954 Walter Cronkite emceed a variety program, *The Morning Show,* on which he was obliged to play straight man to a lion puppet named Charlemane. (*The Morning Show* was an early attempt by CBS to compete with NBC's highly popular *Today* show, which then featured Dave Garroway playing straight man to a spirited chimpanzee named J. Fred Muggs. But Cronkite and his puppet were no match for Garroway and his chimp, and *The Morning Show* soon faded into oblivion, leaving Cronkite free to pursue endeavors more suited to his natural bent.) Even the eminent Edward R. Murrow, the patron saint of integrity in broadcast journalism, was not above lending his presence to such an enterprise. Indeed, the program that made him a star on television in the 1950s was not his great documentary series, *See It Now,* but *Person to Person,* a celebrity-oriented broadcast that was essentially little more than a gossipy talk show.

There was, however, a fundamental difference. In the eyes of their peers, Cronkite and Murrow and others of their stripe were first and foremost journalists who merely dabbled in the show-biz side of television. But that was hardly the perception of Mike Wallace in the early fifties. Although he was starting to make a name for himself on national television, it was as a personality, a breezy raconteur who was most frequently seen on talk shows and similar programs. Moreover, the image left a stigma on Wallace's reputation. Many years later, long after he had established his credentials as one of the best news correspondents on television, he would wince in exasperation whenever an outside reporter or in-house colleague brought up the past and asked him snide questions about *Mike and Buff* or—worse—the various TV commercials he had done in Chicago and New York. Even in an admiring profile of him in a 1978 book about CBS News, it was written that during his early year in television, Wallace had "practically wallowed in schlock."

That assessment was not entirely fair; throughout the forties and early fifties, he kept one hand in news and public affairs programs at every stop along the way. But it is also true that journalism was not his principal concern in those days, and it was certainly not the image he conveyed in most of his early work in radio and television. In fact, Wallace's growing reputation as a personality or entertainer was so pronounced that in 1954 some of his theater friends in New York urged him to audition for a role in a Broadway play. Intrigued by this opportunity, he pursued it and got the part, that of an idealistic art dealer in a Harry Kurnitz comedy called *Reclining Figure*.

When *Reclining Figure* opened in New York in October 1954, the critics greeted both it and Broadway's new leading man with what Damon Runyon liked to call "the medium hello." Still, it was enough of a boost to give the play a run of nearly one hundred performances. Early on, long before the final curtain, Wallace was wishing that he had remembered, in time, what happened to Pinocchio when he followed the advice of *his* companions and went off singing. "Hi-didilee-dee, an actor's life for me." For Mike discovered that an actor's life was not for him. In particular, he found the night-after-night repetition tedious, and in all other respects the storied enchantments of the theater—the smell of the greasepaint and the rest of that malarkey—left him cold. He was determined that come what may, he would never go through *that* again.

Yet by then, Wallace was having a tough time on other fronts as well. Earlier in 1954, before he got involved with the theatrical venture, *Mike and Buff*, having run its course, was taken off the air, leaving him with no source of steady income. And the show's demise signaled the end of his partnership with Buff in more ways than one.

One of the appealing features of *Mike and Buff*, which had been part of the couple's routine since their days in Chicago, was their eagerness to find fault with each other. They often bickered on the air, much to the amusement of viewers who naturally assumed that it was just an act, not unlike the "dingbat" and "meathead" rantings of Archie Bunker on *All in the Family*. But much of the time they weren't kidding. The marriage had been a stormy one almost from the beginning, and by the end of 1954 it was over.

The unexamined life is not worth living, and in the early weeks of 1955 Mike Wallace took a long, hard look at himself. He was thirty-six, his personal life was a shambles and his career was going nowhere. To pay the bills that winter, he signed on to do commercials for a new Procter and Gamble shortening called Fluffo. It was not at all the kind of work he was looking for, but there were no other offers coming in and, with two sons to support from his first marriage, he needed the money. He now began to recognize that he had spread himself around in too many directions. He had been too willing to try his hand at any game in town, just to drift along from one free-lance job to the next. As a result, his professional life had no focus, no coherence, no clear sense of purpose. To paraphrase the title of Pirandello's most famous play, Mike Wallace—at that juncture in his career—was six characters in search of an identity.

In mulling over the multitude of chores he had performed since his days as an apprentice in Grand Rapids, Wallace realized that the job that had given him the most satisfaction, in terms of self-esteem, was his work as a newscaster and reporter on *The Air Edition of the Chicago Sun*. And he had been similarly stimulated by the occasional news assignments that had come his way when he was working at CBS in New York. True, the money in news had not been much, which was the main reason why he had taken on other, more lucrative projects. But news was challenging, he enjoyed it and, equally important to him, it was stable. Entertainment programs were constantly at the mercy of the ratings system and the whims of sponsors, and even those that did capture the public fancy—the solid hits—eventually turned stale. But news had its own built-in process of regeneration. The fact that it changed every day, at least to some degree, kept it fresh and that made it an enduring staple. In the swirling, topsy-turvy world of radio and television, news was a constant, a bedrock of fixed values. And so Wallace decided, during this period of self-examination, that he would do what he could to make journalism the focal point of his professional life.

It wasn't long before events took a dramatic turn for the better, first in his personal life and then in his career. In February 1955, Mike spent a few days in Puerto Rico where he met a gifted and attractive painter named Lorraine Perigord, who was running an art gallery in San Juan. Like Mike, she was divorced and had two children from a previous marriage. Courtship ensued and a few months later, Mike married again. For most of the next twenty-nine years, theirs was a happy and stable marriage.

One day, a few weeks before he married Lorraine, Mike ran into an acquaintance, Ted Cott, who had recently left his job as manager of Channel 4, the local NBC station, to take over the operation at Channel 5, the Dumont television station in New York. Cott was full of high hopes for Channel 5. He told Mike that even though he didn't have much of a budget to work with, he wanted to build a strong, independent news department there. And when Wallace then revealed that he would like nothing better than to be part of the Channel 5 effort, Cott responded with enthusiasm. Mike was hired to anchor the 7:00 P.M. and 11:00 P.M. newscasts, and Cott brought over a bright young man from NBC named Ted Yates to serve as news director. This trio, Wallace, Cott and Yates, formed the nucleus of a team that was destined to make a big splash in television, the shock waves of which would eventually be felt through the entire industry.

The new team, with Wallace in the anchor slot, went on the air in September 1955, and over the next few months built up a substantial following. But the best was yet to come.

In the summer of 1956, Ted Yates had an idea. Instead of airing two newscasts a night, at seven and eleven, he suggested replacing the later show with a new kind of interview program. What he had in mind was an innovative and provocative broadcast, one that would go out of its way to stimulate controversy rather than avoid it, as had been the pattern in television up to that time. Both Mike and Ted Cott were quick to embrace the proposal and plans were launched.

Mike does not remember if it was Yates who also came up with the title for the new show, but he does recall how pleased he was when he first heard it. For he thought that *Night Beat* had just the right ring and snap for the kind of broadcast they were preparing to put on the air. And in all other respects, his memory of that breakthrough experience is precise and to the point.

CHAPTER

TWO

FROM THE MOMENT we put *Night Beat* on the air—live—at 11:00 P.M. on October 9, 1956, we had a hunch that we were caught up in something special. There was a chemistry, a sense of drama in that velvet-dark studio, with its klieg lights stabbing into the faces of our interviewees, that told us New Yorkers were going to watch. Simplicity, candor, irreverence—those were the qualities we were after. And that first night, as I peered into the camera, smoke curling from my cigarette, I stated our premise: *"Night Beat* is designed to get the story directly from the people who make New York exciting, interesting and important. Even if our *Night Beat* steps on the toes of some of these people, we will try to get you their stories of successes and sorrows, trials and errors, hopes, follies and frustrations. We will dig out gossip, expose gripes, study conflicts, hear opinions and extract predictions. *Night Beat* will be offbeat only in that it will get you news at its source—from people."

It was melodramatic, self-conscious, even corny. But it was destined to strike a nerve among the jaded viewers in New York City and its environs.

I had been working with Ted Yates for about a year when he came up with the notion for *Night Beat*. A lanky ex-marine with a fiercely independent streak, Ted was only twenty-six, twelve years younger than I. He had moved around a good deal while growing up and had spent part of his youth in Cheyenne, Wyoming, where he came under the influence of the locals and decided he was a natural-born cowboy. Eager to prove it, he entered the bronco-busting contest at the Cheyenne rodeo. On the first day of competition, his horse threw him and Ted broke his back. It mended.

That escapade was characteristic of Yates, who was a kind of cowboy in everything he did, one of the few men I've known who seemed to be totally fearless. I don't think Ted understood fear the way most of us do. In 1967, long after *Night Beat* had passed into history and he and I had gone our separate ways, he was working as a correspondent for NBC News. In the early hours of the Six-Day War in the Middle East that year, while under fire in East Jerusalem, Ted raised his head at one point so that he could see more of the action. He was shot in the forehead and died the next day.

Ted Yates did more than come up with the idea for *Night Beat;* it was his spirit that animated the rest of us as we embarked on our new adventure. Prior to *Night Beat*, interview programs on television had been mostly verbal minuets, dull and ritualistic exercises in puffery and excessive discretion, or what one critic described as "the bland leading the bland." I should know, for I had served up my share of pablum on *Mike and Buff*. What Yates persuaded me we should do on *Night Beat* was to hurl a thunderbolt into that smug and placid world.

Our guests would be thoroughly, painstakingly researched and then, once we got them on the air, I'd go at them as hard as I could. If they appeared to be hiding behind evasive answers, I'd press them—or cajole them—to knock it off, to come clean. If, in response to pressure, they became embarrassed or irritated or sullen, I'd try to exploit that mood instead of retreating into amiable reassurance. Oversimplified, that was the formula we had in mind: candor, ours and theirs, with enough time to draw them out.

Moreover, we wanted *Night Beat* to be as radical in form as it would in content. Not for us the traditional and cheerful living room set, with the standard soft lights, the comfortable sofa and fake flowers. Instead, our studio was stark, pitch black except for that white klieg light glaring over my shoulder into the guest's eyes—and psyche. Nor was that all. Just as interviewers never cut too close to the bone in those days, neither did the cameras. They had always kept a decorous distance, a medium close-up, to assure the guest that he or she would be seen in the most flattering way. On *Night Beat* we used searching, tight close-ups to record the tentative glances, the nervous tics, the beads of perspiration—the warts and all. Not to put too fine a point on it, but in the context of American television in the mid-fifties, this was revolutionary.

The night we made our debut, the guest who led the broadcast was Robert Wagner, the mayor of New York. Projected on a huge screen behind him was a *Herald Tribune* editorial bitingly critical of his performance at City Hall, and my opening question to him was: "How do you feel when the *Herald Tribune* calls you a do-nothing mayor?" Wagner, an amiable though colorless politician, refused to be provoked; he took refuge in platitudes and generalities. He may or may not have been a do-nothing mayor, but he was surely a say-nothing interviewee. We gulped in disappointment, but learned something, too: If the questions are provocative enough, even pallid answers can reveal a good deal about the character and personality of an interviewee.

If that first effort failed to ignite any memorable sparks, it wasn't long before we began to hit our stride. The trick, of course, was to land the right kind of guest, one who, unlike Mayor Wagner, could be induced to enter into the spirit of candor and confrontation. When that happened, *Night Beat* came alive. One such encounter occurred one night later that winter when Mike Quill, the pugnacious head of the Transport Workers Union of America, played bull to my picador.

A short, beefy Irishman, Quill was fiercely proud of the fact that he had fought in the Irish rebellion as a rifleman with the Kerry Number Two Brigade. He also was fond of recalling that he first set foot in the United States on Saint Patrick's Day in 1926. Since then, Mike Quill had risen through the rough-and-tumble ranks of the labor movement to become one of the most powerful union leaders in America. That was reason enough to have invited him on *Night Beat*. But I also knew that Quill was reputed to have a hair-trigger temper and I was wondering that night if we might set it off.

The camera peered at closeup range into Quill's pudgy, mischievous face as the smoke from my cigarette clouded the illuminated air between us. There was a kind of tension of anticipation, and the moment I brought up the religious question, I could hear his deep brogue begin to rumble:

> WALLACE: Do you consider yourself a religious man? Do you go to church regularly?
>
> QUILL: Mike, I am a Catholic, I'm a practicing Catholic. But you know, I resent your raising the religious question.
>
> WALLACE: Why?
>
> QUILL: Because, because it causes confusion and tension. It was through raising the religious question that Hitler caused all the trouble that the world is suffering from today. And it was through raising the religious and racial question that Stalin carried on his dictatorship in the world. And I think it is a bad thing for one layman to challenge the religious feelings of another.
>
> WALLACE: But I'm not challenging...
>
> QUILL: Oh, I know you're not, but let me finish.
>
> WALLACE: Surely.
>
> QUILL (adopting the tone of a stern schoolmaster): Leave that to a priest and to a rabbi and to a minister, as somebody ordained by God to propagate that respective faith. I am a Catholic, I have answered your question, but I believe that as one layman to another, you should never raise the religious question with another layman.

I thought I knew why he was so sensitive on the subject. Back in the 1930s, when Quill began to organize the transport workers, he had been labeled "Red Mike." There was no evidence to back up the charge; it was, unfortunately, all too typical of the smears that were directed at union activists in those Depression days of labor unrest. But Quill still bore scars from that stormy period in his life, and he apparently thought that—on this night, some twenty years later—I was trying to set him up for questions aimed at the implicit contradiction between his Catholicism and those old calumnies about his subversive past. That was something to be concerned about in the fifties when the poison of McCarthyism was making its wretched presence felt in so many ways. I appreciated his concern, but at the same time, I knew that it was not my intent to Red-bait him. So I declined to go along with his suggestion that the subject be dropped:

> WALLACE: We know so much about Mike Quill the labor leader, but we know very little about Mike Quill the man. I simply asked, do you consider yourself a religious man? Are you a churchgoer?

> QUILL: I'm a churchgoer, but I still say it's a lowdown question to ask of another layman. I do not believe you should raise it over this microphone.

> WALLACE: Certainly it's nothing to be ashamed of?

> QUILL (wagging his finger and finally shouting): The question of religion should be left to the priests and the rabbis and the ministers and it should not be bandied about on a *peep* show like this.

The famous Mike Quill temper had flashed for all to see. After the interview, he stood up and shook hands with me. Then, as he walked off the set, he passed a member of our staff, an Irish lass named Rita Quinn, who had been in the control room. "Well," Quill asked Rita, "did we give 'em a good show, girlie?"

Much of the time there was no need to goad a guest into giving me the kind of lively response we wanted. Once it became clear that *Night Beat* was attracting a large and attentive audience, we discovered there were people who welcomed the chance to make outrageous comments in public on assorted subjects, usually themselves. This was especially true of that peculiar breed of celebrity whose claim to fame does not go far beyond a cunning flair for self-promotion. So it was the night I interviewed Elsa Maxwell, the party-giver and self-anointed doyenne of high society, or the jet set as it was *not* yet called in those propeller-driven days. With hardly a nudge from me, she merrily explained why her hyperactive social life was confined to the drawing room and did not extend to the boudoir:

WALLACE: Elsa, how come a warm person like yourself, an outgoing person, has never married?

MAXWELL: I was never interested in sex, quite frankly. It never interested me. I was never interested for one minute, ever...

WALLACE: And yet you wrote that sex is the most important drive in the world, that women should marry and bear children for their emotional fulfillment, that sex is the natural manifestation of love.

MAXWELL: But my love was another kind of love. It was a love for the whole world: for music, for art, for artists, for people. The world was my husband. I married the world. I couldn't subject myself, I'm very frank with you now, for a few isolated moments. I never liked the idea. I suppose I was attractive. I had two or three—only two—proposals in my life. At seventy-three, I don't wear glasses, my teeth are my own, my life is my own, my vitality. Why am I so young, why have I so much force? Because I've had no sex, the most tiring thing in the world. I found out by watching others.

WALLACE: You mean to say that we spend too much of our time, that we are too much taken up with it?

MAXWELL: Yes, entirely. We don't do it well in America, we don't do it well.

WALLACE: In what sense? What do you mean?

MAXWELL: We are too—our tempos are so great. We are so quick with everything. We go so fast with everything.

Everything's got to move faster and faster, quicker and quicker, harder and harder, over and over.

I am aware that that sort of chitchat would have little shock value nowadays when people are willing to be seen on television lobbying for their favorite perversions. But at the time—1956—it had such a bombshell effect that for days after the broadcast, Elsa Maxwell was the talk of the town. On second thought, it's entirely possible that if uttered today, Miss Maxwell's comments would set the gossip mills churning, for after all, in the jaded climate of the 1980s nothing could be more startling than the public confession of a seventy-three-year-old virgin.

Another flamboyant character was Salvador Dali, the painter. He used to watch *Night Beat* regularly, told friends he was fascinated by it and asked to be invited. We accommodated him, and he lived up to his reputation as the reigning eccentric of the contemporary art world:

> WALLACE: Max Ernst has called you the racketeer of surrealism. *Time* magazine says: "Most of his fellow artists regard Dali as a practical joker who will do anything for a laugh, even if it means creating bad art."
>
> DALI (smiling slyly): Is one very simple question of jealousy. Myself attracts one tremendous quantity of money for my genius. The thermometer of my success is the jealousy of the people around me . . .
>
> WALLACE: Tell me this, what do you think will happen to you when you die?
>
> DALI: Dali not believe in my death.
>
> WALLACE: You will not die?
>
> DALI: No, no. Believe in general in death, but not in the death of Dali. Believe my death becoming very, almost impossible.

For me, the drama and excitement of *Night Beat* was in its total unpredictability. The show was broadcast live, of course, and I never really knew what an interviewee might suddenly blurt out; in that sense, I was as much in the dark as the viewers were. And while I always enjoyed the daring and colorful outbursts, like those from Elsa Maxwell and Salvador Dali, there also were times when I was deeply moved by some unexpected disclosure. For example, I shall never forget the night the black actress Ethel Waters revealed in a low and tortured voice that she had been conceived in an act of rape that her father had inflicted on her mother.

Another somber moment occurred when I interviewed Earl Browder. The former head of the American Communist party, Browder had been a rather romantic figure back in the 1930s when it was fashionable, in certain literary and intellectual circles, to view Communism as the wave of the future. By 1956, however, the Red Hope had turned into the Red Menace, and Browder had become a lonely old man living on Social Security and what money he received from his sons. When I asked him about his sons, he made no attempt to hide his remorse: "My wife wouldn't let the boys come under the Communist influence and I'm happy they escaped that."

But if Earl Browder was a repentant voice from the past, there were new voices being heard on the political landscape in the mid-fifties, and *Night Beat* tuned in on them too. One such guest was an erudite and self-assured young man named William F. Buckley, then just emerging as the most engaging spokesman for the conservative cause. In those days as now, the overriding foreign policy concern was the aggressive designs of the Soviet Union, and I asked Buckley what steps we should take to gain the upper hand in what was still known as the Cold War:

BUCKLEY: By accepting certain goals and preparing for those goals irrespective of the cost. To list a simple program: Liberate Albania. Unification of Korea. Extirpation of Communist influence in Syria. Unification of Germany.

WALLACE: These things are devoutly wished but impossible of accomplishment.

BUCKLEY: I don't think they're impossible of accomplishment necessarily, but one of these days somebody might say we've got to cede Florida to the Soviet Union because it's impossible to keep it—short of war. So that this inhibition you mention must be considered in the context of what it is that the Soviet Union intends to do.

WALLACE: Also in the context of what is possible. And you equate Albania with Florida. That's kind of asinine. Look, you know as well as I there is no way successfully to unify Germany, liberate Albania, unify Korea.

BUCKLEY: You are a defeatist and I reject your pessimism.

Yes, he was like that even then, long before he had to contend with Gore Vidal.

Self-assured is far too modest a term to describe Norman Mailer, who at one point in 1957 deigned to grace *Night Beat* with his presence. Mailer was then known primarily as a novelist. He had only just begun to branch out into the kind of highly charged, intensely personal journalism that would become his literary forte in the sixties and seventies. Nor had he yet developed his outsize television persona—part guru, part buffoon—that would make him, variously, an object of mirth, admiration and wonder in later years. But there is no doubt that when he appeared on *Night Beat* he was starting to move in that direction.

The big hero in Mailer's life at that time was Ernest Hemingway. In fact, he had proposed in a newspaper article that Hemingway run for President because "this country could stand a man for President since for all too many years our lives have been guided by men who were essentially women." Needless to say, I referred to the article in our interview:

WALLACE: What do you mean by that—men who were essentially women? Who among our leaders is so unmasculine that you regard him in that light?

MAILER: Well, I think President Eisenhower is a bit of a woman.

WALLACE: What do you mean by *that?*

MAILER: Well, he's very passive . . . If we're entering a crisis, he's not exactly the kind of man, I believe, who would have any imagination, any particular grasp of how to change things.

It's worth noting that three years later Mailer wrote a provocative and celebrated essay for *Esquire* magazine called *Superman Comes to the Super Market,* in which he extolled John F. Kennedy for possessing the macho virtues he found so lacking in Eisenhower. But even the romantic Kennedy, with his moviestar looks and record of heroism in World War II, was a disappointment to Mailer, who later soured on Camelot because it failed to live up to his yearnings for a "superman" as President. Indeed, the day finally came when Mailer decided he had no choice but to set an example by entering the arena himself as a maverick candidate for mayor of New York in 1969. He lost of course, as did William Buckley when he embarked on a similar ego trip, making *his* run in the New York mayoralty race of 1965. I must admit that back in 1957, when I interviewed them on *Night Beat,* I would have found the prospect of Norman Mailer and Bill Buckley running for mayor public office almost as mind-boggling as the bizarre notion that a journeyman actor named Ronald Reagan, who was then doing television commercials for General Electric, would someday be elected President of the United States.

Although it was Ted Yates who struck the spark that lifted *Night Beat* off the ground, the program would never have become a reality had it not been for the encouragement of our boss at Channel 5, Ted Cott. He was the one who bore the brunt of the risk we were taking. If the reaction to *Night Beat* had been overwhelmingly negative and hostile—and that was a possibility we had to consider—it was Cott who would have had to explain to his superiors at Dumont Broadcasting why the fiasco had been put on the air in the first place.

Cott's support was especially critical during the early weeks when we were unable to generate any revenue from commercials. In those days (and to some extent it's still true), sponsors shied away from television shows that set out to be controversial because they felt that such programs would have a perverse effect on viewers—that is, on potential buyers of their products. In the eyes of most sponsors, the ideal TV show tried to please everybody, and in as inoffensive a way as possible. It wasn't until a few weeks before Christmas, after we had been on the air a couple of months, that we landed our first sponsor, and a less likely benefactor could not have been imagined. A small publishing firm, Hawthorne Books, bought time on *Night Beat* to sell a handsome and expensive edition of the Bible called *The Heirloom*. Soon thereafter we were happy to learn that we also had a friend at Chase Manhattan, which became our second sponsor—a bank to go along with our Bible. Once we had God and Mammon in our corner, there was no resisting us. Controversy was suddenly deemed to have commercial appeal, and by the middle of January we were sold out.

But even after *Night Beat* began to make money, we continued to operate on a tight budget, which was appropriate to the lean-and-hungry image we tried to project. The Spartan style was reflected in our cramped working quarters. Ted Yates shared an office with Marlene Sanders, our booker and all-around handywoman who later went on to become a correspondent and, in recent years, has been a colleague of mine at CBS News. What they shared actually was not an office so much as a tiny cubicle that had space only for two desks and two chairs, which they had to climb over each time they wanted to leave or enter. My cubicle was not much larger, and although it was ostensibly my private office, I had to share it with the teleprompter man. Every night when he began to pound away at the script that had to go on the prompter for our broadcast, it made a racket like a Gatling gun, driving me up the wall and out of there, fast.

As I've said, it was sometimes the questions on *Night Beat,* not the answers, that gave the show its bite, its cutting edge. And those questions evolved out of a process of research, presided over by our lead writer, Al Ramrus.

A slender, curly-haired young man (he was only twenty-five and looked much younger), Al was made to order for the job. First of all, he loved to dig; he had the zeal and perseverance needed to spend hours sifting through newspaper clips and other biographical data. But beyond that, he had a keen eye for the embarrassing quote, the indiscreet or ill-advised remark that a prospective guest probably wished he or she had never uttered. One of Ramrus's duties was to preinterview the guests. Sometimes on those occasions they would say things that contradicted observations they had made in the past. Ramrus never let on that he had caught the discrepancy, but once the preinterview was over he would return to the office in a state of high exuberance. Chortling over his reportorial coup, he'd crow: "Hey, this is hilarious. This is the answer the guy gives *now*, but wait till you get him on the air because just take a look at what he *used* to say six months ago about the same thing." Even more than the rest of us, Al Ramrus relished the sight of interviewees hemming and hawing in their attempts to perform unnatural acts of reconciliation.

And we had no qualms whatsoever about putting our guests on the spot. After all, as we frequently reminded each other, no one was ever subpoenaed to appear on *Night Beat*. In the beginning perhaps, we might have caught one or two people unawares, but once we had established our identity, everyone who accepted our invitation knew more or less what to expect, for our tactics were out in the open for all to see. This was why no one ever took excessive umbrage at questions that under different circumstances might have led to mayhem. Questions, for instance, like the one I put to Mr. John, the famed New York fashion designer and milliner: "Since it is common knowledge that homosexuals make up a large part of the fashion field, isn't it true that an unconscious hatred of women—so typical of homosexuals—has been the force responsible for the dress absurdities of recent years?" One critic wrote after that encounter that "Mr. John could have stuck Mr. Wallace with a hatpin."

So why then were our targets willing, even eager, to make themselves available for interviews on *Night Beat?* The main reason, I believe, was that by the mid-fifties, celebrities had discovered, under the guidance of their press agents, that television was the greatest promotional medium ever invented. They coveted invitations to appear on interview programs because they had something to sell: a book, a movie, a political idea or, all too often, simply themselves. Fair enough, we decided, but only so long as there was a quid pro quo, that in return for the exposure we were giving them, we had the license to try to penetrate the facade, to probe beneath the layers of carefully constructed public image.

Every now and then we were criticized for our unseemly preoccupation with the three subjects that were supposed to be taboo in polite conversation: sex, religion and politics. Our response to such complaints was a quote from George Bernard Shaw that we treasured to the point of regarding it as sacred writ, our own special credo. Shaw had written that it was only the "common and less cultivated people who make a rule that politics and religion are not to be mentioned, and take it for granted that no decent person would attempt to discuss sex." On the other hand, he averred, "the ablest and most highly cultivated people continually discuss religion, politics and sex. It's hardly an exaggeration to say that they discuss nothing else with fully awakened interest."

We were a brash and merry group, we band of brothers and sisters who worked on *Night Beat*. We reveled in a spirit of camaraderie and self-righteous zest as we sat in our crowded cubicles plotting how we were going to nail this pompous ass or that fatuous blowhard who would be stepping into our lair later that night. To this day one of my most cherished possessions, which I keep on display in my study, is a photograph of Ted Yates, Al Ramrus, my wife, Lorraine, and me, huddled together in my three-by-six-foot office just before we went on the air one night. It is a picture of gleeful co-conspirators caught up in the euphoria of a mischievous revolution.

I must confess, however, that there were times when in the heat of battle we went too far. For example, it gives me no pleasure at all to look back on the night I interviewed Al Capp, the cartoonist who created *Li'l Abner*. Capp, it should be said, richly enjoyed playing the gadfly. In particular, he loved going on television and saying things he knew to be outrageous, almost as though he were speaking less from conviction than from a churlish desire to antagonize the audience.

When Capp appeared on *Night Beat*, I noticed that each

time he fired one of his broadsides, he giggled self-consciously, a kind of nervous, reflexive semilaugh that followed almost every acid remark. After it had happened half a dozen times, I said to him: "You know something, Mr. Capp? You say things that are really quite cutting about political leaders or social conditions. And then you giggle, as though to assure us in a backhanded way that you're not really serious. It's almost a nervous tic, your giggle."

"I don't know what you're talking about," he replied with a tight, rather anxious smile. But no giggle.

I asked another question. Capp said something calculatedly offensive, and he giggled again. So I asked:

WALLACE: Didn't you hear it that time, Mr. Capp?

CAPP: No.

WALLACE: Why do you laugh that way, Mr. Capp? It seems compulsive, doesn't it?

CAPP: Why do I laugh what way? Hahahaha.

WALLACE: That laugh . . .

As I pressed on, Capp was palpably unnerved; sweat broke out on his face, and his hands and arms began to shake in jittery, jagged motions. The viewers were suddenly looking at a man in public torment as he tried to cope with some contradiction within himself. That nervous laugh was apparently a signal from his psyche and I had called attention to it on television. In doing so, I had caused him pain and embarrassment.

Yet Capp's distress had a mesmerizing effect on me and I persisted; I didn't let up because I felt we were getting close to the bone. I was hoping to prod him into making some fascinating revelation about himself. It was of course an utterly callous thing to do, as indefensible as sticking pins in a butterfly.

Distress also befell the brilliant Irish actress Siobhan McKenna the night she came on the show; but unlike Al Capp, she had no one to blame but herself. Miss McKenna was appearing on Broadway at the time in one of her greatest roles—

Shaw's *Saint Joan*—and most of my questions dealt with her distinguished career in the theater, dating back to her early days as a member of Dublin's famed Abbey Players. But at one point, I abruptly shifted the conversation to another subject: the then Lord Mayor of Dublin, Robert Briscoe, who happened to be Jewish. I really wasn't fishing for a provocative response. I simply found it intriguing that a man like Briscoe could become mayor of the capital of the Irish Republic, so I asked Siobhan about Ireland's Jewish community.

"Most of the Jews in Ireland stay in Dublin," she explained. "They are mainly merchants and they are rather prosperous. Irishmen, generally speaking, aren't very good businessmen. The Jews of Ireland are the best businessmen there. They are the ones who own the money-making businesses. They are the ones who are prosperous." And she went on to say that the concentration of Jews in Dublin "is one reason why things are not so good elsewhere in Ireland."

As she spoke, I could not help but notice an edge in her voice. Not that she meant to be snide, but the tone of Miss McKenna's remarks apparently conveyed to viewers with highly sensitive ears a strong subliminal message that in its way was kin to the scorn Portia leveled at Shylock in *The Merchant of Venice*. As soon as we went off the air, angry calls came flooding in to the switchboard, and they were followed by a barrage of telegrams and letters. Siobhan McKenna was accused of everything from gross insensitivity to blatant anti-Semitism.

The poor woman was stricken. Her main purpose in coming on *Night Beat* was to publicize the fact that *Saint Joan* was moving from one theater to another; and now she feared that our interview had alienated large segments of the audience she had hoped to attract. Our superiors at Channel 5 were also concerned. The morning after the broadcast, Ted Cott urged us to ask Siobhan to go on the program again that night and apologize, or at least explain herself. Through her friends in New York's Jewish community, she relayed this proposal to the Anti-Defamation League of B'nai B'rith, the Jewish fraternal organization. A spokesman for the group sent word back to us that it would be a mistake for her to go on television again, that it would only cause more trouble. Instead, he suggested that Miss McKenna and Mr. Wallace present themselves at the Waldorf Towers that evening at six o'clock for an audience with Mrs. Chaim Weizmann, the widow of one of the founding fathers of the modern state of Israel, who was visiting New York.

I had serious misgivings about making such a courtesy call. As far as I was concerned, Miss McKenna was entitled to her own opinions and if some people perceived them to be offensive, then so be it. On the other hand, if she felt she had been misunderstood, then she was fully capable of clearing the air herself without the benefit of outside sanction or counsel. What made me most uneasy, however, was the question of principle raised by my own participation in the proposed visit to Mrs. Weizmann. As the on-air representative of the Channel 5 news operation, I did not want to give the impression that I was seeking guidance or intercession from a powerful pressure group, no matter how worthy its intentions. But on a more human level, I was sympathetic to the dilemma Siobhan found herself in and I wanted to help. So, with some reluctance, I accompanied her to the Waldorf Towers apartment of Vera Weizmann, who promptly greeted us with soothing words of reassurance: "Siobhan, you said nothing. Chaimchik always said we were good at business."

That matter settled, Mrs. Weizmann fixed her gaze on me and, apparently recognizing a co-religionist, proceeded to ask a rather ethnocentric question: "I understand you come from Brookline, where the president of the United Jewish Appeal is from. Was your name always Wallace?"

(The answer to that one was both yes and no. Which is to say that *my* name has always been Wallace, but when my father left his native Russia at the age of sixteen to come to America, *his* name was Frank Wallak. When he arrived at the port of Boston, an immigration officer, motivated no doubt by some vague, Yankee-bred sense of duty, arbitrarily translated Wallak to Wallace on my father's entry papers.)

Actually the Siobhan McKenna affair was not yet settled. Emboldened by Vera Weizmann's blessing, Miss McKenna chose to make a second appearance on *Night Beat*, and a few hours after we left the Waldorf, she was telling our viewers: "I'm not here to apologize because I have nothing to apologize for. I just want people to listen to what I said. Since more of the Jews live in Dublin, there is economic hardship elsewhere in Ireland because there aren't enough good businessmen out in the countryside."

That triggered a fresh outburst of angry calls and telegrams, this time from the Irish who decided it was now *their* turn to be offended. Their complaint was that "certain groups" had pressured Miss McKenna into betraying her own people by depicting them as fey morons who wouldn't know how to balance a checkbook, much less run a shop or invest in commodities.

By this time, Siobhan was convinced that the people who watched our show were quite mad. All she wanted to do was make her escape from the martyr's role she had inadvertently assumed on *Night Beat* and return to the one she was playing on Broadway. Getting burned at the stake every night was no fun, but at least when she was interrogated as the Maid of Orleans she knew what to expect from her audience.

The flap over the Siobhan McKenna interview was just one example of the feedback *Night Beat* generated. Most of the time it didn't hit us until we went to work the next day. But then, if the previous night's program had been a winner, we'd hear about it from almost everyone we encountered, cabdrivers and elevator operators, waitresses and bank tellers. From friends and acquaintances I would hear that my interview with Norman Mailer or Mike Quill or Elsa Maxwell had been the chief topic of conversation at this private cocktail party or that public watering hole; and all of us who worked on the program rejoiced in the feedback. It gave us reason to believe that *Night Beat* was the hottest show in town, at least on television.

Since most of the other members of our team were several years younger than I and had been in the business only a short time, I'm not sure they fully appreciated how rare all the attention was. But I surely did. It was heady stuff, this first big success, especially since it came after years of comparative anonymity. When it bestows its gift of recognition, New York is a rewarding and immensely satisfying place to work, and as the accolades poured in during that sunny fall and winter of 1956 and 1957, all of us who labored on *Night Beat* were on a continual "high."

CHAPTER

THREE

IN GOING OUT of his way to acknowledge the contributions of his *Night Beat* colleagues—Yates, Cott, Ramrus, et al.—Wallace was not merely being gracious. He was telling the truth, for television is by definition a collaborative enterprise, a team effort, and the work that is done behind the scenes, off-camera, is essential to the success of any show. To be more specific, *Night Beat* was a crisply produced, well-researched program. But it should be emphasized that more than anything else, it was the combination of talents that Wallace himself brought to the broadcast which made it work as well as it did.

As several critics pointed out at the time, Mike not only had a knack for asking the right questions, but for knowing *when* to ask them. Like all good reporters, he had a shrewd sense of timing; he knew how to pace and develop an interview so that it built to a point where the critical questions would elicit the best and most revealing replies. In addition, Wallace had skills that enabled him to meet the peculiar demands of television.

When a print journalist conducts an interview, he can usually relax a bit and indulge in discursive interludes. Unless he is severely pressed for time, he can allow an interview to veer off on an irrelevant tangent as long as he eventually steers it back to the main subject. But in the 1950s, when everything was broadcast live within a rigid time frame, television interviews could ill afford such a luxury, which is one reason why so many of them rambled off into aimless chatter. They desperately needed some kind of editing device to give them pith and focus. To get around the problem on *Night Beat,* Wallace assumed the role of on-the-spot editor. If a guest began to veer off the subject or lapse into a long-winded response, Mike would not hesitate to chop him off—even in midsentence—and exhort him to keep his answers concise and to the point. That was yet another *Night Beat* innovation and there were those who found it boorish. But the jarring interruptions contributed greatly to the brisk pace and pungent tone of the interviews.

What Wallace also had going for him was his strength as a personality or performer. In this respect, his varied background, his broad range of experience clearly worked to his advantage. Some of the tricks he had learned while toiling in nonjournalistic vineyards, where the emphasis was on style and personality, were put to effective use on *Night Beat.* As he listened to a guest's answer, Mike would often react with telltale facial movements: a frown to express puzzlement, a grimace to convey disagreement, raised eyebrows to indicate skepticism. The primary purpose of such gestures was to assure the interviewee that he, Wallace, was listening intently to every word. This could be dismissed as a routine courtesy were it not for the fact that a common failing of television interviewers is that they often seem to be distracted by other concerns, such as the next question they plan to ask or how much time they have before the next commercial break. Mike's facial reactions also were intended as a signal to the viewers, the raised eyebrows being a silent way of saying to them: "I don't believe what this guy is saying now and neither should you."

Like his more illustrious contemporary of that period, Edward R. Murrow, Wallace frequently smoked during an interview. But the similarity ends there. In Murrow's hands the cigarette was a benevolent prop, a relaxed symbol of drawing-room urbanity. As for Wallace, he was inclined to smoke aggressively—in quick, nervous puffs—and with the cigarette clutched in his fingers, he often brandished it while jabbing the air to punctuate a point being made. Then, too, the plumes of smoke rising in the glaring white light on that stark set served to enhance the aura of menace, the disquieting sense that *Night Beat* was the television equivalent of an interrogation room at a tough New York police station.

These various elements—the brusque interruptions, the exaggerated facial gestures, the cigarette as weapon—were all part of the performance, and none of it was unconscious. Wallace had a clear understanding of what he was doing and what effect he was trying to achieve. And being a true connoisseur, he was quick to recognize similar gifts in others.

Many years later, when he was working with Dan Rather on *60 Minutes,* Mike said to a mutual friend: "I'll tell you one thing that makes Dan so good. When he comes on the screen, you're caught up by the strength of his personality. You immediately react to him; you want to *know* what he's going to ask or say. Like any good performer, he knows how to take stage."

That is a classic example of the pot calling the kettle white. What he said about Rather was true enough, but Wallace could just as easily have been talking about himself and the strength of *his* television personality, which had come to the fore some twenty years earlier on *Night Beat.* So at its best, *Night Beat* was good journalism *and* absorbing theater, and Wallace, having passed his exams in both schools, had the right blend of talents to make it happen.

It's true that his constant striving for the dramatic confrontation, the heightened effect, sometimes carried him into excess, as his lamentable badgering of Al Capp demonstrated. But in a fascinating way, even the occasional lapses in taste and judgment were part of the appeal. That there were nights when viewers caught a glimpse of Wallace's darker, disagreeable side—*his* warts and all—only underscored the fact that there was nothing slick or rehearsed about *Night Beat.* Even the host, the dread interrogator, was vulnerable to the merciless unpredictability of the show's format.

The feedback that *Night Beat* generated was by no means confined to morning-after comments by cabdrivers and the like or to casual conversations at cocktail parties and trendy midtown bars. Not long after the program went on the air, the reviews began coming in. Most of them were favorable, and some of them perceptive. Harriet Van Horne of the *New York World-Telegram and Sun* had this to say: "Any man's conversation is a clue to the texture of his soul. But appearing on this program, it seems to me, is an acid test of character . . . If you're a guest, this is the time when your convictions have to stand up and be counted. Dissemblance is instantly detected."

On the negative side, *Night Beat* was accused—predictably—of "sensationalism." Among those who seemed to be irritated by the banality of that contention was Jack Gould, the influential television critic for *The New York Times*. In one of his daily columns, Gould wrote: "The *Night Beat* trademark, of course, has been the much advertised toughness of the inquiries. But many of them are 'tough' only by the television norm. It has been regrettable that so much attention has been paid to the relatively few minutes of what could be construed as 'sensationalism.'"

Some of the show's disparagers could not resist the temptation to indulge in a little creative name-calling. Wallace was labeled "Mike Malice," which was a model of alliterative restraint compared with the shrill excess of another epithet—"The Terrible Torquemada of the TV Inquisition." But of course even the negative reactions had a positive effect, a point not lost on Mike, who had a savvy appreciation of a cardinal principle in commercial television—to wit: Neglect and low ratings may break my bones, but names will never hurt me. *Night Beat* and its star also attracted a bevy of feature writers who, with their recurring need for fresh material, were naturally drawn to a new television show that had stirred up controversy; and the newspaper and magazine articles they wrote helped to keep the pot boiling. But the ultimate blessing in terms of status came when *The New Yorker*—then as now the bible of sophistication—published a cartoon depicting a sad-faced man lying on a couch in the office of his analyst, who is saying to him: "As soon as we find out what you're trying to hide, we'll find out why you're running away from an interview with Mike Wallace."

Given all this attention, it was no doubt inevitable that at some point one of the networks would come courting. This is what happened in the early spring of 1957 after *Night Beat* had been on the air for only six months. The offer came from ABC, and while Mike was naturally flattered, he was also wary. He and Ted Yates were not at all convinced that the *Night Beat* team would have enough freedom to do what they wanted on a network program. They knew that the pressures at the network level were far more severe than they were at a local station, and Wallace and Yates feared that because of those pressures, efforts would be made to stifle the bite and edge and zest for confrontation that had made *Night Beat* what it was. The prospect of a nationwide broadcast in prime time obviously appealed to them, but not if it meant that they would be forced to do an emasculated version of *Night Beat*. That was too high a price to pay.

The ABC executives assured Wallace that that was not what they had in mind, and he found their siren song too sweet to resist. For the first time in his career, he was being wooed on a grand scale. The courtship included an invitation to break bread with the head of the ABC corporation, Leonard Goldenson, in his private dining room. At that luncheon, Goldenson urged Wallace to be as controversial at ABC as he had been at Channel 5. Or, as he put it rather vividly: "Mike, you will not be doing your job properly unless you make this building shake every couple of weeks."

However, in the negotiations that followed, a serious snag developed. The problem was not money; the two sides reached an early accord on that. Nor did the network have any objections to Wallace's demand that three other members of the *Night Beat* team—Ted Yates, Al Ramrus and Rita Quinn—accompany him in the move to ABC. The conflict was over air time and the question of commitment. Mike and his agent, Ted Ashley, not only wanted a weekly show in prime time, but also a firm guarantee that it would be kept on the air in the same time slot for at least one year. They strongly believed that the program needed a year in a regular time slot to build up a national audience. The ABC lawyers argued that such a guarantee was "unheard of" and could never be granted, especially for a risky interview show like *Night Beat*. And on that sticking point, the negotiations stalled.

The two sides were locked in stalemate for the next several days. Finally, a weekend session was scheduled at the offices of the ABC attorneys. The talks resumed fairly early on Saturday, but dragged on, hour after hour, with little or no progress being made. By eight o'clock in the evening, both sides were still unable to agree on the final language of the guarantee. At that point, an exhausted Ted Ashley lay down on the floor, took off his shoes, put his feet up on a chair and said: "Gentlemen, we're getting no place. Why don't we take a break and watch the Sid Caesar show?"

To appreciate what happened next, it should be pointed out that at the time Caesar and his gifted playmates—Imogene Coca, Carl Reiner, Howie Morris, et al.—were the hottest comedy team on television. Their forte was parody, and few accolades delighted producers, directors and actors as much as seeing their current movie, play or TV show become the target of a Caesar spoof. It was a special kind of recognition, an honor to be treasured. When the Caesar show was turned on that night in the ABC office, no one paid much attention to it until, several minutes into the program, it suddenly became apparent that Caesar and Co. were doing a takeoff on *Night Beat*. Sid Caesar was sitting in a stark, forbidding studio and, with an insolent sneer, was blowing smoke into the face of Carl Reiner. The expression on Reiner's face was one of lip-trembling terror, which steadily grew more acute as Caesar/Wallace assailed him with a flurry of nasty questions. A local program on a small independent station in New York was being parodied by the biggest comedy show on television.

The ABC lawyers began to chuckle. Responding to this cue, Ashley took his feet down, put his shoes back on and said: "Well, gentlemen, I guess that decides it."

And it had. The deal was struck, the contract signed, and in the midst of his euphoria, Mike Wallace forgot all about the concerns that had nagged him when he first heard of the ABC offer. But it wasn't long before he would have occasion to remember them with more than a twinge of regret, for he soon discovered that his fears had been justified. In making the move to ABC and a national audience in prime time, *Night Beat* turned into nightmare.

CHAPTER

FOUR

THE ABC VERSION of *Night Beat*—rechristened *The Mike Wallace Interview*—was scheduled to make its debut on April 28, 1957, and of course we wanted to make that opening punch a knockout if we could. It was imperative, therefore, that we book the right kind of premier interviewee, someone who had both a provocative personality and a national reputation. Our choice was one of the most controversial figures of the time—Senator Joe McCarthy. True, he was no longer the power and menace he had been a few years earlier. The credibility of his shrill campaign against Communist influence in high government circles had been undermined by a series of events, notably by Edward R. Murrow's incisive look at McCarthy on the CBS documentary program *See It Now;* and by 1957 he was damaged goods. But Ted Yates and I felt the Wisconsin senator still had plenty of moxie left in him, and that his presence on our first network program would enable us to show our style to those millions of viewers across America who had heard about us but had not yet seen us in action.

The initial response to our invitation was encouraging. McCarthy's staff did not give us a firm commitment, but we were led to believe that we could count on his appearance. What we didn't realize was that those close to the senator did not want to acknowledge to the public (or, perhaps, to themselves as well) just how gravely ill McCarthy was. As it turned out, he died just four days after our first ABC broadcast. But by the time his staff finally got around to telling us he wouldn't appear, our opening show was only two weeks away and we had to scramble for a suitable replacement. This led to more frustration. Several people to whom we had made overtures turned us down, and we were surprised by the sudden resistance we encountered. It was the first indication of the problems that would beset us now that we had moved into a network showcase. For even some of the intrepid souls who had been willing to come on our local program balked at the prospect of exposing themselves to the risks of what might develop in front of a nationwide audience.

So the list of appealing and amenable candidates shrank rapidly until it came to an unlikely choice between actress Gloria Swanson and Philip Wylie, the acerbic social critic who had lambasted "Mom" and other sacred cows in his iconoclastic book, *Generation of Vipers*. We opted finally for Swanson primarily because she was better known and thus would be more likely to attract a larger audience. Besides, our third broadcast was scheduled for Mother's Day, and that, we figured, was the time to interview the celebrated scourge of Momism.

Our decision to lead off with Miss Swanson was a mistake. Although she was, to be sure, a charming and attractive guest, her memories of Hollywood during the silent-film era (fanny pats from Francis X. Bushman and that sort of thing) and her preoccupation with the wonders wrought by health foods hardly provided the fireworks our new audience had been led to anticipate. As a result, our all-important first show was a dud and we were seized by an overwhelming sense of letdown. Critics and viewers who had never seen us before shrugged their shoulders and asked: Is that all there is to it? So what was all the shouting about?

We knew we had to do better, and quickly. Yet that was part of the problem, for we were locked into a far more inflexible format. *Night Beat* had been a one-hour program aired four nights a week with two guests per broadcast. If the first guest proved to be dull, the second one, waiting in the wings, could be summoned to the rescue. Or even in the unlikely event that both guests were weak, we could still take comfort in the fact that most of the time we had the opportunity to clean up our act the very next night. But now at ABC we were limited to a half hour a week and everything depended on the appeal of our one weekly guest. That put a lot more pressure on us, and of course we were playing for much higher stakes.

Our second show was an improvement. The guest was Eldon Lee Edwards, Imperial Wizard of the Ku Klux Klan, who displayed the closed and twisted mind of a true-blue bigot. He came on like an advertisement for paranoia with his charges that *The Atlanta Constitution* and other major newspapers in the South were "controlled" by the Anti-Defamation League of B'nai B'rith, and that the NAACP took its orders from Communists and other foreign groups which were out to destroy America. When I challenged him to provide even a shred of evidence that would support such reckless accusations, Edwards merely smirked in a way that implied that he regarded me— a northern Jew in the employ of a network in New York—as part of the sinister conspiracy. His most striking observation, in terms of revealing how his mind worked, came in response to my question about racial purity:

WALLACE: In one piece of Klan literature that you furnished us, it is charged, quote, "One drop of Negro blood in your family destroys your white blood forever." I take it that you believe that?

EDWARDS: Well, I wouldn't define it down to one drop now. But here it stands to reason, as common sense, that mongrelization means destruction. It means the destruction of the white race. It means the destruction of the Nigra race. I sure will believe in segregation for the simple reason we believe in preserving and protecting God's word. He created the white man. He intended for him to stay white. He created the Nigra. He intended for him to stay black. And we believe that mongrelization destroys both races and creates a mongrel which is not a race.

The next week was Mother's Day and Philip Wylie's turn. We all had been looking forward to that and Wylie did not let us down. In honor of the occasion, I opened the interview with a long question about his favorite *bête noire:*

WALLACE: Fifteen years ago, in *Generation of Vipers,* you described Mom this way: You said, "Men live for her and die for her, dote upon her, and whisper her name as they pass away. In a thousand of her, there is not enough sex appeal to budge a hermit ten paces off a rock ledge. She plays bridge with the stupid voracity of a hammerhead shark. She couldn't pass the final examinations of a fifth grader." That was written in 1942. The obvious question is: In view of the furor and protest that the essay—that chapter—caused, is that still your opinion today, Mother's Day, fifteen years later?

WYLIE: Well, let me say that if you had read on through those pages of indictment you'd have realized, Mike, that I was talking about not mothers, all of them, but a certain kind, whom I classified as I did and whom I outrageously lampooned, deliberately, from a psychological background that was well informed.

WALLACE: Yes, but it seemed to me, from what you said, that you were talking about millions and millions of American mothers, not just half a dozen of them.

WYLIE: Oh, I wouldn't talk about just half a dozen. If you could have read my mail, which came in by the tens of thousands of letters, and still does, you would know that I was talking about more than I thought. But somewhere later on I said, "Any woman who is not roaring with laughter now ought to take a sharp look at herself." And what I meant is, if you have these attributes, then I don't think you're a good mother.

WALLACE: But you were fairly serious about what you were writing, and I got the impression that you felt that this was true—what you wrote was true about the majority of American mothers.

WYLIE: No, I just thought it was true about too many and it was becoming true about more, so I ought to say, "This kind of Mom is sure a jerk." And I have not changed my opinion in that sense.

Toward the end of the interview, I shifted the conversation to some scattershot:

> WALLACE: I would like from you a quick opinion on some controversial issues—the State of Israel.
>
> WYLIE: I've always opposed my Zionist friends from the time it was set up—building one more righteous group of religionists who have only one belief and are fanatical about it, and putting them in a little nation. We should have taken them in, in the West.
>
> WALLACE: Mercy killing.
>
> WYLIE: That's okay.
>
> WALLACE: Liberace.
>
> WYLIE: Well, seeing the streets blocked with morons, and having to drive around these swarms of hysterical middle-aged gals, I thought of getting a bunch of the last few male men left in the continent and stoning him to death with marshmallows.

The Wylie broadcast gave us a momentary lift, but that sanguine mood lasted exactly one week—until our next program, when disaster struck in the form of ex-mobster Mickey Cohen.

In his heyday Mickey Cohen had been a big shot in the underworld, especially on the West Coast where his operations were based. His specialties were gambling and bootlegging, but he was no stranger to other, rougher games. He readily admitted that he had killed a few people along the way. But now, Cohen insisted, all that was behind him. He had gone straight and was making a modest living as a florist. Instead of bookmaking and illegal booze, he specialized in tropical plants. As part of his rehabilitation, he even had become a friend of the Reverend Billy Graham, or so he claimed.

The decision to invite a shady character like Cohen into the limelight of our new broadcast was in keeping with our overall plan. Neither Ted Yates nor I wanted our guest list to be confined to conventional celebrities; to be sure, we intended to present show-business personalities and literary lions and supplicant politicians. But in addition to the star attractions, the household names, we wanted to offer our viewers an occasional guest who was not so well known and who came not from the mainstream but from the murky backwaters of society. The Imperial Wizard, Eldon Lee Edwards, was one such, and repugnant though his ideas may have been, they represented a dark corner of the American soul. So, too, in his way did Mickey Cohen.

What we wanted from Cohen were his recollections of the Bad Old Days. We were hoping he would talk about his past in a way that would give our audience some understanding of how a gangster lived and what organized crime was like on the inside. When we contacted him, Cohen said he would be happy to give us "the lowdown." He didn't go into any specifics, so we weren't sure exactly what we would be able to get out of him. But we felt certain that what he had to say would be colorful—and, perhaps, even explosive. In that regard at least, he did not disappoint us.

We were told that our guest, the florist, would be flying in from Los Angeles under an assumed name and that secrecy was of the essence. Al Ramrus was dispatched to the airport to meet him. He waited at the gate, immediately recognized Cohen and—thoroughly enjoying this cloak-and-dagger ritual—greeted him in the prescribed manner: "Are you Mr. Dunn?"

"Nah," came the reply. "My name ain't Dunn. It's Cohen."

He was accompanied by a couple of characters known to us only as Arlene and Itchy. We checked the trio into a suite at the Hampshire House, but Cohen did not find it acceptable. Evidently this ex-racketeer had a fetish for cleanliness and was so fastidious that he couldn't bring himself to share a bathroom with anyone else. So we moved them into a larger suite, one that offered more discreet plumbing arrangements. Ramrus guided Cohen through the customary preinterview session and came back to the office in high spirits. Having apparently succumbed to our guest's charm and lingo, Al assured me that Cohen was "ready to sing." All I had to do was push the button.

Ramrus was right. Cohen did talk freely about his life of crime, though in a rather self-serving way. For example, he piously asserted that he never had anything to do with narcotics or prostitution, and he seemed to take considerable pride in having steered clear of those activities. That struck me as just a bit much, and so I called him on it:

> WALLACE: Well, wait just a second. You say you've never mixed with prostitution, you've never mixed with narcotics.
>
> COHEN: That's right.
>
> WALLACE: Yet you have made book, you have bootlegged. Most important of all, you've broken one of the Commandments—you've killed, Mickey. How can you be proud of not dealing in prostitution and narcotics when you've killed at least one man, or how many more? *How* many more, Mickey?
>
> COHEN: I have killed no man that in the first place didn't deserve killing.
>
> WALLACE: By whose standards?
>
> COHEN: By the standards of our way of life. And I actually, in all of these killings—in all of these what you would call killings—I had no alternatives. It was either my life or their life.

At another point, while we were discussing his bookmaking operation, Cohen claimed that he knew politicians who had been bribed, and he strongly implied that he personally had slipped large sums of money to high-ranking officials in order to protect his gambling empire. It was then that I should have had my wits about me. For the next thing I knew, Cohen was talking about a *specific* official—the Los Angeles chief of police, William Parker—and he filled the air with slander.

"I'm going to give him much to bring a libel suit against me," he said prophetically. "He's nothing but a thief. This man is as dishonest politically as the worst thief that accepts money for payoffs. He's a known alcoholic. He's been disgusting.

He's an old degenerate. In other words, he's a sadistic degenerate of the worst type..."

I broke in, not to inject a cautionary note or disclaimer, but to seek clarification. I asked him to repeat the name of the man he had just called "a sadistic degenerate."

Thus the peril of live television. In print journalism or in the film reports I do now for *60 Minutes,* such remarks would be checked carefully for reliability and weighed for discretion before being published or broadcast. But Cohen's abusive comments—unedited and unverified—were heard by the public at the moment they were uttered. But that was no excuse. After all, I was hardly new to this game; I had been working in the format long enough to know that what I should have said at that moment was something like: "Now, wait a minute, you're calling him a sadistic degenerate and that's undoubtedly actionable. I want to dissociate myself from all such statements unless you can prove to me at this instant that he is indeed a sadistic degenerate. Give me a book, chapter and verse. Otherwise, let's move on to something else."

But that's not what I said. I was caught up in the drama of the moment and proceeded to talk my way further into trouble. I remember thinking that no one would say what Cohen was saying unless he had his man nailed. And so, referring to his target as "the apparently respectable Chief William Parker," I urged Cohen to elaborate on his charges. Not that he needed any encouragement from me. Having warmed to his subject, he extended his allegations beyond Parker to other law-enforcement officials in Los Angeles, including the Police Intelligence Department, which Cohen labeled "the Stupidity Department."

It wasn't until after we were off the air that I began to grasp the magnitude of the problem—or potential problem—that we faced. Ted Yates was also concerned; and, after reviewing the broadcast, he and I decided to have another talk with our loquacious guest. A few minutes later, we were in Cohen's suite at the Hampshire House.

Mr. Clean had just taken a shower, a baptismal rite he apparently performed several times a day, and greeted us wearing a pair of wooden clogs and a towel wrapped around his ample midriff. Ted and I told him how upset we were about what he had said during the interview.

"Mike, Ted, forget it," he replied. "Parker knows that I know so much about him, he wouldn't dare touch me. He won't sue. I have so much on this guy, he wouldn't dare sue."

Almost as reassuring as the words themselves was Cohen's serene manner. Sitting there, wearing nothing but a towel, he did not appear to have a care in the world. By the time Ted and I left the Hampshire House, we both believed—or desperately *wanted* to believe—that Cohen had enough information, enough witnesses, enough hard evidence to keep Parker off our backs.

That hope was shattered the next day when Chief Parker held a press conference at which he said: "I am not concerned about the specific comments of such a person. However, I am concerned about the authority of a television station to use that type of slander. A slanderous magazine story must be picked up at a newsstand, but TV enables slander to be brought into the living room."

At ABC meanwhile, the mood had escalated from concern to dismay to panic, and the following week we tried to make amends. Prior to my next interview (with Senator Wayne Morse), Oliver Treyz, the president of ABC Television and Leonard Goldenson's chief deputy, went on the air and solemnly intoned:

Last Sunday night something most unfortunate, unexpected and profoundly regrettable occurred while Mr. Wallace was questioning Mickey Cohen. Leonard Goldenson, our president, joins me most earnestly in stating that the American Broadcasting Company retracts and withdraws in full all statements made on last Sunday's program concerning the Los Angeles city government, and specifically Police Chief William H. Parker, Captain James Hamilton of the Department Intelligence Squad, former Mayor Fletcher Bowron, and former Police Chief Clarence B. Horrell. The American Broadcasting Company knows of no facts which reflect upon the official and personal reputation of these gentlemen, or upon their integrity and loyalty to the highest ethics of law and law enforcement. The American Broadcasting Company deeply regrets the matter and offers its sincere apologies . . .

To which I lamely added: "I join sincerely and earnestly in the statement of retraction and apology."

Treyz and I could have spared ourselves the trouble, for the humble pie we gulped down on national television was not enough to mollify Parker and Hamilton who called the retraction "inadequate." Cohen, on the other hand, thought it was "spineless." And once again, on the telephone, he uttered the refrain that he had injected into every conversation we had had over the past week. "Mike," he assured me yet again, "not to worry. I have so much on this guy Parker, he wouldn't dare sue."

He sued. He sued for two million dollars, and Hamilton sued for one million. Before he appeared on our program, Cohen had signed the usual document indemnifying us against any libel suits, but it was a worthless piece of paper. I thought of Cohen's reputation as a well-heeled hood who in his bookmaking days had apparently forked out lavish sums in bribe money. Now he was pursuing a more respectable though far less lucrative line of work, and it occurred to me, with some bitterness, that our friendly florist would offer to pay us off in roses.

The suit never came to trial. Six months after the Cohen interview, Parker settled out of court for $45,000 and Hamilton for $22,500. Seaboard Surety, the insurance company that held the libel policy for ABC, wanted to settle as quickly and painlessly as possible. And soon thereafter, Seaboard Surety disengaged itself from us and was replaced by Lloyd's of London. But since we were suspect now, Lloyd's would not take over the policy until we agreed, in writing, to the following condition: Each night we went on the air, a lawyer would sit in the studio where, facing me, he would hold up cue cards at sensitive moments warning me to BE CAREFUL or STOP or RETREAT. Like a baby with its bib and a dog with its leash, I was judged to be in need of a legal teleprompter.

Mickey Cohen did not contribute to the settlement; nor was he a party to the agreement. But several months after it was all over, I was in Los Angeles and I ran into him at the Beverly Hills Hotel. To judge from the hearty, effusive way he greeted me, one would have thought we were bosom buddies who had known each other since college days or the war years. My own response to our reunion was less enthusiastic. Cohen brought up the interview, as I figured he would, and proceeded to tell me that he had lined up certain witnesses who would now testify to the truth of his allegations. They would be perfectly willing, he said, to come forward and reveal what they knew about Parker. When I asked him who they were, Cohen named a couple of call girls and a gangster friend. So much for reformed racketeers who go straight as florists.

The Mickey Cohen episode did not endear us to our new employers. Yet the case could be made that we had simply carried out our instructions. I had not forgotten what Leonard Goldenson had said to me during the happy days of courtship: "Mike, you will not be doing your job properly unless you make this building shake every couple of weeks." Well, with a big assist from Mr. Cohen, we had shaken things up to a fare-thee-well. But for some reason, Goldenson neglected to tell us what a great job we had done; in fact, I didn't hear from him for several months. The man we really had to worry about, however, was not Goldenson or his second-in-command, Oliver Treyz, but rather the head of the ABC news department, John Daly—or John *Charles* Daly, as he was sometimes called.

In the mid-1950s, John Daly was a power and a presence in the television industry. In addition to running the network news operation, he was the anchorman on ABC's evening news broadcast; and as if those two major responsibilities weren't enough, he also appeared once a week on CBS as moderator of its highly popular panel show, *What's My Line?* It was as though—to put it in the context of 1984—my colleague Dan Rather not only anchored the *CBS Evening News,* but also was president of CBS News and played host once a week on a panel show on ABC.

Daly made no attempt to hide his displeasure when the *Night Beat* team was hired by ABC. At the time the offer was made, he either had not been consulted or his advice had been rejected. In any case, he vowed that I would have no participation whatever in the ABC news operation, even though Goldenson had promised that I would eventually find a niche there. Daly contended that I was not a "real" journalist, but merely an interviewer. I also was told by several people on Daly's staff that he had warned Goldenson and Treyz that Wallace and his crew were bound to bring trouble to the network. In the aftermath of the Cohen experience, he was able to say "I told you so" —and he did.

But neither the Cohen misfortune nor Daly's disdain and opposition made us gun-shy. True, we did not extend any more invitations to mobsters, reformed or otherwise, but we continued to go after controversial subjects. One issue in particular that could not be ignored was the racial turmoil then erupting in many parts of the South. What set it in motion was the landmark Supreme Court ruling in 1954 that segregation in public schools was unconstitutional. Following the lead of that decision, federal courts were issuing directives to segregated school districts in several southern states to comply with the law of the land. Many southerners viewed this legal change as a social disruption, a threat to what had been their way of life since Reconstruction, and they were determined to resist it. (The prevailing mood in most northern communities was a certain smug superiority, but their day of reckoning would come a few years later over such volatile issues as busing and open housing.)

The alleged evils of racial integration—or "mongrelization," as he phrased it—had been an obsession of Eldon Lee Edwards when I interviewed him. But as the leader of the generally discredited Ku Klux Klan, Edwards could be dismissed as a deviant, a social outcast. Respectable southerners, even those who embraced the principle of segregation, were quick to disavow the Klan and its various wizards. In the summer of 1957, some three months after the Edwards interview, we turned our attention to a staunch defender of segregation who at the same time was an honored member of society, a pillar of the southern power bloc in Washington—Senator James Eastland of Mississippi.

At the end of each broadcast, I announced who was scheduled to be my guest the following week, and I often previewed the kind of questions I intended to ask. The Sunday before the Eastland interview, I told our audience: "Next week we go after the biggest fight the Confederate states have had since Bull Run—the battle for civil rights. We will get the story from the controversial, outspoken senator from Mississippi. He's James

Eastland, you see him behind me. We will try to find out why Senator Eastland charges that, quote, 'the Negro is an inferior race,' unquote, and why he described the United States Supreme Court as, and I quote again, 'a crowd of racial politicians in judicial robes.' Unquote."

The next morning I received a call from a member of Eastland's staff, who informed me that the senator had changed his mind about appearing on our program. He had seen my preview the night before, the aide explained, and he didn't want to answer "those kind of questions." Yates and I promptly flew down to Washington to confront Eastland in person. Having proclaimed on the air that he was to be our next interviewee, I didn't want to renege on that promise.

When we arrived at his office, Eastland greeted us correctly, even cordially. He was in fact still smiling when, after the usual introductory chitchat, he raised the question "So what is it, really, that you're going to ask me next Sunday night?"

We prided ourselves on never divulging our questions ahead of time so that I could say, legitimately, that the interview the audience was about to see was unrehearsed. It's true that from the preinterviews with Al Ramrus, most of our guests knew the general areas we planned to explore, what our line of attack was likely to be—but *not* the specific queries. Eastland surely knew that we wanted to talk about segregation, but apparently he was hoping to intimidate us a bit. We talked around the subject for a moment or two, then Eastland suddenly inquired: "Mr. Wallace, who is your sponsor?"

"I don't know why you ask, Senator. You know it's the Philip Morris Company."

But I *did* know why he asked; or at least I thought I knew. At that time of mounting racial tension, Philip Morris was being portrayed in the South as an equal opportunity employer, and those who spread that word were not paying compliments. What's more, the company had given money to the Urban League and had bought advertisements in Negro newspapers. The result was that Philip Morris's sales in the South had suffered.

"Yes, Philip Morris," Senator Eastland said in response to my answer, "yes, that's what I understand." He paused, his honeysuckle smile broadening into a gloating grin.

"Mr. Wallace, should you ask me questions which I find inimical, I just might find it necessary to point out that Philip Morris, that cancer-bearing agent, is regarded in the South as a Nigra-lovin' cigarette." Once again he paused, this time to study our reaction. "So perhaps you would now care to be guided by that in framing the questions which you intend to put to me. As a matter of fact, Mr. Wallace, would you care to tell me now what questions you *do* intend to put to me?"

Yates and I were stunned. "Nigra-lovin' cigarette"? *This* was the voice of the civilized, respectable South? As far as I was concerned, the senator's observations were every bit as primitive as those of Eldon Edwards and his fellow Klansmen. But we resisted his threat, and Eastland eventually agreed to appear on *The Mike Wallace Interview*—on our terms. And not once during our broadcast the following Sunday did he mention Philip Morris or cancer or the cigarette's alleged reputation in the South. Moreover, the interview did indeed revolve around the kind of questions I had previewed—the kind I was told he did not want to answer—and Eastland, to his credit, did not fudge or equivocate:

WALLACE: Senator, if a Negro maid or nurse is good enough to care for a white infant in the South—live with that infant, feed that infant, et cetera—why is not that same Negro maid allowed to eat in the same restaurant with southern whites?

EASTLAND: It's a matter of choice.

WALLACE: Choice by the whites?

EASTLAND: No, it's a matter of choice by both races.

WALLACE: Are you suggesting—?

EASTLAND: You know that in Mississippi, it was a Reconstruction legislature composed principally of Negroes that enacted our segregation statute.

WALLACE: Are you suggesting the Negro—?

EASTLAND: I'm suggesting that the vast majority of Negroes want their own schools, their own hospitals, their own churches, their own restaurants . . .

WALLACE: Are you saying that the Negro in the South wants segregation?

EASTLAND: I'm suggesting, certainly.

WALLACE: The Negro in the South wants segregation?

EASTLAND: Ninety-nine percent—yes, sir!

The next day *The New York Journal-American* reported our encounter under the headline: "Eastland to Wallace: The Southern Negro Prefers Segregation."

In the fall of 1957, Little Rock, Arkansas, became the first major battleground in the struggle over school integration. Citing "evidence of disorder and threats of disorder" as his rationale, Governor Orval Faubus called out the Arkansas National Guard to prevent nine Negro students from desegregating Central High School in Little Rock. His action contravened a federal court order and, even worse, it greatly exacerbated an already tense situation. Emboldened by their governor's act of defiance, diehard segregationists converged on the school, where they jeered and cursed at the Negro students and, in some cases, resorted to violence. It was a sorry spectacle, and eventually President Eisenhower had to send in federal troops to enforce the desegregation order and protect the students as they entered and left the school each day.

From beginning to end, the man at the center of the Little Rock story was Faubus, who until then had been an obscure figure on the national stage. Critics accused him of being an unprincipled cynic who had exploited the fears and resentments of segregationists for his own political gain. In a similar vein, *Time* magazine described him as "a sophisticated hillbilly." We offered Faubus a chance to speak for himself on nationwide television, and he accepted. So at the height of the disruptions—before the federal troops were ordered into the fray— we took our cameras to Little Rock and interviewed Faubus at the governor's mansion:

WALLACE: Governor, what's your opinion of the crowds of white adults who gather outside Central High School each weekday morning? They curse at any Negro who happens to pass by. They call Negroes animals. And almost to a man they say Governor Faubus has done the right thing. What do you think of these people?

FAUBUS: Well, malice, envy, hate is deplorable in any place or in any circumstance. But as President Eisenhower has said himself, "You can't change the hearts of people by law."

WALLACE: Governor, we, of course, all know that the Supreme Court has ruled that there must be integration. You have said that you respect that ruling. Tell me this: Personally, do you favor Negro and white children sitting together in classrooms?

FAUBUS: I have never expressed any personal opinion as to the matter.

WALLACE: Why not?

FAUBUS: I felt that it is best not to.

WALLACE: Why?

FAUBUS: I am the governor of a state, pledged to uphold its laws, to keep the peace and order and also the laws of the nation. My personal views are not relevant to the problem.

WALLACE: You will make no further statement than that?

FAUBUS: No.

But if James Eastland was an ardent segregationist and Orval Faubus came across as a shifty opportunist who refused to declare where he stood on the issue, there were other white southerners who were strongly committed to another point of view. This truth was vigorously demonstrated when Tallulah Bankhead expressed her views for my newspaper column, which was then running in the *New York Post*. Tallulah no doubt had expected questions that focused on her lively career in the theater, but I knew, of course, that in addition to being an accomplished and flamboyant actress, Miss Bankhead came from a distinguished political family in Alabama. Her grandfather and uncle had been U.S. senators and her father—William

Brockman Bankhead—had been Speaker of the House of Representatives. And knowing that encouraged me to ask her about the political and racial turmoil that was sweeping across her native region:

> WALLACE: Tallulah, as a southern belle from Alabama and daughter of a long line of southern legislators, do you consider yourself a typical southerner?
>
> BANKHEAD: I'm not typical of anything. I'm Tallulah Bankhead.
>
> WALLACE: How do you feel about our most prominent southern senators?
>
> BANKHEAD: Strom Thurmond? Remember me? I was for Truman, which automatically outlaws all Dixiecrats! Eastland? Talmadge? Senators should uphold and respect the law of the land...
>
> WALLACE: Are you sympathetic with the nonviolence tactics of Martin Luther King?
>
> BANKHEAD: I think he has behaved magnificently. The wisdom of the Negro race has been outstanding.
>
> WALLACE: What is the basic thing that separates black and white in the South? Is it fear of intermarriage?
>
> BANKHEAD: Oh, years ago they took a survey and found that almost no Negroes had any thought of intermarriage in their minds. My secretary comes from the South. She has some Indian and white blood, and some colored blood. She says, "Well, Miss Bankhead, my grandmother didn't rape anybody..."
>
> WALLACE: Are you proud to be a southerner?
>
> BANKHEAD: I *am* proud to be a southerner. I *am*. I am not ashamed of the South. I am ashamed of *situations* in the South, things that have *happened* in the South.

It was a difficult and harrowing time, and, as everyone who lived through the 1960s in America knows, it was destined to get a lot worse before it finally got better.

• • •

Another woman of "the theater" I interviewed that year was the celebrated stripper, Lili St. Cyr. When she appeared on our ABC program, she began with a spirited defense of her strip-tease act, especially against the charge that it was lewd and immoral. Then, quite abruptly, her mood changed and she revealed herself as a disenchanted and rather forlorn young woman:

WALLACE: Are you proud of what you're doing?

ST. CYR: No.

WALLACE: You're not?

ST. CYR: No. No, I'm not.

WALLACE: Are you ashamed of what you do?

ST. CYR: I would rather be doing something else.

WALLACE: Ah, you're a married woman. How does your husband feel about his wife disrobing and dancing pro-vocatively in public?

ST. CYR: My husband is very anxious to go into business and have me stop it.

WALLACE: I gather from what you say you don't like show business really at all and you don't like show-business people very much either.

ST. CYR: Well, it's a false sorta business. When you are acting in any form you must be false because you're acting, you're not being yourself, you're not contributing anything really to—to anything . . .

WALLACE: You don't like yourself very much.

ST. CYR: No.

WALLACE: Do you know why?

ST. CYR: Maybe because of what I'm doing.

WALLACE: When you quit, do you intend to raise a family?

ST. CYR: No.

WALLACE: Is it possible that with your preoccupation with

your business, your body, your beauty—are you afraid of growing old or growing ugly?

ST. CYR: Yes.

But the most remarkable woman I interviewed that winter of 1957–1958 was Margaret Sanger, the founding mother of the birth-control movement in America. Arguments over birth control don't stir the passions much nowadays. Thanks to the sexual revolution—and in particular to the widespread use of the Pill—it has become a common and accepted practice. But twenty-five years ago, birth control was as stormy an issue as, well, abortion has been in the seventies and eighties. In fact, the pros and cons of the question are essentially the same, except now the dispute is centered on the next procreative level: the couple who have failed for whatever reason to prevent a pregnancy. Do they then have the right to abort it? The combatants haven't changed much, either. For the most part, the groups that opposed birth control back in the fifties are now in the forefront of the fight against abortion, and vice versa. As for Margaret Sanger, she was such a fervent crusader for birth control that she was jailed eight times for her beliefs; and the night she appeared on *The Mike Wallace Interview,* she was in no mood to mince words on the subject:

WALLACE: You have said often that originally the opposition to birth control was in law, and you had to fight against that. Today your opposition stems mainly from where, from what source?

SANGER: Well, I think the opposition is mainly from the hierarchy of the Roman Catholic Church.

WALLACE: Well, let's look at the official Catholic opposition to birth control. I read now from a Church publication called *The Question Box.* In forbidding birth control, it says the following: "The immediate purpose and primary end of marriage is the begetting of children. When the marital relations is so used as to render the fulfillment of its purposes impossible (that is, by birth control) it is used unethically and unnaturally." Now what's wrong with that position?

SANGER: It's very wrong, it's not normal. It's—it has a wrong attitude toward marriage, toward love, toward the normal relationships between men and women.

WALLACE: Your feeling is what, then?

SANGER: My feeling is that love and attraction between men and women, in many cases, is the very finest relationship. It has nothing to do with bearing a child. That's secondary many, many times. We know that. You see your birth rates and you can talk to people who have very happy marriages and they're not having babies every year.

WALLACE: According to the tenets of Catholicism, they rule that birth control violates a natural law, therefore birth control is a sin no matter who practices it. Certainly you can take no issue with the natural law—

SANGER: Oh, I certainly do take issue with it, and I think it's untrue and I think it's unnatural. It's an unnatural attitude to take. How do they know? I mean, after all, they're celibates. They don't know love, they don't know marriage, they know nothing about bringing up children nor any of the marriage problems of life, and yet they speak to people as if they were God.

Yet of all the interviews that season, my favorite was with the giant of modern architecture—Frank Lloyd Wright. Wright was more than a great architect. Like Philip Wylie, he was an astute and caustic social critic; yet even when he was playing the curmudgeon, he did so with humor. Wright's trenchant opinions on life and art came from a richly original mind, and I quote now from our interview at some length because so many of the observations he made that night, a quarter century ago, are as relevant today as they were then:

WALLACE: What do you think of church architecture in the United States?

WRIGHT: I think it's of course a great shame.

WALLACE: Because it improperly reflects the idea of religion?

WRIGHT: Because it is a paragon-monkey reflection and not a reflection of religion.

WALLACE: Well, when I walk into St. Patrick's Cathedral, and I'm not a Catholic, but when I walk into St. Patrick's Cathedral here in New York City, I am enveloped in a feeling of reverence.

WRIGHT: Sure it isn't an inferiority complex?

WALLACE: Just because the building is big and I'm small, you mean? Ah, I think not.

WRIGHT: I hope not.

WALLACE: You feel nothing when you go into St. Patrick's?

WRIGHT: Regret.

WALLACE: Because of what?

WRIGHT: Because it isn't the thing that really represents the spirit of independence and the sovereignty of the individual. Which I feel should be represented in our edifices devoted to culture...

WALLACE: You said many years ago that you would someday be the greatest architect of the twentieth century. Have you reached your goal?

WRIGHT: You know I may not have said it, Mike, but I may have felt it.

WALLACE: You do feel it?

WRIGHT: But it's so unbecoming to say it that I should have been careful about it. I'm not as crude, as arrogant, as I'm generally reported to be.

WALLACE: What is arrogance?

WRIGHT: Arrogance is something a man possesses on the surface to defend the fact that he hasn't got the things he pretends to have. He's a bluff, in other words.

WALLACE: Let me ask you this: As an intellectual yourself, Mr. Wright, what do you think of President—?

WRIGHT: I deny the allegation, and I refuse to marry that girl. I don't like intellectuals.

WALLACE: You don't like intellectuals. Why not?

WRIGHT: Because they're superficial. They're from the top down, not the ground up. I have always flattered myself that what I represented was from the ground up. Does that mean anything?

WALLACE: What do you think of President Eisenhower as an intellect?

WRIGHT: Well, now, don't ask me as an intellect, because how would I know? But he's a hell of a nice fellow and one of the nicest things I know about him is that my wife voted for him, and I voted for Adlai Stevenson.

WALLACE: The *Philadelphia Inquirer Magazine Section,* October 18, 1953, said as follows: "Some quarters have denounced Wright as an impractical visionary and pompous windbag."

WRIGHT: Yes.

WALLACE: How do you feel about such criticism, Mr. Wright?

WRIGHT: You always have to consider the source from which these things come. Now if somebody I deeply respected had said such a thing, I would be worried. I would feel hurt. But as a piece in the newspaper blowing into the gutters of the street the next day, I don't think it counts much.

An interview like that helped to compensate for all the problems that continued to beset us at ABC, even after the furor over the Mickey Cohen fiasco had died down.

Our interview with Orval Faubus at the governor's mansion in Little Rock was the only one we did on the road; all the others were broadcast from the ABC studio in New York or in Washington. We didn't have the budget then to transport camera crews around the country and to foreign capitals the way we do now on a routine basis for *60 Minutes*. But in the late fall of 1957, we pursued an opportunity to break out of that pattern. The object of our quest was a bearded Cuban revolutionary named Fidel Castro.

Castro had not yet come to power. Hiding out in the mountains of Cuba's Oriente province with his ragged band of guerrillas, he was portrayed in the U.S. press as a mysterious and rather quixotic figure. We really didn't know much about him, including whether or not he was a Communist, but that question was not yet perceived to be of major concern. For it was generally assumed that Castro's lonely and courageous struggle to overthrow the regime of Fulgencio Batista was doomed to fail.

Ted Yates and I had established contacts with some Cubans then living in Miami who claimed to be in close touch with Castro. One of them was Carlos Prío Socarrás, who had been president of Cuba before Batista. We eventually received word from Prío that if we came to Miami, he would get us across to Cuba for an interview with Castro at his rebel camp in the mountains.

Yates and I were elated, but John Daly didn't share our enthusiasm. As head of the ABC news department, he had jurisdiction over the expense money we would need to carry out this ambitious project. Knowing how Daly felt about Yates and me, I hardly expected him to congratulate us for our journalistic enterprise, but I thought that surely he would recognize the value to ABC of an exclusive interview with a man whose attempt at revolution—whether it turned out to be successful or not—was capturing the imagination of so many Americans. Instead, Daly accused us of naïveté and gave us a lecture on news judgment: "Wallace, Yates, this is simply another indication of the fact that you people just don't know what you're up to. Fidel Castro is a has-been. He's no longer a figure of importance. Let me tell you you're chasing a will-o'-the-wisp."

I've often wondered whether Daly really believed that, or was simply anxious that we not score a reportorial coup that his ABC news department couldn't manage. In any case, Yates and I decided to go ahead without Daly's budget approval; with our own money, we hired a camera crew, flew to Miami and began to wait. It was like waiting for Godot. Day after day we had conversations with our various contacts there, including Carlos Prío Socarrás, until finally it became clear that they were not going to be able to take us to Castro.

The frustration we felt, as we flew back to New York empty-handed, was made all the more galling by the realization that we had given Daly and his faction more ammunition to use against us. Our failure to deliver the Castro interview made us vulnerable to the charge that we were gullible amateurs who had wasted time and our own money on a snipe hunt. But as it turned out, that was the least of our worries, for we were soon up to our necks in more hot water.

December 7, 1957, happened to fall on a Sunday, just as it had sixteen years earlier when the Japanese attacked Pearl Harbor and it became known—in President Franklin D. Roosevelt's phrase—as "a date that will live in infamy." This no doubt should have alerted me to the prospect of trouble, but, alas, I have never viewed the calendar with a superstitious eye. To me, Friday the thirteenth has always been just another payday, and I have never been nervous about venturing into public to conduct my affairs on the ides of March.

My guest that first Sunday in December was Drew Pearson, the muckraking Washington columnist. Pearson's specialty was digging for dirt in the dark corners of the political establishment, and he frequently found it. As a result, he was perhaps the most feared and even hated journalist in Washington at that time. (The hard-hitting style and tradition he established has been carried on in more recent years by his protégé and successor, Jack Anderson.) I admired Pearson's bold and aggressive reporting, but I wanted to see how he would react under pressure. He had few peers when it came to dishing it out—but could he take it?

WALLACE: President Roosevelt once called you a chronic liar. President Truman called you an s.o.b. at one time and a vicious liar at another time. The late Tennessee senator Kenneth McKellar called you, quote, "an ignorant liar, a pusillanimous liar, a peewee liar, a liar during his manhood, a liar by profession, a liar in the daytime and a liar in the night time." End quote.

PEARSON: He used up six pages of *The Congressional Record* calling me different types of liar.

WALLACE: Could it be that you are a liar?

PEARSON: I—I *hope* not.

WALLACE: Well, what is it about Drew Pearson that inspires such bitterness in Presidents and other statesmen?

PEARSON: I don't believe that I've ever knowingly told a lie. But I have made some mistakes...

Pearson went on to defend his integrity. He dismissed the name-calling as an occupational hazard and said it didn't bother him as long as he knew that his own conscience was clear. Our conversation shifted then to politics and the next presidential election. I noted that Vice-President Richard Nixon was the current front-runner for the Republican nomination and that "the Democratic glamour boy would seem to be Senator Jack Kennedy." That led to a question about Kennedy and his controversial father:

WALLACE: In your column on October 27, you wrote that Senator Kennedy's—and I quote—"millionaire McCarthyite father, crusty old Joseph P. Kennedy, is spending a fortune on a publicity machine to make Jack's name well-known. No candidate in history has ever had so much money spent on a public-relations advance buildup." Unquote. What significance do you see in this, aside from the fact that Joe Kennedy would like to see Jack Kennedy President of the United States?

PEARSON: I don't know what significance other than the fact that I don't think we should have a synthetic public-relations buildup for any job of that kind. Now, Jack Kennedy's a fine young man, a very personable fellow.

But he isn't as good as that public-relations campaign makes him out to be. He's the only man in history that I know who won a Pulitzer Prize for a book that was ghostwritten for him, which indicates the kind of a public-relations buildup he has had.

WALLACE: Who wrote the book for him?

PEARSON: I don't recall at the present moment.

WALLACE: You know for a fact, Drew?

PEARSON: Yes, I do.

WALLACE: That the book, *Profiles in Courage,* was written for Senator Kennedy?

PEARSON: I do.

WALLACE: By somebody else.

PEARSON: I do.

WALLACE: And he, Kennedy, accepted a Pulitzer Prize for it?

PEARSON: He did.

WALLACE: And he has never acknowledged the fact?

PEARSON: No, he has not. You know, there's a little wisecrack around the Senate about Jack, who is a very handsome young man, as you know. Some of his colleagues say, "Jack, I wish you had a little less profile and more courage."

Kennedy did not see the broadcast, but some of his friends called to tell him about it, and the next day, Kennedy's office called ABC and asked for a copy of the transcript. I could understand why the Kennedy clan was sensitive about the Pearson allegation. For if true, it meant that the senator was resorting to dishonest tactics in his expensive and image-oriented campaign for the 1960 Democratic presidential nomination, which by the end of 1957 was already well under way.

A few days after the Pearson interview, there was a meeting—to which I was not invited—in the ABC executive suite of Oliver Treyz. Later I was told that Bobby Kennedy had been there with Clark Clifford, the eminent Washington lawyer hired to represent the family. Ostensibly they were there to discuss the matter, but in truth they had come to dictate their terms: an on-air apology the following Sunday.

In the meantime, I had prodded Pearson to specify who, if not Kennedy, had written *Profiles in Courage*. Drew did some more checking with his sources and came up with the name of Ted Sorensen, a legislative aide to the senator who at that time was unknown to the general public, but whom Kennedy had credited in the preface to the book for "his invaluable assistance in the assembly and preparation" of the material on which *Profiles in Courage* was based. Pearson refused to make the desired apology and so did I, for by now I was convinced that he was sure of his ground. But the network brass did not back us up; faced with the threat of another libel suit, they offered an official ABC apology, to be delivered by Treyz prior to our next program, and the Kennedy people were willing to settle for that.

I was furious at my employers for the way they caved in to the Kennedys. I had fully supported the earlier decision to retract and eat crow after the Mickey Cohen interview, but this was different. Drew Pearson was no raffish gangster who had spewed forth a torrent of reckless and abusive slander. He was an influential journalist who had made a precise and measured allegation about a specific event in the career of an ambitious politician. And he was an old pro at this game; over the years Pearson had survived several libel suits with his honor intact. As for the Kennedys' libel threat, it would not have taken much fortitude to call their bluff. The last thing in the world they would have wanted was a highly publicized court fight over the question of who had written *Profiles in Courage*. The way I saw it, the ABC apology was a craven gesture and an insult to Pearson.

A postscript: In 1965 in *Kennedy*, Ted Sorensen wrote, "I was not the author of Jack Kennedy's book," and in the years since then, he has never wavered, in public, on that point. But Sorensen's disavowal has not gone unchallenged. To cite just one example: In 1980 in *Jack: The Struggles of John F. Kennedy*, Herbert Parmet detailed his thorough investigation of the manuscript and dictation tapes of *Profiles in Courage* and arrived at the conclusion that it had been essentially ghostwritten. "The research, tentative drafts and organization were left to the collective labors of others," Parmet wrote, "and the literary craftsmanship was clearly the work of Ted Sorensen."

At the end of our first year at ABC, Philip Morris severed its connection with *The Mike Wallace Interview*. What with the Cohen and Kennedy imbroglios and ratings that were less than robust, the company understandably decided to take its money elsewhere. The completion of that first year also released ABC from its obligation to put me on the air once a week in prime time. But I had signed a firm two-year contract with the network and it had to pay me for the second year whether I worked or not; so I was anticipating a year of lucrative inactivity when, out of the blue, I received a call from the Fund for the Republic.

An adjunct of the Ford Foundation, the Fund for the Republic was the most imposing think tank in America. It was the brainchild of Robert Hutchins, former president of the University of Chicago and a highly esteemed figure in intellectual and academic circles. Under his guidance, the Fund gave stipends to scholars to delve into a variety of complex subjects in ways that might lead to a deeper understanding of freedom and justice in American life. And now, in the spring of 1958, this august group wanted to experiment with television. Hutchins appreciated the importance of communication, of the need to transmit ideas from the ivory towers to the populace; he believed that if exploited properly, television—the ultimate mass medium—could become a vehicle for education and enlightenment. Specifically, the Fund for the Republic offered to assume the cost of *The Mike Wallace Interview*, including the salaries for me and our production team, for a nineteen-week period. In return for this largess, we would alter the tone and content of the broadcast to make it more cerebral, more in keeping with Dr. Hutchins's vision of a coast-to-coast classroom.

I was willing to give it a try and so were my superiors at ABC. They felt, and I agreed, that our chances of finding a commercial sponsor to replace Philip Morris were practically nil, and as long as the Fund was going to pick up the tab, the

network would furnish the air time. Besides, it no doubt occurred to Oliver Treyz and Leonard Goldenson that the kind
of program Hutchins and his cohorts had in mind would bring
a touch of prestige to a prime-time schedule that, for the most
part, was a potpourri of sit-coms and quiz shows and the like.
According to the agreement that was drawn up, I would interview "people of substance in the community" suggested by me
or by the Fund, with ABC having final approval. The guests
would appear on the program for "the purpose of stimulating
the discussion of basic issues of survival and freedom." In fact,
that was the name of the new series—*Survival and Freedom*.
Our intentions were nothing if not noble.

It was understood that for this venture I was to eschew the
role of adversary. A spokesman for our new patron explained,
gently but firmly, that the Fund did not want me to probe into
the personal lives of my guests; nor was I to confront them
with contradictions or indiscretions from their past. Instead,
my job was to explore their views in a positive way, to help
them in their efforts to be "insightful and illuminating." In my
chastened mood, I had no objection to this decorous, kid-glove
approach. And so during the summer and fall of 1958, I con-
versed with such distinguished personages as Reinhold Nie-
buhr, Aldous Huxley, Erich Fromm, Cyrus Eaton, Justice
William O. Douglas, Adlai Stevenson and a short, bespectacled
Harvard professor with a thick German accent who at the time
was unknown outside academic circles. His name was Henry
Kissinger, and he had just written a book called *Nuclear Weapons and Foreign Policy.* In our interview Kissinger expounded
his theory of "limited nuclear war" and contended that America
must be willing to make some nuclear weapons a "usable instrument of policy" if it hoped to deter the Soviet Union. Although neither of us had any way of knowing it then, Kissinger
and I would be seeing more of each other in the years to come.

The *Survival and Freedom* series had its moments. Some
of the discussions *were* illuminating, and at the end of the run,
our highbrow sponsor expressed satisfaction with the way it
had gone. But neither the Fund nor ABC came up with a
proposal to extend the series, which was fine with me because
I was growing restless in the *Survival and Freedom* format.
Whatever else they may have been, the lofty colloquies with

scholars and statesmen were a far cry from the combative drama of *Night Beat*, which had been our appeal to ABC in the first place.

By the fall of 1958, I had reached the conclusion that there was no real future for me at ABC. I knew that as long as John Daly remained in charge of the news operation, I and the other members of the *Night Beat* team who had gone over to ABC— Ted Yates, Al Ramrus and Rita Quinn—would be regarded as interlopers. So as 1958 drew to a close, the four of us decided to try to set up shop elsewhere.

And once again, it was Ted Cott, our old friend from Channel 5 and the godfather of *Night Beat*, who took us in.

CHAPTER

FIVE

TED COTT did not perform the ritual of slaughtering fatted calves to celebrate the event, but in all other respects he welcomed his prodigal children home with open arms. Home, however, was no longer Channel 5, the birthplace of *Night Beat*. Cott had recently moved on to another small independent station, Channel 13 (the same Channel 13 that later became the New York outlet for public broadcasting), where the reunion took place in the early weeks of 1959.

Wallace and his group were glad to be free of the pressures and frustrations that had plagued them at ABC, but they could hardly pretend that their return to local television was a triumphant one. The experience at ABC had been severely damaging, especially for Wallace, who—as the on-air presence, the star of the show—had to bear the brunt of the blame just as earlier, when *Night Beat* was showered with praise, he had received most of the credit. Critics and other powerful voices in the industry chose to overlook the positive achievements of *The Mike Wallace Interview*: the stimulating exchanges with Philip Wylie and Frank Lloyd Wright and the forthright treatment of the civil rights struggle in the interviews with Senator Eastland and Orval Faubus. Instead, they persisted in dwelling on the isolated contretemps, the Mickey Cohen episode and the flap over Drew Pearson's slam at Senator Kennedy. Even some of the reviewers who previously had commended Wallace for his candor and enterprise now turned on him. He had come to be regarded in many circles as a reckless hip-shooter whose thirst for sensationalism had embarrassed his network. Certainly in the eyes of most executives at the three networks, Mike had become a pariah and several years would pass before he would be given another opportunity—on the network level—to demonstrate that he was a solid and responsible journalist.

But now in February 1959, Wallace was eager to put all the bitterness and disappointment of the ABC ordeal behind him and concentrate on the challenge of his new assignment. Under the guidance of a new owner, Channel 13 was about to embark on a bold and fascinating experiment that still stands as one of the most ambitious attempts ever made to upgrade the quality of TV programming. The force behind the experiment was a thirty-nine-year-old advertising man and syndicator named Ely Landau. In recent years Landau had made a lot of money, mainly from selling films to television stations around the country. But he wanted more—prestige as well as prosperity—a combination difficult to achieve in commercial television, then and now.

Landau's company, National TeleFilm Associates, purchased the small and nondescript WNTA-TV, Channel 13, for four-and-a-half-million dollars. (The station's headquarters was actually in Newark, New Jersey, but its signal blanketed the entire New York metropolitan area.) Landau then hired Ted Cott to program the station with broadcasts that would offer viewers a clear alternative to routine television fare. His hope was that New Yorkers would respond to the nonformula, adult programs, and that the impetus would lead to wide syndication of those broadcasts to independent, nonnetwork stations across the country. It was a daring gamble, but Landau and his backers did not hedge their bet. Among the projects to which they committed themselves were: David Susskind's discussion program, *Open End,* Bishop Fulton Sheen's lecture series, and offbeat exercises in wit and irreverence featuring the droll talents of Alexander King and Henry Morgan. Another highlight was the splendid dramatic series *Play of the Week,* which provided a steady diet of theatrical classics, such as Shaw's *Don Juan in Hell* and O'Neill's *The Iceman Cometh.* All those programs were aimed assertively at an intelligent and sophisticated audience, which alone was enough to make them a radical departure from the norm.

Wallace and Ted Yates were given a generous budget and a free rein to produce five interview shows a week plus New York's first half-hour evening news program. The latter broadcast, *News Beat,* was yet another innovation, for at the time all the other nightly newscasts on television—local and network—were still confined to the fifteen-minute format that had been in effect throughout the 1950s. The networks, in fact, did not get around to expanding their evening news shows to a half hour until 1963, and when they finally did, it was with a great deal of fanfare and self-congratulation. Almost everyone had forgotten that a local New York newscast anchored by Mike Wallace had beaten them to the punch four years earlier.

Channel 13 unveiled its new look in March 1959, and most of the critics applauded the experiment. Jack Gould of *The New York Times* offered this observation:

"By all odds the season's most interesting development on the local television scene has been the emergence of Channel 13 as an outlet that is consciously trying to break out of the usual video pattern. Operating on a comparative shoestring, WNTA-TV has become the darling of the avant-garde viewer, generated more talk—both on and off the screen—than any other single TV undertaking of the year and raised some interesting speculation about possible new economic approaches to TV. In many ways, the station is a practical laboratory test of whether a TV station must bow to the concept of a mass audience or whether it can succeed theatrically and financially by cultivating its own type of following."

The laboratory test proved to be too great a challenge. Channel 13 did indeed become the darling of the avant-garde viewer, but the cult following was minuscule. Because of its failure to make an appreciable dent in the huge New York market, the station was unable to enlist the support of the big spenders—the sponsors who invested heavily in television—and Ely Landau's own financial resources were not enough to keep the ambitious format going indefinitely. Hence, the high hopes that Landau and Ted Cott had entertained for the project eventually gave way to the bleak reality of their economic status, and gradually, over the next couple of years, one innovative program after another was pulled off the air. Wallace's two shows were among the casualties. *News Beat* lasted a year, and the less costly interview series hung on for a little more than two years.

The "last hurrah" phase of *The Mike Wallace Interview* was something of an anticlimax. The broadcast itself had not changed in form or content; it continued to attract lively guests and Mike continued to hammer away at them with his customary verve. Nor had the show lost its knack for igniting unexpected moments of emotional drama. (For example, when Mike interviewed the sultry black singer Eartha Kitt, she suddenly burst into tears while reminiscing about her unhappy childhood.) The difference was that by now viewers had become all too accustomed to such theatrics, and in that sense the program had become a victim of its own success. The interviews no longer conveyed the freshness and shock value that had made *Night Beat* such a conversation piece when it exploded on the scene in the fall of 1956. As a result, when the show finally went off the air in the spring of 1961, its departure was scarcely noticed. Like the world in the T. S. Eliot poem, it ended not with a bang but a whimper.

During the two years that he worked at Channel 13, Wallace was active on other professional fronts as well. He remained on friendly terms with the president of Philip Morris, Joseph Cullman, even after the tobacco firm dropped its sponsorship of the interview program at ABC; and through this association Wallace began doing commercials for the company's new filter cigarette, Parliament. That pleased his banker and broker, not to mention the Internal Revenue Service, for the commercials were a lucrative source of income, but they hurt him in other ways. At a time when news correspondents at the three networks were extricating themselves from any direct involvement in commercials so as to avoid even the appearance of a conflict of interest, Wallace became a highly visible spokesman for a product that was being cited by numerous medical authorities as a principal cause of cancer. Not exactly the ideal image for someone who yearned to be taken seriously as a journalist.

But during that period, Wallace also took on other jobs that helped to enhance rather than damage his reputation. In the summer of 1959, he received a call from a stranger who introduced himself as David Wolper. Like Ely Landau, Wolper had made a bundle selling syndication films to television stations, but—again like Landau—he was eager now to try his hand at something more ambitious. In the years ahead, Wolper would find plenty of outlets for his ambition as he went on to become a giant in the industry, the producer of *Roots* and other milestones in TV programming. When he telephoned Wallace in 1959, Wolper was preparing to produce his first documentary. The space age had dawned (the first sputnik had been launched by the Russians two years earlier) and Wolper was gathering film for a detailed look at the emerging Soviet-American rivalry in space exploration. He wanted Wallace to narrate the program and conduct the interviews that would be woven into it. Mike accepted the offer, and *The Race for Space* was aired in April 1960.

The success of *The Race for Space*—the program was sold to ninety-five television stations across the country—led to other fruitful collaborations with Wolper, notably on the award-winning broadcast *Biography,* a series of sixty-five profiles of world-famous figures from Mao Tse-tung to Babe Ruth. Many of those *Biography* films are still shown in rerun on stations throughout the United States and around the world, and high school teachers also use them as supplemental guides in history and other courses.

The Parliament commercials and Wallace's work with David Wolper were moonlighting diversions that in no way interfered with his regular duties at Channel 13. But in the summer of 1960, Wallace took a leave of absence from the station and embarked on a special assignment for the Westinghouse broadcasting chain. It began with the political conventions. With the news director of Westinghouse, Jim Snyder, he co-anchored Kennedy's hard-earned, first-ballot victory in Los Angeles and Nixon's preordained nomination by the Republicans in Chicago.

Then, following the conventions, Wallace and a Westinghouse camera crew spent the next two months traveling around the country in a station wagon for a series of on-the-road reports called *Closeup U.S.A.* From Chicago they drove west through the Rockies to Portland, Oregon, then down the Pacific coast to Los Angeles, then back across the continent through the Deep South, then up the Atlantic coast to Boston, and finally wound up in Pittsburgh. Along the way, Wallace renewed his acquaintance with Arkansas Governor Orval Faubus in Little Rock, and he also interviewed—among many others—Roswell Garst, the Iowa farmer whom Nikita Khruschev had visited the year before, a Pottowatamie Indian chief in Indiana, a steel-worker in Pennsylvania, an atomic-energy worker in Idaho, a lumberman in Oregon, a Brahmin banker in Boston and an auto worker in Cleveland. The pace was hectic (every day a radio piece and, almost that often, a television story were fed to Westinghouse stations throughout the country), but for Mike it was a richly rewarding experience. It marked the first time in his broadcasting career that he had a chance to work exten-sively as a correspondent in the field, and he would be given a similar, even more ambitious opportunity two years later when Westinghouse sent him around the world to produce and deliver a series of radio reports from Tokyo, Taipei, Hong Kong, Sai-gon, New Delhi, Cairo, Nairobi and London. The experience Wallace gained from those two assignments helped prepare him for the globe-trotting grind that would later become his way of life as a correspondent for *60 Minutes*.

His last chore for Westinghouse in 1960 was to co-anchor the election-night coverage; then it was back to Channel 13 for what turned out to be the final season of *The Mike Wallace Interview*. Ely Landau's high-risk venture had been on the ropes for the past several months, and by the winter of 1960–1961 it was going down for the count. News of its impending demise had spread through the industry, and shortly before Wallace's interview series went off the air for good in April 1961, he received another call from Dick Pack, the head of programming at Westinghouse. Pack was excited about a new broadcast he was putting together—a talk show to be called *PM East*—and he wanted Mike to co-host it with an attractive young woman from Canada named Joyce Davidson. (In later years the young woman would become known to viewers as Joyce Susskind following her marriage to another native son of Brookline who had made a big name for himself in television.)

To borrow a line from the late Billy Rose, Wallace was "underwhelmed" by the offer. The program Pack had described to him sounded uncomfortably similar to the entertainment shows he had worked on in earlier years, and he had no desire to get back on that kind of frivolous treadmill. Yet he did not feel he was in a strong enough position to reject it out of hand. He could count on a certain amount of free-lance income from the Parliament commercials and his projects with David Wol-per, but for the first time since he married Lorraine six years earlier, he had no steady job, no regular paycheck; and there were bills to pay and children to support from two previous marriages, his and hers. He also could not help but notice that neither the networks nor anyone else was pounding at his door with an offer of a serious interview program or a job as a news correspondent. The only other proposal that had come his way in recent weeks was from a producer of game shows who had wanted Wallace to host a trifle called *To Tell the Truth*. He had turned that offer down without hesitation but he realized he could not continue saying no to everything. And so, after mulling it over for several days, Mike decided to say yes to Dick Pack and *PM East*. Yet even as he accepted the offer, he had the disquieting sense that he was making a mistake, that he was locking himself into the wrong kind of vehicle.

His apprehensions were justified. *PM East* went on the air in June of 1961 and ran for a year; from beginning to end, Mike wallowed in embarrassment and frustration. Alexander King once observed that a talk-show host must have a gift for being able to "drench people with the slime of his amiability," and Wallace was no longer any good at the gush-and-prattle routine. In the years since he had done that sort of thing with Buff Cobb, he had grown into a formidable television personality, and his presence now was too strong, too intense, too heavy for the breezy format of a talk show. At one point, the producer of *PM East* brought in Abe Burrows from the Broadway theater world to "help lighten Wallace up." Burrows had directed Wallace in *Reclining Figure*, his one brief fling as a Broadway actor, and now on *PM East* Abe assumed the role of Mike's ego-stroker, his Ed McMahon; but Mike continued to come across as a miserably inept Johnny Carson. Jack Gould wrote in the *Times* that watching Wallace on *PM East* was like watching "Walter Lippmann try to do a buck-and-wing." That was a bit of an overstatement (Wallace was as far removed from the Olympian pronouncements of Lippmann as he was from the zippy one-liners of a deft stand-up comic like Carson), but Gould's general point was on target.

Every now and then, Wallace tried to inject flashes of the old *Night Beat* fire into the happy-talk atmosphere of *PM East*. One such attempt occurred the time Burt Lancaster came on the show to plug his latest movie, *Birdman of Alcatraz*. While doing his homework in preparation for that visit, Wallace was struck by the plethora of stories—some funny, some not so funny—about Lancaster's explosive temper. So instead of confining his interview to flattering, flack-inspired questions about *Birdman of Alcatraz*, he pursued the following tack: "It has been said that Burt Lancaster is the nicest fellow that you could meet *until* he loses his temper, and then watch out! Really? Do you have that bad a temper?"

Lancaster was not amused. He accused Wallace of being "self-consciously sensational" and said that he "resented" being asked about matters that were nobody's business. Mike thoroughly enjoyed the testy response; he was glad to be back in his element, trading verbal punches with a spirited adversary. He told Lancaster that asking direct questions in television interviews had been his stock-in-trade for the past several years, but then he made a tactical mistake that left him wide open for a cutting rejoinder. "I daresay," he ventured, "that you have a certain familiarity with my work."

"Very little," Lancaster replied with a steely grin. A few moments later, he walked off the show, the only time in Wallace's long broadcasting career that that ever happened.

The irony is that many viewers who *were* familiar with his best work—the serious interviews—were, in fact, wondering what Wallace was doing on a show like *PM East*. His "buck-and-wing" stint, along with his frequent appearances as a pitchman for Parliament cigarettes, served to overshadow and undermine all his solid achievements of the past five years: on the interview programs, on the documentaries he did with David Wolper, as anchorman on *News Beat* and as a news correspondent for Westinghouse. All of a sudden he was back in show business and there was every reason to believe that he was stuck in that rut for good.

During this period Mike was inclined to be defensive about his work. When well-meaning friends gingerly suggested that he might be misusing his talents on commercials and talk shows, he would bristle and point out that he had four kids to support and educate. There was certainly no denying that. In addition to his two sons from his first marriage, Peter and Chris, he had assumed paternal responsibility for Lorraine's two children, Pauline and Anthony. In his dual role as divorced father of two kids and stepfather of two others, Mike took care not to play favorites, but by the summer of 1962 he had reason to be especially proud of his eldest son, Peter.

At the age of nineteen, Peter Wallace was a young man of high prospects. He had distinguished himself at prep school and in his first two years at Yale, and, as a reward for his academic achievements, he was given permission to spend the summer in Europe. Mike and Lorraine also were abroad that summer (1962 was the year he made the globe-circling tour of foreign capitals for Westinghouse), and when they returned to New York in late August, they learned that more than two weeks had elapsed without a letter or card from Peter. That was unusual, for Peter had always been a reliable correspondent. The last news his mother had from him was that he had left France and was planning to rendezvous with some college friends in a Greek town on the Gulf of Corinth. When another week passed with still no word from their son, Mike and Peter's mother decided that he should fly to Greece to find out what, if anything, had gone wrong.

The American Embassy in Athens assigned a consular officer to help in the search, which led to the village of Camari. There a man told Mike that he remembered seeing a young stranger set out about two weeks earlier to investigate a monastery situated atop a small mountain just outside Camari. On the backs of donkeys, Mike and the consular officer followed the path the young stranger had taken, and after three hours or so they came to a narrow ledge where they could see that something had happened, that someone had slipped. Mike looked down and there, some fifty feet below, was Peter's body.

Peter's death had a devastating effect on Wallace, not only in the usual sense of intense bereavement, but also in terms of the course his professional life had taken. Peter had expressed a desire to pursue a career in journalism and Mike had encouraged that aspiration, telling his son that it was both a stimulating and honorable profession. (In fact, Peter had worked as a copy boy at Channel 13 the previous summer.) And now in the desolate days following Peter's death, as he struggled to cope with the loss, Mike regretted that he had not set a better example in his own work.

It's true that by the conventional standards of American materialism, Wallace had no cause to complain. He could command top dollar to perform on talk or game shows, and there were other sponsors besides Philip Morris who would have been willing to pay him large fees to deliver their commercials on television. But he knew that this was not the kind of work he could take pride in, and his customary justification for accepting those jobs—that he had the future of his kids to consider—had a rather hollow ring now that Peter was gone. He recalled that eight years earlier, during another bleak period in his life (following the breakup of his marriage to Buff Cobb and his ill-advised, demoralizing romp on the Broadway stage), he had made a promise to himself to concentrate his energies on journalism. That resolve had led him to Ted Cott and Channel 5 and the fulfilling experience of *Night Beat*. But in the past couple of years he had allowed himself to be distracted by the lure of easy money, and now the time had come to reaffirm his earlier commitment. And so, in the dark autumn of 1962, Wallace vowed to transform his grief into something positive, to restructure his life in a way that would honor Peter's memory.

To begin with, he would give up doing the Parliament commercials; that was the essential first step. Next, he would spread the word that he was no longer available for talk shows or game shows or anything else in the show-business sphere of TV programming. And finally, he would inform the heads of the news divisions at the three networks that he was "going straight" in the hope that one of them would be willing to hire him as a correspondent. This sequence of moves would entail a big financial risk and sacrifice, but he knew he could rely on Lorraine's support and encouragement. As a matter of fact, Lorraine had been trying, in her quiet, subtle way, to nudge Mike in that direction even before Peter's death, for by the early 1960s she had formed strong opinions about what her husband should and should *not* be doing in his television career.

This had not been the case in the early days of their marriage. When she first met Mike in the winter of 1955, Lorraine knew nothing about his professional world. There was, after all, no connection whatever between the dash and hustle of the broadcasting industry in New York and the kind of tranquil life she had created for herself and her children in the Caribbean.

The daughter of a French professor at UCLA, Lorraine Perigord was born and raised in southern California, where she eventually became disenchanted with the Hollywood-inspired values and life-style that characterize the region. By the time she was twenty, she found herself agreeing with Oscar Levant's sardonic assessment of the LA area, to wit: "Beneath all that phony tinsel is real tinsel." An aspiring artist, Lorraine wanted to get away from all of that; so in 1948, not long after her first marriage broke up, she and her two children moved to Haiti to start a new life. With its natural beauty and exotic culture, Haiti is a marvelous setting for a painter and Lorraine soon fell in love with the land and its people. To support her family and her painting, Lorraine developed a business that complemented her vocation perfectly. In partnership with another painter, a Spaniard named Angel Botello, she opened an art gallery in Port-au-Prince, and once it became a thriving concern, they opened a second gallery in San Juan, Puerto Rico, which is where the vacationing Mike Wallace found her in February 1955.

At the time, Wallace was a minor celebrity, but this meant nothing to Lorraine, who was totally insulated from the popular culture then being transmitted over American airwaves. Mike discovered that one afternoon shortly after they had met. They were having drinks with some friends from New York at his hotel in San Juan. Mike and the others in the group began talking about Arthur Godfrey's recent public firing of his young protégé, singer Julius LaRosa. Godfrey was then a television superstar with an enormous following—the Johnny Carson of that era—and his brusque dismissal of LaRosa had stirred up a big fuss in the newspapers back home. As Mike and his New York friends continued to debate the pros and cons of Godfrey's action, Lorraine listened quietly with a puzzled expression on her face. Finally, she leaned over to Mike and whispered a question that brought a smile to his lips: "Who's Arthur Godfrey?"

Mike already had been impressed by Lorraine's more obvious attributes—her beauty, her talent, her gentle charm. And now, in addition, she had revealed an ingenuousness that he found endearing. By the time he left Puerto Rico, Mike was thoroughly smitten. Over the next few months he made several return trips to the Carribbean—to keep the fires of courtship burning—and by the summer of that year, he had persuaded Lorraine to leave her beloved Haiti and move to New York with her two children. They were married on July 21, 1955.

In the years that followed, Lorraine did not entirely lose her innocence about Mike's professional life. Even after they had been married twenty years or so and he was the senior correspondent on *60 Minutes,* she would express concern to his secretary that some of his producers were making too many demands on his time and energy. The problem, as she saw it, was Mike had such an accommodating nature that it was easy to take advantage of him, but she wished that certain producers would make more of an effort to ease up on the pressures they imposed on him. Such complaints, which were not frequent, were always good for a merry little laugh around the offices of *60 Minutes,* for the truth of the matter was invariably just the opposite. One would be hard-pressed to name anyone else in the television news business who is as demanding of his associates as Mike Wallace has been of his support troops over the years. Those who have worked for him on *60 Minutes* and other programs generally have lived in dread of his blunt assertions that they were not pushing themselves hard enough to get a certain story or a specific angle on a story. The notion of Wallace as a man easy to take advantage of, secretly yearning for a respite from the pressures that came with the job, would have struck most of his co-workers as a consummation devoutly to be wished, but God help them if they ever made the mistake of acting on that premise. Lorraine's touching belief that the stress and burdens were being inflicted on Mike instead of the other way around can be attributed in large part to the fact that he was inclined to shield her from the more abrasive realities of his working personality.

Yet in other respects, she developed her own kind of savvy about his career. *Night Beat* came into existence during the second year of their marriage, and she could plainly see the satisfactions he derived from the show and the other interview programs that followed. Then in the late 1950s, when he reverted to the pattern of his early years in broadcasting and began to vacillate between journalism and other assignments—commercials and entertainment programs—she could not help but notice the sharp contrast in his attitude: how happy he was when he was working in news and how restless and bored when he was performing the other chores. In the spring of 1961, when he told her about the offer to co-host *PM East,* Lorraine urged him to reject it and wait for something to turn up in news. But she acquiesced to his practical argument that the money was too good to pass up, especially since there was no guarantee that he would be able to land a suitable job in journalism. She suffered with him through that year-long ordeal, during which time she observed that when he watched the news at home, he often did so with a mixture of admiration and envy for the various network correspondents—Walter Cronkite, Eric Sevareid, David Brinkley, et al. From his reaction to their work, she came to realize more clearly than ever before that they were the men whom he regarded as his natural peers.

So it was against this background that Mike went to Lorraine in the fall of 1962, at a time when his grief over the loss of Peter was so intense that he could scarcely bear to speak of it, and told her why he wanted to forsake all the easy-money work and try to make another fresh start in journalism. He had expected her to be supportive, but Lorraine's response was so positive and enthusiastic that it prompted him to say to her: "You've wanted me to do this all along, haven't you?"

"Yes," she replied, "I have. Because this is what you should be doing. It's the only kind of work that makes you happy."

Planning a course of action is one thing; putting it into effect is quite another, and Wallace was under no illusion that it would be easy to induce one of the networks to hire him as a news correspondent. He knew exactly what he was up against.

First, there was the age factor. Wallace was now forty-four, clearly a disadvantage in an industry that placed so much emphasis on youth. Then, too, his reputation was still tainted by the bruising experience at ABC. Because of the Mickey Cohen libel suit and other controversies, the network executives he would be contacting were apt to regard him as a headline-seeking troublemaker who could not be trusted to behave with dignity and discretion. He was prepared to defend himself against such a charge, to point out that the overwhelming majority of his ABC interviews had been responsible and well within the bounds of journalistic propriety.

Most damaging of all, however, was his close association with Philip Morris. He recalled that in 1960 when he was working with David Wolper on *The Race for Space*, Wolper had tried to sell the documentary to the networks. All three turned him down, primarily because the networks have always been reluctant to grant air time to free-lance producers. (Broadcasting the work of outsiders tends to have a demoralizing effect on staff producers, who have a difficult enough time getting their own documentaries on the air.) But there was another reason why the networks were wary of *The Race for Space* program. As one CBS News executive put it to Wolper: "We wouldn't want the man who measures the quarter-inch filter on a Parliament cigarette measuring the missile gap between the Soviets and the Americans."

So Wallace's first move in the fall of 1962 was to go see Joseph Cullman, the head man at Philip Morris. Cullman was sym athetic when Mike told him why he had to quit doing the Parliament commercials, but speaking strictly as a friend he wondered if perhaps it wasn't too great a financial risk. He suggested an alternative: "Why don't you make inquiries at the network news divisions and hold on to your income-producing jobs until you hear back from them?"

"Because they won't believe me," Wallace replied. "They won't even listen to me unless I can give them proof that I'm serious about this."

Mike also paid a visit to Mark Goodson, a producer of entertainment programs for whom he had worked on occasional game shows over the years. In fact, Goodson now wanted him to host a new one he had just put together called *Match Game*. When Mike explained why he had to turn down the offer, Goodson said he understood and wished him luck in his quest for a job in news. In those two conversations with Cullman and Goodson, Mike had talked himself out of about $150,000 in income for the 1962–1963 television season. He hoped the men who ran the network news divisions would appreciate that, and now the time had come to find out.

In the letters he wrote to Dick Salant of CBS, Jim Hagerty of ABC and Bill McAndrew of NBC, Wallace acknowledged that his career had been a checkered one, but he said he wanted to work exclusively in news now, and as a necessary first step toward that goal, he had cut himself off from all other sources of income. He ended each letter with a request for an appointment, and all three men greeted him cordially when he went to see them. But except for polite handshakes and a few moments of pleasant conversation, they had nothing to offer. He was told at all three shops that there were no openings, and he was not encouraged to anticipate any in the near future.

The winter months stretched before Mike like a prison sentence. He was not accustomed to the prolonged idleness he had imposed on himself with his decision to steer clear of all opportunities outside journalism. Ever since the summer of 1939 when, fresh out of college, he began his first job at the small station in Grand Rapids, he had always been employed, often working on two or three projects at the same time. Given his high level of energy and restless temperament, Wallace thrived on work—it was tantamount to a psychic need—but now, for the first time, he had nothing to do, nowhere to go, no deadlines to meet, no interviews to conduct, and no colleagues with whom to share ideas and laughs and honest toil. The long, empty hours of sitting around at home waiting for the phone to ring made each day a misery, and in his frustration he became sullen and snappish. What's more, his life had become a social embarrassment. His close friends were privy to what he was trying to do, but mere acquaintances were not, and Wallace began to dread running into them. For invariably they would ask in all innocence: "Hey, Mike, what are you up to these days?" In the past, he had always had positive answers to such a question, but now all he could reply was: "Nothing."

Yet even if he had been temperamentally equipped to play the waiting game over an extended period of time, he could not have done so indefinitely. He had some money set aside— enough to get him through a year or perhaps a little longer— but at some point, he realized, he would either have to generate fresh income or adopt a far more austere life-style than the one to which he and his family had become accustomed. In that sense, time was also working against him. Throughout this difficult period, Lorraine remained serenely confident, and she would say later that she never had any doubt that Mike would eventually get the kind of job he wanted. But he did not share her sanguine view; with each passing week that winter, he grew more despondent.

Then one day in early February, a call came from out of the blue—from California. It was an offer to anchor the evening and late-night newscasts at a local station in Los Angeles, KTLA. To be sure, it was *not* the kind of job he wanted; he had his sights set on a position at one of the networks, and, in fact, he had not responded to a couple of feelers he had received from local stations in New York. Moreover, he knew that Lorraine, having made her escape from southern California fourteen years earlier, would not be overjoyed by the prospect of returning to the LA area. Indeed, Lorraine's first reaction was dismay; but she quickly recovered and encouraged Mike to accept the offer as a step in the right direction. This is exactly how he saw it: as a means toward an end. In a pep talk he gave himself, Mike embraced the notion that if he put in a couple of good seasons in the Pacific coast league, this would persuade one of the networks to give him a chance to play in the majors.

That chance was coming his way much sooner than he realized. Just as he was on the verge of making a firm commitment to the job at KTLA, he received a call from Dick Salant. Salant had heard through the grapevine that Wallace was going to Los Angeles. He also had heard—and this impressed him even more—that Mike told the Philip Morris people he was willing to buy up his Parliament commercials to keep them off the air. This did not happen to be true; once Joe Cullman learned about Mike's desire to kick the Parliament habit, he gave his assurance that the commercials would be pulled out of circulation. Yet the rumor about Mike's offer to buy them was in keeping with the spirit of his decision, and it worked greatly to his benefit. For it was that reported gesture, more than anything else, which induced Dick Salant to change his mind and give Wallace a call.

Never one to waste time on aimless preambles, Salant got right to the point: "Mike, what's this about your going to KTLA to do their news?"

"Yes, Dick, I'm probably going. Why?"

"Why don't you come in and see me before you make up your mind?"

"I'll be there in half an hour."

Salant's offer was hardly generous. He told Mike he could not expect to come in at the top, as one of the network's star correspondents. Salant suggested he do some break-in work on the local TV station, WCBS, and he gave his okay to an interview series on the radio network that they had discussed at their earlier meeting. As for salary, Mike was told he would have to start at forty thousand dollars a year, which was roughly one fourth what he would have made had he chosen to continue doing commercials and entertainment shows. But he had already made peace with himself on the money question; therefore, all he asked Salant was: "Where do I sign?"

With that, the matter was settled, and, at long last, so was Mike Wallace. Once again he was working for a network and he was in journalism—this time for keeps.

Many years later, in the summer of 1977, a visiting reporter had the good fortune to catch Dick Salant in a reminiscent mood. Salant was then approaching the end of his long and distinguished reign as president of CBS News, and he talked about all the sweeping changes that had taken place during his years at the helm. He cited the expansion of the *CBS Evening News* to a half-hour format; the birth and spectacular growth of *60 Minutes;* the elevation of Walter Cronkite to the post of anchorman on the *Evening News* and the superb leadership he had given the network in that role; and the careful nurturing of other careers that, in time, transformed the likes of Harry Reasoner, Dan Rather, Morley Safer, Roger Mudd and Charles Kuralt into correspondents of stature and influence. Then he said: "But of all the moves I was involved in, none has given me more personal satisfaction than my decision to bring Mike Wallace in here. It sounds ridiculous now, but at the time there was a lot of resistance to that around here, and I sort of had to muscle it through on my own."

Indeed, he did. Salant's decision to hire Wallace clearly did not sit well with many of his colleagues, and Mike felt the resentment when he went to work for CBS News in March 1963. Even *The New York Times* made a point of reminding him—and its readers—that he was a man on probation. The story the paper printed about his new job said, in part: "Mike Wallace, intent on regaining his stature, is joining the Columbia Broadcasting System's news department under an arrangement whereby he has agreed not to do any more spot commercials ... Most recently Mr. Wallace has been host on the *PM* series seen over independent TV stations. He has admitted to being uncomfortable in the role of entertainer."

Wallace's response to the chilly reception was to maintain a low profile—to play down the fact that he had made a big name for himself in television—and to concentrate his energies on doing a good job. He worked especially hard on the radio interview series, *Personal Closeup.* Among the guests he interviewed on that program during his first weeks at CBS News were Noël Coward, Jimmy Hoffa, Jack Benny, Moshe Dayan and a then-emerging young writer named Gloria Steinem. *Personal Closeup* was so well received that it became an enduring staple in the radio program schedule. The name of the broadcast was later changed to *Mike Wallace at Large,* and for the next twenty years it was a regular feature on the CBS radio network. He also lent his talents to various news shows on the local television station, including a stint as a summer replacement for Robert Trout, then the regular anchorman on the evening newscast at WCBS-TV. But these assignments were merely a prelude to a much larger challenge, one that seemed destined to make or break his career at CBS News. Later that summer a new program, the *CBS Morning News,* was to make its debut on the television network, and Mike Wallace was picked to anchor it.

This decision only served to exacerbate the in-house irritation his presence had aroused. The anti-Wallace faction believed the *Morning News* assignment was far too choice a plum to be given to a newcomer who had such a checkered background. A leader of this faction was Harry Reasoner, who actually had a right to be miffed. By 1963 Reasoner had risen through the ranks to the point where now he was the number two man in the hierarchy of CBS News correspondents; as visible confirmation of that status, he had recently become the backup anchorman on the *Evening News,* the correspondent who invariably took over when Cronkite was on vacation or pursuing an out-of-town assignment. In addition, for the past two years Reasoner had been the host on a midmorning news and feature program called *Calendar,* which in its tone and format was similar to NBC's *Today* show. But now *Calendar* was being pulled off the air to make room for Wallace and the *Morning News,* and Reasoner made no attempt to conceal how he felt about *that.* In later years, long after Reasoner had changed his mind about Wallace and the two men had become close friends, Mike had a favorite line which he laid on reporters when they interviewed him about his early days at CBS News. "Harry," he would fondly recall, "used to look at me like I was a hair in his soup."

What's more, Reasoner had become a highly popular fellow

within the shop, and the local admirers he had cultivated over the years were influenced by his attitude toward Wallace. When one member of his coterie, a talented young news writer named Joan Snyder, was assigned to work on the *Morning News,* she viewed the prospect with disdain. "Oh, we were all quite contemptuous," Snyder confessed many years later. "Why on earth, we wondered, had this sleazy Madison Avenue pitchman been chosen to anchor a CBS News broadcast? As long as we were going camp, I would have preferred Johnny, the Philip Morris bellhop."

Snyder and the other skeptics on the *Morning News* staff soon learned the hard way that the "Madison Avenue pitchman" was no insecure stranger to the news. They discovered that Wallace was a demanding and excellent editor, both in overall news judgment and frank handling of copy. He did not hesitate to toss stories back to his writers for revision, and his favorite epithet for copy that displeased him was "baby shit." The writers assigned to the *Morning News* came to dread that phrase, and to avoid having it—and their copy—hurled at them, they began putting more care into their craft.

Wallace's new colleagues were also impressed by his work on the air. Drawing on his years of experience in all forms of programming, he projected a poise and authority that quickly stamped him as an anchorman of the first chop. Viewer response was most encouraging, and once it became evident that the *Morning News* was attracting a large and loyal audience, Mike began to relax and enjoy his newfound success as a full-time journalist. He had proven his point, and all around him within the world of CBS News, he could feel the ice melt, the resentment give way to approval and acceptance. There was one moment, in particular, that he cherished for a long time afterward. He was standing in the newsroom one morning in the spring of 1964 when Harry Reasoner walked up to him, extended his hand and said: "Look, this is silly. I can't stay sore at a guy who's doing as good a job as you're doing. Let's be friends."

Among those who had misgivings when they learned that Wallace would be anchoring the *Morning News* was the show's executive producer, Av Westin. Westin had been on the CBS payroll since 1948, when he worked as a desk assistant while still a student at New York University, and in recent years he had built up a solid record as a field producer. But now for the first time, he had been given a chance to develop his own broadcast, to preside over his own special domain, and he knew that if he failed in that assignment, he might never be offered another opportunity. So for Westin as well, the *Morning News* posed a critical challenge and, given his druthers, he would have preferred a more conventional correspondent in the anchor slot. But when he was summoned home from London, where he had been working as the network's chief European producer, in the early summer of 1963 he found out that the decision was final and that he had no say in the matter. Dick Salant told him that Wallace came with the offer to produce the *Morning News*, and Westin's only choice was to take it or leave it.

He took it, and a few days later he met Wallace for the first time. They were among a select group of correspondents, producers and executives invited to lunch at the East Side town house of Blair Clark, who was then Salant's chief deputy. The ostensible purpose of the luncheon meeting was to discuss the two major programming changes that were about to take place: the expansion of the *Evening News* to a half hour and the advent of the *Morning News*. But the *Morning News* was hardly mentioned at all. From the appetizer through dessert and coffee, the conversation revolved around the new format of the *Evening News* and what a great and glorious milestone that was going to be in the evolution of TV journalism. This focus was quite understandable in view of the fact that the Cronkite show was the flagship of the CBS News operation. More to the point, the move to enlarge the scope of the *Evening News*, along with NBC's decision to follow suit and expand *The Huntley-Brinkley Report* to a half hour, was indeed a major breakthrough in the history of television news. So the priority being what it was, Wallace and Westin were obliged to sit below the salt, and they resented being treated like stepchildren whose views and concerns were of no interest to the rest of the family.

When the luncheon ended, Wallace and Westin walked back to the office together. That was the first real opportunity they had to talk in private and size each other up. Both of them griped about how they had been snubbed and how none of their colleagues seemed to give a damn about the *Morning News*. They spoke of their determination to make their new show such a strong and innovative broadcast that their superiors and associates—especially those who now only had eyes for the *Evening News*—would have to sit up and take notice. The more they talked, the more animated they became and the more they realized that, whatever their differences in background, they were both proud and ambitious men who welcomed the fire of competition. Having thus established their bond, there soon developed between Wallace and Westin the kind of rapport that Mike had enjoyed with Ted Yates during the years they worked together on *Night Beat* and the other interview programs that followed.

Like Yates, Westin was a creative producer who was not afraid to break with convention. Not that he overdid it, for in many respects the *Morning News* was an orthodox news show. It opened and closed with the headlines, the latest developments in breaking stories, and it presented film reports on timely, hard-news subjects—from the various power struggles in Washington to the unceasing clamor of strife and revolution in foreign lands. And on some occasions, the broadcast provided live coverage of events as they were unfolding, such as space shots and Senate hearings.

But this is not what gave the program its distinctive character, for by 1963 all that had become standard fare in network journalism. After all, the new, half-hour edition of the *Evening News* was offering a similar blend of "tell" stories and longer film reports, and at an hour when there was much more to choose from—a full day of news and related events. Westin realized that a news show that went on the air at 10:00 A.M. would have to cope with two special conditions: (1) a paucity of fresh, domestic news at that hour, and (2) the need to recruit viewers from a much different kind of market, one largely composed of housewives and other stay-at-homes. Early on, he stated his conviction to Wallace and others that the broadcast would have to "grab people by the ears and not the eyes" because midmorning viewers were apt to have their sets on while doing household chores and the like. To capture their attention, Westin flooded the *Morning News* with consumer-oriented stories and back-of-the-book features deemed to be of particular interest to women. For example, the show dealt quite candidly with sexual subjects: birth control, infidelity, venereal disease, menopause, Pap smears and other delicate matters.

This may not seem like much to a generation accustomed to the conversational gambits on the *Phil Donahue* show, but viewers were far less jaded in the mid-sixties, and some of the topics aired on the *CBS Morning News* were a daring departure from the norm. In the words of Bill Crawford, a CBS News producer based in Washington, it was "the only television news show that had to be sent out in a plain brown wrapper because it was in constant danger of being hauled into court on charges of appealing to prurient interests."

For two years the *Morning News* flourished in its mid-morning time slot. But then in August 1965, it was suddenly shifted to a 7:00 A.M. starting time. This decision was imposed on the news division by the corporate brass, the bottom-line worshipers who discovered that CBS could make a million dollars more a year by airing reruns of *I Love Lucy* each morning at ten o'clock. Wallace, Westin and their superiors on the news-division level vigorously protested the change. They argued that the *Morning News* had built up a strong and loyal audience in the 10:00 A.M. slot, and that the program was bringing a measure of prestige to a daytime schedule that for the most part was a wasteland of game shows and soap operas. But they were up against an invincible force. As long as there were sponsors who loved *Lucy* to the tune of an extra million bucks a year, prestige and loyal viewers had as much chance of prevailing as a camel that tries to squeeze its way through the eye of a needle.

With the shift to the 7:00 A.M. time period, when it had to compete against NBC's well-established powerhouse, the *Today* show, the *Morning News* lost its special identity and most of the audience it had courted and nurtured over the past two years. And it also lost the two men who had done the most to shape that identity and attract the audience.

Av Westin was the first to go. He guided the *Morning News* through its transition into the new time slot, then left the broadcast to produce documentaries and special reports. In fact, he eventually left CBS altogether and moved on to a brilliant career at ABC News. Since he went to work at ABC in 1969, Westin has been at one time or another the executive producer of every major news program at the network—from the *ABC Evening News* in the early seventies to the magazine show *20/20* in the early eighties.

As for Wallace, he anchored the 7:00 A.M version of the *CBS Morning News* for the better part of a year, but then he, too, decided it was time to move on to something else. For one thing, his enthusiasm for the broadcast itself had waned, in large part because, with Westin gone, it had lost much of its zest and vitality. But most of all, Mike could no longer stand the wretched hours; the early-to-bed, early-to-rise regimen of the past three years had worn him to a frazzle. Ever since his early days in broadcasting, most of his on-air work had been at night, and over the years his metabolism had adjusted to those hours. He had become a night person, and he was not able to turn his body chemistry around to make a similar adjustment to the *Morning News* schedule. It had been bad enough getting up every morning at five o'clock, as he had done during the first two years when the show went on the air at 10:00 A.M. But now under the new schedule, Mike had to drag himself out of bed at 3:00 A.M., an ordeal he found utterly hateful and one that was taking its toll on his nerves and even his health. As a matter of fact, his system was a long time recovering from his three-year stretch on the *Morning News*. For several years thereafter, he was bothered by a kind of lingering sleep lag.

So in the summer of 1966, Wallace gave up anchoring the *CBS Morning News*, and since there was no comparable position available to him, he had to join the ranks of general-assignment correspondents. This was quite a comedown in the pecking order, and it also entailed, once again, a drastic cut in his paycheck. Anchormen in those days received special fees over and above their base salaries, and for a five-day-a-week anchor slot, like the one Wallace occupied, the fees were so generous that they almost doubled his income. But he didn't care so much about the reduction in stature and income. He was more than willing to make the sacrifice in order to resume a normal life that would enable him to meet friends for dinner at a civilized time and to luxuriate in the bliss of six or seven hours of undrugged sleep every night.

As a field correspondent based in New York, Wallace covered a wide range of stories over the next several months, including Richard Nixon's vigorous campaigning on behalf of Republican candidates in the 1966 midterm election. That was the start of Nixon's remarkable comeback; and one year later, when he launched his drive for the GOP presidential nomination, Wallace was one of the few reporters who zeroed in on this campaign during its early stages. It was such a low-key effort then—the fall of 1967—that almost all the media attention was focused on other candidates. But as the Nixon campaign picked up steam in the early months of 1968 and breezed through the primaries, Wallace began to suspect that he had latched on to the ultimate winner. This, in turn, led to the happy speculation that following the November election, he would be sent to Washington to cover the Nixon White House. He coveted the assignment, in large part because he had never worked in Washington and he wanted to add that experience to his background.

In the meantime, within the confines of CBS News, a far less publicized comeback was unfolding, one that was being engineered by a dynamic producer who, in years past, had made an enormous contribution to the growth of television news. His name was Don Hewitt, and, as fate would have it, it was *his* comeback—not Nixon's—that would dictate the future course of Mike Wallace's career.

The millions of Americans who watched television in the 1960s had no idea who Don Hewitt was, but within the industry he was highly esteemed as one of the pioneers of TV journalism. For more than sixteen years, from the fall of 1948 until the end of 1964, Hewitt had been the creative force and driving whip behind the evening news broadcasts at CBS. During that period he nursed the format through its primitive, Stone Age phase—when it was nothing more than a visual version of a radio newscast—and developed it into the complex, tightly structured sequence of film reports it became in the early 1960s.

More than anything else, it was Hewitt's technical innovations that changed the face of television news and gave it an enduring new look. Yet his protean gifts extended to all other aspects of the craft as well, from the editorial focus of each night's program to the difficult logistics of putting together film reports in the field at a time when camera crews and correspondents were still learning how to merge their respective talents into a coherent pattern. Indeed, it was mainly to define Hewitt's sweeping authority over the daily news operation that the term "producer"—and later "executive producer"—came into common usage at CBS News. For he was the puppeteer who pulled all the strings. Or in the words of Av Westin, one of his many protégés: "Don Hewitt is the guy who invented the wheel in this business."

Hewitt's talent was more than matched by his extravagant personality. Flamboyant and freewheeling in his approach to every challenge he encountered, he once said of himself: "I am the original 'Smilin' Jack' of TV journalism. I fly by the seat of my pants. I operate by visceral reaction." That was true, and some of those visceral flights sent him soaring into a never-never land where others, less intrepid and less intuitive, refused to follow.

During most of Hewitt's reign as producer of the *CBS Evening News*, the show was anchored by Walter Cronkite's predecessor, Douglas Edwards. Back in the days before script prompters were mounted on studio cameras, Edwards (like all other anchormen at that time) found it almost impossible to maintain steady eye contact with the camera. He could not be expected to memorize the script—the crush of late-breaking stories ruled that out—and when he read directly from his hand-held copy, as he was accustomed to doing on radio, he glanced down so often that viewers spent half the time looking at the top of his head. It was a real problem. One day, in a flash of inspiration, Hewitt came up with a solution. "Doug, I've got it!" he exclaimed. "What you should do is learn *Braille.*" That way, he elaborated, Edwards could simply gaze into the camera and read the news—with his fingers.

Edwards was usually receptive to his producer's schemes, for he greatly admired Hewitt's flair for innovation. But on this occasion he drew the line. He would *not* take up the study of Braille. As for Hewitt, he could not understand why over the years so many of his friends and colleagues dined out on that story. "What's so goddam funny about it?" he replied defensively many years later when a reporter asked him about the Braille proposal. "Look, we were desperate at the time. Nothing else was working. And you know something? I *still* think it was worth a try."

As far as Hewitt was concerned, just about anything within the realm of his fertile imagination was worth a try in those early, experimental days, especially if it helped give CBS News an edge over the other two networks. For he was also intensely competitive. One of his heroes was Hildy Johnson, the brash and unscrupulous reporter in *The Front Page*, the classic play about big-city newspaper life in the 1920s. When the Hildy Johnson spirit was upon him, Hewitt would resort to almost any tactic to outfox the opposition.

He had a special aptitude for devious pranks, as he demonstrated in the summer of 1959 when Nikita Khrushchev, then in the midst of a coast-to-coast tour of America, visited the Iowa farm of Roswell Garst. It was a very big story that year and had captured the public fancy, so Hewitt flew to Iowa to take over as field commander of the CBS News coverage. Shortly after he arrived, he struck up an acquaintance with a retired sheriff through whom he was able to get his hands on an official-looking badge. Then Hewitt purchased a five-gallon hat, a sartorial touch designed to underscore the authority of his badge, and, doing his best to affect the swagger of a cornbelt constable, began to masquerade as a sheriff's deputy. In that guise, Hewitt made frequent visits to the NBC News remote trucks, where he asked all kinds of questions about NBC's plans for coverage of the event. The occupants of those trucks may have been puzzled by the inquisitive nature of this rural lawman who kept pestering them, but, not wanting to get in Dutch with the local sheriff's office, they gave him all the information he wanted. They must have been even more puzzled when CBS News seemed to anticipate and frustrate their every move, to such an extent that NBC wound up getting clobbered on the story. Hildy Johnson himself could not have pulled it off any better.

During those early years, Hewitt's superiors were inclined to indulge or overlook his more outlandish antics and brainstorms. They recognized that his strengths as a producer far outweighed his occasional excesses and lapses in judgment. Even more to the point, television news was struggling through its growing pains, a recurring process of trial-and-error to find its proper identity, and Hewitt's youthful exuberance and spontaneity (he was only twenty-five when he began directing the *Evening News* in 1948) was in keeping with the carefree spirit of that developmental period. But by the early 1960s, TV journalism had come of age. Television had begun to rival newspapers as the prime source from which Americans received their daily dose of news. And within the news divisions of the three networks, the climate became increasingly serious and self-important, as Mike Wallace discovered when he knocked at their doors and was spurned (until Dick Salant underwent his change of heart) because he had not come to them as a simon-pure journalist. In a somewhat different way, Don Hewitt also had to contend with this shift to a more lofty attitude, and it eventually did him in. Some of his superiors gradually adopted the view that for all his talents as a producer, Hewitt's hotshot style and brash capers were unseemly and out of tune now that television had become a mature and responsible medium. Instead of a "Smilin' Jack" who flew by the seat of his pants, they wanted a more sober and steady pilot at the controls, especially now that Douglas Edwards had been replaced and their flagship broadcast had become the *CBS Evening News with Walter Cronkite*.

Hewitt remained in charge of the *Evening News* after Cronkite moved into the anchor slot in 1962, and he was still at the helm the following year when the show was expanded to a half hour. (Even those CBS News executives who had begun to sour on Don Hewitt were savvy enough to realize that his skills and experience were needed to guide the broadcast through those two critical transitions.) But in the summer of 1964, at the time of the Republican convention in San Francisco, Hewitt acted on one of his wild impulses and soon came to regret it. At a meeting of news executives and producers from the three networks, the purpose of which was to discuss the new computer techniques that were revolutionizing election coverage, he spotted a copy of the NBC election handbook on the floor, and—Hewitt being Hewitt—he grabbed it and managed to smuggle it out of the meeting. Then, accompanied by a few CBS cronies, he repaired to his room at the Fairmont Hotel and began to leaf through its contents. An hour or so later, a distraught young man from NBC News showed up at Hewitt's room and moaned that if he did not get the handbook back, he would lose his job. Hewitt, having discovered by this time that the handbook was utterly worthless as an enemy document, gladly turned it over. Then the young man said, by way of thanks: "I would have thrown you out of that window to get it back." Hewitt and his pals thought that was pretty funny, but they were no longer laughing the next day when a story about the "theft" and the "threat" to hurl Hewitt out a window at the posh Fairmont Hotel was given a big play in the *San Francisco Chronicle*. A number of CBS executives read the story with even less amusement; and a few months later, in December 1964, Don Hewitt was sacked as executive producer of the *Evening News*.

Hewitt was so demoralized by their decision that he came close to leaving CBS. But instead, he rallied his spirits and spent the next three years producing documentaries, a period he later referred to as "my time in limbo." Still, he turned out several first-rate documentaries during those years, and, perhaps more important, he toned down his act. He did not completely repress the Hildy Johnson fantasies that triggered his more flamboyant exploits, but he kept them in reasonable check most of the time. As a result, he gradually worked his way back into good order.

In the process, Hewitt discovered that—for him, at least—producing documentaries left much to be desired. He felt that very few stories or subjects warranted the full-dress treatment of an hour-long broadcast in prime time, and the snail's pace of documentary production (it generally took several months to get just one project on the air) grated on his restless temperament. In earlier years, before he was pulled off the Cronkite show, Hewitt often said that one of the many things he liked about producing the *Evening News* was the challenge of having to "get it up" every day. No matter how good the broadcast had been the night before, he had to go in the next day and start all over again. Documentary work offered no such challenge, and now he yearned to get back to a more active and stimulating regimen, one that would compel him to get it up more often. Yet he knew that the only way he could do it would be to create his own action—which is precisely what he did.

At some point in 1967, there began to evolve in Hewitt's mind an idea for a different kind of broadcast. If the *Evening News* was the television equivalent of a daily newspaper—the electronic front page, as it were—and a documentary was comparable to a nonfiction book that thoroughly examined one subject, then the program he envisioned could properly be described as a magazine. It would be a weekly or biweekly broadcast consisting of several stories on a wide range of topics—from politics to the arts, from interviews with world

leaders to profiles of movie stars, from in-depth reports on the
latest crisis at home or abroad to light features on scuba diving
or health spas. Hewitt even came up with a title for the program.
He wanted to call it *60 Minutes*.

Hewitt took the idea to his immediate superior, Bill Leonard,
who was then vice-president in charge of documentaries. Leonard
instantly gave the project his full and hearty blessing. Indeed,
his response to it was so enthusiastic that one might have
thought that Hewitt had come to him with a design to *re*invent
the wheel in television news. (Which, in a way, he had, for
60 Minutes was to become another major milestone in the
evolution of TV journalism.) Leonard's strong support was
crucial because Dick Salant's initial reaction to the proposal
was negative. He was concerned that such a program, being
neither fish nor fowl, would encroach on the domains of both
the documentary unit and the daily news operation, which, in
turn, would foment all kinds of intramural bickering over territorial rights and privileges. Salant had a precise and orderly
mind and he preferred to keep everything neatly compart-
mentalized. But Leonard eventually won him over, and in February 1968 Salant gave Hewitt the green light to produce a
pilot. It was understood that if the pilot was well received,
Hewitt would then be given a budget to put the new program
into production for the fall season.

Hewitt had conceived of *60 Minutes* with Harry Reasoner
in mind. Having steadily strengthened his position as Cronkite's
regular backup on the *Evening News*, Reasoner had acquired
by now what is known in the trade as "marquee value." In
other words, he had become a star, a household name. Beyond
this, Hewitt believed that Reasoner was ideally suited for a
program like *60 Minutes*, that he would bring to the multisubject
format the right combination of talent and experience. His solid
background as a hard-news reporter gave him authority, yet he
also had a special knack for the lighter stuff, the feature stories
that would help give the show its distinctive tone. Leonard
agreed that Reasoner was the perfect choice for *60 Minutes*.
But at some point, after he and Hewitt had discussed the program in more detail, Leonard suggested that it might benefit
from a dual on-camera presence, especially if the second correspondent's style and personality sharply contrasted with the
dry humor and relaxed urbanity that Reasoner projected on the

air. Hewitt thought this was a splendid idea. He recognized at once that the broadcast would take on an added and appealing dimension if Reasoner was given a foil to play off, a heavy who would wear the black hat and patrol the dark alleys in search of stories while Harry, all smiles and charm, worked the sunny side of the street. And once they had defined the role in those terms, Hewitt and Leonard had no trouble deciding who should play Darth Vader to Reasoner's Obi-Wan Kenobi. Clearly, the man for that assignment was Mike Wallace.

Reasoner would have preferred doing a solo, but he had no strong objection to sharing the *60 Minutes* limelight with another correspondent. And when Hewitt and Leonard explained to him why they wanted to pair him with Wallace, Reasoner wryly observed that if they were looking for his exact opposite, someone who—in contrast to his, Reasoner's, acknowledged attributes (wit, charm, warmth and fundamental decency)—would come across as dour, humorless, abrasive and relentlessly ill-mannered, then yes, of course, he had to agree that Mike Wallace was tailor-made for the part. (This was said in a spirit of good fun, for by 1968 Reasoner and Wallace had become close friends and admirers of each other's work. But they were both compulsive needlers and seldom passed up an opportunity to stick it to each other.) So now that Reasoner had accepted the arrangement, the time had come for the next step—to sell the idea to Wallace.

CHAPTER

SIX

I WAS NOT that easily sold. In the early spring of 1968, when Don Hewitt finally got around to telling *me* about his scheme to produce a magazine program in prime time, my sights were firmly set in another direction. Having covered Richard Nixon's presidential campaign since its misty origins (when most of the veteran, Washington-based reporters were dismissing his candidacy as a joke, something akin to a Harold Stassen fantasy), I wanted to see it through to its climax. For by April of 1968, it was—to borrow one of his favorite phrases—"perfectly clear" that Nixon was going to have the last laugh, at least in terms of that year's contest for the Republican nomination. He had by then reduced the GOP primary elections to a mopping-up operation, and although Nelson Rockefeller and even Ronald Reagan were gearing up to challenge him at the convention that summer, I was convinced that Nixon now had the momentum and mainstream support he needed to win. Looking beyond the convention, I also thought he stood an excellent chance of winning in November, and if that happened I wanted to move to Washington and cover the Nixon White House. This prospect struck me as far more promising than an iffy new broadcast that had not even reached the pilot stage.

Of course, there was no guarantee that I'd be offered the Washington assignment. But I knew there was a kind of unofficial policy at CBS News to change White House correspondents every time a new administration took over, and the reporter who had covered the winning candidate's campaign was usually given prime consideration; which made sense because he was the one who had built up the sources and contacts within the new President's inner circle of advisers and confidants. (I also felt certain that the current man on the beat, Dan Rather, would understand that decision—if it came to pass—because he had been the beneficiary of a similar switch five years earlier when, following the Kennedy assassination, he was brought in from Texas and assigned to the Johnson White House.) True, I had to face the possibility that Nixon might be defeated, either at the convention or, more likely, in the general election. But I had seen enough over the past few months to persuade me that this was a chance worth taking. After all, he already had confounded the experts by coming back as far as he had, and like any gambler who plays a hunch on a long shot and cashes in, I congratulated myself for having been among the handful of reporters who had covered his political resurrection from the beginning.

When I first began to follow Richard Nixon around in the fall of 1966, I knew him only by reputation. Which is to say that I knew only the worst about him. He was known as "Tricky Dick," the devious opportunist from whom no one in his right mind would buy a used car. He was the blundering campaigner who had entered the 1960 presidential race as the heir presumptive of the enormously popular Dwight Eisenhower, and who then proceeded to blow that election to an opponent who had to overcome the handicap of being a Catholic at a time when no member of that church had ever been elected President, and when many still clung to the view that no Catholic ever should be. Yet as damaging as the narrow loss to John F. Kennedy had been, it was nothing compared with the disaster Nixon inflicted on himself two years later. When he ran for governor of California in 1962 and lost again—this time by a wide margin—he had made the horrendous mistake of capping that campaign with a bitter valedictory to the reporters assembled at his election-night headquarters, uttering words that would haunt him for many years thereafter: "But as I leave you, I want you to know, just think how much you're going to be missing. You won't have Nixon to kick around anymore because, gentlemen, this is my last press conference..."

With that graceless performance, Richard Nixon's public career hit rock bottom. The enemies he had acquired over the years of hard, political combat openly gloated over his misfortunes. He had become, in their eyes, an object of scorn and ridicule: not only an inept loser who had snatched defeat from the jaws of victory in 1960, but even worse, a sore loser who had blamed the press for the crushing rejection he had been dealt at the polls in his home state. Then came the years of exile—the move to New York and a new life as a lawyer with the Wall Street firm of Mudge, Rose, Guthrie and Mitchell. He had chosen to live in hostile territory (the Republican turf in New York was then the sole property of his longtime rival, Governor Nelson Rockefeller) where he had no realistic hope of building a new power base. By setting himself up in New York of all places, Nixon seemed to acknowledge that he was through with politics forever.

Such then were the burdens that Nixon had to shoulder when he took his first tentative steps up the comeback trail in the autumn of 1966. I covered a few of his campaign appearances that fall as he traveled around the country beating the drums for various Republican candidates who were running in that midterm election, and I asked to interview him one morning at LaGuardia Airport just before he flew off to another campaign stop in Waterville, Maine. It was a routine piece, utterly predictable, Nixon contending that Lyndon Johnson's landslide victory over Barry Goldwater in the 1964 presidential contest had been an aberration that did not accurately reflect the relative strengths of the two parties, and expressing confidence that the Republicans would redress the balance by making sizable gains in the 1966 House, Senate and gubernatorial races. Boilerplate stuff. The producers of the *CBS Evening News* evinced no interest in the story, which did not surprise me; in fact, I had to agree with their judgment that party-line clichés voiced by a political has-been hardly qualified as news. So I filed a couple of pieces for the radio network and figured that was the end of that.

But it must have been a slow news day because the wire services picked up portions of my interview and *The New York Times* also published a separate story on Nixon that day. It wasn't much, but that coverage was more attention in the press than Nixon had been getting up to that point—and it was just enough to arouse the displeasure of the Leader of the Free World.

The next day, at a presidential news conference, Lyndon Johnson was asked to comment on Nixon. From time to time during his career, Johnson had displayed an occasional weakness for retaliatory overkill, for bashing an adversary with a sledgehammer when a discreet and concise karate chop that left no mark would have been more effective. Now, in reply to a reporter's question, he launched into an anti-Nixon tirade, denouncing the former Vice-President as a "chronic campaigner . . . who never did really recognize what was going on when he had an official position in the government." LBJ's intemperate remarks *did* qualify as front-page news; all of a sudden, Cronkite's producers were interested enough in the political has-been to dispatch me and a camera crew to Maine to get Nixon's response to Johnson's response.

Nixon was delighted. He realized that a lightning flash of presidential irritation had just propelled him back onto the national stage and that my interview had helped, inadvertently, to trigger the chain reaction. Would he consent to another interview? You bet he would, and this time he put more bite into his answers. Nixon sensed that now he had been given license to step up his attack on Johnson, so he weighed in with the assertion that the main reason the Republicans would make dramatic gains in the upcoming election was because the voters were growing disenchanted with the President's policies: his Great Society programs at home and the way he was prosecuting the war in Vietnam. (Since Nixon was aware that his own party was sharply divided on the Vietnam question, he took care not to align himself with either the hawk or dove faction, both of which had begun to criticize Johnson's handling of the war.)

That second interview was aired on the Cronkite news, and from then on Nixon's campaign speeches began to receive a bigger play in the press. Nixon himself later referred to that episode as the first break, an early turning point, in his comeback, and he never forgot it or the reporter who had helped bring it about. A few months later, he sent me (and who knows

how many other reporters who had covered him that year) a
little memento of the 1966 campaign: a small piece of molded
plastic with, for some unknown reason, a Winston Churchill-
Queen Elizabeth coin inside. Inscribed on it were the words
"Birdwatchers of 1966—Mike Wallace" and Richard Nixon's
signature.

Yet even without the unexpected assist from Lyndon Johnson, Nixon had other advantages working for him in 1966.
One of the effects of the Barry Goldwater debacle in 1964 was
to take some of the curse off Nixon's hairbreadth loss to Kennedy four years earlier. At least Nixon had made his 1960 race
close enough so that other Republicans running that year had
a fighting chance to save their own necks, and many of them
did, while in 1964, Goldwater and his inflexible, do-or-die
brand of conservatism led the Republicans to slaughter. In the
ruinous aftermath of that election, the party looked like Georgia
after General Sherman made his march through it. Moreover,
the disaster had left a gaping vacuum in the Republican leadership, and with his eye fixed on filling it, Nixon had demonstrated again in 1966—as he had during his vice-presidential
years—that he was a potent spokesman for the party. Most of
the GOP candidates running that year welcomed his efforts on
their behalf, and by campaigning as a concerned veteran from
past wars who had come out of retirement to help others instead
of merely seeking office for himself, Nixon was able to recast
his battered image. In fact, this was the unveiling of what his
cohorts would soon be promoting as "the new Nixon." Finally,
and most important, the Republicans did indeed rack up impressive victories that fall—gaining seats all across the board—
and Nixon could rightly claim credit for predicting the outcome,
and for helping to achieve it.

I spent the next several months on other assignments, including
a two-month tour of duty in Vietnam and a few weeks in Israel
following the Six-Day War. In both places I ran into the peripatetic Mr. Nixon, who was reinforcing his overseas credentials in those two trouble spots. When I returned to New York
in the early summer of 1967, I began to anticipate the forthcoming battle for the Republican nomination. (At that time
everybody assumed that all the fireworks would be on the

Republican side; no one foresaw the stormy distruptions in the Democratic party which would lead to Johnson's abdication and, two months later, to the assassination of Robert Kennedy.) The man being touted as the Republican front-runner that summer was George Romney. As the thrice-elected governor of a key swing state, Michigan, Romney was a proven vote-getter, and for the past several months he had been leading all prospective candidates including the President, in the public-opinion polls. But I suspected that Romney might not have the "legs," the staying power, to survive the bruising ordeal of a national campaign. Nor did I think much of Nelson Rockefeller's chances; for all of his popularity in the East, the rest of the Republican party was still strongly conservative, and I did not think that wing would ever accept him. Yet the conservatives themselves were still on the defensive, still chastened by the Goldwater nightmare they had foisted on the party three years earlier. The governor of California, Ronald Reagan, was emerging as their new leader; but since he was another hardcore conservative, I thought it unlikely that the party would nominate a man who could so easily be nailed to Barry Goldwater's cross.

This left Nixon who, for all his stigma as a shopworn loser, was perhaps the one candidate who could unite the two factions. He might not be their first love—as Rockefeller or Romney was to one group, and Goldwater or Reagan to the other—but at worst, he was acceptable to both wings of the party. I'm not saying that I had a premonition of what Nixon would accomplish in the year ahead. I knew that most Washington reporters who covered politics full time were writing him off on the grounds that once a politician is perceived as a chronic loser (which is probably what Johnson *really* meant to say), it is almost impossible for him to shake that image. I respected that prognosis, and to a large extent agreed with it. But I still thought that, given the rest of the field, Nixon at least had a chance, and I was curious to see how far his comeback attempt would carry him. Besides, he was based in New York and so was I, which gave me easy access to him and to the men helping him chart his strategy.

I resumed contact with the Nixon operation over lunch one day in September 1967. My companion was Len Garment, one of Nixon's law partners and a recent convert to what was then only a small cult of believers in the New Nixon. Perhaps I should mention that it was not just any day in September but Yom Kippur, and although both Len Garment and I are Jewish, it did not deter us from breaking forbidden bread together while our more pious brethren observed the traditional rites of prayer and fasting. And to add to the vague aura of blasphemy, Garment talked about Nixon with all the zeal of one who—in political terms, at least—had been inspired to abandon the faith of his fathers.

"You're looking at a lifelong Democrat," he told me. "A couple of years ago I would have been the last person in the world to come to the aid of Richard Nixon. But he's changed. The years in exile have made him a better man, a more thoughtful and more compassionate man. But don't take my word for it. Judge for yourself. All I ask is, if you do decide to take this assignment, please come to us with an open mind."

Garment's enthusiasm whetted my curiosity, and although I could tell that my superiors at CBS News agreed with the prevailing view of Nixon's prospects, they indulged my desire to follow him around that fall. It was not yet much of a campaign when I joined the tiny press corps covering it. My companions on that early Nixon watch were: Bob Semple of *The New York Times*, Herb Kaplow of NBC News, Jayne Brumley of *Newsweek* and Don Irwin of the *Los Angeles Times*. Nor were many aides traveling with Nixon. In addition to Len Garment and John Sears, another young lawyer from Mudge, Rose, Guthrie and Mitchell, there were a couple of speechwriters, Pat Buchanan and Ray Price; the candidate's longtime personal secretary, Rose Mary Woods; his appointments secretary, Dwight Chapin; and a colleague of mine from CBS, Frank Shakespeare, who would soon leave the network to work for Nixon full time. The campaign manager was yet another partner from Nixon's Wall Street law firm named John Mitchell. He was, in those days, something of a mystery man who seldom traveled with the Nixon entourage, apparently preferring to direct the operation from behind the scenes in New York. But of course we would get to see plenty of John Mitchell in the months—and years—to come.

The slow and subdued start was in keeping with Nixon's

"game plan," as he called it. He purposely chose to maintain a low profile at that stage of the campaign and let the front-runner, George Romney, absorb most of the heat and glare of day-to-day scrutiny. "I want him to get the exposure," Nixon exhorted his aides as he moved toward a showdown with the Michigan governor in New Hampshire's first-in-the-nation primary. "We have to keep him out at the point." Convinced that he had been savaged in the past by excessive and unfair press coverage, Nixon now wanted that kind of media firepower directed at Romney instead. And as a matter of fact, the heavy exposure was already taking its toll on the governor's campaign. At one point that fall, when a Detroit interviewer asked him about his recent visit to Vietnam, Romney blurted out that the U.S. Command in Saigon had subjected him to "the greatest brainwashing that anybody can get . . ."

Properly understood, Romney's accusation had plenty of merit, for as we all would learn, American leaders were lying about the war in Vietnam, giving the impression that the enemy was being slowly but relentlessly ground into submission, when in reality the North Vietnamese were gearing up for the Tet offensive, which—when it came in the early weeks of 1968—would expose the folly and deceit of the official claim that the conflict was under control. But poor George Romney had chosen to describe his grievance with a most unfortunate phrase, one that had distressing connotations dating back to the wretched treatment of American prisoners during the Korean War. If he had said that he had been given a snow job or even if he had allowed the word "bullshit" to escape his pious Mormon lips, it's unlikely his offhand remark would have caused such a furor. But in the aftermath of what he *did* say, George Romney was scorned as the only presidential candidate in history who confessed to having been "brainwashed," and that remark plunged his campaign into a tailspin from which it never managed to recover. The more he tried to extricate himself, to explain what he really had meant, the more he came across as a naïve bungler who didn't know what he was talking about. Or in the acidly graphic words of a fellow Republican, Governor James Rhodes of Ohio: "Watching George Romney run for the presidency was like watching a duck try to make love to a football."

In the meantime, the Nixon campaign was gliding almost

serenely along on its chosen course of caution and restraint. And as the weeks passed, I came to appreciate Len Garment's assessment of the candidate. I had no way of knowing if Nixon had "changed" all that much because I had not been with him during the earlier campaigns; but I did not find him cold or double-dealing or paranoid or any of the other negative things I had heard or read about him over the years. I was impressed by his intelligence, his grasp of history and his clear under- standing of the difficult problems he would face in the White House, especially in the area of foreign policy, which is where he intended to concentrate his efforts. I grew to respect him and even to feel a kind of affection for him. The affection part was not easy because, as so many others have observed, Richard Nixon was an intensely private man who did not welcome attempts at intimacy and who was no good at small talk or breezy camaraderie. His personality was the antithesis of that of a compulsive extrovert like Hubert Humphrey, to cite a rival whose sunny disposition was a large part of his political appeal. But Nixon was cordial enough, in his stiff and formal way, and I found him to be more courteous and considerate than I had expected.

In view of the barriers that were erected later between Nixon and the press, it's worth noting that he made himself readily available to the reporters who were covering him then. Access was never a problem in those days. In fact, there were times when Nixon himself made the overture. I recall, in particular, a long flight to Oregon in November 1967 (that state's primary the following spring was looming as a critical test). I was the only reporter present. Not long after we took off from New York, Nixon invited me to sit with him for an hour or two and just talk, in a relaxed way, about the campaign, the issues and what he hoped to achieve as President. He sensed that because our small group—Wallace, Semple, Brumley, et al.—had not covered his past campaigns, we did not bring an anti-Nixon bias to our current assignment. Unlike the old Washington crowd and the California clique, we were not out to "kick him around," as he put it so vividly in his so-called last press conference in 1962. Not that we were soft on him. God knows I've never been accused of avoiding tough questions, and I didn't avoid them during the months I covered Nixon in 1967 and 1968, but he seemed to appreciate that at least we were giving him a fair shake. Nixon was responsive and remained open in his relations with the press until the summer of 1968 when H. R. Haldeman and John Ehrlichman, two California cronies from the bad old days, joined the campaign. For it was then that construction began on what later was to be known as the "Berlin Wall," the sullen shield that Haldeman and Ehrlichman (with the help of Rose Mary Woods) formed to seal Nixon off from direct contact with reporters or anyone else—including, ultimately, members of his own Cabinet— whose presence he might find disturbing.

Throughout the waning weeks of 1967 and the first two months of 1968, George Romney continued to flounder in his frantic struggle to make love to a football. By late February, all the polls indicated that he was going to get trounced in the New Hampshire primary; one survey had Nixon in front by an astounding six-to-one margin. Originally Romney had been drawn into the contest by all those nationwide polls in the early months of 1967 that pointed to him as the Republican with the best chance of winning the 1968 presidential election. But now that support had crumbled—brainwashed away, as it were—not only in New Hampshrie but in other key primary states as well. He who lives by the polls must die by the polls, and so, rather than subject himself to the humiliation of getting clobbered by Nixon, the celebrated loser, Romney decided to call it quits— two weeks before the voters in New Hampshire registered their official verdict. I was with Nixon at a Grange hall in New Hampshire when the word came in that Romney had pulled out of the race. He did not gloat over the news (he had far too much control over his emotions to allow himself that luxury), but he clearly savored the moment.

Nixon had known from the start how critical New Hampshire was for him. A defeat there or in any of the early primaries would have been fatal, for it would have confirmed all the suspicions that, New Nixon or no, he was still a loser, and the party's power brokers would have moved quickly to pledge their support to other candidates. But Nixon no longer had to worry about that. He was assured now of his first *meaningful* triumph since being elected to the Senate in 1950. (In his two vice-presidential campaigns, he rode to victory on Eisenhower's coattails, and when he breezed through the GOP primaries in 1960, he did not even have to contend with the kind of feeble opposition that Romney had provided in this campaign.) In addition, Nixon must have been gratified by the actual turnout in New Hampshire, for when election day came, he received more votes than any candidate in any presidential primary in that state's history, a stunning show of support that went far toward obliterating his loser's image once and for all.

Romney's withdrawal also upset the furtive plans of Nixon's two remaining, though as yet undeclared, rivals for the nomination. Both Rockefeller and Reagan had been counting on Nixon and Romney to cut each other up in the primaries, to engage in a prolonged and stormy battle from which there would emerge no clear winner. Then, as the focus shifted from the primaries to the convention, Rocky and Ronnie would present themselves as fresh alternatives who had not been bloodied in intraparty combat. But Romney's collapse foiled the strategy of the other two governors, and by the time each got around to mounting his challenge, it was too late to enter any of the primaries—and therefore too late to inflict any serious damage to Nixon.

On the night of the New Hampshire primary, I caught a glimpse of Richard Nixon I never saw again. I was covering his New York headquarters, where he was awaiting the returns, and as his margin mounted he came out of a back room with Mrs. Nixon. After a short interview with him for an election special later that evening, I put the microphone in front of a visibly shaking Pat Nixon. She answered an innocuous question about that day's big victory; I thanked her and went back to the CBS studio to do a live report. No sooner was I off the air than a phone call came in from the candidate. "I just wanted to thank you, Mike, for being nice to Pat," he said. That was all, but in my dealings with Nixon it was the closest he ever came to revealing a personal feeling.

A week or so later, Len Garment and Frank Shakespeare brought me a message from Nixon. "The boss would like you to join up, to come aboard and work with us," Garment said.

I was floored; until that moment, such a thought had never occurred to me. "To do *what*, exactly?" I asked.

Garment shrugged. "We're not sure. You know we're not that well organized yet. But I imagine it would be press secretary or communications director, or something like that."

I confess that I gave the offer serious consideration. Power may or may not be "the great aphrodisiac" that Henry Kissinger once claimed it to be, but it does have a strong and compelling attraction. And for an American interested in government and politics, no seat of power is more compelling than the White House, and no opportunity more enticing than the prospect of being involved in the adventure of a new presidency. Lorraine and I talked it over at some length, and we also discussed it with a few close friends. But I still couldn't make up my mind, and so I decided to seek the advice of Frank Stanton, then the president of CBS and a man who had thoroughly earned his reputation as the premier statesman of the broadcasting industry.

Stanton said he could understand why I was tempted to go to work for Nixon. But he warned me that if I accepted the offer, I would be taking a risk that could compromise my standing as a journalist. If I were drawn into the partisan passions of a campaign, then later became a spokesman for the policies of a strong-willed and controversial President, I might find it very difficult to get my job back as a news correspondent.

That was all I needed to hear. I wasn't about to run such a risk, not after all I had gone through to get back into journalism. So I wrote Richard Nixon a letter telling him how much I appreciated the offer, but added that I was happy at CBS News and, after thinking it over, I preferred to continue in my present job. It wasn't long before I fully grasped the wisdom of Stanton's counsel. Even now, many years later, I shudder to think how I might have fared in the role of Ron Ziegler.

Which reminds me of the *other* proposal that came my way that spring: that I team up with Harry Reasoner on a prime-time magazine broadcast Don Hewitt was hoping to put on the air. I didn't see this as my future either, and not just because I wanted to keep myself available for a possible assignment as White House correspondent. To be frank, I thought Hewitt was off on a pipe dream.

I knew that even the established forms of news programming,

the documentaries and live specials, did not do well in prime time, and I doubted seriously that the CBS management would give its blessing to a venture that was new and experimental. Then, too, there was Hewitt's reputation to consider. I liked Don personally, and although I had never worked with him, I knew how able and creative he was. I don't think I would go so far as to echo Av Westin's claim that he "invented the wheel in this business," but I would give him credit for contributing the hub and a few vital spokes. Yet I also knew that he had fallen out of favor at CBS and been languishing in a backwater since 1964, when he was relieved of his command as executive producer of the Cronkite show. That being the case, I felt it most unlikely that the CBS brass would entrust him with the authority to produce the kind of ambitious program he had in mind.

But in the spring of 1968 when Hewitt came to me with his grandiose scheme, I kept my reservations to myself. I didn't want to rain on his parade, and, besides, when Don Hewitt is in full cry, there is no resisting him; you simply let his words wash over you. And so, more or less in self-defense, I feigned enthusiasm when he began to bombard me with the details of his proposal.

"This is going to be a radical departure in both form and content," he proclaimed. "Our documentaries are so damn stuffy. They take themselves much too seriously, and most subjects don't deserve the full-hour treatment we give them on *CBS Reports*. Some stories are worth ten minutes, and some are worth twenty-five. They're too long for the Cronkite news and too short for *CBS Reports*. Those are the stories we'll be doing."

He paused to let that sink in, then, having reloaded, he opened fire again: "Not only that, but you know as well as I do that television practically ignores what the newsmagazines call the back-of-the-book. The arts and sciences and all that stuff. We'll be going into those subjects and there will be features and profiles of personalities from all walks of life. The idea is to strike a balance between those pieces and the more serious, conventional stories we'll be doing. And Mike, listen to this: You'll have a chance to do your long interviews again. How about *that?*"

That certainly appealed to me, as Hewitt knew it would,

and having played his king, he now played his ace: "You and Reasoner will be just great together. Harry will be the white hat and you'll wear the black hat."

I knew what he meant and we shared a chuckle over the prospect for I confess it also appealed to me. I thought it made eminent sense to have Harry work on the soft stuff—the wry and casual pieces he did so well. This would leave me to concentrate on the front-page stories—politics and civil rights and world affairs—which would be of interest to the grownups in our audience.

I still wasn't sold on the idea, but I did agree to work on the pilot for the broadcast that Hewitt had dubbed *60 Minutes*. A rather pedestrian title, I thought, for I had no way of knowing that Hewitt would dip into his fertile imagination and come up with the ticking stopwatch motif, which was to become the show's trademark, its visual signature. As for the pilot, it hardly lived up to Don's glowing sales pitch. It was little more than a banal pastiche of leftovers and outtakes from pieces that had already been on the air, the content so trivial that the so-called highlight of the model program Hewitt slapped together was footage from an old Robert Kennedy film called *Bobby and His Kids Go Skiing*. The Reasoner-Wallace contribution was confined to introductions and tag lines. When Hewitt asked me what I thought of the pilot, I assured him emphatically that it was "the nuts." But the truth was that I hadn't even watched it all the way through.

I went back on the road with the Nixon campaign as it wound up its sweep of the primaries. Rockefeller and, to a lesser extent, Reagan were in hot pursuit of the nomination, and although they were getting lots of media attention, it was not translating into delegates. Quietly and methodically, Nixon and his agents had locked up the commitments of Republican leaders in various non-primary states; and by the middle of June—some seven weeks before the convention assembled in Miami Beach—they knew they had the necessary votes to secure the nomination on the first ballot. In the meantime, as I traveled with Nixon around the country, Hewitt kept phoning me with gossipy updates on how the pilot was being received by our superiors. Although I was still skeptical, Don was more confident than ever that he would be given a budget to put *60 Minutes* on the air in the fall.

Spring faded into summer, and over the next few weeks, Hewitt's relentless optimism became so contagious that I gradually succumbed to it. In fact, the more I thought about it, the more I began to welcome the prospect of working on a broadcast that would put me in such amiable and stimulating company: an inventive Hewitt at the controls, a team of first-rate field producers to help us find and develop stories, and my amusing pal, Harry Reasoner, as on-air partner. I figured that if the network executives gave us the go-ahead, *60 Minutes* would run for at least a season, maybe two, enough to make it a worthwhile experience. Besides, neither Dick Salant nor anyone else had so much as hinted that I would be given the White House assignment if Nixon won the election. What if they decided to keep Dan Rather on the beat? Or what if Nixon lost?

So I was already leaning toward a commitment when the word came down that *60 Minutes* had been approved for the new season as a biweekly broadcast to be aired on Tuesday night at ten o'clock. Soon thereafter, Hewitt and I and scores of other CBS News personnel descended on Miami Beach to prepare for our coverage of the Republican convention. By then I had definitely made up my mind. I told Hewitt that he could count on me to be with him in the fall. He gave me a puzzled look and said: "Sure, Mike, sure. I knew that." It was obvious he had never doubted what my eventual decision would be.

Then I offered a suggestion for our first broadcast in September. "What about setting up cameras inside Nixon's suite at the Hilton on the night of the balloting? We could film him as he watches himself being nominated."

"Terrific," said Hewitt. "And we'll do the same thing in Chicago with Hubert or whoever the Democrats pick. Then we'll play them back on the first show. Great idea."

Nixon granted our request, and on the evening of August 7, CBS News cameras were in his hotel suite filming his and his family's reaction to the long-awaited moment of triumph. The next night Nixon came to the convention hall to deliver his acceptance speech, and as he made his way to the podium, he passed a cluster of reporters. He peered into the group looking for familiar faces and after spotting them, tossed greetings to those of us who had been with him since—as he liked to put it—"the snows of New Hampshire and before." When my turn came, he said: "Hi, Mike, I'll see you in California next week. We'll be out there planning the campaign."

"No, Mr. Nixon, I'm afraid not. I thought you understood. Those cameras in your suite last night were for *Sixty Minutes,* the new television series I'm working on. I'm peeling off the campaign after tonight."

Nixon looked at me as though I had lost my mind. He obviously could not comprehend how I, one of the early heralds of his political comeback, could leave the campaign at this momentous juncture, with the general election coming up and the strong possibility of a White House assignment to follow. He seemed to take my remarks almost as a personal affront, as if I were saying in effect that I had no confidence in his ability to beat the Democrats, and therefore had decided he was not worth covering after the convention. He promptly sought to disabuse me of that notion.

"We're going to win this thing, Mike," he declared. Then came a cryptic non sequitur: "And later, after we get to Washington, we're going to take some great trips."

At the time that struck me as an odd, rather frivolous inducement. But a few years later, when Richard Nixon became the first American President to visit the Communist capitals of Peking and Moscow, I realized that he had envisioned those historic missions early on, back in the campaign summer of 1968, and that that perhaps was what he was trying to tell me the last night of the convention. But of course Nixon had more important things on his mind that night than offering career guidance to a wayward reporter; so he quickly moved on to the podium where, arms outstretched, he drank in the cheers and applause and jubilation of the party faithful. And as I stood there watching him in the happy din, I could not help but wonder if I had made the right decision.

CHAPTER

SEVEN

WALLACE DID PEEL off the Nixon campaign after the 1968 Republican convention had run its course, but he still had one more major assignment to carry out before he would be free to devote all his time and energy to *60 Minutes*. For him, as for scores of other political reporters that August, the road from Miami Beach led directly to Chicago, where later in the month the Democrats gathered to nominate their candidate. Wallace was among the small and elite group of CBS News correspondents who had been assigned to cover the floor at both conventions. In the hierarchy of network convention coverage, floor reporters outrank all other correspondents except the anchormen. They are entrusted with the grueling task of patrolling the various delegations in search of news, any tidbit of information to justify the saturation, gavel-to-gavel coverage the networks give to these spectacles, which Murray Kempton once described as "the quadrennial assault on decency and reason."

Wallace first won his spurs as a floor reporter in 1964 when he was still a newcomer to CBS News, having been hired by the network the previous year. The opportunity came his way more or less by happenstance during an outbreak of panic at that summer's first convention, the Republican conclave in San Francisco at which Barry Goldwater was nominated. Earlier in the year, when the CBS executives drew up their list of as-

signments for the conventions, Wallace was passed over. He
was not yet recognized as a correspondent with a feel and an
aptitude for politics. (The fact that he had co-anchored coverage
of the 1960 conventions for the Westinghouse broadcasting
chain cut no ice with his new employers, who snobbishly be-
littled almost any experience outside the sphere of network
journalism.) Indeed, there still existed within certain circles at
CBS a lingering suspicion that Wallace was not a bona fide
reporter. Yes, he had proven his worth as a studio interviewer,
and, yes, he was doing a good job as anchorman on the *CBS
Morning News*. But his detractors believed that his success as
an anchorman was largely the result of his marquee value; in
their view, he had merely capitalized on the celebrity status he
had acquired as a TV personality before he joined CBS News.
Thus, even after he had been with CBS for more than a year,
Wallace still had to contend with echoes of the disdain he had
encountered at ABC seven years earlier when John Daly dismissed him as something less than a "real" journalist.

The only reason Mike was in San Francisco that summer
was because it had been decided to have the *Morning News*
originate there during the week of the Republican convention.
However, these were harrowing times for CBS News, and Mike
had the good fortune to benefit from the misery being inflicted
on the network by its chief competitor, NBC News. Led by
the able and appealing anchor team of Chet Huntley and David
Brinkley, NBC was riding high as the dominant force in TV
journalism. Four years earlier, at the 1960 political conventions, NBC had clobbered CBS in the ratings, and on the heels
of that victory, *The Huntley-Brinkley Report* opened up a commanding lead over the *CBS Evening News* in their fierce rivalry
for the dinner-hour news audience. NBC continued to lord it
over the other two networks at the 1964 conventions (though
ABC was then so deeply mired in third place that it scarcely
figured in the competition), and in its desperate effort to mount
a more effective challenge, the CBS management took a number of drastic steps, including the public humiliation of its
premier correspondent. For it was in the summer of 1964 that
Walter Cronkite was banished from the anchor chair he had
occupied since the landmark conventions of 1952, the first year
they were televised coast to coast.

The dumping of Cronkite after the Republican convention was the big headline in media news that summer, but it was just one of several impulsive moves made by the panic-driven CBS brass. At one point during the convention week in San Francisco, a harried news executive approached Wallace and asked: "Mike, how would *you* like to cover the floor?"

"Nothing I'd like better," he replied. And, like a scrub who comes off the bench with an eagerness to show his stuff in a game already lost, Wallace went charging into the fray. He soon demonstrated that he possessed the requisite attributes of a good floor correspondent: a thorough knowledge of the issues being debated, the stamina to work long hours on his feet, the moxie to barge through a cluster of unruly delegates to get to a possible story, and the capacity to ad-lib with clarity and relevance in the midst of unrelenting chaos. He strengthened his hand by turning in another solid performance on the floor of the Democratic convention in Atlantic City later that summer. In fact, it was his work at the 1964 conventions, even more than his success as anchorman on the *Morning News,* that convinced the few remaining skeptics at CBS that he was a real journalist who could handle himself under fire.

But Wallace was not the only silver lining in the ratings nightmare that befell CBS in 1964. Two other relative newcomers to the network, Dan Rather and Roger Mudd, made their debuts as floor reporters and also came through the initiation course with high marks. Moreover, their collective performance in the summer of 1964 augured a dramatic shift in the power struggle between the two networks. Over the next twelve years—at the 1968, 1972 and 1976 conventions—the trio of Wallace, Rather and Mudd would form the nucleus of the CBS team of floor correspondents; and it was during those years that CBS overtook NBC and established itself as the perennial leader in broadcast journalism. As for Walter Cronkite, his fall from grace was so short-lived it was soon forgotten. He was back in the CBS anchor booth during the 1968 conventions, and has anchored the network's coverage of every convention since then—that is, until 1984, when the assignment devolved on Dan Rather as part of his inheritance when he succeeded Cronkite on the *Evening News.*

But if the Goldwater convention of 1964 was Wallace's

baptism, then the Nixon convention of 1968 was his confirmation. His coverage of the Nixon campaign and other aspects
of Republican politics over the previous two years gave him a
decided advantage over most of his colleagues and competitors,
and Wallace was quick to exploit it. Even before he swung into
action at the convention itself, he had scored an impressive
beat over the opposition.

In the final days leading up to the convention, Nixon se-
cluded himself in a beach house at Montauk Point on the eastern
tip of Long Island. His aides passed the word that he was
working on his acceptance speech, and under no circumstances
would he be available to the press during this period of intense
concentration. But Nixon made an exception to this firm edict
when he received a request for an interview from Wallace, the
early "Birdwatcher" who had been with him since "the snows
of New Hampshire and before." Two days before the convention opened for business, Wallace and a camera crew flew to
Montauk and were ushered in to Nixon past a group of highly
resentful reporters whose requests for an audience with the
prospective nominee had been denied. Their sullen murmurs
of discontent were, of course, music to Mike's ears. And when
the convention opened the following Monday, the highlight of
CBS's coverage that first day was Wallace's exclusive interview
with Nixon.

By then Wallace was back in Miami Beach, working the
floor and doing his energetic best to keep the main story on
target in the face of misleading rumors and speculation. In his
book on the 1968 political *Sturm und Drang*—the third in his
superb series on modern presidential campaigns—Theodore
White noted that some reporters, both print and electronic, were
temporarily mesmerized by what he called "the mirage in
Miami."

That mirage was the notion that the pincer movement waged
against Nixon's mainstream support—Rockefeller boring in
from the left and Reagan exerting pressure from the right—
had a realistic chance of blocking Nixon's first-ballot nomination, and thereby would throw open the convention to a
free-for-all. Such a scenario was never more than a fantasy,
and Wallace knew it from day one. It was not just that he was

plugged into the Nixon apparatus, for the propagandists there were no more reliable than those in the rival camps. But he also was in close touch with other sources he had built up over the past few months, and through them Mike knew that the power brokers who controlled the critical delegations—such as Governor Spiro Agnew of Maryland and Senator Strom Thurmond of South Carolina—were not wavering in their support of Nixon. So while other reporters pursued the mirage, using trendy words like "erosion" and "slippage" to describe the alleged dispersion of Nixon's delegate strength, Wallace hammered away at what he knew to be the reality: Richard Nixon had come to Miami Beach with a lock on the nomination and the lock was holding fast.

The following week, in *Time* magazine's review of how the media covered the Republican convention, Wallace was singled out as the one floor reporter who was on top of the story from opening gavel to closing benediction. Buoyed by this and other reactions to his work, Mike moved on to Chicago and the Democratic convention, where he took it on the chin—literally.

In contrast to the competitive edge he had enjoyed in Miami Beach, Wallace was not close to the players who had taken part in the events that led the Democrats to their rancorous showdown in Chicago in 1968. The Republicans had been his meat, his main area of concern. Hence, it was with a certain detachment that he had viewed the upheavals that rocked the Democratic party during the winter and spring of 1968: the insurgent candidacies of Eugene McCarthy and Robert Kennedy; the stunning decision by Lyndon Johnson to renounce his bid for another term in the White House rather than face repudiation at the polls in the Democratic primaries; the belated entry of Johnson's captive, Vice-President Hubert Humphrey, into the race; and finally, as the primary season came to an end, the assassination of Bobby Kennedy in California just after he had scored a decisive victory over McCarthy in their internecine battle for the peace vote that spring.

Vietnam was the catalyst that had unleashed those disruptive forces; and it was Vietnam—that is, Johnson's prosecution of the war there—which continued to divide the Democrats when they assembled in Chicago that August. Johnson was by then so roundly despised by the antiwar faction of his own party that he dared not run the risk of even making an appearance at the convention. However, as President he still controlled enough of the party machinery to deliver the prize to his hand-picked successor. It was the inevitability of the outcome—Humphrey's nomination—that brought the swarm of frustrated antiwar demonstrators to Chicago, where they would raise their cries and flaunt their banners of militant protest.

There is no need to dwell here on the appalling spectacle that followed: the brutal scenes of violence which a study commission later characterized as "a police riot." Which it was—no question of that—but there also is no question that the police were provoked to riot by the angry protesters who had come to town itching if not for a fight, then at least for a breakdown in order and civility. Nor is there any question that the antiwar groups chose to make the streets their battleground because they felt betrayed by a political process that was about to nominate a man who had aligned himself with the war policy of a rejected President.

The reporters who covered the violence in the streets that week had a very tough time of it; when police resort to rioting, they are not fussy about whose heads they bash with their nightsticks. But even for those who were working inside the convention hall, there was no guarantee of safety. The ugly mood of confrontation that pervaded the city infected the security guards Mayor Richard Daley had assigned to maintain order in the hall, and—like the cops outside on the streets—they began to overreact to delegates or anyone else who seemed to question their authority. For their part, many of the delegates resented the heavy-handed methods of the guards, and as these two groups became more hostile toward each other, scuffles broke out on the floor of the convention. The reporters who tried to cover these skirmishes did so at their peril. On the second night of the convention, one of Daley's goons punched Dan Rather in the stomach and knocked him down. Observing the assault from his aerie in the anchor booth, Walter Cronkite lost his temper—one of the few times in his long career he ever did while he was on the air—and said in a voice shaking with rage: "It looks like we've got a bunch of thugs in here

... If this sort of thing continues, it makes us, in our anger, want to just turn off our cameras and pack up our microphones and our typewriters and get the devil out of this town and leave the Democrats to their agony."

Of course, CBS News did not pack up and leave, and the next night Mike Wallace got his. When Alex Rosenberg, a McCarthy delegate from New York, was dragged off the floor for speaking rudely to a security agent, Wallace tried to tag along, to follow through on the story. However, as they moved off the floor and out of camera range, one of the police officers shouted at Wallace to stay away. "This is none of your business," the officer snarled.

"Certainly it's my business," Wallace replied. "This is a public place." This only made the cop more livid, so Wallace quickly shifted to a more cajoling tack in an effort to calm him down. Flashing a broad smile, he asked: "Officer, what are you getting so upset about?" To underscore the affable tone of his question, Mike chucked the man under the chin in an avuncular gesture of goodwill. The cop, an ungrateful nephew, responded by slugging Wallace on the jaw. Mike buckled but did not go down (later, like Jake LaMotta, he prided himself for having stayed on his feet), but the blow stunned him.

At that point, the unlikely melodrama turned into farce. Another cop, clearly unnerved by what his fellow officer had done, but driven by panic to try to justify it, rushed over to Wallace and said: "You're under arrest."

"*I'm* under arrest? *Me?* What the hell have *I* done?"

"Assaulting an officer."

"Assaulting an officer? For crissakes, I chucked him under the chin. What the hell . . . ?"

Mike heard the officer who had belted him explain to another reporter that he, Wallace, was under arrest because "he slapped me." By the time two other cops had grabbed Wallace under each arm and were brusquely leading him away past a group of still photographers who gleefully recorded this latest example of frontier justice, Chicago style; and the next day the picture of his arrest appeared in newspapers across the country.

Wallace did not remain in custody for very long. When Dick Salant found out what had happened, he quickly arranged a meeting with Mayor Daley. Daley offered no apology; in fact, he defended the cop who had hit Wallace as well as the actions of all the police and security guards under his command. But he did agree that under the circumstances the decision to arrest Wallace was a bit much. Mike was told he was free to resume his duties on the convention floor, and, after washing his face and combing his hair, he did just that—in time to witness one of the highlights of the convention: the dramatic confrontation between Senator Abraham Ribicoff of Connecticut and Mayor Daley who, after giving the order to release Wallace, had returned to his seat in the Illinois delegation. Speaking from the podium, Ribicoff glared down into Daley's pudgy, defiant face and denounced the "Gestapo tactics" being used by the mayor's police force on the streets of Chicago.

Compared with the people who were caught up in those tactics and beaten bloody in the process, Rather and Wallace had little to complain about. However, they were struck by the sheer stupidity of the attacks. For they knew that even those cops who did practice "police brutality" (a frequently heard phrase in those days, even before Chicago) seldom made the mistake of slugging reporters, especially in front of cameras and/or other witnesses.

The immediate effect of all the violence that week was to throw the Democrats into such bitter disarray that they scarcely had any fight left in them for their common opponent. It was, indeed, something of a miracle that Humphrey, coming out of that tumult, was able to close the gap to the point where he came within a whisker of beating Nixon, who once again demonstrated his gift for taking a big early lead and driving it to the edge of the cliff. Yet the ultimate and enduring victim of the so-called police riot was Chicago itself and its reputation as the favorite convention city of both political parties. Ever since 1860, when Abraham Lincoln was nominated there, Democrats and Republicans had assembled in Chicago more often than in any other city. But after 1968 it became *"urbana non grata,"* a city shunned by both parties as a national convention site.

In the meantime, there was no rest for the wounded as the summer drew to a close. When Wallace returned to New York at the end of August, he had to commence working at once on projects for *60 Minutes,* which was scheduled to make its debut in less than a month. He was assigned to do the "cover story" for the show's first broadcast, and the subject could not have been more appropriate. Called "Cops," it dealt with the break-down in trust between the police and their fellow citizens in major cities across the country.

Yet even at this late date, Wallace was still ambivalent about the commitment he had made to the new broadcast. In the aftermath of the Democratic convention, he was more con-vinced than ever that Nixon was going to win the election, and he continued to suspect that he had blown a golden opportunity to become the White House correspondent for CBS News. He was willing to bet that the Nixon presidency would last a lot longer than *60 Minutes*. But having made his decision, he now strove with customary diligence to make the new program a success. With any luck, he kept telling himself, *60 Minutes* should have enough appeal to run for at least a season, and maybe two.

CHAPTER

EIGHT

IT WAS ON TUESDAY evening, September 24, 1968, that our ticking stopwatch was heard for the first time in homes across America. Those comparatively few viewers who were curious enough to look at the first edition of *60 Minutes* saw a broadcast dominated by stories that evolved from the two political conventions. Naturally we led with our exclusive, for our cameraman was the only one allowed in the hotel rooms of Nixon and Humphrey on the nights they were nominated. There was a certain fascination in observing the two nominees watching the hubbub on the convention floors as their delegate counts mounted. Nixon conducted a kind of on-camera political seminar for his family in his hotel suite as the balloting unfolded; and Humphrey jumped up and kissed the TV screen when he saw his wife, Muriel, in the convention hall.

Our story on cops was built around my interview with the man who was then the nation's top cop—Attorney General Ramsey Clark. A few days before our broadcast, Clark had alluded to the "police riot" that had taken place in Chicago during the convention. In his statement, which I quoted by way of introducing him to our viewers, he had said: "Of all violence, police violence in excess of authority is the most dangerous. For who will protect the public when the police violate the law?" However, I wanted to know what Clark thought about the average cop, so I began our interview on a fairly provocative note:

> WALLACE: I think Dick Gregory has said that today's cop is yesterday's nigger. Do you understand that?
>
> CLARK: Yes, I understand that, and it's, you know, you've got to be able to recognize wisdom and truth where you find it. I find a lot of truth to that.
>
> WALLACE: How so?
>
> CLARK: I think what he means is that the policeman today is a man who is put upon from every standpoint. He's not paid well, he's not trained well. He finds little opportunity to improve himself. He lives a life that causes very considerable risk to his safety. His relationships with the community he serves have become so strained in so many parts of our cities that he is living and working in a hostile environment.

To round out the broadcast, we showed an offbeat film called *Why Man Creates*. It was the work of an inventive filmmaker named Saul Bass, and it came to us from Kaiser Aluminum, which had commissioned the film. Then Harry and I signed off with a few self-conscious remarks in honor of the occasion:

> WALLACE: And there you have our first *Sixty Minutes* broadcast. Looking back, it had quite a range, as the problems and interests of our lives have quite a range. Our perception of reality roams, in a given day, from the light to the heavy, from warmth to menace, and if this broadcast does what we hope it will do, it will report reality.
>
> REASONER: The reality, as we have suggested, is various. The symphony of the real world is not a monotone. This doesn't necessarily mean you have to mix it all up in one broadcast, but it seems to us that the idea of a flexible attitude has its attractions. All art is the rearrangement of previous perceptions, and we don't claim this is anything more than that, or even that journalism is an art,

for that matter. But we do think this is sort of a new approach. We realize, of course, that new approaches are not always instantly accepted...

WALLACE: We'll see. I'm Mike Wallace.

REASONER: We will, indeed. I'm Harry Reasoner. *Sixty Minutes* will be back two weeks from tonight.

And so we began. By today's standards it was a fairly pedestrian program, but we were on our way and finding our way. The immediate reality we faced that fall was the presidential race, the final chapter in a long season of political turmoil, so the campaign and the candidates dominated the first few broadcasts of *60 Minutes*. Harry did a long interview with Hubert Humphrey, and I made sure we did not overlook George Wallace, who was making his run as a third-party candidate that year. After I reminded Governor Wallace, on-camera, that many Americans regarded him as a demagogue or a racist or a fascist—or even a combination of all three—he chose to have a little fun with the fact that we were namesakes. "Now, Mr. Wallace, cousin Mike," he said, then added: "I might get you in trouble by calling you that." Governor Wallace always seemed to enjoy his jousts with us "pointy-headed" correspondents from up north.

My major story that fall was on the candidate I'd covered for most of the past year. When I sat down with Nixon in early October, it was the first time I had seen him in person since his parting shot to me from the podium about "great trips" at the Republican convention. Many of my questions dealt with the campaign, but I also asked him about critical turning points in his past, such as the Alger Hiss affair and his narrow loss to John F. Kennedy. In talking about that defeat, he readily admitted that he had made several serious mistakes in 1960, notably his decision to debate the lesser known Kennedy at a time when he, Nixon, was leading in the polls. I pressed him about his personal feelings toward his opponent that year:

WALLACE: There are those who suggest that you were awed, almost overawed, by Jack Kennedy's money, social grace, position.

NIXON: Oh, I don't buy that. I think everybody tries to rewrite history in terms of what the book should read, but while I do not have money and perhaps while I am not blessed with particular social grace, I have a confidence that comes from a different source. I fought my way up all the way and I don't mean that somebody who didn't have to fight his way can't make it, too, but believe me, when you've gone through the fires of having to work your way through school, of having to fight campaigns with no money, of having to do it all on your own, you come out a pretty strong man and you're not in awe of anybody.

WALLACE: There's been so much talk in recent years of style and charisma. No one suggests that either you or your opponent, Hubert Humphrey, have a good deal of it. Have you given no thought to this aspect of campaigning and of leading?

NIXON: Well, when style and charisma connote the idea of contriving, of public relations, I don't buy it at all. As I look back on the history of this country, some of our great leaders would not have been perhaps great television personalities, but they were great Presidents because of what they stood for, because of their principles, their courage, their character.

The question of style versus character clearly intrigued Nixon, because he continued in a vein that in retrospect takes on considerable irony:

NIXON: Some public men are destined to be loved and other public men are destined to be disliked, but the most important thing about a public man is not whether he's loved or disliked, but whether he's respected. *And I hope to restore respect to the presidency at all levels by my conduct.* [Italics are mine.] And as far as the charisma and all the PR tricks and everything else that's supposed to make you look like a matinee idol, forget it. If that's what they want in a President, I'm not the man.

WALLACE: But the name Nixon is anathema to millions of American voters. To them Richard Nixon is a political opportunist to whom the desired political end has justified just about any political means. How does Richard Nixon, if elected by a majority, go about reconciling the doubts of the skeptics?

NIXON: I do have, based on a hard political career going back over twenty-two years, some people in this country who consider me as anathema, as you pointed out. But on the other hand, I believe that I have the kind of leadership qualities that can unite this country and that at least can win the respect if not the affection of those who have a very bad picture of Richard Nixon.

From our post-Watergate perspective, it's a little too easy, perhaps, to sit back and scorn such pious pronouncements. At the time there were millions of Americans—and I was one of them—who also believed that Richard Nixon had the "kind of leadership qualities" that would enable him as President to "win the respect if not the affection" of his detractors. But in the end, the detractors were right about Nixon, just as they were right about the man he had chosen to serve as his Vice-President—Spiro Agnew. I must confess that Agnew was another politician whose character I misjudged at the time. Like Nixon, he fooled me, just as he did so many others.

I first met Ted Agnew in the fall of 1966 when he was running for governor of Maryland. Although a Republican, he was the liberal candidate in that race. His Democratic rival, George Mahoney, was a fervid opponent of open housing for blacks; he built his entire campaign around this single issue. His campaign slogan—"Your home is your castle, vote to protect it"—was sung to the tune of *The Bells of St. Mary's,* thereby proving once again that in politics nothing is sacred. In addition to following Richard Nixon around in the fall of 1966, I filed reports on some of the major senatorial and gubernatorial races in that midterm election. Maryland was one of the stops on my beat, and Agnew had every reason to be heartened by the story I did on his campaign. In truth, I was impressed by the ad hoc alliance he had formed with black leaders, organized labor and white liberals. And I was not surprised when he won the election with heavy support from those normally Democratic blocs of voters.

Nor did Agnew renege on his campaign promises. He put more blacks on the state payroll than had any Maryland governor before him, and he pushed through the first state open-housing law south of the Mason-Dixon line.

But Agnew's love affair with Maryland's black community came to an abrupt end in April 1968. When Martin Luther King was assassinated, angry blacks rioted in Baltimore, as indeed they did in other American cities. Agnew was furious. He summoned Baltimore's moderate black leaders to a public meeting where, in front of reporters and TV cameras, he denounced them for their failure to exert their influence to maintain law and order in the ghettos. He told them that he had put himself on the line for them, but they had not lived up to their end of the bargain. "Do you repudiate black racists?" he shouted. "Are you as willing to do that as I am willing to repudiate the white racists?" And when they refused to give him the answer he wanted, he berated them again.

The Baltimore riots and his stormy showdown with the black leadership had a devastating effect on Spiro Agnew. The two events radicalized him to the right; and in retaliation his black and liberal supporters turned against him. Not long afterward, Agnew met privately with Richard Nixon in New York, and a few days later Nixon announced that he had added Agnew's name to his list of vice-presidential possibilities. When the lightning struck that summer, Agnew was still virtually unknown to the vast majority of American voters. In fact, when he held his first news conference in Miami Beach after Nixon had anointed him, I was the reporter who said to him: "You have to admit, Governor, that the name Spiro Agnew is hardly a household word."

I could have added—but chose not to—that another reporter had conducted an impromptu survey that day along the beaches of Miami's Gold Coast and had discovered, among other things, that one befuddled sunbather thought *a* Spiro Agnew was "some kind of shellfish." Anyway, Agnew instantly sensed that I had tossed him a cue he could exploit to his advantage. "That's right," he replied with a grin, "I have to admit that Spiro Agnew is hardly a household word." The press pounced on the quote, which is how all that business got started. In one campaign speech after another, he joked about how Spiro Agnew was not a household word—and in the process he became one.

However, some of his other, more spontaneous one-liners during the 1968 campaign—dubbed "Agnewisms"—made him an object of ridicule. At one point, when asked about the nation's urban problems, he shrugged and said, "If you've seen one slum, you've seen them all." On another occasion he awakened echoes of the strident rhetoric the "Old Nixon" used in the early 1950s when he helped to create the climate for McCarthyism. "Hubert Humphrey," Agnew blustered, "is squishy soft on Communism." And there were the Archie Bunker-like slurs. He described one fellow as a "dumb Polack," and humorously referred to a Japanese American journalist covering his campaign as "that fat Jap," thus conjuring up the bizarre image of a Sumo wrestler in his traveling party.

Agnew came across to newcomers among the reporters covering him, and therefore to the public, as an insensitive fool, which puzzled and dismayed me, for the Ted Agnew I knew was a better man than that, and certainly a brighter man. By this time he and I had become friends of sorts, in that wary, arm's-length way that reporters and politicians allow themselves to become friends, and I couldn't understand why he was making such a fool of himself. After the election was over and he was about to be sworn in as Vice-President, I interviewed Agnew for *60 Minutes*. I did not go at him very hard; for one thing, we were still in the honeymoon period that reporters always accord a new administration; and besides, as I said, I liked him. When he contended that his impromptu campaign remarks had been taken out of context and that he had been misinterpreted, I let it go. I was more interested in talking about the future, and what he—a one-term governor with no experience in foreign affairs—was doing to prepare himself for the burdens of national office. At the end of our interview, Agnew averred that "I'm equipped to handle this job," and I followed with this summation:

It is no overstatement to suggest that there is some skepticism among Americans, Republicans and Democrats alike, on just that point. They know Spiro Agnew principally for the Agnewisms he uttered off the cuff during the campaign. They don't know his substantial record as governor of Maryland. They don't know whether he is equipped to handle the job of Vice-President, and the possibility of the presidency in the mid-twentieth century. His chore now is to persuade the doubters.

No one expected him to adopt such a bellicose method of persuasion. Agnew, who had gone through more transformations in a couple of years than most politicians do in a lifetime, now took on yet another identity. He became the hard-hitting point man for the Nixon administration's attacks on the media and on other, less clearly defined targets, whom Agnew characterized in such vivid terms as "effete snobs" and "nattering nabobs of negativism." This phase reached its climax in the fall of 1970 when he swung the heavy club for Nixon in the midterm election campaign. By then, his combative style on the stump had made Agnew a figure of great controversy—a hero to those who welcomed his divisive message and a villain in the eyes of others, including many of my co-workers at CBS News and the other two networks. Yet even at that late date, I was still inclined to defend him, if only on the grounds that we of the media were not above criticism ourselves and that the First Amendment protected his right to speak out as much as it did ours. At the same time, I didn't think we should let him intimidate us, so I heartily agreed with my *60 Minutes* colleagues that he had earned the honor of being subjected to the full glare of our scrutiny. Therefore, in February 1971 we broadcast a profile of Spiro Agnew, and this time we took a much closer look.

We traced his career in Maryland from his early years as a struggling lawyer and personnel director at a supermarket (where, like the other employees, he wore a smock with the words *No Tipping Please* stitched on it) to his election as Baltimore County Executive, the post he held when he made his successful run for governor in 1966. We also strongly suggested that Agnew, who had been a registered Democrat, became a Republican not so much out of ideological conviction as opportunism. I interviewed an old friend of his who said, on-camera, that Agnew switched parties "because there was little hope of being recognized and achieving anything in the mass of Democrats in Baltimore County." We also probed into his early life, his youth in a Baltimore suburb, and reported some things about him that were not generally known and that he would have preferred not to have broadcast over national television:

> WALLACE: His grades at Forest Park High School were mediocre at best. We asked to see the grades, but school principal Charles Michael told us Agnew's record was pulled from the file when he became Vice-President . . . Young Spiro played the piano at assembly, but he belonged to no clubs, won no honors. Since graduation, though, he has never missed a class reunion. Spiro, it seems, was a fun-loving adolescent. A friend since high school, Attorney Lee Harrison, recalls those early days.

> HARRISON: We'd go to football games. We'd got out to clubs or things of that sort that we could be admitted to as teenagers in those days and perhaps have a drink illegally. We cheated a little bit, too, I suppose the way kids do nowadays . . .

What we reported was hardly character assassination, the lurid stuff of yellow journalism, but Agnew seemed to think it was. He was furious; he felt that I had done a hatchet job on him and, even worse, that I had betrayed our friendship. He failed to understand that when a reporter and politician become friends (and we were never really *that* close), it does not mean the reporter abandons his principles and becomes the politician's lackey.

As I look back on our profile of him, I suspect the quote that bothered him the most was his high school friend's offhand remark that they had "cheated a little bit." At the time, of course, neither I nor anyone else—except Agnew himself and his Baltimore County accomplices—knew how large a role "cheating" still played in his life. Even as Vice-President, he continued to accept the illegal payoffs that eventually led to the indictment which, in the fall of 1973, forced him to resign his office in disgrace. But as I said, he sure fooled me.

Of all the men who came to power in Richard Nixon's Washington, no one was closer to the President in those early years than his attorney general—John Mitchell. More than anyone else at that time, Mitchell set the tone and direction of domestic policy; and because he was also the chief spokesman and lightning rod for that policy, he was every bit as controversial as Agnew. During most of the first term, Mitchell ranked next to Nixon himself in power and influence.

I've never forgotten my first conversation with John Mitchell. By February of 1968, I had been covering the Nixon team for more than four months and Mitchell, the campaign manager, was still a mystery man to me, as he was to most of the other reporters in our group. So I went to Frank Shakespeare, who was partially responsible for Nixon's press relations, and said, "Hey, isn't it about time that I met John Mitchell?" He agreed, and a few days later I was invited to an off-the-record, get-acquainted lunch with Shakespeare and Mitchell at the "21" Club in New York. It happened that we met on the day that Hubert Humphrey had come to town to address a convention of black newspaper publishers. I knew the Nixon people were going to great lengths to win the support of white southerners (a political calculation that came to be known later as "the Southern Strategy"), so I made a point of asking my luncheon companions if Nixon intended to follow Humphrey's example and make a speech to the black publishers. Mitchell's answer could not have been more direct. "I don't want Dick to go over there," he grumbled. "You can buy those monkeys, anyway."

I did my best to keep a poker face, but Frank Shakespeare turned pale and I could see him kick Mitchell under the table. Even though the luncheon conversation was off the record, they quickly shifted to another subject.

I soon discovered that Mitchell was seldom so indiscreet. As I got to know him better, I also discovered a side to him that bore little resemblance to his dour public personality. He had a dry sense of humor and could be on occasion quite gracious and charming, especially when relaxing over cocktails. For there is no denying that John Mitchell was, in the Irish phrase, a man who liked his glass.

But Mitchell's public image remained stern and forbidding, the perfect symbol of the tough law-and-order message the Nixon White House was determined to convey. And the image was fully backed up by performance. Within weeks after the new administration took over, Mitchell had established himself as the strongman in Nixon's Cabinet, the only department head with regular easy access to the White House, and the only one whose advice and influence extended far beyond areas under his official jurisdiction, the Justice Department. But it was within that department that he registered his biggest impact. Critics of Nixon's domestic policy pointed to Mitchell as the culprit, the sinister force behind the move to undermine federal guidelines for school desegregation. In addition, he was accused of misusing the power of his office to encroach on the civil liberties of dissenting citizens who were not part of Nixon's Middle-American constituency, the so-called silent majority. In his quiet way, Mitchell seemed to enjoy his reputation as a tough cop, and to take an almost perverse pleasure in being Nixon's heavy, the favorite target of liberal wrath.

In the meantime, his impulsive and garrulous wife, Martha, suddenly began to speak out in public. Like her husband, Mrs. Mitchell was fond of the sauce, and from time to time, when she had downed a few drinks, she would telephone one of her favorite reporters—often in the middle of the night—to discuss various matters currently in the news. Her opinions were always colorful, and sometimes outrageous. (In the fall of 1969, when opponents of the war in Vietnam organized an observance they called "Vietnam Moratorium Day," Martha Mitchell likened the peaceful protest to the Russian Revolution, a diverting analogy which, if extended to its full implications, would have cast Nixon as Czar Nicholas II and her husband in the role of Rasputin.)

Therefore, in the spring of 1970, I suggested to Mitchell that *60 Minutes* broadcast a joint interview with him and his wife at their home in Washington. What we had in mind, I explained, was a free-wheeling conversation that would touch on their personal relationship as well as explore their political views. To my surprise, Mitchell agreed, and the result was one of the liveliest interviews ever aired on the show.

A date was set, and when I arrived at the Mitchells' duplex apartment with our production crew, Martha was wearing a pair of old slacks and her hair was in curlers. Perhaps they had both assumed I was kidding about including her in the interview. We quickly persuaded her to go along with our plan, and she dashed upstairs to change into something more appropriate. While Martha was getting ready, we turned on the cameras and I began interviewing Mitchell about his performance and reputation as attorney general. I brought up the allegation that some of the law-enforcement measures he had championed— for example, wiretapping, preventive detention, no-knock searches—constituted the greatest threat to civil liberties since the days of Joe McCarthy. Mitchell dismissed the charge as "rhetoric," and then he said:

> MITCHELL: And if by chance that somebody along the line had made a mistake, the attorney general or the Congress that enacts these laws, we still have the courts to take care of them under our concept of judicial review. So I have no fear of anybody invading our civil liberties.
>
> WALLACE: You don't think that the majority might demand the limiting of certain civil liberties if violence continues and expands on college campuses and in the cities?
>
> MITCHELL: Well, the majority might talk about it, Mike, but we, under our system of government, do not have the mechanics for them to provide their wishes . . .
>
> WALLACE: So everybody that suggests that John Mitchell may be a harbinger of a new McCarthyism is simply dead wrong?
>
> MITCHELL: Mike, if you've never said anything with more truth in your life than that, I would agree that you have said it now. There's no question about it.

It wasn't long before Mrs. Mitchell returned, all gussied up. I took one look at her and detected that she had taken a couple of belts to fortify herself. She promptly broke into my conversation with her husband to proclaim: "Look, either you people are going to interview *me* now, or I'm going to bed."

I was only too happy to oblige. I turned to her and said: "Mrs. Mitchell, please sit down." We adjusted the cameras to set up a two-shot picture of the Mitchells sitting together, and I began to interview Martha, if indeed "interview" is not too formal a term for the verbal frolic that followed:

WALLACE: Have you been outside listening?

MRS. MITCHELL: Yes, I definitely have.

WALLACE: Did you get angry at any of it?

MRS. MITCHELL: Yes, I did.

WALLACE: What part?

MRS. MITCHELL: I got angry because I think that the American people don't know what a wonderful husband I have. I think that I have been angry for a long, long time, my darling, because my husband is probably one of the most intelligent men in this whole country.

MITCHELL: You see?

MRS. MITCHELL: In the *world*, I would even say.

WALLACE: Now, Washington generally seems to feel that you really liven up an otherwise dull administration. How do you feel about the effect that you've had on this town?

MRS. MITCHELL: I think it's tremendous. As long as you can bring a laugh into a society and all the problems and troubles that we have, it's marvelous. Even at my expense . . .

WALLACE: But the question everybody asks is, where was John Mitchell when those telephone calls were going on?

MRS. MITCHELL: Oh, really?

WALLACE: Yes.

MRS. MITCHELL: Why would people ask something like that?

WALLACE: They feel, perhaps, that he wouldn't have permitted it.

MRS. MITCHELL: My husband permits me to do what I feel I would like to do. And I can tell you that one hundred percent.

At the time of this interview, in May of 1970, there was a lot of speculation in Washington that Mitchell was hoping his friend in the White House would eventually appoint him to the Supreme Court. So I asked Martha about that:

WALLACE: How would you like to see—honest now— how would you like to see this man on the Supreme Court? Your husband.

MRS. MITCHELL: I wouldn't.

WALLACE: Why not?

MRS. MITCHELL: He isn't the type of man to be on the Supreme Court.

WALLACE: You mean he's not a strict constructionist? Why isn't he the kind of man who ought to be on the Supreme Court?

MRS. MITCHELL: Because a man on the Supreme Court needs to be the type of person that can go through piles and piles of—of—what do you call it, darling?

MITCHELL: Briefs.

MRS. MITCHELL: Briefs, briefs, unbelievable! You take our Chief Justice, he sits up all night long going through all these briefs. And John's just not that kind of person.

WALLACE: He's not a student? He's an activist?

MRS. MITCHELL: He is definitely a student, but I don't think that would be interesting to my John.

WALLACE: Mr. Mitchell, candidly, how much real difficulty has Martha Mitchell caused by her comments and
telephone calls and interviews and things like that?

MITCHELL: None whatsoever. It's all been on the plus
side.

MRS. MITCHELL: He's had a chance to laugh. Isn't that
wonderful?

There was no doubt Mitchell was enjoying himself that evening.
As his wife continued to chatter on, he sat there sucking on
his white meerchaum pipe and chuckling until his belly shook.
Of course, the Mitchells had no idea how soon their days of
laughing together would come to an end. Four years later, their
marriage was in ruins, Martha Mitchell was dying of cancer
and her husband was on his way to prison for the part he played
in the Watergate cover-up.

During the years when John Mitchell was riding high as attorney
general and as President Nixon's close confidant, I often recalled my first, off-the-record meeting with him in New York
when he let me know what he thought of America's black
publishers. "Monkeys," he had called them. This was the period—the late sixties—when the Black Panthers were making
their militant presence felt across the land and were spewing
forth their own choice epithets. Their favorite word for the
police was "pigs." So when Mitchell was named Attorney General of the United States, I found myself thinking about the
appointment in sardonic, zoological terms. The man who referred to blacks as "monkeys" had become, in the abusive
rhetoric of the "Panthers," the nation's "Top Pig." The times,
alas, were not conducive to rational and civilized discourse
between the races.

Through a fortuitous circumstance, I happened to be one of
the first white reporters to become aware of the harsh, antiwhite
rhetoric and attitudes that pervaded large segments of the black
community in the sixties. Back in 1959, when I was anchoring
News Beat on Channel 13 in New York, a black reporter named
Louis Lomax came to me with a proposal that began with a

question: "Mike, what do you know about the Black Muslims?"

"I don't know what you're talking about," I replied. I had never even heard the term "Black Muslims." In those days blacks were still called Negroes, and Moslems—spelled with an *o*, not a *u*—were Arabs who lived in the Middle East. Lomax explained: "The Black Muslims are black supremacists. They are totally opposed to integration. They're a hate group. They hate white people."

Remember, this was 1959—a time when the average American Negro was—in Ralph Ellison's phrase—"the invisible man," a second-class citizen who knew his place, minded his manners and brought great peril on himself if he dared challenge white authority. It's true that there were a few signs of the revolution to come. The valiant Martin Luther King had launched the civil rights movement in the South, but he and his followers were preaching a message of racial harmony, of blacks and whites working together to achieve equality and integration. We assumed, in our condescending way, that the cherished goal of all black folks was to live with and be like white folks. So I was highly skeptical when Lomax insisted that the Black Muslims were a rapidly growing army that already had drawn more than 200,000 blacks into its ranks. I contended that such a large and hostile organization could not have escaped the attention of the press; yet I had not read one word about the Muslims in any major newspaper or magazine.

"That's right!" Lomax exclaimed. "The white press isn't covering this story because the white press can't get near these people. And that's what I want to talk to *you* about."

Lomax then proposed our doing a documentary on the Black Muslims for Channel 13. He would be the reporter (as a black man, he could gain access to the group and its leaders), and we would provide the camera crew and other technical and editorial assistance. The report would include film coverage of a Muslim rally plus interviews with the head of the movement, Elijah Muhammad, and its chief New York minister, Malcolm X. Ted Yates and I, who were running the news operation at Channel 13, would have full control over the editing process, and if we decided to put it on the air, I would anchor the documentary. This meant I would introduce Lomax's interviews and narration and would have the right to comment on them. Finally Lomax said the main reason he had come to us was because Yates and I had a reputation, dating back to *Night Beat,* for taking on provocative subjects.

I was intrigued by the prospect and so was Yates. We knew that if Lomax was right—or even half right—it would make an extraordinary story; and as Lomax pointed out, that kind of controversy was right up our alley. Moreover, as a local station with modest resources, we rarely came upon such an opportunity to score a beat over the major news organizations. So, after getting the green light and budget approval from management, we hired a camera crew to work with Lomax and told him to proceed under our supervision.

It was a difficult assignment that stretched out over several months. The Muslims were extremely wary at first, not of Lomax but of us, his white collaborators. However, Lomax was persistent and eventually was able to get everything we wanted. The material he obtained was startling and, in the context of that innocent time, more than a little terrifying. The atmosphere we recorded at the Muslim rally was one of pure hatred. In scathing language made all the more menacing by the cold, unemotional tone of the delivery (the Muslim leaders had disciplined themselves not to rant and bluster), Malcolm X and other speakers excoriated the Caucasian race as "white devils" who had committed every heinous crime in the book against black men and women. "The white man was the serpent in the Garden of Eden," Malcolm told Lomax in an on-camera interview. "By nature he is evil." And in his interview with Lomax, Elijah Muhammad predicted that in the next ten years there would be a "general insurrection" of black Americans and "plenty of bloodshed."

We called the story *The Hate That Hate Produced* and gave it a very big play. Instead of a one-shot, single-night broadcast, the customary fate of most documentaries, we cut the report into five separate pieces and featured it on *News Beat* every night for a week. This gave the story a cumulative impact which, in a lesser way, was not unlike the powerful, night-after-night effect that *Roots* had on a later generation of viewers. Then, at the end of the week we patched the pieces together and broadcast *The Hate That Hate Produced* as a one-hour documentary.

The report struck a nerve, no question of it. Moderate black leaders, like my friend Roy Wilkins of the NAACP, accused us of grossly exaggerating the size and importance of the Black Muslims. That charge was picked up by most of the reviewers, including Jack Gould of *The New York Times,* then the most influential television critic in the country. In the past Gould had been generally sympathetic to my work, first on *Night Beat* and then at ABC, but this time he wrote: "Mike Wallace's penchant for pursuing sensationalism as an end in itself has backfired." Our reporting, he asserted, was "not conscientious or constructive." Our reply to this and other criticisms from the power centers of the white media (all of which had been thoroughly scooped on the story) was a defiant challenge: "All right, don't take our word for it. Go see for yourselves." They did. In the months that followed, the *Times,* the three networks, *Time* and *Newsweek* magazines and other major organs of American journalism ran stories on the Black Muslims that corroborated the basic points we had made in *The Hate That Hate Produced.*

In terms of becoming a media star, the chief beneficiary of all this exposure was not the head of the movement, Elijah Muhammed. A remote and impassive man, he shunned the press and was not very articulate on the rare occasions he did talk to reporters. Instead, the man who came to be identified in the public mind as the face and voice of the Black Muslims was Malcolm X who, unlike Muhammad, was a skilled and powerful communicator. When he appeared on television, he came across as an intelligent, forceful and magnetic presence. Although Malcolm invariably delivered his diatribes against the white man in a steady, even-tempered voice, there was no mistaking the strength and passion of his convictions. The anger and sense of menace he conveyed were palpable and riveting. Hearing him say things about white America that no black man had ever before dared to say in public was for many viewers a disturbing and visceral experience.

Neither Elijah Muhammad nor Malcolm X would consent

to be interviewed by me when we were putting together *The Hate That Hate Produced*. They were willing to sit down with Louis Lomax, but they would not allow themselves to be seen talking to a "white devil" on television. However, as time went on and Malcolm began to make himself available to the white press, I was one of the first white television reporters to interview him. Perhaps he felt he owed me that, for he had begun to appreciate the publicity he and the Muslims were receiving, and he knew that our report on Channel 13 had been the first shot in the barrage of press coverage. As it turned out, I did several pieces on Malcolm over the next few years, first at Channel 13 and later at CBS, and we gradually developed a mutual respect, a friendship. He was an excellent source; he fed me information and insights about the black community that few white journalists were privileged to get in those days; and I, in turn, made a special effort to be fair in my dealings with him. It would have been easy to prejudge him, dismiss him as a morbid hatemonger or a headline-seeking troublemaker, but I tried not to. And I must admit that I was touched when, in the autobiography he wrote with Alex Haley, he cited me as one of the few white reporters he felt he could trust.

Over the years, as he traveled in the United States and abroad, Malcolm began to modify his views and temper his searing hatred of white America. His celebrity status brought him into more frequent and closer contact with white people; he was invited to lecture before mixed audiences at universities across the country. All of this had an effect. He came to recognize that there were at least some white Americans who were not devils, who instead were truly sensitive to the historic wrongs that had been inflicted on their black compatriots and whose commitment to social and economic change went beyond the liberal cant he had scorned for so many years. Guided by his fresh outlook, Malcolm moved toward a more flexible position, though he did not go so far as to embrace the interracial idealism that motivated Martin Luther King and other civil rights leaders. He remained more militant than they, but became more tolerant than his doctrinaire brothers in the Black Muslim movement. This shift in attitude inevitably brought him into conflict with Elijah Muhammad, a conflict aggravated by the resentment Muhammad and his advisers felt toward the media attention then being showered on Malcolm. The upshot was that the two men eventually turned against each other, and in 1964 Malcolm broke with the Muslims and formed a rival group called the Organization of Afro-American Unity.

Muhammad was understandably concerned that the charismatic Malcolm might lure members and financial support away from the Black Muslims. But that was the least of his apprehensions, as I learned from Malcolm the last time I saw him. That was in the late fall of 1964. We were sitting in my office at CBS News, talking about a story I was planning to do on the black community. When I mentioned his former comrades, the Muslims, Malcolm suddenly glowered and said: "They're out to get me, Mike. They're going to try to kill me."

I didn't take him seriously. An element of paranoia had always been evident in his fear and hatred of the white man, and now he seemed to be focusing on the Muslims as the sinister force in his life. "Oh really," I said with a touch of sarcasm, "why would they want to do that?"

"Because I know too much about Elijah."

"What do you know about Elijah?"

"Mike, he is not the man he is cracked up to be. His morals aren't what he would have you believe. He has weaknesses of the flesh that disillusioned me. This man Muhammad who paints himself as an ascetic, who paints himself as a holy prophet of God, is a lecher. A *lecher!*"

"Oh Malcolm, come on."

"I can tell you that he takes girls as secretaries, girls within the movement, and gets them pregnant, and then farms them and their children out. Elijah Muhammad is the father of several children by several different teenage girls."

In response to my look of disbelief, he said that he had solid proof to back up the charge. In imparting this kind of information to a reporter with whom he felt friendly, Malcolm obviously was trying to alert me to the danger he was in. He simply knew too much about his former associates.

On February 21, 1965, Malcolm was addressing a meeting at the Audubon Ballroom in Harlem; shortly after he began his speech, he was gunned down by three men who were later identified as Black Muslims. Many years later, in January 1982, *60 Minutes* broadcast a piece called "Who Killed Malcolm X?" In it, producer Allan Maraynes and I came to the conclusion that of the three men sentenced to and still serving life terms for Malcolm's murder, two—Norman Butler and Thomas Johnson—were very likely innocent of the crime. We came up with evidence that strongly suggested that two other Black Muslims, who were never apprehended, had been among the trio that shot and killed Malcolm that Sunday afternoon in February 1965. But Manhattan District Attorney Robert Morgenthau found our evidence insufficiently compelling to reopen the case. Whoever the guilty Muslims were, it was no small irony that Malcolm X—a man who had risen to prominence by preaching a message of hate for the white man—was slain by members of his own race and adherents of the faith he had done so much to propagate.

Malcolm X was killed just as the black revolution was about to turn militant and destructive. The anger and frustration that had been building in the urban black ghettos for so many years could no longer be contained. The first major riot of the sixties—in the Watts section of Los Angeles—occurred six months after Malcolm's death, and it set off a chain reaction of violence in black communities that persisted through the rest of the decade. Those ghetto uprisings were a sharp departure not only from the organized, nonviolent demonstrations of the civil rights movement, but also from the highly disciplined tactics of the Black Muslims. For all their verbal attacks on white America, the Muslims did not translate inflammatory rhetoric into action. Although Elijah Muhammad had prophesied the racial bloodshed of the sixties, both he and Malcolm counseled their followers to avoid violent confrontations with the "white oppressors." They were realistic enough to know that blacks would suffer far more than whites in that kind of direct and open rebellion. But when the riots began to erupt in one city after another, other, less responsible black leaders emerged who condoned the disorders. "Violence," exulted one of them, a young radical named H. Rap Brown, "is as American as cherry pie." From other voices came similar battle cries—"black power" and "burn, baby, burn"—and in the midst of this stormy climate the Black Panthers burst upon the scene.

The forces of black militancy that swept across America in the middle and late sixties reached their crest in the rhetoric and actions of the Black Panthers. Unlike the Muslims, they were not black separatists; they espoused a kind of primitive, street-oriented Marxism that cut across racial lines. When the Panthers raised their clenched fists and shouted, "Power to the people!" they claimed to be speaking out on behalf of all poor Americans, black and white. In other words, "black was beautiful," but white was okay, too, as long as one was not a member of the white power structure—the despised "pigs" who were responsible for the social and economic oppression of "the people."

In portraying themselves as revolutionaries, the Panthers went out of their way to dress the part. With their black leather jackets and berets and the beards and dark shades adorning their faces, they looked like a cross between Fidel Castro's guerrillas and Haiti's Tontons Macoute. They also brandished guns for the avowed purpose of protecting "the people from the brutality of the pigs." Along with the National Rifle Association and other opponents of gun-control legislation, the Panthers fervently believed in the constitutional right to bear arms. They did more than simply bear them, however; during 1968 and 1969, the years when they were most prone to violence, they had several gun battles with the police, and at least ten Panthers and three cops were killed in the shoot-outs. By the end of 1969, the leadership of the Black Panther party was in total disarray. Its co-founders, Huey Newton and Bobby Seale, were in jail and its Minister of Information, Eldridge Cleaver, was living in exile in Algeria.

Eldridge Cleaver was the Malcolm X of the Black Panthers, their most forceful and articulate spokesman. A confessed rapist who had spent several years in prison, he was a hard-bitten product of the ghetto streets. But Cleaver was also a man of considerable intelligence and a gifted writer. His polemical memoir, *Soul on Ice,* was to the Panthers what *Das Kapital* had been to an earlier generation of Marxists. Even some critics who deplored Cleaver's revolutionary views—his call to arms and violence—were impressed by the power and clarity of his prose.

Cleaver had no qualms about practicing what he preached. In the spring of 1968, he and another Panther, Bobby Hutton, engaged in a shoot-out with the police at Panther headquarters in Oakland, California. Hutton was killed and Cleaver was arrested when he walked out of the bullet-scarred house naked to show that he was unarmed. That resourceful tactic probably saved his life. Booked on a charge of assault with intent to kill, he later jumped bail and fled, first to Cuba, then to Algeria.

In the late fall of 1969, when producer Paul Loewenwarter and I were preparing a profile of the Black Panthers for *60 Minutes,* we decided to try for an interview with the party propagandist who had chosen exile over prison. Through a contact in New York's radical community, I was able to obtain Cleaver's telephone number in Algeria. When I placed the call I had no trouble getting through; in fact, he answered the phone himself. After listening to my proposal, Cleaver said: "I might be interested. Talk to my agent."

"Talk to your *what?*"

"Talk to the person who represents me."

"Who would that be?" I asked.

"Ellen Wright. Richard Wright's widow. She's in Paris."

Before calling Mrs. Wright, I paused to reflect on what a fascinating world we were living in. Here was a Marxist revolutionary, an ex-convict and fugitive from justice, who insisted that our request to interview him on national television be negotiated through his agent. Nor did Ellen Wright hesitate to lay it on the line. When I made the call to Paris, her first question was: "How much money?"

I told her emphatically that under no circumstances would *60 Minutes* pay for an interview with Eldridge Cleaver. Mrs. Wright passed the message on to her client, who eventually scaled his demands down to a condition that I could meet without troubling my conscience or putting a strain on our budget. "Eldridge is willing to participate," Mrs. Wright informed me later, "but only if you can bring to Algiers a new pedal for his Uher tape recorder. He needs it so he can transcribe what he's taping for his next book." I figured that even the most fastidious critic of checkbook journalism could hardly have objected to that.

I flew to Algeria on New Year's Day, 1970. As I left my Manhattan house that morning, I spotted Jane Fonda outside her father's home in the next block about to get into a taxi with several pieces of luggage. She and I were acquainted, and since we were both headed for JFK Airport we decided to ride out together. Jane had to catch a flight to California, and when I told her where I was going—and why—she began asking me about Cleaver and the Black Panthers. It was obvious that she knew little about them; but since she seemed to be genuinely interested, I gave her a rundown on who the Panthers were and what they had been doing over the past couple of years. I should emphasize that Miss Fonda had not yet become a voice of radical protest, a critic of U.S. policies in Vietnam and social injustices at home. In those days she was known to the public only as a promising and very attractive young actress, and as the daughter of one of America's most esteemed actors. Even so, as we rode out to the airport that New Year's morning, I thought it odd that a bright young woman like Jane Fonda should have so little awareness of a phenomenon like the Panthers, who had been in the headlines so often during the past year. Yet it was not more than six months later that Miss Fonda, a quick study once her attention began to focus, was hip-deep in radical politics. I viewed her sudden conversion skeptically at first, thinking that here was a rebel in search of a cause. But I was disabused of that notion when, as the years went by, it became clear that her political commitments were genuine and enduring.

When I arrived in Algeria, on that first day of 1970, I went directly to Cleaver's apartment overlooking the waterfront. Eldridge and his wife, Kathleen, greeted me cordially, and I spent several hours that night in casual conversation with them. Both were eager for the latest news from America, and I detected in the wistful tone of their questions a trace of homesickness. It was evident that they found their life in exile to be a lonely one.

Cleaver's subdued demeanor did not surprise me, for it was consistent with the chastened mood of other Panthers I had talked to over the past few months. All the killings and arrests and the constant pressure they felt from various law-enforcement agencies had taken their toll. The members of the party I met in California and New York seemed dispirited, intimidated and very much on the defensive. In my interviews with them, they played down the violence and belligerent rhetoric that had been the Panther hallmark; instead, they emphasized the positive, constructive activities they were involved in, the special schools and free breakfast programs they were running in the ghettos. So when I returned to Cleaver's apartment the next day with a camera crew to do the interview, I fully expected him to echo this new, conciliatory line. I could not have been more mistaken, as I discovered early in our interview when I asked him about Panther threats against America's political leaders:

WALLACE: What purpose is served by talking about shooting your way into the Senate of the United States, taking off the head of Senator McClellan and shooting your way back out? What purpose is really served by that kind of talk and what would be accomplished—?

CLEAVER: The goal is to take Senator McClellan's head. Now the process of getting his head has to rely on a strategic technique. I mean I just won't walk in and take his head and walk out, you see. I have to get past the guards and get past those who might try to protect his pig head, so to me I think that would mean shooting my way in and shooting my way out because I wouldn't want to go in, take his head and just sit there.

WALLACE: But right now, we are at the point of trying to understand. When the American people hear that you want to shoot your way into the United States Senate, take off the head of a senator—

CLEAVER: Into the White House and take off the head of Richard Nixon, you see.

WALLACE: What does that mean? This is rhetoric?

CLEAVER: This is not rhetoric. I'm telling you that Richard Nixon, J. Edgar Hoover, Senator John McClellan, et al.—not just them, but all of the pigs of the power structure—have to be apprehended, and I feel myself, you see, that the fate that they receive will depend upon the resistance that they put up. I feel that they are criminals, that they are the decision-makers who are programming oppression and destruction not only in the United States but around the world.

Even as he was speaking, I sensed that he was playing to the balconies back home. It was a macho performance, an act of bravado, a self-conscious message to his craven comrades back in the States that he, at least, had not abandoned the true Panther creed of Violent Revolution and Death to All Pigs. Of course, it was infinitely easier to spout that kind of tough talk from the refuge of political asylum four thousand miles beyond the reach of U.S. law. Once the interview was over, Cleaver quickly reverted to the pleasant, mild-mannered host who had welcomed me into his home the night before. And later that day, after we had packed up our equipment and it was time to leave for the airport, he seemed truly sorry to see us go. It wasn't so much that he wanted us to stay, but rather that we were flying home and I could tell from the forlorn look on his face as he waved good-bye that a part of him wished very much to be going with us.

The basic point of our *60 Minutes* profile was that the Black Panthers should be viewed in perspective and without undue alarm. We pointed out that they were few in number (not more than a thousand party members throughout the country), and that the vast majority of black Americans did not support their bellicose Marxism. We also noted that even within the ranks of the Panthers themselves, there was a concerted effort to move away from violence and toward more constructive pursuits like the free breakfast programs. The interview with Eldridge Cleaver took up less than five minutes of our twenty-four-minute report; but it came at the end of the piece, where it had such an impact that it overshadowed the main theme of our story. The reaction to the interview was heavy and emotional. Cleaver's crude threats seemed to intensify the fears of some viewers who already felt imperiled by the rise of black militancy. Others accused us of exploiting those fears and took us to task for airing Cleaver's barbarous rantings on national television. As on other occasions over the years when I had done controversial interviews, I was reproached for having indulged in what some critics regarded as my favorite vice— sensationalism.

However, Attorney General John Mitchell and other officials in the Justice Department acted as though such fears were justified; in one public statement after another, they portrayed the Black Panthers as a dangerous revolutionary force, a serious threat to law and order. A few days after our Panther broadcast, government lawyers subpoenaed our outtakes, the notes which producer Paul Loewenwarter and I had compiled, and even our expense accounts. Because CBS's lawyers were not on the ball in that particular instance, they turned over to the Justice Department all the material it requested. What we should have done, of course, was insist on our constitutional right to deny the government access to such privileged and confidential information. Nor were we alone; other journalists who did stories on the Panthers during that period were hit with similar subpoenas. Such actions made it clear that Mitchell and his deputies were going to extreme lengths in their pursuit and harassment of the Black Panthers. This did not surprise me, for I knew that even though they did not have the tangible power to back up their rhetoric, the Panthers were not the sort of people that John Mitchell was inclined to toy with.

There is a postscript to this Black Panther affair. In my Algiers expense account, turned over to the Justice Department by the CBS lawyers, the following item appeared: "$300 for services rendered," with the names of three young women, two of them Americans, who had received one hundred dollars each. During my interview with Mitchell at his Watergate apartment (before Martha joined us and stole the show), he brought up that expense account and asked me, in a sly and knowing tone, to specify the services that had been rendered. I found it difficult to believe that the Attorney General of the United States had gone through my travel tabs and various jottings, and I was tempted to tell him what he apparently wanted to hear about my Algerian peccadilloes. Instead, I played it straight: I told him, though it was no legitimate concern of his, the truth was that the three women had performed secretarial services for us in Algiers.

Among the leaders of the black revolution one man towered above all the others: I'm referring, of course, to Martin Luther King, whose eloquent voice was tragically stilled by an assassin's bullet in April 1968.

I had interviewed Dr. King on numerous occasions through the years and had come to admire him more deeply than any other American figure of that period. It is a pallid understatement to say that King had the courage of his convictions. He understood that if he broke the law, he would have to pay the penalty. With that understanding, he deliberately did break the law to wake America's conscience; and he went to jail. But King took on more than the burden of his black brothers. He despised what the United States was doing in Vietnam; and though he knew it would hardly help the civil rights cause were he to speak his mind on Vietnam, he refused to be silent on that issue.

On Christmas Eve in 1968, eight months after King was killed, *60 Minutes* broadcast an interview with his widow, in the course of which Coretta King talked about the loss she shared with millions of other Americans who revered her husband. At one point, I asked Mrs. King what that first Christmas without her husband would be like in the King household. Here, in part, was her reply:

> It doesn't mean that we will sit around and bathe in our grief. I think that very often a time like this causes people to really reflect on the deeper meaning of, say, Christmas or any other occasion. I remember Easter 1963, when my husband was jailed in Birmingham. I had just had my fourth child and was still confined to my house, and he had gone to jail on Good Friday, and Easter I had not heard from him. And I was very depressed, but somehow that was the most meaningful Easter I have ever experienced because, you know, Easter's a time for suffering, but it's creative—it can be creative suffering. So I think if we can look on this Christmas season as a time for reflecting and a time to think of the deeper meaning and the real spirit of Christmas, which should be the spirit of giving and giving unselfishly. And I think if we think of my husband's life and his death in those

terms, then we will not be as sad. We will be hopeful because
in his death there is hope for redemption.

Martin Luther King was not the only American clergyman who
embraced controversial stands on political issues in the sixties
and seventies. Another was Archbishop Fulton Sheen, whom
I interviewed on *60 Minutes* in the fall of 1969.

Bishop Sheen was the first (and no doubt the last) Roman
Catholic prelate to star on a hit television show in America.
This was back in the 1950s when his weekly sermons attracted
a large and faithful audience. At a time when the enormously
popular TV comic Milton Berle was known as "Uncle Miltie,"
Bishop Sheen was affectionately called "Uncle Fultie." A man
of wry humor, he often made a point of paying tribute "to my
four writers—Matthew, Mark, Luke and John." During that
period Sheen generally refrained from speaking out on sensitive
political issues. But in 1967, after he had stepped down from
the television pulpit and was serving as Bishop of the Diocese
of Rochester, New York, he exhorted President Johnson unilaterally to withdraw all U.S. forces from Vietnam. This public
statement did not sit well with American Catholics who supported LBJ's policies and who felt that a bishop of the Church
had no right to meddle in secular politics. When I interviewed
Sheen two years later, Johnson was no longer President, and
although his successor was taking steps to wind down the war,
Richard Nixon firmly opposed unilateral withdrawal, which he
equated with surrender. So I asked the archbishop if he was
still committed to that view:

> SHEEN: Yes, I am. First, it is not a political action. It's
> a moral action. If we are to be the moral leaders of the
> world, we must give an example . . . So I suggested that
> we withdraw for the sake of winning, or winning the
> approval of the world. And furthermore, this war is cost-
> ing too much. In Vietnam, it costs a million dollars an
> hour, twenty-four million a day. If we kill twenty-four
> men a day—and sometimes that is all that is killed—
> that means a million dollars a man. So that from a moral
> and economic point of view, withdrawal from Vietnam
> is to be very much recommended.

WALLACE: Now?

SHEEN: Now.

WALLACE: Immediately?

SHEEN: Immediately.

WALLACE: Among the most unrelenting of the South Vietnamese are the Catholics, some of whom came down from North Vietnam in the middle fifties. Surely you worry about their safety should U.S. forces withdraw?

SHEEN: No, I do not, Mr. Wallace. I believe that if we pulled out unilaterally, that the moral opinion of the world would sustain us. The other nations would resent any attempt on the part of the northern Vietnamese to come down to destroy the people of South Vietnam.

In that interview we also touched on the arcane subject of ecclesiastical politics. In response to my question about his career ambitions within the Catholic hierarchy, Sheen said that the reason he had not been elevated to the rank of cardinal was because "I refused to pay the price." He declined to specify except to say that the "price" of a red hat would have entailed "disloyalty to my own principles and I think to Christian practice."

The war in Vietnam was very much on my mind in the spring of 1971 when Don Hewitt and I flew to Texas to do a story on the opening of the Lyndon Baines Johnson Presidential Library. A little more than two years had elapsed since Johnson left the White House, an embittered man who felt he had been betrayed by members of his own party and even by some high-ranking officials in his administration. Cut off from the center of action and power in Washington—a world he had dominated for so many years, first as Senate majority leader and later as President—he spent almost all his time at his ranch, brooding over his fate and nursing his grievances. Anti-Johnson feeling was still running high throughout the country in 1971, and nowhere was it more evident than within the Democratic party, the controls of which were passing into the hands of the antiwar forces that helped to bring about his downfall. (Indeed, some of the demonstrators who had clashed with police on the streets of Chicago during the 1968 convention would become delegates committed to the nomination of George McGovern at the next Democratic convention.)

Johnson's bitterness extended to the press, which he blamed for having fanned the flames of protest that flared up against him during the last two years of his presidency; as a result, he was rarely receptive to reporters who sought him out at the ranch. But the opening of his presidential library drew him out of his shell. He viewed that project as the vindication of his performance in the White House, a lasting memorial to the Civil Rights Act, the Great Society programs and other achievements in domestic policy during his administration. And now that the library was finished and ready to open its doors to the public, Johnson was more than willing to cooperate with the media in their coverage of the event. In fact, such was his eagerness that when he learned that Hewitt and I were planning to do a *60 Minutes* piece on the opening, he invited us to be his guests at the ranch. Not only that, but when we arrived at the airport, Johnson and his wife, Lady Bird, were there to greet us and take us in tow. Even by the extravagant standards of Texas hospitality, that was a red-carpet welcome—and the best was yet to come.

A professional chauffeur had driven the limousine that brought us to the ranch from the airport; but the next day, when Don and I and a couple of other guests were herded into a white convertible for a sightseeing drive around the LBJ ranch, Johnson himself was at the wheel. At one point during that high-speed tour of his spread, the former President suddenly swerved onto the shoulder of the road, near a trash bin, and came to an abrupt halt. Something had caught his eye that displeased him. "Hewitt," he barked, "you want to pick up that candy wrapper?"

Hewitt, sitting next to me in the backseat, lurched forward as though he had been hit with a rabbit punch. "Mr. President?" he said in a startled tone.

Johnson turned and glared at Don, then gestured toward the object in question. "That candy wrapper," he repeated, "how about picking it up?"

Apparently he had decided to have a little fun at Hewitt's

expense. Yet it seemed to me there was more to it than that. Yes, he was glad that we had come to Texas to do a story on his library, but he also wanted us to understand that since this was his turf, his domain, he was the one who called the shots, no matter how petty. As for Hewitt, he decided that under the circumstances he had no choice but to comply. His main concern was getting the best possible story, and toward that end we needed Johnson's full cooperation. What would he have gained by challenging our host's command? So, while the rest of us sat in the white convertible and watched with amused approval, the executive producer of *60 Minutes* jumped out and did his bit to combat the crime of littering at the LBJ ranch.

We later drove over to the Lyndon Baines Johnson Presidential Library, which is situated on the campus of the University of Texas in Austin. We intended to structure our piece in the format of a tour. The plan called for Lady Bird Johnson to show us around those areas that dealt with the social and ceremonial aspects of the presidency; then, as we turned our attention to matters of substance—policies and programs— Johnson would take over as tour guide. We went through a couple of dry runs to get our bearings and set up camera angles. Johnson rambled on like a proud father as he steered us past exhibits honoring such hallmarks of his administration as civil rights, Medicare, the war on poverty and other achievements of the Great Society. In the sphere of foreign policy, there was a prominent exhibit on the 1967 Six-Day War in the Middle East, but I couldn't help noticing that there was nothing about the war in Vietnam, and when I asked Johnson about that, the proud papa suddenly turned surly. "Don't ask me about Vietnam," he rasped. "I don't want to talk about Vietnam."

Hewitt and I protested that we couldn't ignore Vietnam, that it was an essential part of the story, a centerpiece in Lyndon Johnson's presidency. Johnson was adamant. He warned me that if I brought up Vietnam while the cameras were rolling, he would cut off the tour on the spot and "send you boys packing." That was enough to alarm Hewitt; wanting no more of the argument, he backed away and went off to discuss some technical details with one of the camera crews.

Standing alone with Johnson, I decided to try another tack.

I told him that I had been a longtime admirer of his, dating back to the Eisenhower years when he had been such an effective majority leader in the U.S. Senate. Then I reminded him of an eloquent speech on civil rights that he had given as Kennedy's Vice-President before a Jewish group in New York City. I said that I remembered thinking at the time that he was just the kind of leader the country needed—a white southerner with progressive views on the racial question—and what a shame it was that because he was from the South, he could probably never be elected President. But then the tragedy of assassination had given him the opportunity, I went on, and for a while he lived up to my expectations of him. That is, he did more to advance the cause of civil rights than any President since Lincoln. "But then," I said, "everything turned sour, Mr. President, and you know why?"

"Why?" he snapped.

"Because you let that war get out of hand." I drew a breath and continued, man to man. "Vietnam fucked you, Mr. President, and so, I'm afraid, you fucked the country. And you've got to talk about that!"

Johnson looked at me first in disbelief, then his gaze turned withering, and he stalked off without saying a word. For a moment I feared that he had gone to find Hewitt to tell him the deal was off, that Wallace had stepped way out of line, and that he would not cooperate with a *60 Minutes* story. But he did nothing of the sort. We proceeded with the shooting as scheduled, and when the time came to walk with Johnson through the exhibits, I honored his request and did not mention Vietnam. Much to my astonishment, however, he himself brought up the subject. We had just finished talking about the Middle East crisis and the burdens that a Commander in Chief must shoulder in the nuclear age when suddenly—without warning or preamble—he let it all out:

Throughout our history our public has been prone to attach Presidents' names to the international difficulties. You will recall the War of 1812 was branded as Mr. Madison's War, and the Mexican War was Mr. Polk's War, and the Civil War or the War Between the States was Mr. Lincoln's War, and World War I was Mr. Wilson's War, and World War II was Mr. Roosevelt's War, and Korea was Mr. Truman's War, and President Kennedy was spared that cruel action because his period was known as Mr. McNamara's War. And then it became Mr. Johnson's War, and now they refer to it as Mr. Nixon's War in talking about getting out. I think it is very cruel to have that burden placed upon a President because he is trying to follow a course that he devotedly believes is in the best interest of his nation. And if those Presidents hadn't stood up for what was right during those periods, we wouldn't have this country what it is today.

Quoting from the transcript does not convey the almost physical intensity of Johnson's outburst. In particular, I was struck by the bitter, derisive tone that came into his voice when he noted that "President Kennedy was spared that cruel action because his period was known as Mr. McNamara's War." Even though it had been Johnson's decision to escalate the military action in Vietnam—to transform it into a full-scale American war— he obviously felt that he had been unjustly blamed, that it was Kennedy who had set the course there, and that he, Johnson, had merely followed it. Later, after we finished shooting and the cameras were turned off, he said to me: "Well, goddammit, Mike, I gave you what you wanted. I hope you're satisfied."

"Oh I am, Mr. President, I am." When we aired the piece a few days later, I summed it up with the following comment on the man and his presidency:

What he hopes most is that he will be remembered for his Great Society and not for Vietnam. But the tragedy of Lyndon Johnson is that, although he accomplished so much for so many while he was in office, historians are bound to write of him principally as the President who bogged his country down in Vietnam. It is some measure of the man, I think, that on that matter—Vietnam—he has not wavered. He still believes that he was right, and that history will prove it.

He apparently clung to that belief until the day he died in January 1973. Yet the past decade has brought little of the vindication Johnson anticipated as his due. Most Americans still regard the war in Vietnam as a monumental blunder and a tragic waste of lives.

And so it went during the early years of *60 Minutes* as we struggled to gain a foothold on prime-time television. And it was a struggle, no question of that. Most of the critics were in our corner; the reviews of our programs during those first few years were favorable, with rare exception. In addition, we were heartened by the Emmys and other awards that came our way. And if it's true that imitation is the sincerest form of flattery, then NBC paid us the ultimate compliment. A few months after *60 Minutes* went on the air, our chief rival introduced a similar broadcast, *First Tuesday,* the first of many efforts by NBC over the years to come up with a winner in the newsmagazine format. At least we could take pride in having become a *succès d'estime*.

But the ratings were another story, for in those days we did not attract a large audience, at least not by prime-time standards. Part of the problem was a program we had to compete with on the 10:00 P.M. slot on Tuesday. Pitted against us on ABC was *Marcus Welby, M.D.*, then the most popular show on television—the *Dallas* of its day. As a result, *60 Minutes* consistently finished at or near the bottom of the heap in the weekly tabulations. Therefore, if ratings alone had been the criterion, we would not have survived those lean, early years. But the CBS brass kept us on the air, one of the rare occasions when network executives in charge of prime-time programming allowed themselves to be influenced by considerations other than ratings. Or who knows, maybe there was a visionary or two in the CBS hierarchy who had a premonition that we would eventually justify their faith and become a popular success. But if so, that foresight certainly flew in the face of the conventional wisdom of the time. For the most part, we were tolerated in much the same way that publishers tolerate those slim volumes of poetry and obscure first novels that occasionally appear on their lists of new books: offerings good for the

soul, no doubt, but let's not forget that it's the best sellers—
the literary equivalents of *Marcus Welby* and *Dallas*—that
bring in the bucks.

Frankly, I had not expected our superiors to be as indulgent
as they were; I figured that *60 Minutes* would be lucky to make
it through a couple of seasons in prime time. But when we
were given the green light to launch a third season in the
Tuesday night slot, I began to entertain the notion that we just
might be in for the long haul; that having established a modest
beachhead, we had a chance of becoming an enduring fixture
in the CBS schedule—and that was fine with me, for I was
thoroughly enjoying myself. The work was stimulating and the
critical response to our efforts was satisfying. Thanks to Hewitt's creative talents and those of the field producers and film
editors he had recruited, we were delivering the diversity and
quality we had set out to achieve. And despite our low ratings,
we were managing to make our presence felt. The right people
were watching. Best of all, from a personal standpoint, Harry
Reasoner and I were having a fine time as a team. When we
began our third season in the fall of 1970, I had every reason
to believe that the team was intact, that the Reasoner-Wallace
combination would last as long as *60 Minutes* remained on the
air. But the day was fast approaching when I would have to
face the prospect of doing the program with someone other
than Harry.

CHAPTER

NINE

THE PAIRING OF Reasoner and Wallace went far toward giving
60 Minutes its special focus and identity. If Don Hewitt had
gone ahead with his original plan to structure the broadcast
around one correspondent—Harry Reasoner—it would never
have evolved in quite the way it did. Reasoner himself often
made the point in later years that if he had embarked on the
venture alone, without Wallace, he would have been largely
confined to the studio-bound role of a host or anchorman who
merely introduced and commented on reports gathered in the
field by other correspondents. His would have been a passive
presence, similar to the one later assumed by Hugh Downs on
the ABC magazine program *20/20*. In fact, even with the two-
man format, there were times when Harry and Mike simply
played host to stories that had been put together by various
CBS News colleagues. Among those who made periodic contributions to *60 Minutes* during the first few months of its
existence were Eric Sevareid, Charles Collingwood, Robert
Trout, Hughes Rudd and Heywood Hale Broun. Although Reasoner and Wallace could rightly claim that *60 Minutes* was their
show, for a while during those early days it was not *exclusively*
theirs.

As time went on, however, they discovered that by sharing
the load and relying heavily on their field producers to handle

the research and preliminary legwork, they could do all the on-air reporting themselves. Thus was established the pattern that would become a distinguishing feature of *60 Minutes* and one of the key ingredients of its success. Starting with Reasoner and Wallace and extending to the three men who later became regulars on the program—Morley Safer, Dan Rather and Ed Bradley—the *60 Minutes* correspondents came across to viewers as engaged, peripatetic reporters who spent most of their time on the road, at home and abroad, in direct contact with the stories they presented. That personal involvement—"I was there, and here's what happened"—gave them and the program a credibility and dash of drama that it otherwise would have been lacking. (To cite two vivid examples from later years: Rather trudging around the hills of Afghanistan with anti-Soviet guerrillas and Wallace going eyeball to eyeball with the Ayatollah Khomeini in the early days of the hostage crisis in Iran.)

Beyond the general advantage of a two-man format, there was the specific appeal of the Reasoner-Wallace duo. It wasn't just a case of "Mike the Black Hat" versus "Harry the White Hat," although there was some of that and both men were willing, even eager, to exploit the contrast in their on-air personalities. On a couple of occasions during those first two years of *60 Minutes,* they even assumed adversarial roles on the same story. In a report on the continuing turmoil in the Middle East in early 1969, Reasoner viewed the conflict from the Arab perspective while Wallace focused on the Israelis; then a few months later, in a story on the religious strife in Northern Ireland, Harry concentrated on the Catholics and Mike dealt with the Protestants. In effect, that put them in direct competition with each other, which they welcomed. Since both Reasoner and Wallace were skilled in the art of one-upmanship, each was quick to seize on any opportunity to gain an edge and needle the other about it. This was especially true of their off-camera relationship, which was spiced by frequent bantering and jocular insults. On one occasion, when Mike taunted his co-star with a fan letter he had received expressing a preference for his work over Reasoner's, Harry dismissed the kudo, claiming that it must have been written by "your hair colorist." (This was something of a tender point with Reasoner, who professed to believe that Wallace resorted to all kinds of elaborate facials, hair dyes, diet pills and glandular injections to maintain the trim, energetic appearance that made him look younger than the gray-haired, stockily built Reasoner even though Mike was in reality five years older.)

The two correspondents generally played it straight on the air, but every now and then they indulged themselves a bit. For example, in September 1969 Reasoner did a feature story on a new breed of panhandlers that had cropped up on the sidewalks of New York: middle-class youths fresh out of college who buttonholed pedestrians not out of desperate need for food and survival, but simply because it was a relatively easy way to make a buck. Some of them boasted that they took in more than two hundred dollars a week in loose change hustled from soft touches—all of it tax-free, of course. At the end of the piece, while he was filming his on-camera close in front of the posh "21" Club in midtown Manhattan, Reasoner was suddenly accosted by Wallace, who until then had not figured in the report. In a pushy, abrasive tone that completely captured the brazen spirit of the story, Mike said: "Pardon me, sir, I wonder if you could let me have a hundred dollars for lunch at the 'Twenty-one'?"

Harry gave him a haughty, scornful look and replied: "Why don't you get a decent job—like me!"

In building up to that exchange, Reasoner had made this observation:

> The trouble with panhandling as a career is that you cannot expand indefinitely, and there are no fringe benefits like hospitalization or a pension. But it has certain advantages for young people: healthful work in the open air, flexible hours and a chance to meet a lot of interesting people.

That was vintage Reasoner. The droll treatment of offbeat subjects was Harry's forte: highly personal pieces on such topics as whiskey, small cars and miniskirts—journalistic side dishes that he served to viewers with his own special brand of "wry." More than anything else, it was Reasoner's urbane features on manners and mores that broke new ground and gave *60 Minutes* its distinctive flavor, setting it apart from the excessively earnest tone of documentaries and other television news programs. And largely for this reason, it was Harry who was regarded in those days as the show's top banana.

Wallace was aware of that prevailing sentiment and to a large extent he agreed with it. This was not a humble posture on his part. He had a clear appreciation of his own skills as a reporter and interviewer, and he was not at all shy about drawing attention to his contributions to *60 Minutes*. But at the same time, he recognized and admired the special gifts Reasoner brought to the broadcast, and he was among those who believed that if *60 Minutes* lost Reasoner, it would lose much of its distinctive appeal. Hence, Wallace shared in the dismay that swept through CBS in November of 1970 when Harry Reasoner disclosed that he would soon be leaving the network to commence a new career at ABC News.

His decision was not prompted by any dissatisfaction with *60 Minutes*. On the contrary; like Wallace, Reasoner viewed it as a choice assignment that gave him an opportunity to make full use of his talents. However, *60 Minutes* was just one of several hats that Reasoner was wearing at CBS in 1970. Since the early sixties, he had anchored his own Sunday night news show, and, as Walter Cronkite's regular replacement, he frequently anchored the *CBS Evening News*. The exposure he gained in those two assignments over the years enabled Reasoner to build up his own reputation as an anchorman. Indeed, an audience-research survey taken in 1970 revealed that the network anchorman who ranked next to Uncle Walter in overall viewer preference was not one of Cronkite's evening-news rivals—NBC's David Brinkley or John Chancellor, or the ABC team of Howard K. Smith and Frank Reynolds—but Harry Reasoner. Aware of the stature he had acquired, his superiors at CBS were fond of boasting that in Reasoner they had a number two man good enough to be number one at any other network. And Harry had a gracious way of returning the compliment: he often said during this period that he would rather be number two at CBS than number one anywhere else. It was gracious, yes, but not altogether honest.

For the truth was that Reasoner had become increasingly frustrated in his role as Cronkite's substitute. He yearned for a chance to be captain of the flagship in his own right rather

than merely a reliable first mate who manned the helm only
when the skipper was on vacation or away from New York on
another assignment. Yet Reasoner knew that given Cronkite's
sturdy constitution and strong aversion to sharing the *Evening
News* anchor seat with another correspondent, he would be
lodged in the backup slot for many years to come. Moreover,
when it came to the salary offer made him when his contract
came up for renewal in 1970, Reasoner had the sour feeling
that the CBS brass did not fully appreciate his worth. The words
of praise were nice to hear, but as far as Harry was concerned,
CBS was not willing to put its money where its mouth was.
So, like those disgruntled major league baseball players who
put themselves on the free-agent market in the hope of landing
a better deal elsewhere, Reasoner began shopping around in
the early autumn of 1970; a few weeks later, he signed a five-
year contract to co-anchor the *ABC Evening News* with Howard
K. Smith. "I took this job," he told a reporter, "because Walter
Cronkite was showing no inclination toward stepping in front
of a speeding truck."

Among the beneficiaries of Reasoner's defection to ABC were
the three correspondents who inherited the assignments he vacated. Roger Mudd settled in as Cronkite's regular replacement
on the *Evening News* and Dan Rather was given the anchor
slot on the Sunday night news show. Those promotions came
as no surprise, for by 1970 Mudd and Rather already had been
groomed to the point where, with Reasoner gone, they were
in position to start competing with each other for the role of
crown prince, heir to the throne that Cronkite would eventually
relinquish. However, in picking Reasoner's successor on *60
Minutes*, Don Hewitt and the other executives involved in that
decision had to consider other factors besides rank and future
value as an anchorman. They had to think in terms of blend
and harmony, of someone who would counterpoise Wallace's
black-hat approach to the stories he chose to focus on.

After talking it over, Hewitt and the others agreed that the
correspondent whose casual style and varied background in
hard news and features most closely resembled Reasoner's was
Charles Kuralt. But when the job was offered to Kuralt, he

turned it down. At the time he was so deeply immersed in the *On the Road* pieces he was doing for the *Evening News* that he did not want to give up that vagabond assignment, even for the opportunity to co-star on a prime-time program like *60 Minutes*. And the chief beneficiary of *that* decision was the person whose name came next on Hewitt's list of candidates— Morley Safer.

Safer was primarily known as a war correspondent whose reporting from Vietnam in the mid-sixties was so strong and distinguished that it inspired Fred Friendly, the documentary producer and onetime president of CBS News, to christen the conflict "Morley Safer's War." Yet because of his reputation as a hard-hitting combat reporter, he seemed an unlikely choice for the white-hat role on *60 Minutes*. At the time of his appointment, several people at CBS News expressed concern that the broadcast would lose the delicate balance in tone that Reasoner and Wallace had achieved. Hewitt took a different view. Since leaving Vietnam in 1967, Safer had been based in London, where, in addition to other duties, he had turned out a succession of feature stories in recent years. Hewitt had been impressed by Morley's deft touch. He regarded Safer as a man of sophisticated sensibilities who aspired to a certain elegance in manner and craft. His reporting in Vietnam had overshadowed that side of Safer's working personality, but Hewitt was confident that it could be brought to the fore on *60 Minutes*.

As usual, Hewitt knew what he was doing. Safer soon demonstrated that he could handle the diversified format of a magazine broadcast as effectively as he had covered search-and-destroy assaults on peasant villages. More to the point, his on-air persona was sufficiently different from Wallace's to provide the desired contrast. Yet in one significant respect, he was at a disadvantage. Unlike Reasoner and Wallace, both of whom had become seasoned veterans with established identities before they teamed up on *60 Minutes,* Safer was a relative newcomer to American television. A native of Toronto, he had served his apprenticeship in TV journalism at the Canadian Broadcasting Corporation before joining CBS News in 1964. And although his work in Vietnam had captured the attention and respect of his peers, Safer was not a familiar figure to the millions of casual viewers who watched the news desultorily. Partly for that reason, Wallace now became the dominant presence on *60 Minutes,* and the complexion of the program began to change to reflect his more aggressive style. It became harder in tone and more investigative in subject matter.

Safer accepted this state of affairs with good grace, in part because he respected the fact that Wallace was his senior in age and experience, and also because he knew that Mike had enthusiastically supported the decision to bring him aboard as Reasoner's successor. While the rapport between them was never as close as it had been between Mike and Harry, Mike and Morley got along well during the early years they worked together. But as time went on and it became more and more evident that Wallace was perceived as the star of *60 Minutes,* the correspondent whose pieces invariably made the big waves, an element of strain began to infect their relationship. The situation was aggravated by some of the show's producers, who, out of misguided loyalty to one correspondent, made disparaging remarks about the other. However, none of this was imparted to viewers because both men, adhering to the professional code of their craft, took pains to project a positive attitude toward each other on the air. Still, the friction was there, and many years later, following a dispute they had over a story Safer wanted to do on Haiti, the two correspondents would go several months without speaking to each other— except in the line of duty.

But they did hit it off in the beginning, which helped make a smooth transition from Reasoner to Safer. Unfortunately, the program itself continued to languish in the ratings as it struggled through its third season as a Tuesday night broadcast. By the time the season drew to a close in the spring of 1971, the CBS programming executives had run out of patience. Three years of prestige and low ratings on a precious hour of prime time were enough; so, when *60 Minutes* began its fourth season that fall, it was in a new time slot—6:00 P.M. on Sunday. To soften the blow of being banished from the prime-time schedule, the network gave the show more air time. Instead of being a bi-weekly program, it was broadcast once a week, except during football season when it was often preempted.

Hewitt, ever the optimist, chose to fix his gaze on the bright side. "Anything to get us away from *Marcus Welby*" was his primary reaction to the change. But Wallace and others at CBS News were apprehensive, fearing that the shift was a first step toward eventual cancellation. As it turned out, however, the switch was just the tonic that *60 Minutes* needed. Benefiting from being broadcast at a less competitive hour as well as from the increased air time, the weekly exposure, the show not only grew in critical esteem over the next few years, but gradually attracted with each passing season a larger audience. By the end of 1975, *60 Minutes* had built up such a strong and loyal following that it was ready to make a dramatic and triumphant return to prime time.

The changes on *60 Minutes* were not the only new developments Wallace had to confront in the early 1970s. There was also a sequence of events called Watergate. During that long season of discontent from the spring of 1973 until the denouement in August of 1974, when the Watergate Affair was nothing less than a national obsession, it was often said that the chief victims of the scandal were the avid supporters of Richard Nixon, those millions of Americans who had voted for him because they believed him to be a man of honor and dignity. Included in that vast group—that not-so-silent majority—was Mike Wallace.

Having been drawn into Nixon's orbit during the early stages of his political comeback, Wallace came to know the man at his best. At that critical point in his career, Nixon needed all the help he could get. So as part of his genuine effort to court the reporters covering his campaign, he managed to suppress the darker aspects of his complex personality: the petty suspicions, the festering sulks and the vindictive eruptions that had caused him so much trouble in the past. In a striking about-face from previous behavior, he strove to be attentive and aboveboard in his dealings with the press. It was an impressive performance, and it worked. Wallace was just one of several reporters who heralded the birth of the New Nixon, the chastened loser who, having learned from his past mistakes, had acquired enough wisdom and character to make him an appealing candidate. At one point in the early days of the 1968 campaign, shortly before the New Hampshire primary, Mike arranged for Nixon to make a speech at a small CBS News luncheon. He helped set it up because he wanted some of his skeptical colleagues at the network—Sevareid, Mudd, Rather, and others—to see the New Nixon in person and judge for themselves. The get-together was a huge success. Most of the skeptics agreed that Nixon seemed to have changed for the better, and some of them even told Wallace privately that— on the basis of what they had heard Nixon say that day—they could be induced to vote for him in the fall. Wallace was far less tentative and discreet. Years later, a colleague would recall: "I know for a fact that Mike was not the only CBS News correspondent who voted for Nixon in 1968, but he was the only one who *bragged* about it."

In his dealings with friends and associates, Wallace became an apologist for Nixon, which revealed a certain perversity, a characteristic desire to go against the grain of fashionable opinion and liberal cant. Although he espoused liberal positions on some issues, notably civil rights, Wallace disdained the elitist, cocktail party liberalism that flourished in Manhattan and Georgetown, the two centers of social and political chic on the East Coast. (In the fall of 1971, when the controversy over school busing was at its height, Mike did a *60 Minutes* piece on how some prominent Washington liberals got around this problem. The report noted that even such staunch advocates of compulsory busing as Senators Edward Kennedy and George McGovern sent *their* kids to schools—private or public—where there was no busing and almost no racial integration whatsoever; the schools in question were about 95 percent white. Needless to say, the story did little to allay the resentment of white parents who did not have such a choice.)

Many of the liberals Wallace knew, socially and professionally, were inclined to be Kennedy cultists, promulgators of the Camelot myth, and they had long regarded Nixon as their *bête noire*, the sullen heavy who had tried to prevent their hero from settling the New Frontier. Wallace was proud of the fact that he had never succumbed to the Kennedy mystique, and he took perverse pleasure in the distress that swept through

the Camelot crowd when Nixon made his triumphant march to
the White House. This is not to suggest that he was merely
indulging himself by playing devil's advocate for the sport of
it. There was much in Nixon that he genuinely admired—his
intelligence, his tenacity, his grasp of history and foreign affairs—but at the same time he did rather enjoy the exasperation
that came over his liberal friends whenever he launched into a
spirited defense of the man they loved to loathe.

In return, they chided Wallace for being a patsy who had
been duped by Tricky Dick and his operatives into swallowing
all the malarkey about the New Nixon. The political baiting
back and forth was seldom malicious—it generally took the
form of good-natured ribbing—and Wallace welcomed it because he felt that his was the stronger position. He did not
concur with all the actions and policies that Nixon initiated
during his first term in the White House, but he did believe
that his overall performance was eminently defensible. Moreover, he could make the case—and often did—that, Manhattan
and Georgetown notwithstanding, most of the country was supporting the President. Convincing proof came in November of
1972 when, thanks largely to his achievements in foreign policy
and the ineptitude of his Democratic opposition, Nixon was
reelected by a landslide.

But then, *le déluge*. When the Watergate storm finally broke
in the spring of 1973, the liberals who had always despised
Nixon reacted with predictable smugness, a gleeful litany of
I-told-you-sos. Conversely, those were difficult days for Nixon
apologists, especially if they worked in the media, where they
were so vastly outnumbered. During that spring and summer,
when there seemed to be no end to the revelations that the
White House had become a citadel of paranoia and criminal
deception, the "Nixon patsy" charge took on ramifications that
were downright humiliating. And to make matters worse, Wallace had not been alert in seeing through the cover-up. Of
course, he was hardly alone. Almost all the veteran political
journalists who were reputed to be perceptive observers of the
Washington scene shared in the embarrassing failure to pick
up the Watergate scent until it became a stench one could no
longer ignore. (It's worth noting that the two reporters who

came up with the major beat on the story, Bob Woodward and Carl Bernstein of *The Washington Post,* had no prior experience in covering national politics. Watergate was their debut on that center stage, and they wound up stealing the show.) But if— like most of his journalistic brethren in both print and broad- casting—Wallace was a latecomer to the Watergate story, it's also true that once he turned his attention to the unfolding drama, he tore into it with all the ferocity of a betrayed lover. Some of the Watergate-related interviews he put together in 1973 and 1974 were as tough and incisive as any he has ever done. And in many ways, the first one—a close encounter of the best kind with John Ehrlichman—was the most riveting.

CHAPTER

TEN

ONE DAY IN JUNE 1973, John Ehrlichman telephoned me to say that after mulling it over, he had decided to grant my request for an interview on *60 Minutes*. I could scarcely believe it, for at that particular "point in time," John Ehrlichman was very much a man of the hour, and bagging him for an interview was a coup.

That spring had been a period of severe upheaval in the lives of both Ehrlichman and his longtime crony, Bob Haldeman. Just five months earlier, at the time of Nixon's second inaugural, they had seemed to be utterly secure in the positions they had carved out for themselves in the White House. Along with Henry Kissinger, Haldeman and Ehrlichman ranked next to the President in power and influence in Richard Nixon's Washington. Autocratic, rigorous and often vindictive in their dealings with subordinates, "Hans and Fritz" (as they were sneeringly referred to behind their backs) were the hard-line instruments of the President's will and, as such, they inspired fear and loathing in some quarters of the administration, and in much of the press corps as well. But then, barely two months into the second term, the Watergate cover-up began to crack and then shatter in a fusillade of stunning disclosures. By the end of April, government prosecutors had accumulated so much evidence implicating Haldeman and Ehrlichman that Nixon had no choice but to banish them from the White House, which he did with great reluctance. The night he went on national television to announce their resignations, he described them as "two of the finest public servants it has been my privilege to know."

By then the legal investigation—which would lead in time to their indictment and conviction—was just one of the pressures bearing down on them. In May a special Senate committee, chaired by Sam Ervin, opened hearings into the Watergate crimes, an event that, via television, brought the scandal into millions of homes across the country. Along with others involved in the cover-up, Haldeman and Ehrlichman were about to be summoned into the glare of public scorn. The most explosive testimony at the hearings came, of course, from John Dean, who had been a key figure in the cover-up until he broke under the strain and began to cooperate with the prosecutors. For an entire week in late June, Dean sat before the committee—and the nation—and spelled out the sordid details of what John Mitchell aptly called "the White House horrors." In fact, the weekend before Dean was to commence his testimony, Ehrlichman called to inform me that he was willing to be interviewed for *60 Minutes*.

It was a call, as I said, that I had not expected. Of course, I was just one of many reporters who had been trying for several weeks to get to Ehrlichman or one of the other principals in the story. But ever since early April, when the disclosures began to dominate the headlines, Ehrlichman had been shunning the press. Still, I could understand why in late June Ehrlichman was choosing that moment to go public. He knew that Dean's upcoming testimony was going to be extremely damaging to him, and he obviously wanted to get his rebuttal on the record as soon as possible. I could also understand why he had chosen *60 Minutes* as his forum, and some of the likely reasons behind his decision made me just a little uneasy.

First, I could offer him a national platform on a program that by 1973 had built up a substantial audience. Second, although I had never been close to Ehrlichman himself, I was still in good order with the Nixon people. I doubt that even during the innocent, upbeat days of the 1968 campaign they had me pegged as a Nixon patsy, but they did regard me—quite accurately—as one of the few reporters who did not carry a grudge against Nixon and who was, in fact, generally sympathetic to him, both before his election and throughout most of his first term. Finally, since I was not based in Washington and was no longer covering politics full time, I had not been focusing on the Watergate investigations and was therefore probably less familiar with the minutiae of the subject than were some of my colleagues. For all these reasons, Ehrlichman and others close to Nixon may well have concluded that I and *60 Minutes* could be exploited to serve their purpose. Hence, the phone call accepting my invitation to appear on the broadcast.

I must say that being sized up in this way—as a relatively safe interviewer, a soft touch—was an uncommon experience for me, and I was determined to disabuse Ehrlichman of that comforting notion. Toward that end, I prepared as thoroughly for the interview as for any I have ever done.

The encounter with Ehrlichman was scheduled for the weekend following the completion of Dean's testimony. Fortunately, my Washington producer, Marion Goldin, had immersed herself in the Watergate story, and we spent most of the intervening week in her office boning up on every facet of the scandal. By the time I sat down with Ehrlichman, I was ready. But I soon became aware that he had not prepared himself for a thorough going-over. When he arrived at our Washington studio, Ehrlichman was in a cordial, almost insouciant mood. Clearly, he was anticipating a light workout, a chance to tell his side of the story without having to contend with much in the way of challenge or contradiction:

> WALLACE: John Dean put on the record a list of the administration's enemies compiled by various White House people, enemies in various categories—some hard-core enemies, for lack of a more precise term, and some enemies less reprehensible. Could you tell me how you arrived at categorizing these various lists?
>
> EHRLICHMAN: Now, this may surprise you, but I didn't know there was such a list. That's something that was developed totally out of my sight and hearing...
>
> WALLACE: Well, let me just read what he says.

EHRLICHMAN: All right.

WALLACE: To you and Bob Haldeman, among others, a memo entitled "Dealing with Political Enemies."

EHRLICHMAN: To me?

WALLACE: Yes, sir. He [Dean] was White House counsel and he explores the means of—to use his words—how can we use the federal machinery to screw our political enemies through withholding federal contracts, through litigation of income tax audits, and so forth.

EHRLICHMAN: Well, I must say that surprises me. I don't recall seeing that memo, and I particularly don't recall seeing a list of enemies. Now—

WALLACE: You don't know about Colson's lists or Caulfield's lists?

EHRLICHMAN: I'm sorry, I didn't. And—

WALLACE: You never saw that memo?

EHRLICHMAN: I don't recall seeing it, no.

.WALLACE: A pretty important memo.

EHRLICHMAN: Well, I'm sorry . . .

Later we talked about the break-in at the office of Daniel Ellsberg's psychiatrist, which occurred in September 1971, nine months before the Watergate burglary. The field generals of the Watergate break-in, Gordon Liddy and Howard Hunt, were also the culprits in the Ellsberg "bag job" (as Liddy called it), which was carried out under the direct supervision of Egil Krogh, one of Ehrlichman's chief deputies. Ehrlichman insisted that he didn't know about this criminal action beforehand, but that he was told about it shortly afterward:

WALLACE: Look, you were involved to some degree with Hunt and Liddy. When I say you were involved, I don't mean that you were looking over their shoulder.

EHRLICHMAN: I met them once.

WALLACE: Well, you knew what they were doing in the Ellsberg business and you told—you said it was a pretty poor idea. Wouldn't it be logical then to believe that when you learned of their involvement in the Watergate business—and you knew immediately after it happened, even before it hit the press, that Liddy and Hunt were involved—wouldn't it be logical to believe you'd want to cover up your own prior dealings with them?

EHRLICHMAN: I can't think why.

WALLACE: Well, you didn't—

EHRLICHMAN: My own prior dealings with them didn't give me any trouble at all.

WALLACE: Well, you knew that they had broken in—

EHRLICHMAN: No. Well, I knew after the fact.

WALLACE: I know, but you knew by this time. That was back in 1971, in September, that they broke into Ellsberg's psychiatrist's office.

EHRLICHMAN: That didn't seem to come home to me. I didn't send them out there to do an illegal act.

WALLACE: No, no, but you knew . . . And suddenly the same two fellows are involved in Watergate. It was—it becomes apparent that people who hear about that are going to say, "Well!" They'll put two and two together. That crowd worked on Ellsberg, that crowd worked on Watergate, they did it on—at the suggestion of the White House. And so the cover-up began . . .

EHRLICHMAN: The so-called cover-up really did not become evident to me until I got into this thing full steam at the end of March of this year.

That was his main line of defense, that he knew nothing about the cover-up until it began to come apart. So I shifted to another tack:

WALLACE: Look, explain something to me, will you, Mr. Ehrlichman? Why would anybody in the Nixon administration—in the official Nixon family—want to defend, want to raise money to defend the guys who burglarized the Watergate?

EHRLICHMAN: Certainly for no reason of self-interest, other than perhaps Mr. Dean. There may have been a— a compassionate motive on somebody's part. I can't answer that.

WALLACE: Compassionate?

EHRLICHMAN: But the—the—in terms of self-interest, protecting one's own interest, and so on, that's a question that comes back to this whole cover-up thing. Cover up what? The White House had no interest, as such, in covering this thing up. It had no exposure.

WALLACE: Look, the information that we have is that Herbert Kalmbach got—channeled to Anthony Ulasewicz from the end of June to the end of September—$219,000. For what?

EHRLICHMAN: I'm—

WALLACE: For the Watergate defense fund?

EHRLICHMAN: You simply cannot get an answer from me 'cause I don't know.

And so it went—a steady stream of clumsy evasions, sudden attacks of amnesia and transparent lies. Yet even more revealing than the answers he gave was Ehrlichman's demeanor: the grimaces, the constant fidgeting and the beads of perspiration that glistened on his face and brow. To counteract those visible signs of stress, he adopted at times a tone of defiance, of smirking arrogance that was as unconvincing as it was unappealing. Nor was any of it lost on our viewers, for Hewitt had chosen to photograph Ehrlichman in extreme close-up, a tactic reminiscent of the warts-and-all scrutiny that Ted Yates used to impose on guests back in the *Night Beat* days. The upshot was that Ehrlichman came across not only as a liar but as a man who knew, even as he stammered through his answers, that he was being perceived as a liar. It was a devastating exercise in self-incrimination. Finally, toward the end of the long interview—it ran more than thirty minutes on our next broadcast—there was this exchange:

> WALLACE: Did you see Senator Weicker enumerate a list of the illegal or unconstitutional or unethical acts committed by various persons, either in the White House or employed by the White House?
>
> EHRLICHMAN: No, I didn't.
>
> WALLACE: Let me read them . . . Breaking and entering. Wiretapping. Conspiracy to foster prostitution. Conspiracy to commit kidnapping. Destruction of government documents. Forgery of State Department documents and campaign letters. Secret slush funds. Laundering money in Mexico. Payoffs to silence witnesses. Perjury. Plans to audit tax returns for political retaliation. Theft of psychiatric records. Spying by undercover agents. Bogus opinion polls. Plans to firebomb a building. Conspiracy to obstruct justice. And all of this by the law-and-order administration of Richard Nixon.
>
> EHRLICHMAN: Is there a question in there somewhere?

Was there a question in there somewhere? The question, as I promptly informed Ehrlichman, was the one that millions of Americans had been asking for the past several weeks: How did all this happen? Why was it allowed to happen? Ehrlichman replied lamely that to raise the question that way was "to misstate the association of a number of areas." Not much of an answer, but then I could understand why he would shy away from the conclusion that I and many others had reached. To wit: that the crimes of Watergate grew out of an unhealthy insulation, a climate of suspicion and hostility, an us-versus-them mentality that took root in the White House in the early months of Richard Nixon's presidency; and that along with the President himself, Ehrlichman and especially Haldeman were chiefly responsible for having created that atmosphere of paranoia.

There is of course nothing like hindsight to clear the vision, and as the Senate Watergate hearings continued to dominate

the news during the summer of 1973, I began looking back
over the early Nixon years. My purpose (and there was nothing
systematic about it) was to scan the pre-Watergate record for
signs or signals which, if we had been alert to them, might
have tipped us off to the sickness that had infected the White
House. At one point, I found myself recalling the events which
in 1970 led to the public firing of Nixon's first Secretary of
the Interior—Walter J. Hickel.

In the spring of 1970, Richard Nixon had been President a
little more than a year and by then the honeymoon was definitely over. His decision to expand the Vietnam conflict into
Cambodia touched off the biggest and angriest wave of antiwar
demonstrations since the stormy last months of the Johnson
administration. Most of the protests erupted on college campuses, and in an ill-advised, off-the-cuff comment to a reporter,
Nixon characterized the demonstrators as "these bums . . .
blowing up the campuses." Much was made of this inflammatory remark a few days later when National Guard troops,
who had been dispatched to Kent State University in Ohio to
quell a demonstration, opened fire on a milling crowd of students, killing four of them. It was also during this difficult
period, when the divisive forces behind the generation gap
seemed to be tearing the country apart, that Interior Secretary
Hickel wrote a letter to Nixon. In the letter he accused the
administration of setting out "consciously to alienate our young
people." In addition, Hickel implied that much of the problem
was the President's own isolation. This was a direct slap at the
so-called Berlin Wall that Haldeman and Ehrlichman had erected
to seal Nixon off from direct contact with dissenting points of
view, and even from members of his own Cabinet. Indeed, one
of Hickel's complaints was that he was having trouble getting
through the Wall to gain access to the President who had appointed him. When a copy of the letter was leaked to the press,
it caused such a furor that Hickel suddenly became the most
controversial man in America. A few days after the letter was
made public, I interviewed him for *60 Minutes*.

WALLACE: Have you heard from the President since you wrote him the letter?

HICKEL: No, Mike, I haven't. I'm sure he's been busy, but I have not heard from the President since I wrote him the letter.

WALLACE: Not a word?

HICKEL: No, not a word.

WALLACE: What was the reaction to the letter? I'm sure you got a reaction from the White House, from a staff member?

HICKEL: I think that's the understatement of the year.

At the time, since he was struggling to hold on to his job, Hickel declined to elaborate on the White House reaction. But later I found out that just one day before our interview, Haldeman had called Hickel to *dis*invite him to the regular White House religious service that Sunday. This was the kind of petty snub Haldeman loved to inflict on members of the administration who had fallen out of favor at the White House. Hickel demanded to know if the ostracism had been ordered personally by Nixon. Haldeman's reply was cryptic and tantalizing in its implications. "The President," he told Hickel, "was in the room when the decision was made."

Later it was disclosed that Haldeman and others wanted to fire Hickel immediately—that spring. But they decided to hold off, in large part because of the upcoming midterm election. With the winds of protest already sweeping across the political landscape, the last thing the White House wanted to see in the campaign ahead was Hickel barnstorming the country as a martyred Cabinet officer, speaking out against the President. Once the 1970 election was over, however, rumors began to spread through Washington that Hickel was being pressured to resign. When I interviewed him again that fall, he declared he would not allow himself to be ousted from his post by a spate of rumors, innuendos and snubs. He would resign only if Nixon personally demanded his resignation. Or as Hickel put it to me in a rather florid turn of phrase: "If I go away, Mike, I'm going away with an arrow in my heart and not a bullet in my back."

The day after that broadcast, Nixon accommodated him. Hickel was summoned to the Oval Office, where the deed was done: an arrow straight through the heart.

Walter Hickel had tried to alert the President—and the rest of us—to the dangers of the isolation and climate of suspicion that had begun to prevail inside the Nixon White House. But his words of warning went unheeded. Both the sacking of Hickel and the critical letter that led to his downfall were soon overshadowed by other events. In the months that followed, the Nixon presidency made a strong recovery from the setbacks it had encountered in 1970. The major stories out of Washington in 1971 and the early months of 1972 were the China breakthrough and other bold foreign-policy initiatives that Nixon and Kissinger were taking. But then in March 1972 another signal flashed that something was rotten—or at least fishy—in the Nixon administration. The central figure was a woman named Dita Beard.

Dita Beard was a Washington lobbyist for International Telephone and Telegraph, which had been involved with the Justice Department in an antitrust case. The company wanted to acquire the Hartford Fire Insurance company, and after a long study, Justice approved the transaction. Then columnist Jack Anderson and his associate, Brit Hume, uncovered a memo, allegedly written by lobbyist Beard, indicating that Justice had gone easy on ITT in return for a promise to kick in $400,000 to help finance the 1972 Republican convention.

The day the story broke, everyone began looking for Dita Beard but she was nowhere to be found. Apparently she had gone into hiding. That was enough to arouse my interest and competitive juices, so I joined in the search for the elusive lobbyist. I spent several hours that day working the phone, pursuing one lead after another, and finally I tracked down her attorney in California. He informed me that Mrs. Beard had suffered a mild heart attack and was recuperating at an osteopathic hospital in Denver. I told him I wanted to talk to her, and he agreed, with some reluctance, to relay the message and get back to me.

I had met Dita Beard once before, at a National Governors
Conference in Oklahoma several years earlier. I remembered
her as an outspoken, rather bawdy woman who liked to sprinkle
her conversation with salty, four-letter words. When her lawyer
called me back, he said Dita had fond memories of our one
and only meeting and that she'd be happy to hear from me. I
placed a call to her hospital room in Denver, and when I introduced myself, her throaty voice crackled with enthusiasm.

"Hey, Mike, how are ya? How're you feeling?"

"I'm fine. But how are *you* feeling?"

"Well, things aren't so bad, darlin'. Things are going to be
all right."

When I proposed flying out to interview her for *60 Minutes*,
she said she would have to think it over and get back to me.
But she did make a point of saying: "If I talk to anybody, Mike,
I'll talk to you, darlin'. We go back a long way together." (As
I hung up, I tried to remember what she and I had talked about
when we met at that governors conference, but the details were
foggy. I could only conclude that I must have been even more
affable than usual.)

A week or so later, some members of the Senate Judiciary
Committee flew to Denver. Crowding into her hospital room,
they questioned Dita Beard about the now-famous memo and
about reports that she had personally discussed the ITT antitrust
case with Attorney General John Mitchell. As Dita was presenting her testimony, her heart suddenly began to beat irreg-
ularly, and her doctor called an abrupt halt to the hearing. When
I heard about this, I assumed it scotched whatever chance I
had of interviewing Mrs. Beard. But again Dita surprised me.
A few days after the senators had visited her, she sent word
through her attorney that she was willing to talk to me—but
not on-camera. One-concession-at-a-time has always been my
motto. The next move was to get to Dita, establish personal
contact and *then* try to coax her into an on-air interview. Don
Hewitt and I flew to Denver that day, and the next morning
we walked into Dita Beard's hospital room.

Dita was sitting up in bed and wearing a turquoise nightgown
so loosely buttoned that it failed to cover her ample bosom.
She gave us a big, cheery hello as she puffed away on a
cigarette. Her room, in fact, was thick with cigarette smoke,

and it occurred to me that chain-smoking was an unorthodox form of therapy for someone recovering from a heart attack. Another thought that crossed my mind was that perhaps Mrs. Beard wasn't quite as sick as we had been led to believe.

We exchanged pleasantries, then Hewitt and I launched into our sales pitch. Dita was a hard sell. Being a lobbyist, she was wise to all the tricks of persuasion, but we hammered away at the argument that *60 Minutes* offered her the best opportunity to get her story across to the American people. "You don't want just a bunch of senators to be your only link to the outside world," I told her. "You want a dispassionate reporter, a man whom you know and trust"—I was doing my best to take advantage of all those "darlin's" she had bestowed on me over the phone—"to interview you so you can clear the air in your own words. Not somebody else's version of your words, Dita, but your own *actual* words on film." It took us about half an hour, but we finally won her over.

Then we had to confront another hurdle. Hospital regulations forbade the use of television cameras on its premises, and the doctors could not be persuaded to bend the rule, not even for the few minutes we would need for our interview. Fortunately, there was an alternative. We had been told earlier that Dita's son had rented an apartment in Denver where she could convalesce after leaving the hospital; so we proposed escorting Dita there. We would do the interview, then bring her back. Her doctor seemed horrified by the suggestion, but the ultimate decision was Dita's as long as she was willing to assume full responsibility. By this time she was entirely on our side, eager to do the interview, so she agreed readily to make the move in defiance of her doctor's advice. Hewitt dashed off to pick up our rented car and the camera crew while Dita prepared herself for the little outing we had cooked up. She put on a kimono over her nightgown, and I helped her into a wheelchair. Five minutes later, we had her out of the hospital and were on our way to the apartment.

I had no trouble justifying the course of action we were taking, but nevertheless it made me a little nervous. What if she were sicker than I suspected? (Just before we left the hospital, her doctor had pressed a couple of digitalis pills into my hand, just in case.) What if—heaven forbid!—something *dramatic* happened while I was interviewing her? This thought filled me with such alarm that, like Philip Roth's hero in *Portnoy's Complaint*, I began having visions of the lurid headlines such a calamity would provoke: "Grilling by 'Mike Malice' Too Great a Strain for Ailing Lobbyist" or "Noted TV Interrogator Sinks to New Low in Sensationalism."

By the time we arrived at the apartment, I had made up my mind to go easy on her. I would ask the questions that had to be asked, but I would not press her if she showed any sign of getting upset. As a result, the interview turned out to be basically what we had discussed: a chance for Dita Beard to explain herself on national television. She admitted that when she ran into John Mitchell at a social gathering, she had foolishly tried to engage him in a conversation about the ITT antitrust case. But Mitchell, she said, had refused to discuss the matter. As for the celebrated memo, Mrs. Beard flatly denied that she wrote it and raised the intriguing possibility that someone inside ITT may have been trying to set her up to put her out of business as a lobbyist. That, in essence, was her story; and although I challenged a point here and there, I was not as insistent as I would have been under other circumstances. And toward the end of the interview, I injected a playful note to give our viewers at least a hint of the way Mrs. Beard normally talked when she did not have to deal with the intimidating presence of a camera and microphone:

> WALLACE: One hears that you are addicted to the use of four-letter words and this conversation, Dita Beard, has been pure as the driven snow.
>
> BEARD: It's been a chore, Mike. But for you I'd do anything.

Less than an hour later, Dita was safely back in her hospital room and Hewitt and I were on a flight back to New York. The following night we went on the air with the interview, and since it was an exclusive—Mrs. Beard's first public appearance since the ruckus began—a number of newspapers ran stories on it. Some chose to deplore the fact that Dita Beard had defied her doctor to accommodate *60 Minutes*. We were grateful that that was *all* they had to fuss about.

• • •

After the interview with John Ehrlichman in June 1973, producer Marion Goldin and I turned our attention to other characters in the Watergate story There were plenty to chose from, for the squalid drama had a large cast; and as the crisis deepened through the months that followed, moving inexorably to that day in August 1974 when the impending threat of impeachment would force Nixon to resign, we took a look at several of them on *60 Minutes*. At one point in early 1974, we even went to Allenwood Prison to interview Egil Krogh, the Ehrlichman protégé who was serving time for having authorized the Ellsberg burglary. And a few weeks later, we persuaded one of the major figures in the Nixon White House—Charles Colson—to sit down with us.

Chuck Colson was a husky, hard-nosed ex-marine who in 1972 boasted that "I would walk over my grandmother if necessary" to get Nixon reelected. This remark was widely quoted at the time; but not so well known was a comment he made to a White House colleague, telling him that he, Colson, wished to be thought of as a "flag-waving, kick-'em-in-the-nuts, antipress, antiliberal Nixon fanatic." He liked to come on as a tough customer in those days, but by the time I interviewed Colson in the spring of 1974 he had forsaken the chest-swelling bravado and pungent language that two years earlier had made him such a forceful presence in the Nixon White House. Around the time that he was being pulled into the Watergate dragnet, Colson disclosed that he had become a "born-again Christian."

"There are no atheists in foxholes" is a phrase I remember from my Navy days in World War II, and one did not have to be a born-again cynic to have some doubt about the total integrity of Colson's "jailhouse conversion." (Some Washington wag started the rumor that when the Dial-A-Prayer people heard that Chuck Colson had jumped into the fold they demanded to be given an unlisted number.) When I talked to Colson for *60 Minutes*, he had recently been indicted, along with Haldeman, Ehrlichman, Mitchell and other less prominent figures, for taking part in the cover-up conspiracy, so I felt obliged to question the sincerity of his new faith:

WALLACE: Mr. Colson, have you done more than pray? Have you made a palpable witness? Have you tried to make it up to those you've hurt?

COLSON: In my own heart, yes.

WALLACE: In your own heart. But have you tried to make it up? Have you gone to—have you apologized to anybody for some of the tactics that you used?

COLSON: There are a couple of instances where that has happened, where it came very naturally.

WALLACE: With whom?

COLSON: I'd rather not say because I don't think it's fair to the individual.

We talked later about the recently published transcripts of the White House tapes, and I asked him to assess them from the standpoint of the Christian morality he now embraced:

COLSON: Oh, I'm not going to try to characterize how I look at those transcripts because I don't think you can. I—

WALLACE: Well, wait—

COLSON: I've sat in many, many meetings in the Oval Office, Mike, and I did not know there was a recording system. I suppose—

WALLACE: Is that moral?

COLSON: I suppose—I'm not going to try to draw a moral judgment on it. I think if you looked at any black-and-white transcript of any conversation, it's going to look an awful lot different when you read it then if you were a participant in it. And—

WALLACE: Wait a minute. Let me understand something about this new Christianity, then. You say that you are a new man in Jesus Christ. It—it seems as though your prior faith takes precedence over your new faith . . .

COLSON: Mike, let me try to address your question in this way. I don't believe that when you accept Christ in your life or when you decide that you're going to live by the teachings of Christ, that you necessarily should set yourself up as a judge of others. As a matter of fact, Christ teaches us exactly the opposite. Only—only God really is our judge.

WALLACE: Well, I—I confess you leave me somewhat bewildered, then, as to the meaning of your faith.

COLSON: The meaning of the faith, Mike, is very simple. It's a relationship between God and myself, and between myself and my brothers and my fellowman.

WALLACE: But what—?

COLSON: And I will judge myself by the standards I think Christ has set for us, but I don't really think it's my business to judge others.

WALLACE: And you know what I'm saying, or—or asking, I guess, is how does it translate into daily life when you are asked to make a value judgment, a moral judgment, about something as, it seems to me, as straightforward as tapes in the White House? It seems to me that a new Christian—a new one particularly—would make a moral judgment about that. Am I—am I wrong?

Colson continued to skirt the issue, but in the aftermath of our interview apparently he gave it a lot more thought. I say that because in his book about his conversion, *Born Again,* he wrote that some of the questions I had raised helped him realize that he had to be more forthright in acknowledging both his own guilt and that of his former employer in the White House.

Chuck Colson's book sold well, as did others that were written by some of the Watergate criminals. For the most part, these books (Jeb Magruder's *An American Life: One Man's Road to Watergate* and John Dean's *Blind Ambition* were typical of the genre) were remorseful in tone, public acts of contrition. But there was one Watergate convict who steadfastly refused to join in the spirit of public confession; one man who, in fact, felt nothing but contempt and loathing for the breast-beating *mea culpas* that were pouring forth from his former partners in crime. I'm referring to G. Gordon Liddy.

In the argot of the hip generation, Gordon Liddy was something else, a real piece of work. He was the man who readily admitted that he once threatened to kill Jeb Magruder and who, according to Magruder, also threatened to "rub out" columnist Jack Anderson. According to John Dean, it was Liddy who, a few days after the Watergate break-in, volunteered to stand on a designated street corner at an appointed hour in case his White House superiors decided that *he* should be bumped off for having bungled his mission. The White House tapes revealed that Nixon himself once described Liddy as "a little bit nuts— I mean, he just isn't well screwed-on."

Be that as it may, Liddy fervently believed that the Watergate burglary and related crimes (including some that he proposed but could not get approved, such as the kidnapping of anti-Nixon radicals and the use of prostitutes to extract information from Democratic politicians) were entirely justified. He refused to plea bargain, refused to cooperate with government prosecutors, refused to acknowledge his guilt and refused, under oath, to answer any questions that would incriminate him or his fellow defendants. Liddy likened himself to a prisoner of war whose duty, even if tortured, was to disclose nothing more than his name, rank and serial number. Among those to whom Liddy refused to talk were reporters; from the time of his arrest in the summer of 1972 and through the months, even years, that followed, he wrapped himself in a shroud of silence. But finally, in the fall of 1974, there appeared a slight crack in the stone wall he had been presenting to the public: "a letter from prison" he sold to *Harper's Magazine* for five thousand dollars. Encouraged by that, we made contact with Liddy and negotiated an interview with him for *60 Minutes.* His one condition, which we accepted, was that he would answer no question about Watergate that he deemed to be substantive. I agreed because I felt that even on those terms, our audience would find Liddy and his outlandish views sufficiently intriguing. When the interview was broadcast in early January 1975, I introduced Liddy as a man who sees himself as a loyal soldier, a true-blue patriot, and then asked him the following questions:

WALLACE: Was it duty, loyalty, patriotism to plan to kidnap anti-Republican radicals from Miami Beach, from the GOP convention, in 1972? Was it duty, loyalty, patriotism to plan to employ call girls to entrap Democratic politicians at their convention?

LIDDY: I don't comment on those tactics. I will comment on the uses of, or the absence of uses of, power. Power exists to be used. The first obligation of a man in power or someone seeking power is to get himself elected.

WALLACE: Is there nothing that cannot, should not be done in the pursuit of power?

LIDDY: Yes, it depends upon what you define. If Watergate is as it's alleged to be, and it was an intelligence-gathering operation of one group of persons who were seeking power or to retain power against another group of persons who were seeking to acquire power. That's all it was. It's like brushing your teeth, Michael. It's basic.

WALLACE: It's like brush— What kind of a—? Explain! It's like—*what's* like "brushing your teeth"?

LIDDY: Well, if one is engaged in a war, one deploys troops, one seeks to know the capability and intentions of the enemy, and things of that sort. If one is engaged in politics, one deploys his political troops, one seeks to learn the capabilities and intentions of the other side, the opposition.

WALLACE: By any means? Even if laws are broken in doing it?

LIDDY: I think that is a fair statement as to fact. That is the way it is.

We then talked about some of his former colleagues in the Nixon White House, which led inevitably to this exchange:

WALLACE: John Dean was the man who recommended you for your job at CREEP. What's your opinion of John Dean?

LIDDY: I think, in all fairness to the man, you'd have to put him right up there with Judas Iscariot.

WALLACE: Judas Iscariot? In other words, he betrayed Christ? Christ being Richard Nixon?

LIDDY: No, he being a betrayer of a person in high office.

WALLACE: And what do you think his motive was?

LIDDY: To save his ass . . .

WALLACE: What do you think of Richard Nixon?

LIDDY: Well, he's evidently a very sick man, and I regret that. I think he has demonstrated toward the end of his presidency that he was insufficiently ruthless in that, in these domestic difficulties in which he was engaged. He did not act ruthlessly.

CBS News had to come up with some money to get the Liddy interview. I don't know how much exactly, because I had nothing to do with the financial arrangements, but one figure mentioned to me was fifteen thousand dollars. Whatever it was, we made no attempt to conceal the fact that we paid Liddy to talk to us, and no one took us to task for having done so. But "checkbook journalism" was to become a hot issue a few weeks later when it was learned that CBS News had agreed to pay Bob Haldeman a considerable sum—a hundred thousand dollars—to be interviewed by me on a special, two-part broadcast.

Of all the high-level officials in the Nixon administration who were convicted of Watergate-related crimes, Haldeman was the most powerful and the most inaccessible. He despised the press; even during the years when he was the stern authority figure in the Nixon White House—"the Abominable No-Man," as he was sometimes called—he almost never gave interviews. And ever since he was forced to resign his post in April 1973, Haldeman had been as resolute as Liddy in his refusal to talk to reporters. Therefore, when one of our executives, Bill Leonard, informed me in the fall of 1974 that CBS News had negotiated a deal to have me interview Haldeman, I was delighted.

Coming on the heels of the Gordon Liddy interview, which already had been set up, a lengthy on-air encounter with Bob Haldeman would be a fitting climax to our coverage of the Watergate story. But that is hardly the way it turned out.

The first tremor of concern hit me when I had a chance to examine an outline Haldeman had put together for a book he was planning to write about the Nixon presidency. I was appalled by the banality of the subjects he seemed to regard as important. Among the major topics he chose to emphasize in his outline were "SECRET NIXON PLAN TO MAKE CONNALLY VICE-PRESIDENT" and "MARTHA REALLY WAS THE REASON MITCHELL QUIT." I had to ask myself, could he be serious? Was this puerile sampling an accurate indication of the inside, penetrating stuff he planned to offer us and, subsequently, the readers of his book? I decided then that it was imperative to talk to him before committing myself to the program.

The cover-up trial was in progress when CBS News signed its contract with Haldeman, and since he was one of the defendants, it was agreed that the interview would be done after the jury had come in with its verdict. But in the meantime, Haldeman was willing to meet with me on an informal, get-acquainted basis. So in December 1974, Executive Producer Gordon Manning and I flew to Washington to spend an evening with him. Like Ehrlichman, Haldeman was a comparative stranger to me. Neither had been active members of the Nixon team during the months I covered the 1968 campaign. They did not come aboard until after Nixon had completed his sweep through the primaries, and by then I was veering away from the campaign to concentrate on getting ready for the start of *60 Minutes*. But in the years since, I had become aware of Bob Haldeman's reputation as the cold and ruthless sentinel of the Nixon White House, the praetorian guard who rejoiced in kicking ass and taking names and meting out retribution to those members of the administration who failed to measure up to his exacting standards of loyalty and devotion to Richard Nixon.

Manning and I met him for dinner at the Hay-Adams Hotel, where from our suite we had a clear view of the White House, across Lafayette Square. Haldeman's manner was correct and businesslike. He made no attempt to be cordial, which was fine with me; I was not looking for camaraderie. My purpose was to assess him as a potential interviewee. Before leaving New York, I had been told by Bill Leonard and Dick Salant that if after talking to Haldeman I thought he would not be worth interviewing, the CBS lawyers would find a way to buy the network out of the contract and the project would be scrapped.

Haldeman assured me that he was worth the effort and the money we had agreed to pay him. He was a camera buff, and during his years in the White House, he had assembled what he called "some fascinating films," which we would be allowed to use on the broadcast. "After all," he added, "while all of your people with all of their equipment were never on the inside, I was always on the inside and my camera was always going." Even more encouraging was another, more provocative comment he made. Nodding toward the window and the flood-lit facade of the White House across the park, he said: "You know something? That man, Richard Nixon, was the weirdest man ever to live in that place." I didn't ask him to elaborate on that statement because I didn't want to run the risk of saying anything that might scare him off. But this spontaneous remark was enough to convince me that this longtime Nixon confidant was prepared to give us some choice and intriguing insights into "the weirdest man" who ever lived in the White House. So I picked up the phone, after Haldeman had left, and called Bill Leonard to recommend that we proceed as planned.

The trial ended in January, and Haldeman was among those found guilty of perjury, conspiracy and obstruction of justice. Released on bail pending his appeal, he returned to his home in California to begin preparing material for our broadcast. By this time, word had spread about the contract between CBS News and Haldeman, and suddenly we stood accused of having committed a sin called checkbook journalism. To be frank, I thought our critics were being more than a little sanctimonious. While checkbook journalism was a trendy phrase, the practice itself was an old and time-honored tradition. For years news organizations, print and broadcasting, had occasionally paid certain newsworthy figures for the exclusive rights to their stories. As far as I was concerned, the deals we made with Liddy and Haldeman (like the later deal CBS News made in 1984 with Richard Nixon and his former aide Frank Gannon) were no different from, say, the fee *Life* magazine paid the astronauts or the one *The New York Times* forked over to Svetlana Alliluyeva for her memoirs about her father, Joseph Stalin.

It could be argued that because Liddy and Haldeman were convicted felons this gave our transactions with them a taint of impropriety. Were they any more ethically reprehensible than the book contracts and lecture fees then being lavished on the Watergate criminals? I think not, especially since the serial rights to some of those books were later purchased by various newspapers and magazines. In fact, I emphatically believe that our arrangements with Liddy and Haldeman did less to violate journalistic principle, for instead of merely offering them space to tell their own stories, we insisted on an interview format, a face-to-face encounter with a detached reporter—me—who would serve as an editorial voice to question and challenge some of their assertions. In any event, at the time of the controversy over our contract with Haldeman, I felt that the best, most effective answer to our critics was to deliver the kind of strong and incisive interview that would justify our venture into checkbook journalism. And it was precisely in that area that we failed.

Gordon Manning was dispatched to California to work with Haldeman, and it wasn't long before he began to have some reservations about the deal. First of all, those "inside" films Haldeman had touted with such enthusiasm were nothing more than vapid home movies: shots of Nixon waving at Haldeman, and Haldeman dutifully waving back, family pictures of the Haldemans and Ehrlichmans relaxing on a porch at Camp David. Almost all of this material was totally useless to us. All that was needed to make the Norman Rockwell-*Saturday Evening Post* scenes complete was a cuddly cocker spaniel frolicking with a bone. I'm sure that if Checkers hadn't been called up to the Great Kennel in the Sky several years earlier, *he* would have been featured in the footage.

Moreover, the anecdotes and behind-the-scenes information Haldeman chose to divulge in the preinterview sessions were as insipid as the home movies. When I learned about the material he was offering, I recalled, with a shudder of dismay, the book outline I had seen a few weeks earlier. In early March,

Marion Goldin and I flew to Los Angeles, where we spent the
next three days in intensive preparation. Then came the interview itself, which turned out to be a bitterly frustrating encounter.

One way to explain what happened is to draw a contrast
between the Haldeman interview and the earlier one with his
sidekick, John Ehrlichman. When I sat down with Ehrlichman
in June 1973, I had done my homework, but he had not done
his. And it showed, especially since that appearance on *60
Minutes* was the first time that Ehrlichman was subjected in
public to a thoroughgoing questioning about Watergate and his
role in the cover-up. But when I interviewed Haldeman nearly
two years later, he had been grilled by the government prosecutors, had testified at length before the Ervin committee, and
had been examined and cross-examined at the cover-up trial.
He was no less evasive and dissembling than Ehrlichman had
been, but the difference was he had his act down cold. On all
the critical questions, Haldeman had rehearsed his answers so
well he could recite them in his sleep. Hence, it was impossible
to catch him off guard.

Beyond that, there was a sharp difference in the public
personalities of the two men. Ehrlichman had a far more volatile
temperament. Although he could on occasion be quite pleasant,
even charming in private, he allowed himself to be easily provoked in his dealings with the press, especially when he felt
that reporters were badgering him with questions that in his
view were out of line. This is what happened when I interviewed Ehrlichman; his abrasive manner and sneering arrogance served only to antagonize viewers and undermine his
credibility.

But Haldeman, whose professional background was in advertising, had an expert understanding of the media—especially television. He recognized that the way to be most effective
on television was to project a calm, bland, low-key image.
Controversy and the more intense emotions, such as anger or
even irritation, were to be avoided at all costs. And by the time
I got around to him, Haldeman had even transformed his appearance to suit the occasion. The military crew cut, that graphic
symbol of his curt, spit-and-polish authority during the White
House years, had been replaced by a softer, more modish hair-

style. Gone, too, was the satorial rigidity of the straight-arrow, no-nonsense business suit, the daily uniform he imposed on himself and his minions at the White House. Now he was sporting a more casual, California look. These not-so-subtle changes were designed to reinforce the notion that since leaving the Nixon White House, the Abominable No-Man, the stern gatekeeper with the cold, laser-beam eyes, had become a relaxed, easygoing fellow who liked to greet the world with a smile.

Throughout our long interview, Haldeman played that role to the hilt. From start to finish, he was unfailingly courteous as he calmly but deftly parried my attempts to pin him down on Watergate and related matters. If he displayed at times a highly selective memory and gave answers that were vague and tentative, nevertheless he succeeded in conveying the impression of a man who was *trying* to be cooperative and forthcoming, and it made his evasions credible. Unlike Ehrlichman, who came across as an angry, uptight liar, Haldeman projected a manner and tone of sincerity, even on those occasions when, based on other information we had, I had reason to believe he was being less than totally honest. Another ploy of his was to take a difficult or provocative question and smother it in such a morass of details or hair-splitting qualifications that the result was confusion or tedium. Very clever, for Haldeman shrewdly understood that a dull and imprecise interview suited his purpose even as it sabotaged ours. All in all, it was from his point of view a masterful performance.

Nor was there any doubt that Haldeman's tactics brought out the worst in me. In my efforts to penetrate his bland facade, to stimulate a lively confrontation, I grimaced with impatience or irritation, which, by way of contrast, only underscored his placid and genial manner. Indeed, there were times during our lengthy sessions (we filmed more than five hours of conversation with Haldeman) when I felt like a frustrated boxer trying to land a solid punch on an elusive, nimble-footed opponent. And the truth is, I barely laid a glove on him. Haldeman even managed to weasel out of his assertion that Nixon was the weirdest man ever to live in the White House. When I reminded him of the off-camera comment he had made to me at the Hay-Adams Hotel in Washington, he replied:

HALDEMAN: What I meant was that he is—as a man, as a human being—one of the least understood, most complex, most confusing men who has ever sat in the White House. The—

WALLACE: But you chose the word "weird" and—

HALDEMAN: Weird—weird in the sense of inexplicable, strange, hard to understand.

WALLACE: All right, help us to understand.

HALDEMAN: (with an imploring sigh): How?

That exchange was, I'm sorry to say, all too typical. Haldeman was determined to play it safe at every turn, and there was nothing I could say or do to draw him out of his self-protective shell.

But the worst was yet to come. Once we had completed the interview, we had to address ourselves to what we should put on the air. To quote a rather inelegant expression that is often heard around our shop when things aren't going right, we now faced the unappetizing task of trying to "turn chicken shit into chicken salad." Yet we had no choice because we had made the stupid mistake of locking ourselves into a big showcase presentation. If the Haldeman interview had been a routine assignment for *60 Minutes,* one that we had pursued quietly and without fanfare, we could easily have made the decision to air only a small piece of it or even not to broadcast it at all, and that would have been the end of that. We could have written it off as yet another promising idea that did not work out, which is something that happens all the time in our business. But given all the commotion that had been stirred up by our contract with Haldeman (with much of it generated by our own publicity apparatus), we had to go through with the show we had ballyhooed: a two-part interview, with each part running one full hour, to be broadcast on successive Sundays in the time slot normally occupied by *60 Minutes.*

The reaction to the Haldeman broadcasts did not surprise me. Some of the same people who had rebuked us with such finger-wagging solemnity for having violated a sacred canon of journalistic ethics now had a big belly laugh at our expense. We were mocked for our folly, and what made *that* so difficult to stomach was that unlike all the pious blather about checkbook journalism, I thought this criticism was valid. Having been flim-flammed into buying a pig in a poke, we deserved the brickbats that came our way. Nor was there any point in trying to fix the blame on Haldeman. Oh sure, I thought he purposely misled me in our pre-interview meeting with all his talk of "fascinating films" and his tantalizing remark about the "weird" man he had served in the White House. But I'm just as certain that Haldeman would be quick to say in his own defense that while he had agreed to answer questions about the Nixon White House, he never promised us the Rose Garden.

The fault was ours. We should have known better.

The Haldeman interview was my swan song to Watergate, and at the end of the second broadcast I made this observation:

> He [Haldeman] is convinced that the activities that brought down the Nixon White House differed only in degree from those undertaken in previous administrations. But that the other devastating difference was that the Nixon men were caught.

In the years since, Haldeman and other Nixon apologists have clung stubbornly to that view. As Victor Lasky asserted in the title of a book he wrote on the subject, *It Didn't Start with Watergate*. To buttress their argument, Lasky and others have cited various acts of wrongdoing in pre-Watergate Washington, such as the illegal wiretapping that was condoned by the White House during the Kennedy and Johnson administrations. Yet I've never understood what the Nixon sympathizers were trying to prove exactly. The covert transgressions committed by previous administrations clearly pale in comparison to the scope of the Watergate offenses; and even if that were not the case, even if the earlier misdeeds had been comparable in magnitude, it would hardly take Nixon and his co-conspirators off the hook. A crime is a crime, and the flimsiest defense of all is to say, "Okay, sure, I embezzled the money, but I'm not the first person to have done that and, besides, a lot of other embezzlers have

never been caught." No jury in the world would be swayed by
such an argument and neither, I suspect, will historians when
they take on the task of explaining Watergate to generations
yet to be born.

One of the cathartic side effects of the Watergate investigations, paradoxically, was to restore and strengthen faith in our
basic political institutions. For when push came to shove, all
three branches of the federal government did their duty, even
demonstrating that the creaky and cumbersome machinery of
the presidential impeachment process could be cranked up and
put to effective use for the first time in more than a century.
The various steps taken by Congress, the courts and the Special
Prosecutor's Office to resolve the crisis impressed even some
of the militant radicals who had railed against "the system"
with such vehemence during the Johnson and early Nixon years.
I encountered a telling example of this change in attitude when
I flew to Paris in the spring of 1975 to do another story on
Eldridge Cleaver.

Five years had passed since our interview in Algiers when
he had boasted about his threat to shoot his way into the White
House and "take off the head of Richard Nixon." Nixon, though
no longer in the White House, was still in possession of his
head. As for Cleaver, he had since worn out his welcome in
Algeria and had spent most of the past three years in Paris. He
was still a fugitive from justice and still a lonely American
living in exile. But when I interviewed him this time, Cleaver
was no longer preaching a message of violence. In fact, he
seemed slightly embarrassed when I brought up the harsh rhetoric he had uttered five years earlier:

CLEAVER: Okay, now I would say this. You see, my
feeling then and my feeling now is that Richard Nixon
absolutely had to be taken out of the White House, you
see.

WALLACE: But the system did it.

CLEAVER: The system did it at long last. I'm very happy
that the system did it. Therefore, I don't feel any need
to talk about going in there and taking him out myself . . .

WALLACE: You said that it was going to be necessary to "fight a war of liberation against the fascist, imperialist United States." You no longer believe that?

CLEAVER: I think that we can solve our problems without fighting a war of liberation, simply because the system itself has reacted to the pressure that was brought upon it by that kind of organizing and that kind of mobilization and that kind of rhetoric. Now, this doesn't mean that by doing that, that solves all of our problems, but it does eliminate, I think, the kind of concentration-camp solution to the black problem that we thought that we were faced with.

WALLACE: Are you telling me, at bottom, that you wish you hadn't said "violence," "gun," "take off the head," "shoot your way into the Senate"? Are you telling me that political action would have been better?

CLEAVER: Well, I'm saying this. Here's—here's what I'm saying. I think it would have been possible, given—and this is all hindsight now, Mike, because at the time I didn't see any alternative. I can say now that I wished that I had a better knowledge of how to deal with our political situation. I no longer am interested in going around talking about guns or advocating just violence in the abstract or calling people pigs.

The wistful tone and manner I had detected when we met in Algiers was far more evident now, five years later. Cleaver was plainly homesick, and in the course of our interview he disclosed that he was making preparations to end his exile and face the music of the criminal charges against him in California. A few months later, he did return to America, where he astonished many of his former cohorts in the Black Panther movement by announcing that he had become a born-again Christian. After serving his time, Eldridge Cleaver began touring the United States with his newfound comrade-in-Christ, Charles Colson. That the likes of these two muscle-flexing firebrands and bitter antagonists—one a Nixon henchman, the other a Nixon headhunter—were now joining hands in a cause that transcended race and conventional politics was just one of the more startling indications of how drastically attitudes changed during the Watergate years.

But to get away from Watergate and on to more *mundane* politicians and their foibles, what is the responsibility of the press in covering them? What are the limitations we should impose on ourselves in the interest of fairness, good taste and sound judgment? Do we have the right to probe into the private lives of public officials, to report, for instance, on their sexual activities and drinking habits?

Those questions came to the forefront of national attention in the summer of 1974 when Wilbur Mills, then the chairman of the House Ways and Means Committee and one of the most powerful men in Congress, was caught misbehaving in public with a lady friend not his wife: a nightclub stripper named Fanne Fox, also known to some of her admirers as "the Argentine Firecracker." Mills was quite drunk when he and Miss Fox jumped fully clothed into the Washington Tidal Basin and engaged in other peace-disturbing actions that brought them into police custody. In the weeks following, a few Washington reporters disclosed that they had known for some time about Mills's philandering and his problems with the sauce. But they did not report any of it because they felt that the congressman's drinking and amorous escapades were his own business and did not qualify as—to quote the famous motto of *The New York Times*—"news that's fit to print."

The Wilbur Mills affair aroused my interest to the point where *60 Minutes* did a story, not on Mills himself but on the general subject, which we called "Private Lives of Public People." Producer Marion Goldin and I structured the piece around a series of interviews with a few prominent Washington journalists, among them Jack Anderson, Ben Bradlee and our own Capitol Hill correspondent, Roger Mudd. Some took the position that the press has the right, under any circumstance, to delve into the off-duty pecadilloes of public officials, while others maintained that such matters should be reported only when they directly affect public performance. Yet even then, it can be a tricky question of judgment. For example, some of the reporters who covered Congress argued that even when he was in his cups, Mills was a more capable and effective legislator than many of his cold-sober colleagues, an opinion that was obviously shared by a majority of his constituents back home in Arkansas. For despite all the unfavorable publicity about his indiscretions, Mills was reelected by a comfortable margin in the fall of 1974. A few months later, however, he quietly retired from public life and sought professional help to cure his alcoholism.

Of all the stories I worked on during this period—the mid-seventies—the most poignant was an interview with Clint Hill, one of the Secret Service agents who had been assigned to President John F. Kennedy's motorcade that dreadful day in Dallas in November 1963. The Kennedy assassination had had such a traumatic effect on Hill that he never really recovered. The harrowing experience continued to sear his memory and turn his dreams into nightmares for many years afterward, and by the summer of 1975 his nerves were so shot that he was given early retirement from the Secret Service. Then, just a few weeks after Hill retired, a couple of incidents occurred in California that rekindled the painful memories of Dallas in all of us who had lived through that tragedy. On September 5, 1975, a young woman named Lynette "Squeaky" Fromme was arrested in Sacramento for pointing a loaded pistol at President Gerald Ford. And seventeen days later, another woman, Sara Jane Moore, fired a shot at the President on a crowded street in San Francisco. Like the shooting of Ronald Reagan six years later, the two attempts on Ford's life served to remind us just how vulnerable an American President is when he ventures out to greet the public in a nation where almost any misfit with a penchant for homicide can get his or her hands on a Saturday night special.

Later that fall, Clint Hill agreed to appear on *60 Minutes* to discuss the difficult problems the Secret Service must cope with in trying to protect a President. He also agreed to answer questions—for the first time in public—about the Kennedy assassination. This part of the interview was so emotional, so full of anguish and unrelieved guilt that it overshadowed everything else we talked about:

> WALLACE: Can I take you back to November twenty-second in 1963? You were on the fender of the Secret Service car right behind President Kennedy's car. At the

first shot, you ran forward and jumped on the back of the President's car—in less than two seconds—pulling Mrs. Kennedy down into her seat, protecting her. First of all, she was out on the trunk of that car—

HILL: She was out of the backseat of that car, not on the trunk of that car.

WALLACE: Well, she was—she had climbed out of the back, and she was on the way back, right?

HILL: And because of the fact that her husband's—part of his—her husband's head had been shot off and gone off to the street.

WALLACE: She wasn't—she wasn't trying to climb out of the car? She was—

HILL: No, she was simply trying to reach that head, part of the head.

WALLACE: To bring it back?

HILL: That's the only thing—

At that point, Hill broke down. The tears came pouring down his face. I said nothing for a moment or two, then quietly asked him if he would prefer we drop this painful subject and switch to something else. But he waved me off, indicating that he was willing to continue talking about Dallas; so, after he had regained his composure, I resumed:

WALLACE: Was there any way—was there anything that the Secret Service or Clint Hill could have done to keep that from happening?

HILL: Clint Hill, yes.

WALLACE: "Clint Hill, yes"? What do you mean?

HILL: If he had reacted about five tenths of a second faster, or maybe a second faster, I wouldn't be here today.

WALLACE: You mean, you would have gotten there and you would have taken the shot?

HILL: The third shot, yes, sir.

WALLACE: And that would have been all right with you?

HILL: That would have been fine with me.

WALLACE: But you couldn't. You got there in—in less than two seconds, Clint. You couldn't have gotten there— You don't—you surely don't have any sense of guilt about that?

HILL: Yes, I certainly do. I have a great deal of guilt about that. Had I turned in a different direction, I'd have made it. It's my fault.

WALLACE: Oh, no one has ever suggested that for an instant! What you did was show great bravery and great presence of mind. What was on the citation that was given you for your work on November twenty-second, 1963?

HILL: I don't care about that, Mike.

WALLACE: "Extraordinary courage and heroic effort in the face of maximum danger."

HILL: Mike, I don't care about that. If I had reacted just a little bit quicker, and I could have, I guess. And I'll live with that to my grave.

I have never interviewed a more stricken and tormented man. Hill's anguish was so acute, so visceral that I had to fight back the tears that were welling up inside me. And the effect on our viewers was just as overwhelming, as we learned from the flood of mail we received in response to that broadcast.

The Nixon years were a watershed experience for me for I was in a position to witness, at first hand, the Nixon comeback as it evolved from its tentative and unpromising origins. That early jump gave me access to some of the principal players who dominated the news during Nixon's first term in the White House.

Then came Watergate, and having been caught up in that drama for the better part of two years, I found it difficult to work up much enthusiasm for the politics-as-usual climate that followed. Compared with its recent predecessors, Gerald Ford's administration seemed bland and uneventful. Nor did the Democrats engage much of my attention. No one then envisioned that Georgia Governor Jimmy Carter, a man scarcely known outside his native region, would be able to mount a serious challenge, much less go on to win it all. Carter's grass-roots surge through the Democratic primaries in the winter and spring of 1976 took me totally by surprise. As the primary campaign drew to a close, I felt so out of touch with the Democratic mainstream, which had suddenly been transformed into a Carter tidal wave, that I asked to be excused from my customary assignment as a floor correspondent at the party's convention. For by then it was obvious that Carter had a lock on the nomination, and I had no feel, no grasp of the candidate or the people around him. But in stepping aside, I did so with more than a twinge of regret; for that was the first political convention since 1956 that I did not cover.

There was another reason why, in the words of Sam Goldwyn, I asked my CBS superiors to "include me out" of the 1976 Democratic convention. Having turned fifty-eight that spring, I was getting a trifle old for the task of spending many hours at a stretch on my feet, chasing delegates and dealing with the clamor and turmoil that make floor reporting at a political convention such a merry but grueling challenge. Like an aging ballplayer, I was confident that I could still hit with the best of them—I could still get around on the fast ball—but I no longer had the legs to cover the ground that had to be covered. Floor work at a convention is a young man's game, and the time had come for me to stop kidding myself.

But I thought I still had enough stamina to handle the burden of one floor assignment that year; so I agreed to go on active duty for the Republican conclave in Kansas City. I preferred the GOP convention in large part because, unlike the Carter Coronation in New York, it promised to be a far more exciting story. Ronald Reagan's strong finish in the primaries that spring had propelled him into a position where he seemed to have a real shot at wresting the nomination away from President Ford. Reagan also was one candidate in 1976 who was not a stranger to me. Indeed, I had a special and privileged connection with him that even his closest advisers had to respect. For I was, I'm sure, the only journalist in America who could boast that I had known Mrs. Reagan—the former Nancy Davis—longer than her husband had.

Back in the early 1940s, when I was jumping around from one radio job to another in Chicago in a helter-skelter effort to find my niche in broadcasting, one of my regular chores was to narrate a program called *The First Line* at the CBS station WBBM. There I encountered an actress named Edith Davis, who was starring in a network soap opera that originated from WBBM. Edie Davis was a warm, gregarious woman, full of vitality, and although she was almost old enough to be my mother (I had just turned twenty-four), we became close friends. Through Edie, I came to know her husband, the eminent neurosurgeon Loyal Davis, and her daughter, Nancy, then a student at Smith College. As time passed, I moved to New York, Loyal and Edie retired to Scottsdale, Arizona, and "sweet little Nancy" (as I then thought of her) went to Hollywood to pursue a career as an actress. Her dream of movie stardom didn't pan out, and the next thing I heard, she was getting married to the well-known actor Ronald Reagan. I didn't give that much thought at the time except to cherish the hope, as I would for any friend, that the marriage would prove to be happy and enduring.

More time passed. Reagan's own acting career began to languish while I struggled through the vicissitudes of my early years in New York—*Night Beat* and the rest of it. Then came the 1960s and, as it turned out, Ronald Reagan's initial plunge into active politics roughly coincided with the start of my new career as a full-time journalist at CBS News. Thus, when I shifted my attention to political reporting on a regular basis, our paths began to cross. The fact that I was an old friend of his wife and her family gave me an advantage I did not hesitate to exploit, and I had no trouble building up solid contacts within the Reagan camp.

Although he had just recently been elected governor of California—in his first time at bat as a candidate for public office—it was apparent even then that Reagan had his eye on the White House. Frankly, I didn't think much of his chances. The Republicans were still reeling from the Goldwater debacle in 1964, and Reagan, who was cut from the same right-wing cloth as his Arizona mentor, struck me as far too conservative for national office, a man out of step with the political temper of the sixties. Beyond that, with his casual, easygoing personality, he seemed to lack the intensity, the all-consuming drive, the Nixonian determination required to make the long-distance run for the presidency. (I certainly was not impressed by his belated, halfhearted bid for the Republican nomination in 1968.) Finally, while his background as a movie actor did not hurt him in California, where actors are almost as plentiful as oranges or surfers, I felt that it would not "play in Peoria" and other less indulgent parts of the country. Still, there was no denying his skill and appeal as a candidate. He had given a convincing demonstration in his smoothly run, triumphant campaign for the governor's chair in 1966, and of course there was no way of knowing what the future might bring.

What the future *did* bring was Watergate and the destruction of Richard Nixon's leadership in the Republican party. Another big loser was John Connally, for it was widely known, before the Watergate dam burst, that Connally was Nixon's personal choice to succeed him in 1976. And even his premature successor was caught up in the tangled web of suspicion. True, Gerald Ford was in no way implicated in the Watergate scandal as such, but he inflicted severe political damage on himself with his decision—just one month after taking office—to grant Nixon a "full, free and absolute pardon." By 1975 many Americans were yearning for a fresh alternative to what they perceived as the corruption and cynicism of Washington politics, which is one reason—perhaps the main reason—why such an outsider as Jimmy Carter was able to take the country by storm.

Like Carter, Reagan could offer himself to the voters as a grass-roots candidate with no strings attached to the political establishment, a man whose experience in government had been confined to the state level, far removed from the poisonous climate in Washington where the crimes of Watergate had been allowed to fester. In the late fall of 1975, a Gallup poll revealed that Ford, even with all the powers of the presidency at his disposal, was *not* the leading contender for the Republican nomination in 1976. The front-runner, by a solid margin of eight points, was Ronald Reagan. This time, in contrast to the tentative, long-shot effort he had made eight years earlier, his challenge had to be taken seriously; and in December 1975 I flew out to California to do a story on Reagan and his family.

That *60 Minutes* piece is all old hat now that the Reagans have been subjected to the unrelenting scrutiny that befalls every family that becomes the nation's First Family. However, back in 1975 much of it was fresh, for our story was the first detailed look at the Reagans on national television. We showed them relaxing at their ranch near Santa Barbara, and I talked to them about their courtship days in Hollywood and their life together since then. At the time, very little had been written or broadcast about the governor's children. So I interviewed Maureen Reagan, the daughter of his first marriage to actress Jane Wyman, who freely admitted that she disagreed with her father on several issues, notably his opposition to the Equal Rights Amendment. In my interview with Reagan himself, we talked about his eight-year record as governor of California and about his political philosophy, which he insisted was not conservative so much as what he termed "libertarian." Then, toward the end of our conversation, we discussed the "poverty of political leadership" in America in recent years, and that led to the following:

> WALLACE: Tell me the last time we had a leader we had a good deal of faith in.
>
> REAGAN: Franklin Delano Roosevelt. He took his case to the people. When the New Deal started, he was faced with a Congress that wouldn't go along. He went over their heads with the "Fireside Chats." They were the most popular program on radio. He took his case to the people and he enlightened the people. And the people made the Congress feel the heat. It isn't necessary to enlighten Congress. Just put the heat on. And he got the things that he wanted.

I recalled those words five years later when, much to the dismay of old-line Republicans who had bitter memories of the New Deal and "that man in Washington," Reagan made a point of praising Roosevelt in his acceptance speech at the GOP convention. As for when he talked about Roosevelt going over the heads of Congress and taking "his case to the people," this is precisely what Reagan did during his first few months in the White House. FDR's style of leadership would serve as Ronald Reagan's model in 1981 as he set out to steer the country away from the social and economic policies that were ushered in by Roosevelt half a century earlier.

All that was to come later. In the meantime, Reagan made his spirited run for the Republican nomination in 1976, demonstrating in the process that he had the stamina and drive to carry out a long and arduous presidential campaign. He kept the pressure on right up to the convention, and even then, in Kansas City, if a handful of votes in a few key states could have been pried away from Ford, it would have been enough to tip the balance in Reagan's favor. However, Ford, having won the battle, went on to lose the war to Jimmy Carter, and when I interviewed Reagan again one month after the 1976 election, he bluntly asserted that if he had been the GOP nominee, he would have beaten Carter:

WALLACE: Where Ford failed, Reagan would have won. How? How would you have put it together?

REAGAN: Well, I think I would have broken into the Solid South, which went for Carter as a native son. I think there were states there—Texas, Mississippi, probably others—that I would have taken. But I believe the main point would be that we found in the polls since that the major issue in the campaign was Watergate. That could not have been an issue had I been the candidate.

WALLACE: The pardon, particularly?

REAGAN: Yes, this was mentioned in the polls very much. Now, I don't say this in derogation of Gerald Ford at all, but I—as I say, I think it left the Democrats with an issue they would not have had.

He spoke with the frustrated confidence of a top-ranked prizefighter who had been denied his rightful shot at a championship bout, and it was obvious that he was already looking forward to 1980 as his year to win it all.

• • •

During the Carter years, I continued to drift away from domestic politics. Most of the Washington pieces on *60 Minutes* in that period were done by Dan Rather, who had joined Morley Safer and me on the broadcast in late 1975. Since Dan had made his reputation as the CBS News White House correspondent during the Johnson and Nixon years, it was only natural that he would take on a heavy load of Washington stories—and that was just fine with me. I had no more feel for the Carter presidency than for the Carter candidacy, so I was more than willing to yield that turf to Rather and devote more of my attention to overseas assignments and back-of-the-book features on movies (Bette Davis), music (Vladimir Horowitz), dance (Mikhail Baryshnikov) and other cultural subjects. Also by this time, having explored a new vein and found it to my liking, I had become deeply involved in investigative reports of one kind or another. I'll talk about all that in the chapters to come.

But I didn't completely turn my back on the Washington scene in the middle and late 1970s. I kept my hand in. I did a few stories on the Central Intelligence Agency during the period when it came under attack on a variety of fronts. Included was an interview with George Bush shortly after he took over as head of the CIA, and another with Bush's predecessor, William Colby, when he wrote a book about his stormy tenure as director of the agency. It was Colby's misfortune to have been in the hot seat when Congress launched its investigations into assassination plots and other covert abuses of power committed by the CIA over the past three decades. He was sacked from his post by President Ford in large part because, as Colby said in our interview, "I was too responsive to Congress." (Colby was a practicing Catholic, a circumstance that once prompted Henry Kissinger to chide him: "Bill, when you go up there you go to confession.")

Then in the fall of 1978, I wrote a letter to the man who, next to the President, occupied the most distinguished office in the U.S. government:

Dear Mr. Chief Justice:
    We on *60 Minutes* would very much like to draw a film

profile of Warren Burger. Now I can almost hear you chortling, "I'll bet you would, and there's not a chance that Warren Burger would cooperate." If I'm right, I ask myself why. Why should the Chief Justice be more reluctant than other high officials in our government to afford his fellow Americans the chance to learn a little more about him? I can see only a few hazards, far outweighed by public benefits, were forty million Americans to get a more personal understanding of the man who sits as Chief Justice of their Supreme Court.

Justice Burger declined to accept what he facetiously characterized as our "intriguing invitation to participate in the premature autopsy of a Chief Justice." But that did not deter us. We proceeded over the next few months to put together a profile of Chief Justice Burger, which we aired in March 1979. The report consisted largely of interviews with various jurists and law professors, some of whom had worked as clerks at the Supreme Court. From their observations emerged a portrait of Warren Burger that was neither puff nor poison; we accorded roughly equal time to his critics and his defenders. Ultimately we sought to measure his performance against that of his controversial predecessor, Earl Warren, and this effort led to the following exchanges with Shirley Hufstetler, then a Federal Appeals Court judge from California, and Scott Powe, a professor of law at the University of Texas:

> WALLACE: The mark of Earl Warren's Court, and Earl Warren, was a social activism which seemed to move the country ahead or back, depending upon your political point of view, but move the country. The same cannot be said—or can it?—of the Burger Court in its first ten years?

> HUFSTETLER: In the first ten years, I don't think you can say that there is a comparable track record. Now in fairness, however, one must say that there have been cycles in which, after a period of very significant activism, we need to relax and restore and mend our ways.

> WALLACE: The Dwight Eisenhower of the Supreme Court?

HUFSTETLER: I think that would not be unfair.

WALLACE: Others have suggested that Burger as Chief Justice might turn out to be Nixon's revenge. I asked Scott Powe about that.

POWE: That depends on what you mean by "Nixon's revenge."

WALLACE: Nixon's revenge was to put in that spot of Earl Warren a law-and-order man, a strict constructionist, a fellow who was going to turn around the direction of the Court. And the Court has not turned around, Professor Powe, has it—that much?

POWE: If that's the definition of Nixon's revenge, then he's not Nixon's revenge.

Of course, it would have been a much more satisfying story if the Chief Justice had agreed to participate, and in that respect I think he missed the point. As long as a man is alive, he has the glorious right to speak for himself; and it was precisely Burger's refusal to exercise that option that gave our profile the rather bloodless tone of an obituary or "premature autopsy."

By the fall of 1979, familiar noises were rumbling across the political landscape as various candidates began to rev up their engines for the next presidential Grand Prix. This time the challenge from within the incumbent's own party would be taking place in the Democratic primaries, where Senator Edward Kennedy hoped to prevail over President Carter. On the Republican side, Ronald Reagan was once again the frontrunner in a crowded field that included John Connally, the former Democratic governor of Texas who had converted to the Republican faith a few years earlier. There was a widespread belief that fall that if anyone had a chance of stopping Reagan's march through the GOP primaries, it was Connally. His candidacy had attracted the support of so many Republican fat cats that he already had close to seven million dollars stashed in his war chest. Connally himself was exuding the hearty confidence of a high-stakes poker player who keeps raising the bet in blithe disregard of what the cards (or polls) presently show, because he intuitively sensed that in the end he would be dealt the winning hand. He was a political high roller, and if nothing else, one had to respect the huge pile of chips he was able to throw into the game. Still, Connally knew that he also needed the kind of media exposure that money can't buy, so he welcomed my request to interview him for *60 Minutes*.

No doubt he had warm memories of a story I had done on him back in 1971 when he was riding high as Nixon's Secretary of the Treasury. That had been, for the most part, an admiring profile, in keeping with the then prevailing view that next to Kissinger, Connally was the strongest and most influential voice within Nixon's circle of top policy advisers. And although Connally was indicted later in the Watergate-related milk-fund case (he was accused of having accepted a payoff from the dairy association in return for urging Nixon to approve a raise in milk prices), a jury found him not guilty. So here he was, in December 1979, a bit bloody perhaps but clearly unbowed as he went flying around the country telling voters that if elected President, "I can begin to turn this country around in forty-eight hours."

Along with his financial clout, Connally's broad experience and demonstrated ability in government were his biggest assets. But on the down side, he was afflicted with a serious image problem. While business leaders were solidly in his corner, polls that fall indicated that many Americans did not trust him. His close association with Nixon was an obvious handicap, but there was more to it than that. An exuberant man with a Texas-size weakness for bluster and bombast, Connally was perceived by many to be a wheeler-dealer in the tradition and style of his onetime mentor, Lyndon B. Johnson. Like Johnson, he had an injudicious tendency to shoot from the hip, and in preparing for our interview, I came across a number of reckless statements that had been attributed to him over the years. Needless to say, they were high on my list of questions when we filmed the interview at his home in Houston.

For example, when Martin Luther King was assassinated, Connally was quoted as having said, "Those who live by the sword die by the sword." He denied he ever said *that*, but he did admit to having said this about the slain civil rights leader: "He contributed much to the chaos and the strife and the confusion and the uncertainty in this country, but he deserved not the fate of assassination." Which, as I suggested, was hardly a glowing epitaph for a man of King's stature and accomplishments.

In the interview I pointed out to Connally that the heavy support he was receiving from the business community was especially interesting in light of the fact that he once said: "There's an amazing amount of mediocrity, even among the top, top businessmen. I know. I've seen them. Ninety percent of them are mediocre, pompous, narrow, stupid Neanderthals." Squirming in irritation (the interview was not going the way he had anticipated), Connally confessed lamely that when he made that statement, he had been guilty of "an exaggeration."

Finally, in going through my research, I read that someone taped a remark Connally made in reference to the nuclear accident at Three Mile Island, which had occurred earlier that year. The comment, if true, could only be construed as a slur against the man who Connally and others believed would become the 1980 Democratic nominee—Ted Kennedy. When I asked him about it, his vexation flared into open anger:

WALLACE: Governor, did you really say: "More people died at Chappaquiddick than at Three Mile Island"?

CONNALLY: No, I did not.

WALLACE: You're sure?

CONNALLY: I'm positive.

WALLACE: If I could show it to you on tape—

CONNALLY: I don't care—

WALLACE: Would you be surprised?

CONNALLY: I—no. If you did, you—you were taping something you shouldn't have been taping.

WALLACE: Ho! Then—then—

CONNALLY: If you did, then you taped a private conversation. Sure, I've repeated it in our own home because it was a joke that's going around, and it's been on bumper stickers. I have never said it publicly. Never.

WALLACE: Publicly.

CONNALLY: No, sir. And if you've taped it, you shouldn't have.

WALLACE: Well, we didn't tape it—

CONNALLY: Okay.

WALLACE: But it has been taped. And you said it.

I'm afraid that our interview, which was broadcast on the last Sunday of 1979, did little to help John Connally with his image problem. He was just one of several Republican presidential contenders who were featured on *60 Minutes* that winter. Dan Rather interviewed both Ronald Reagan and George Bush, and Morley Safer did a piece on John Anderson, who was then still a Republican candidate. (His quixotic, third-party campaign would blossom in the spring, the proper season for romantic pursuits.) Connally complained later that while his rivals were generally presented to our viewers in a favorable light, he was not, and he asserted that *60 Minutes* had purposely singled him out for a hatchet job. He seemed to base this charge on the fact that I was the correspondent who had been assigned to deal with him, strongly implying that if he had been interviewed by Dan or Morley, he would have been treated less harshly. Connally was entitled to nurse whatever grievance he chose, but he had voiced no objections to my approach and treatment eight years earlier when I did a profile of him that, in tone and substance, was largely positive and upbeat. To me, Connally's gripe was reminiscent of Spiro Agnew's reaction back in 1971 when I, whom he regarded as a friend and admirer, probed into aspects of his early life that he did not care to have broadcast over national television. And before the 1980 political season was over, I would incur the displeasure of yet another eminent Republican who thought he had me in his pocket— Ronald Reagan.

Reagan breezed through the GOP primaries and had the nomination sewn up by the middle of May. What little opposition he met came not from John Connally, who called it quits after he was soundly defeated in the early primary tests, but from

George Bush, who scored enough scattered victories here and there to earn the silver medal at his party's Olympiad that summer—the vice-presidential slot on the ticket. The night the Republican convention opened in Detroit, CBS aired a special edition of *60 minutes*. Instead of the usual multisubject format, the entire hour was devoted to one story: an updated portrait of the Reagans, which we called "First Family of the GOP."

I must admit that our first piece on them five years earlier had been fairly soft, more of a feature story than anything else. That didn't bother me much because at the time the Reagans were relatively new to national politics and the national media. In fact, the main purpose of our visit to their ranch in 1975 was to introduce Reagan and his family to viewers outside of California who really didn't know much about them. That, however, was hardly the case in July 1980, for by then the American people had become fully acquainted with Ronald and Nancy Reagan. The only question remaining to be answered was would they deliver the votes in November to put them in the White House. My own opinion, based largely on the anti-Carter mood that pervaded the country, was that Reagan would go on to win the election. Yet I also knew that many Americans were alarmed by this prospect, and in preparing to interview him again, I felt I had an obligation to reflect some of that concern. I told myself this was no time to go easy on Reagan or his wife, my old friend from Chicago. I think sometimes reporters lean over backward to be a bit harder on their friends, and indeed, when I interviewed Nancy separately from her husband, I ungallantly resorted to the dubious tactic of sarcasm. We were discussing the awesome stature of the presidency, and I pointed out that when we look back over the history of the office, "we talk about George Washington and Abraham Lincoln and Franklin Roosevelt." Then, in an exaggerated tone of incredulity, I added: "And Ronald Reagan?"

"Yes," she replied with a vigorous nod. Far from striking her as incongruous, it seemed she regarded the juxtaposition as perfectly natural and appropriate, as if there were no doubt in her mind that her husband would earn his rightful place in that pantheon:

WALLACE: You do believe that, don't you?

MRS. REAGAN: Why of course I do. Of course I do.

I had put the same question to Reagan himself, but phrased it in a somewhat different way. Instead of citing historical perspective, I stressed the contemporary burdens of the presidency:

WALLACE: Isn't there a certain arrogance in a man whose total formal government experience is eight years in Sacramento as governor of California in wanting to take over the direction of the foreign policy and the economic policy and the broad social policy of the greatest superpower in the world?

REAGAN: Well, I don't think it's arrogance and I find myself very conscious of the size of the undertaking, the difficulty. But on the other hand—

WALLACE: And of your limitations?

REAGAN: Yes. But also the fact that at this point in my life I'm not politically ambitious. I am not—

WALLACE: What? Wait, wait.

REAGAN: No.

WALLACE: Not politically ambitious that—

REAGAN: No. I'm not—

WALLACE: —that you want to be President of the United States?

REAGAN: No. In other words, I'm not on any ego trip or glory ride.

I moved on to another subject—his problems with the black community, where distrust of Reagan was running especially high. In fact, just a few days earlier he had antagonized many blacks when he failed to respond to an invitation to address the annual convention of the National Association for the Advancement of Colored People (NAACP). The head of the NAACP, Benjamin Hooks, said it was yet another example of

Reagan's "racial insensitivity" and unwillingness to be seen with black leaders. And in truth, one would detect in the atmosphere of the Reagan camp the unmistakable echoes of "the southern Strategy" that Nixon and John Mitchell had exploited in previous presidential campaigns. We talked about the NAACP contretemps, then I decided to bring the issue closer to home:

> WALLACE: How many blacks are there on your top campaign staff, Governor?
>
> REAGAN: I couldn't honestly answer you. No.
>
> WALLACE: That speaks for itself.
>
> REAGAN: Huh?
>
> WALLACE: I say that speaks for itself.
>
> REAGAN: No, because I can't tell you how many people are on the staff. We've got—
>
> WALLACE: But you can tell black from white.
>
> REAGAN: Oh yes, but I mean we've got a—we've got a mix of volunteers and staff members and—
>
> WALLACE: I'm talking about top campaign staff.
>
> REAGAN: Well, let me put it this way—
>
> WALLACE: Let me not belabor it. I mean—
>
> REAGAN: Yeah.
>
> WALLACE: Apparently there are none.
>
> REAGAN: No, I don't think so. I mean, I'm—I don't— I don't agree with you on that . . .

In the meantime, while I was asking Reagan about his lily-white staff and other sensitive matters, Nancy was lurking around the room, outside of camera range, and there were moments when, out of the corner of my eye, I caught her glaring at me. Then when we took a break in the interview to change the film in our camera, she came striding toward me, her eyes ablaze, and let me have it: "Mike Wallace, what kind of question are you asking? Why are you doing this to Ronnie?"

I glanced over at Reagan, half hoping he would explain in his amiable way that in asking that "kind" of question, I was merely doing my job. But right then he wasn't projecting the amiability that over the years has been such a large part of his political appeal. Instead, his face was set in a grim expression as he lent silent support to the disapproval that his wife, my friend, had just voiced with such vehemence. Well, I thought, here we go again, as memories of the rift with Spiro Agnew and other broken friendships flashed through my mind. With a weary sigh, I began to state the case for journalistic independence, and the next thing I knew Nancy had flung herself on my lap and was giving me a big hug. It was a spontaneous gesture, but the message was clear enough—a reminder that she and I were old friends, and no friend of hers should be "doing this to Ronnie." Anyway, we all burst out laughing and that broke the tension. But the Reagan people were plainly miffed at me. And they were even more upset a few nights later when the interview was broadcast on the special edition of *60 Minutes* inserted into CBS's live coverage of the opening ceremonies in Detroit, where the Republican faithful had gathered to anoint Ronald Reagan as their 1980 presidential nominee.

I was told later that there was one observation of mine that Reagan resented in particular. It came early in the interview when I was trying to explore the reasons why the most recent polls that summer indicated that many Americans still had serious misgivings about his candidacy:

> WALLACE: Can you explain this, Governor? Why should a competent, decent, mainly successful two-term governor of California—a man acknowledged by the reporters who have covered him through the years to be bright and serious and devoted, dead honest—why should that man still have the reputation among some millions of Americans as Neanderthal, or even dangerous, a hip-shooter, lightweight, actorish—in short, probably not up to the job of President of the United States?

REAGAN: Mike, I find the farther away you get from California, the more that image exists ... Now, maybe it started because—

WALLACE: May I suggest that it started, for instance, back in 1965 when you were running for governor and you had a colorful quote about the United States in Vietnam: "It's silly talking about how many years we'll have to stay in the jungles of Vietnam," you said, "when we could pave that whole country, put parking stripes on it, and still be home for Christmas." Now, you weren't a kid at the time. You were fifty-four years old and running for governor.

He replied calmly that such a remark had to be viewed within "the whole context" of the mid-sixties. But Reagan obviously did not enjoy being reminded of that statement in front of a nationwide television audience; especially when he was heading into a campaign against a President who intended to portray him as a kind of simple-minded Dr. Strangelove whose idea of foreign policy was to blacken the skies with missiles and order the citizenry into the fallout shelters. So I understood his resentment, and, in fact, after we broadcast the interview, it occurred to me that in dragging up that old quote, I had taken a cheap shot at Reagan. Not that I had in any way misrepresented him; it was an accurate quote of a statement that, in or out of context, was unconscionably flippant and irresponsible. But the more I thought about it, the more I realized that I could not recall any major American politician from the 1960s who at one time or another had not said something reckless or foolish about Vietnam. Nor were our political leaders alone in their failure to foresee the tragic consequences of our involvement in that war. In their myopia they had plenty of support from the rest of us—or *many* of us, anyway. I know it took me an inexcusably long time to recognize what a dreadful mistake it was for us to intervene in Vietnam.

"History," wrote James Joyce, "is a nightmare from which I am trying to awake." For those of us who lived through those years and were touched, even in a peripheral way, by that wretched war, Vietnam is a nightmare from which we will never fully awake.

CHAPTER

ELEVEN

WALLACE MADE HIS FIRST visit to Vietnam in the relatively peaceful summer of 1962. That was the summer he went on a globe-circling tour of eight foreign capitals for the Westinghouse broadcasting chain, and Saigon was one of the stops on his itinerary. (On that assignment, Wallace also reported from Tokyo, Taipei, Hong Kong, New Delhi, Cairo, Nairobi and London. The series of radio pieces he broadcast from those cities was called "Around the World in 40 Days.") At the time, both the size and mission of the U.S. military presence in Vietnam were still quite limited. The United States had slightly more than fifteen thousand troops stationed in the country, and they were confined for the most part to acting as advisers and support personnel. The men had been sent to train, instruct and provide transport for the South Vietnamese Army in its struggle to defeat the Communist insurgents, the Viet Cong. In short, it was still a very small war in 1962, and Americans had not yet been committed to engage in the actual fighting.

Nor had Wallace yet reached the significant crossroad in his career, the point at which he resolved to devote his efforts entirely to news. In fact, his professional life that summer was at a low ebb. He had just completed his unhappy stint as host on the talk show *PM East,* and insofar as he worked as a reporter at all then, he was merely dabbling on the fringes of journalism. He had almost no experience overseas; so this rather ambitious

assignment for Westinghouse was a venture into unfamiliar
territory.

But in preparing for his week-long stay in Vietnam, he read
enough to acquaint himself with the major events in the recent
history of that troubled land: First, the long colonial war that
ended with the French collapse at Dienbienphu in 1954. Then,
at the Geneva peace conference, the carving up of French
Indochina into three independent states—Laos, Cambodia and
Vietnam—and the further, ostensibly temporary partitioning
of Vietnam itself into North and South, with Ho Chi Minh and
the Communists retaining their political base in the North, and
Ngo Dinh Diem taking on the task of forming a nationalist
government in Saigon. Then, in a move that was utterly predictable and consistent with overall U.N. and U.S. policy, the
Eisenhower administration officially sided with Diem, and Ike
sent a few hundred military advisers to South Vietnam to lend
visible support to the shaky regime in Saigon. It was nothing
more than a token gesture, but it was the first step, and from
it all the others would follow, starting with John F. Kennedy's
decision to escalate the commitment in 1961. In the fall of that
year, the Viet Cong guerrilla raids were having such a disruptive
effect on the Saigon government that Diem appealed to Washington for help, and Kennedy responded with an order to increase the number of U.S. advisers in Vietnam to fifteen
thousand.

From his research Wallace had also learned a few salient
things about Diem. Namely, that he was a deeply religious
Catholic who had spent some time in a monastery in New
Jersey; and that as a result, he was an implacable foe of Communism and in sympathy with Western values. Additionally,
Diem was a nationalist whose professed goal was to establish
a democratic government in a country which for years had
chafed under the burden of colonial rule. Even in those innocent
days, Wallace had no illusions on that score. He was not one
of those romantics who expected to see constitutional democracy take root and flower in the Mekong Delta. From what he
had learned about Diem, Wallace sensed that he was a remote,
autocratic figure who was not in close touch with his people.
But whatever his defects as a man and politician, Diem was
on our side against the Communists and that's what mattered.

For better or for worse, he was our man in Saigon, and like most Americans at the time, Wallace fully concurred with Eisenhower's decision to support him and Kennedy's decision to reinforce that support. Both moves, after all, were in keeping with the Cold War containment strategy that had been the cornerstone of U.S. foreign policy since the creation of NATO.

In particular, it was natural that Wallace would identify, to some degree, with Kennedy, for he and the young President were practically the same age, Kennedy being just one year older. More to the point, they both had served in the Pacific as young Navy officers in World War II, and like most Americans of that generation, they shared certain values and attitudes about their country and its mission in the world.

To some extent, those values and attitudes were shaped by their experiences in the war. The veterans who came home in triumph from World War II were convinced, and with good reason, that America had the strength and resources to accomplish just about anything it set out to accomplish. But if they were supremely confident of America's might, even more did they believe in the virtue of America's cause. The new enemy was international Communism, which was just as despotic and potentially as belligerent as the Axis powers that had just been defeated in Europe and the Pacific. Once again it was up to the United States to assume the initiative in this new struggle to contain and, if necessary, repel the aggressive designs of the Soviet Union and its ideological allies.

It was this spirit of high optimism and moral certitude that the world heard in the bold and militant pledge of the Kennedy inaugural: "Let every nation know, whether it wishes us well or ill, that we shall pay any price, bear any burden, meet any hardship, support any friend, oppose any foe to assure the survival and success of liberty." Then a few months later, he made the decision to assist Diem and deepen the U.S. commitment in Vietnam. In subsequent years, it would be cited as a fateful decision that went far toward assuring that Vietnam would become the place where America would reap the bitter fruit of the Kennedy inaugural. There, in the jungles of that distant land, the hardship would be met, the burden would be borne, the price would be paid.

Yet at the time, only a few—a perceptive, clairvoyant few—

foresaw that it would ever come to that. To the vast majority of observers in 1961, the escalation in Vietnam was no big deal. After all, even fifteen thousand troops were an extremely small contingent compared with the huge force of combat-ready divisions we had stationed on other Cold War fronts, such as South Korea and West Germany. Moreover, as Kennedy and his deputies stressed repeatedly, the young Americans sent to Vietnam that fall were not combat troops but merely advisers. Their limited mission was to guide and counsel the South Vietnamese, who were judged by Washington to be entirely capable of fighting and winning their own war. Thus, even after the initial escalation, Vietnam was still widely viewed as a backwater, an insignificant theater of operations in the global drama of the Cold War. That was the prevailing outlook when Wallace arrived in Saigon in the summer of 1962.

His assignment for Westinghouse was to file a five-minute radio piece every day, and in tracking down stories for those reports, he saw or heard nothing that induced him to question the wisdom of U.S. policy in Vietnam. The war, still in its guerrilla phase, was confined to sporadic skirmishes in the countryside. But they had minimal effect on daily life in Saigon, then still a city of considerable beauty and charm, a lovely blend of Oriental tranquillity and Gallic sophistication.

From an American point of view, the big story in Vietnam in 1962 was the Strategic Hamlet Program, an early effort in the long struggle to win the "hearts and minds" of the people. The brainchild of U.S. officials, the strategic hamlets were designed to protect peasants from Viet Cong attacks. Residents of neighboring villages were herded into central locations behind barbed-wire barricades heavily guarded by military personnel. The peasants would go out each day to work in the fields, then return to the hamlets, where they could eat and sleep in peace without fear of falling prey to the marauding Viet Cong. The American advisers in Vietnam regarded the Strategic Hamlet Program as an astute, non-combative way of thwarting the Communists, and, proud of their handiwork, they were eager to display it. Wallace visited one of the hamlets, did a story on the program, then turned his attention to the Saigon government.

He did not yet have the journalistic clout, the solid credentials to open doors for him in those days; so Diem himself was
inaccessible. But through contacts Wallace had made in Saigon,
he was able to land an interview with Diem's sister-in-law,
Madame Ngo Dinh Nhu, who, since Diem was a bachelor, was
in effect the First Lady of South Vietnam. Madame Nhu had
not yet become known by such choice epithets as "the Dragon
Lady" and "the Spitfire of Saigon." She would earn such notoriety in the summer of 1963 when, as part of a rising protest
against the Diem government, Buddhist monks immolated
themselves on city streets, and Madame Nhu contemptuously
dismissed their public sacrifices as "monk barbecue shows."

The two qualities that most impressed Wallace, when he
interviewed her in 1962, were her feminism and her puritanism.
Madame Nhu was a zealous advocate of women's liberation
years before that term and the revolution it defined exploded
on the American scene. She had founded a progressive group
called the Vietnamese Women's Solidarity Movement, and she
had exerted her influence to make sure that the country's new
constitution included guarantees that, as she proudly put it,
made the Vietnamese woman "the most emancipated woman
in the world." But she was also a dogmatic and highly moralistic
Catholic whose views on sex were so prudish that she even
opposed dancing in public. She considered that and similar
forms of recreation frivolous and counterproductive in a nation
at war. The interview with Madame Nhu, at her summer retreat
in Da Lat, was the high point of Wallace's first visit to Vietnam,
and several months later, long after he had returned to the
States, he wrote an article about her for *McCall's* magazine.
It was published in November 1963, the same month that her
husband and brother-in-law were slain in an anti-government
coup. Barely eluding the same fate, Madame Nhu fled to a life
of exile and bitterness in Europe.

From Saigon, Wallace moved on to New Delhi and Cairo
and then to Nairobi, where he met a young reporter for *The
New York Times* named David Halberstam. Halberstam was
winding up his tour of duty in Kenya and was about to embark
on a new assignment—in Saigon. He briefed Wallace on the
general situation in East Africa, and Mike, in turn, filled him
in on the week he had spent in Vietnam. Soon thereafter,

Halberstam flew to Saigon, where it was his good fortune to be the *Times'* man during the stormy months of 1963 when both the war and the political unrest heated up to the point where Vietnam became a continual, front-page story. The reporting by Halberstam went against the grain of the official optimism: Instead of reflecting the party line of the U.S. Command in Saigon, he wrote in one story after another that the Viet Cong had captured the initiative in the countryside, in large part because the Diem regime did not have the support of the South Vietnamese people. Halberstam's dispatches so infuriated the Kennedy administration that it put pressure on his editors at the *Times* to pull him out of Vietnam. He eventually did leave Saigon (of his own volition), and in 1965 he published *The Making of a Quagmire,* a grimly prophetic book about the early and critical phase of U.S. intervention in Vietnam.

As for Wallace, he completed his global tour for Westinghouse and returned to New York to confront grief and trouble in his own life: the death of his son Peter, and then the long winter of rejection that preceded his going to work for CBS News in March 1963. Then came the years as anchorman on the *Morning News* and the various assignments as a political reporter that brought him into close contact with the start of Richard Nixon's comeback in the fall of 1966. By then the war in Vietnam had become the major story of the decade and Mike wanted a piece of the action. So in March 1967 he returned to Saigon, this time as a correspondent for CBS News.

In the meantime, under the leadership of Lyndon Johnson, America was sinking deeper and deeper into the quagmire. We have no way of knowing what Kennedy would have done if the crunch had come while he was still alive and in the White House. In the years since his death, some of his apologists have insisted that in the last few months of his life, Kennedy had begun to change his mind about the intervention and was starting to look for a way to ease U.S. troops out of Vietnam, to effect a withdrawal through negotiation. Perhaps so, but there is no conclusive evidence to support that claim. What we *do* know is that Kennedy led America to the banks of the Rubicon, and it was left to Johnson to decide whether or not to cross it.

In the early months of his administration, Communist forces, having steadily strengthened their position, were on the verge of a sweeping victory in South Vietnam—another Dienbien-phu. It was then that Johnson had to make the hard and bitter choice: either abandon the commitment that Eisenhower had initiated and Kennedy had enlarged, thereby yielding all of Vietnam to the Communists, or order a massive buildup of U.S. combat troops that would, in effect, transform the conflict into an American war. In deciding on the latter course, Johnson plunged the country into the most divisive ordeal to befall America since the Civil War. By the time Wallace returned to Vietnam in the early spring of 1967, the number of U.S. troops stationed there had swelled to over 400,000, and in the preceding year alone, more than 5,000 Americans had died in combat.

At the age of forty-nine, Mike Wallace was a little long in the tooth to be running around combat zones, dodging sniper fire and other forms of "incoming." And in truth, most of the reporters then in Vietnam were endowed with younger legs and quicker reflexes. Yet Wallace's two-month assignment was in accordance with the policy of CBS News. That policy was dictated in part by the fact that by 1967 so much of the reporting from Vietnam was negative and pessimistic. Halberstam and other early skeptics had set a strong example that emboldened the American journalists who followed them into Vietnam to challenge the official optimism. However, it was creating a problem for the networks and other major news organizations. Older viewers and readers in particular were inclined to resent and reject reports that were critical of the U.S. intervention, especially since so many of those reports were filed by "kids" who were too young to remember Anzio and Iwo Jima and the other sacrifices *their* generation had made for their country. Therefore, executives at CBS News and the other networks deemed it advisable on occasion to send senior correspondents to Vietnam to look things over and judge for themselves. After all, these senior correspondents (Walter Cronkite, Harry Reasoner and Wallace were among those who spent time in Vietnam in the mid-sixties) were older men whose attitudes toward the U.S. military were formed during the heroic, upbeat days of

World War II when there were no ambiguities, no nagging doubts about the cause that sent Americans into battle on foreign soil. Yet invariably these older, presumably more reliable journalists wound up coroborating the gloomy perceptions of their younger colleagues, which helped to sanction and legitimize the unsettling press coverage of the war.

The U.S. brass in Vietnam did everything it could to prevent that corroboration from happening. Whenever a name correspondent from one of the networks or an influential newspaper arrived in Saigon, he was given the big hello, the star treatment, the public-relations equivalent of a twenty-one-gun salute. On the greeting end of the red carpet was the commanding presence of the man in charge of the U.S. combat mission—General William C. Westmoreland. With his erect bearing, his firmly set jaw and his crisply starched fatigues, "Westy" was the very model of military assurance, the embodiment of the can-do spirit that had led American GIs to glorious victories in past wars. And in Wallace's case at least, he proved receptive. Mike was invited to accompany the general on a daylong air tour of firebases, forward positions and field briefings across the length and breadth of South Vietnam. Westmoreland even took time to escort Wallace through the military hospital at Cam Ranh Bay, where wounded soldiers gazed up at their commander in admiration. But most of all, he talked an optimistic game. Yes, he told Wallace and other journalists whose approval he courted, the struggle here has been a very difficult one, but at last we've gained the upper hand, we've turned the corner. (It was this rosy assessment that later prompted Westmoreland to utter the phrase that would haunt Americans for many years afterward, the confident boast that there was "light at the end of the tunnel.")

It was an impressive and highly persuasive performance, but Wallace knew that it was only one version—the *official* version—of the story. For the reporters he talked to were no less convincing in their assessment that the war was going badly. Some of them, such as R. W. Apple of *The New York Times* and William Touhy of the *Los Angeles Times,* had been in Vietnam since the start of the big buildup in 1965, and they had discovered, in one combat zone after another, that the enemy was much stronger and far more resourceful than the

U.S. Command cared to admit. These reporters went out of their way to emphasize that they had not come to Vietnam with antiwar chips on their shoulders. On the contrary; at first they, too, had believed that Washington was pursuing the right course, and they had accepted at face value the smug predictions of a quick and decisive victory. Yet now, based on all they had seen, most of them scoffed openly at Westmoreland's optimism. They told Wallace that if indeed there was light at the end of the tunnel, it was a very long tunnel and the light so faint that Westmoreland must be looking through a very powerful telescope in order to see it. Even more disturbing, several reporters said that the longer they stayed in Vietnam, the more they became convinced that the U.S. combat forces had no business being there; they were intruders in what was essentially a civil war, and their presence had only succeeded in making the war more bloody and more costly.

Having thus been briefed and counterbriefed, Wallace set out to see for himself, and more than anything else, it was the attitude of the GIs—the "grunts," as they called themselves—that made the most chilling impression on him. Many of the young soldiers he encountered seemed disconsolate and bewildered. They evinced little of the patriotism that had bolstered the morale of his generation in World War II. Instead, many of the grunts expressed the sullen belief that the war was never going to end, and that the men who sent them into combat had not leveled with them, had not told them the truth.

At one point during the two months he spent in Vietnam, Wallace shifted his attention from the war to the political story. This time around, as a senior correspondent for CBS News, he had no trouble gaining access to the top man in the Saigon government, President Nguyen Van Thieu. Thieu had recently become the latest hope for democracy in South Vietnam, and Washington was investing as heavily in him as it had in Diem a few years earlier. When he interviewed Thieu in the study of his luxurious home within the military compound, Wallace wryly observed that facing each other, in proud display on opposite walls of the study, were those contradictory icons of Western culture, a crucifix and a *Playboy* nude. Wallace found Thieu to be cunning and evasive, a man adept at paying lip service to democratic ideals but who, beneath the slick surface, seemed to be chiefly interested in clinging to power as well as to the perquisites he had attained through his close alliance with the United States. Mike left the Thieu interview with the sour feeling that in the political sphere as well as the military, the prospects in Vietnam were far less promising than official reports were proclaiming.

Wallace had expected his assignment in Vietnam to be a busy one, but he had not anticipated that his pieces would be featured so frequently and prominently on the *CBS Evening News*. To a large extent, he had a fortuitous circumstance back in the States to thank for that. Shortly after he arrived in Saigon, a strike was called by AFTRA, the broadcasters' union to which the correspondents at all three networks belonged, and their on-air slots were temporarily filled by management personnel unknown to the public. (The Cronkite show was anchored by a self-conscious young man named Arnold Zenker.) But AF-TRA had no jurisdiction over correspondents who were on assignment overseas. Therefore, while Cronkite and Reasoner and other well-heeled practitioners of the craft carried placards on the most affluent picket lines in the history of the American labor movement, Wallace was free to work—and work he did. Because he was one of the few name correspondents not out on the streets singing *Solidarity Forever*, Mike's reports from Vietnam were eagerly sought by the producers of *The CBS Evening News with Arnold Zenker*. His stories became a nightly staple, and much of the time they led the broadcast. So it was that in the early spring of 1967, viewers of the *Evening News* were given, whether they liked it or not, a heavy dose of the "living-room war," as reported by Mike Wallace. Moreover, the constant demand from producers in New York for fresh pieces by Wallace forced him to dig deeper into the story, and in the process his own views of the war underwent a gradual but decisive change.

He had come to Vietnam as a hawk, a firm supporter of U.S. intervention, including the huge escalation ordered by Johnson in 1965. For he was still an unreconstructed cold warrior who believed that America, having led the fight to stop Communist aggression in Korea and contain it in Europe, had an obligation to respond militarily to the Communist challenge

in Southeast Asia. But the realities he encountered in Vietnam—
the unexpected strength and tenacity of the enemy, and the
persuasive evidence that we were interfering in a civil war—
made him question the pat assumptions he had formed back
in the States. The more he saw and heard, the closer he moved
toward the position that the full-scale commitment of American
troops had been a mistake. By the time Wallace returned to
New York in early May 1967, he had come to regard Vietnam
as a tragic waste of lives and resources, as well as a political
and military blunder that was severely damaging our reputation
in the eyes of the world.

Yet even then, Wallace did not become an outspoken critic
of the war, either on or off the air. For all his altered perceptions
of the U.S. role in Vietnam, he did not identify with the passions and rhetoric of the antiwar protesters. Indeed, there was
a strong element of moral arrogance in some of those people
that he found almost as offensive as the bellicose rantings of
the superpatriots who clamored for more and more escalation,
up to and including, in the words of their favorite proposal,
bombing North Vietnam "back to the Stone Age." In turning
against the war, Wallace did so quietly, and more in sorrow
than in anger. For he did not lose sight of the fact that the
political leaders who had steered us into Vietnam, from Eisenhower to Kennedy to Johnson, were men of good faith who
were convinced they had acted in the best interests of their
country and the free world. To paraphrase George Bernard
Shaw's famous aphorism, the road to an American war in
Vietnam had been paved with good intentions.

By the fall of 1967, as his thoughts turned to the forthcoming
presidential election, Wallace felt fairly certain that, good intentions or no, Johnson's war policies were going to cost him
and his party the White House. What's more, he welcomed the
prospect because he believed that a repudiation of those policies
at the polls was exactly the message the American voters should
send to Washington and the rest of the world. In his view a
Republican administration, starting out with a clean slate, had
a far better chance of negotiating a quick and honorable withdrawal from Vietnam. That is one reason why he and millions

of other Americans who shared his belief were attracted to the candidacy of Richard Nixon in 1968.

But those who voted for Nixon that year in the hope his election would bring about a swift resolution, a rapid transit to the light at the end of the tunnel, were in for a big disappointment. It's true that Nixon scaled down the war, at least in terms of American casualties and overall troop strength in Vietnam. (In another sense, of course, he enlarged it by extending it into another country, Cambodia.) But the earnest quest for "peace with honor" proved to be as elusive as victory on the battlefield, in large part because Nixon and Kissinger persisted in the mistake they inherited from the Johnson administration of linking U.S. goals with those of the Thieu regime in Saigon. As a result, the war dragged on through the late sixties and early seventies, and four years after Nixon's election, Americans were still fighting and dying in Vietnam.

In some respects this phase of gradual de-escalation was the most frustrating period of all. There was no longer any talk of winning the war, of achieving a great victory for democracy over the forces of Communism. By the time Nixon took office, the U.S. military mission in Vietnam had been reduced to the thankless task of merely keeping up the pressure, holding the line until the negotiators at the Paris "peace talks" (a phrase that as time went on came to be uttered with caustic mockery) could agree on a settlement. In fact, there were many who felt that because of these altered circumstances, there was less rationale for continuing the U.S. involvement in the war than there had been during the Kennedy and Johnson years, when at least there had been the illusion of progress toward a decisive and favorable military outcome.

It was during the Nixon years that Wallace became involved in stories about Vietnam and its effects that were far more potent and controversial than any he had covered earlier in 1962 and 1967. For example, he did a *60 Minutes* piece on U.S. deserters who had fled to Canada. That story aroused resentment in some quarters, probably because he made an effort to understand the deserters' point of view instead of simply depicting them as cowardly traitors. Then in 1973 came the celebrated and explosive report on Colonel Anthony Herbert that touched off such a bitter and prolonged legal battle (and one that went to the heart of the First Amendment question) that in 1984, more than a decade later, it still had not been resolved. This phase of his work—taking on Vietnam-related assignments that provoked headlines and controversy—began in 1969 when he was drawn into a story that was not really his, but one that had been brought to CBS News by the free-lance journalist who had tracked it down. Yet because of the role Wallace played in reporting that story to the American public, he became a prime target of the anger and revulsion it stirred up. For it was from a Mike Wallace interview on the *CBS Evening News* that millions of viewers first learned about the atrocities committed by American GIs in a small Vietnam village called My Lai.

CHAPTER

TWELVE

I FIRST LEARNED about the massacre at My Lai in November 1969 when Ralph Paskman, then the assignment editor at CBS News, called me into his office and said he wanted me to interview a young man named Paul Meadlo.

"Who's he?" I asked.

"He was a soldier in Vietnam and he's got some incredible things to say about atrocities committed there. We got hold of him through some outfit called Dispatch News Service and this guy, Seymour Hersh. Ever hear of him?"

No, I had never heard of Seymour Hersh, but I soon learned, from Paskman and others, that he was a free-lance reporter who had once covered the Pentagon for the Associated Press and, more recently, had worked as a press secretary for Senator Eugene McCarthy. He also had written a book on chemical and biological warfare, and had started work on another one about the Pentagon. The latter project was promptly put aside, however, when he received the tip that led him to one of the biggest and most disturbing stories to come out of the war in Vietnam. But it wasn't until some time later, after I had met Hersh and become involved in the reporting of his scoop, that I found out about all the frustration he had experienced in trying to get this country's more influential newspapers and magazines to give the My Lai story the exposure it deserved.

Actually the story had surfaced briefly in a tentative way several weeks before Hersh got wind of it. Back in early September, the Associated Press moved a 190-word news item on its national wire that began as follows:

FT. BENNING, Ga. (AP)—An Army officer has been charged with murder in the deaths of an unspecified number of civilians in Vietnam in 1968, post authorities have revealed.

Col. Douglas Tucker, information officer, said the charge was brought Friday against 1st Lieutenant William L. Calley Jr., 26, of Miami, Fla., a two-year veteran who was to have been discharged from the service Saturday.

The dispatch raised a number of intriguing questions that it did not answer, such as: How many civilians had been murdered? How had they been murdered? Why had Lieutenant Calley been charged just one day before he was to leave the Army? The AP's general manager, Wes Gallagher, later admitted that the news service had been "derelict" in its failure to probe into the story more deeply, but he pointed out that the AP did not receive "a single call from an individual paper or from broadcasters" requesting additional information. And so the massacre at My Lai, which already had been kept under wraps for more than a year, remained dormant for another two months.

Then in late October, Hersh received a call from one of his Pentagon sources, who told him: "I've got a fantastic story. There's a guy down in Benning who is being held on a charge of murdering seventy to seventy-five Vietnamese civilians." As Hersh would soon discover, his source had erred on the side of conservatism. He immediately went to work on the story, and after three weeks of digging, he had come up with solid evidence, including firsthand accounts, that in March 1968 Calley's infantry platoon had attacked the village of My Lai, where they slaughtered, in cold blood, more than a hundred unarmed civilians, many of them women and children. (The eyewitness estimates of how many civilians had been killed ranged from 109—the figure later used in the Army's official charge against Calley—to more than 500.) At one point in early November, Hersh even managed to get an exclusive interview with Calley, who confirmed the essential details of what Hersh had learned from other sources.

Sy Hersh would go on to win a Pulitzer Prize for his reporting on My Lai, but this did not seem likely in the fall of 1969 when, in his efforts to sell the story, he ran into resistance at every turn. He pitched it to two national magazines, *Life* and *Look,* and to such important newspapers as *The New York Times*, *The Washington Post* and *The Boston Globe.* They all turned him down, in part no doubt because they were reluctant to be out in front and alone on such a grisly and appalling story, especially one that had come to them "over the transom" from a freelancer who, at the time, had no reputation as an investigative reporter. So in desperation Hersh decided to peddle it through the Dispatch News Service, a shoestring operation run by a couple of young men fresh out of college. Through that channel, Hersh was able to get the story placed in several newspapers across the country, including such major dailies as the *Chicago Sun-Times,* the *Milwaukee Journal* and the *St. Louis Post-Dispatch.* Even then, the story did not make waves; for some reason, even when published, its impact on the public was minimal.

Hersh knew that an earlier, cursory investigation of My Lai, conducted a few weeks after the massacre, had led to an apparent whitewash, an official conclusion that most of the civilian casualties had been victims of random artillery fire and that, therefore, no disciplinary action was warranted. He also knew that Calley had not been formally indicted—no court-martial order had yet been cut—and Hersh was fearful that unless the public was made aware of My Lai, the Army might decide to keep the lid on the story and paper it over. So in late November, David Obst of the Dispatch News Service contacted CBS News and offered Paul Meadlo, one of Hersh's prime sources, for an interview on national radio and television. In return, CBS agreed to pay a finder's fee of ten thousand dollars to the Dispatch News Service. And that, in short, was how I was drawn into the My Lai story.

Ralph Paskman had assigned me to the interview on a Friday, and when I arrived at my office the following Monday morning, waiting there for me were Sy Hersh, Paul Meadlo and his wife. Hersh filled me in on all the background, then left so that I could be alone with the Meadlos. A clean-cut young man from Terre Haute, Indiana, Meadlo had plenty to tell me. He had been a private in Calley's platoon and had participated in the atrocities at My Lai. I also learned that the day after the massacre, Meadlo himself became a casualty of the war when he lost a foot in a land-mine explosion. He said he had cooperated with Hersh and was cooperating with me because he was stricken with remorse over what had happened that day at My Lai. A few minutes later, the camera was set up and I began to interview Meadlo on film.

He explained that he and others in his platoon had killed the civilians under direct orders from Lieutenant Calley. "I want them dead," he quoted Calley as saying. Meadlo also said that his company commander and Calley's immediate superior, Captain Ernest Medina, was "right there and could have put a stop to it if he wanted to." Then we got down to the specifics of what Meadlo did at My Lai. He said he emptied four clips from his M-16 rifle into the civilians, and since each clip carried seventeen rounds, he reckoned that he personally fired sixty-eight shots:

WALLACE: And you killed how many at that time?

MEADLO: Well, I fired them on automatic, so you can't— you just spray the area in on them, so you really can't know how many you killed 'cause it comes out so dog-goned fast. So I might have killed about ten or fifteen of them.

WALLACE: Men, women and children?

MEADLO: Men, women and children.

WALLACE: And babies?

MEADLO: And babies.

WALLACE: Uh-huh. How do you shoot babies?

MEADLO: I don't know. It was just one of them things . . .

WALLACE: And nothing went through your mind or heart?

MEADLO: Many a times. Many a times.

WALLACE: While you were doing it?

MEADLO: Not while I was doing it. It just seemed like it was the natural thing to do at the time. I don't know. It just—I was getting relieved from what I had seen earlier over there.

WALLACE: What do you mean?

MEADLO: Well, I was getting—my buddies getting killed or wounded or—we weren't getting no satisfaction from it, so what it really was, it was just mostly revenge.

His revelations were made somehow more shocking by the bland, matter-of-fact tone in which he told his tale. It was as though he were describing a routine exercise, a commonplace event. Toward the end of the interview, I tried to put the My Lai experience into some sort of historical perspective:

WALLACE: Obviously, the thought that goes through my mind is, we've raised such a dickens about what the Nazis did, or what the Japanese did, but particularly what the Nazis did in the Second World War, the brutalization and so forth, you know. It's hard for a good many Americans to understand that young, capable American boys could line up old men, women and children and babies and shoot them down in cold blood. How do you explain that?

MEADLO: I wouldn't know.

WALLACE: Did you ever dream about all of this that went on?

MEADLO: Yes, I did, and I still dream about it.

WALLACE: What kind of dreams?

MEADLO: I see the women and children in my sleep. Some nights, I can't even sleep. I just lay there thinking about it.

We ran eighteen minutes of the Meadlo interview on radio, and a somewhat shorter segment was aired on the Cronkite show that night. As Hersh had anticipated, that big a play on national radio and television broke the My Lai story wide open. Accounts of the interview with Meadlo appeared the next day on the front pages of newspapers across the country, including most of those which had previously given Hersh the cold shoulder. And in addition to its front-page story, *The New York Times* printed the transcript of the interview, even making room for the longer version that had been broadcast on the radio network. Nor was it the only My Lai story that made headlines that day. In fact, there is ample reason to believe that the Army learned in advance about the deal Hersh had struck with CBS News. I say this because shortly after I interviewed Meadlo, but before we had a chance to get it on the air, a bulletin came in from Fort Benning announcing that the Army had ordered Lieutenant Calley to stand trial before a general court-martial on six charges of premeditated murder in the deaths of 109 Vietnamese civilians. It could have been a coincidence, but I'm inclined to doubt it.

Nor was there any question that the story struck a raw nerve in the country. The reaction to the Meadlo interview was heavy and intense, and almost all of it was hostile to me and to CBS News. First came the abusive phone calls on the night it was broadcast. Then, over the next few days, the mail came pouring in. Of the first hundred letters that were counted, all but two berated me for "giving that boy a hard time" or for "putting words in his mouth" or for "dishonoring the Army and the country." Never mind that Meadlo had come to us of his own accord because he wanted the American people to know what had happened at My Lai. Never mind that the Army itself was (finally) taking criminal action against Lieutenant Calley. Most of the people we heard from simply refused to believe that such atrocities had occurred; if a wrong had been committed, it had been committed by us, the media. This time, it was even worse than the old, familiar response of blaming the messenger who brings the bad news. In this instance we were not just the bearers of ill tidings, but the bad news itself. The reaction was that strong, and that irrational.

Even though I was distressed by all the hostility, part of me could understand why so many viewers had reacted in such a way. After all, by the fall of 1969, the American people had had their fill of traumatic news about Vietnam. It had been difficult enough to accept the harsh realization that the U.S. intervention had been a mistake, and even more so to accept the bitter reality that thousands of young Americans had been killed in a war to which they should never have been consigned. And now, on top of all that, people were being confronted with the harrowing story of My Lai. More than perhaps any other single event, it was the revelations of those atrocities that drove home the ugly, almost unbearable truth of the war and what it was doing to the moral values of the young men fighting it. This certainly was the message of anguish that Paul Meadlo's mother sought to convey in a comment she made shortly after I had interviewed her son. "I sent them a good boy," she asserted, "and they made him a murderer."

The tragedy of My Lai was not soon forgotten. The antiwar groups, always eager to embrace an issue they could exploit, kept the pot boiling in a number of ways—and I, alas, was not spared in their efforts. Not long after the story broke, they began circulating posters of my interview with Meadlo that focused on the question I had asked him about shooting babies. I had to admit that the posters were effective propaganda, but what annoyed me was the implication that I had joined their crusade; for all of my private reservations about the war, I had no intention of going public in protest. I was a reporter, nothing more.

Various legal proceedings also helped keep the story on the front burner. In March 1971, three years after the massacre took place, Lieutenant William Calley was convicted of murdering at least twenty-two Vietnamese civilians, and sentenced to life imprisonment; his sentence was later reduced to twenty years. Some critics of the war contended that Calley had been made a scapegoat. In their view the criminal responsibility for My Lai extended up the chain of command all the way to the President who had ordered U.S. combat troops into Vietnam. But in the judgment of the military courts, it did not extend beyond Calley. Although his company commander at My Lai, Captain Medina, was also tried for murder, he was acquitted, as was his superior, Colonel Oran K. Henderson, who in a related case had been accused of trying to cover up the atrocities. As for Sy Hersh, he was awarded the Pulitzer Prize he deserved; soon thereafter he went to work for *The New York Times* as its top investigative reporter.

• • •

Every war attracts its share of profiteers, men who greedily exploit the golden opportunities that war offers to make a different kind of killing. Such a man was William J. Crum, who came to be known as "the money king of Vietnam." From 1965 through 1970, Crum held sway over the entire U.S. post-exchange operation in Southeast Asia. This was no mean achievement, for the military post-exchange system was then the third largest retail business in the world; only Sears, Roebuck and J. C. Penney were bigger. Crum had cornered the market on almost every product that was sold to the PXs, from whiskey and beer to slot machines and pizza ovens. Not long after the big buildup of U.S. combat troops in 1965, Crum wrote to one of his contacts at a brewing company back in the States: "Dear Tommy: There is nothing but good news from Vietnam—beer-wise, that is."

But what was good news to Bill Crum was not necessarily good news to the U.S. Senate—ethics-wise, that is. In early 1971 the Senate Permanent Investigations Subcommittee was looking into reports that certain high-ranking officers had used their influence to help Crum sew up his lucrative contracts and that, in return, they had received kickbacks. In particular, the senators wanted to question Crum about his relationship with Brigadier General Earl F. Cole, who, according to one of Crum's former employees, had been receiving one thousand dollars a month from the money king of Vietnam. The problem, however, was that Senate investigators had come up empty in their efforts to locate Crum. In a manner reminiscent of another enterprising millionaire, Howard Hughes, financial success had made Crum reticent and reclusive, at least as far as the Senate was concerned. In the meantime, the testimony about his activities had aroused my interest, and in March 1971, *60 Minutes* joined in the search for the elusive entrepreneur.

Most of the credit for what happened next belongs to producer Bill Brown, whom I had first met back in 1962 when I went to Vietnam for Westinghouse. Back then, Brown was working in Saigon as a free-lance reporter, and it was through his contacts with the Diem government that I had been able to get my interview with Madame Nhu. Five years later he was hired by CBS News to work on a documentary on the Viet Cong; and when *60 Minutes* went on the air in the fall of 1968, he joined our staff. In the process of digging into the PX story, Bill discovered that the lawyer who represented one of the generals at the Senate hearing also represented Crum. Through that connection we were able to establish contact with Crum, who it turned out was living on the qt in Hong Kong. Crum sent word that if we came to Hong Kong, he would make himself available for an interview. Although he had no intention of going to Washington to testify before the Senate subcommittee, he was willing to talk to the press. He and his lawyer no doubt decided that *60 Minutes* could serve as a useful forum to get *his* story across to the public.

Brown and I flew to Hong Kong and, in keeping with the plan we had worked out, we took a cab to a seedy, disconsolate-looking yacht club at the far end of Hong Kong Harbor, and there—as promised—Crum was waiting for us. A fifty-two-year-old American born and raised in China, Bill Crum did not have the health to match his wealth. He suffered from muscular dystrophy and cirrhosis of the liver; he also wore a glass eye, which made him look a bit spooky. The first thing Crum did, after we were introduced, was offer us a drink, even though it was only about ten o'clock in the morning. That was a little early in the day for me (especially since I had work to do), but I rationalized that my body chemistry was still on New York time and back home it was ten or eleven at night, or the shank of the evening. We chatted for a while, then filmed the interview in his modest sailboat against the exotic background of Hong Kong Harbor. Since we had not flown ten thousand miles to beat around the bush, I asked Crum if it was true that he had paid General Cole one thousand dollars a month to help him gain control of the PX market in Vietnam. His answer was:

CRUM: General Cole, as I knew him, was always a gentleman. And to insult the man by offering him a thousand dollars is beyond my credulity.

WALLACE: You mean it's not enough or it's too much or—

CRUM: I'd say a million dollars would have been stupid to offer this man.

As soon as the interview was over, Brown and I rushed to the airport and caught the next plane back to New York. And on our next broadcast, viewers of *60 Minutes* were introduced to William J. Crum, the man the Senate investigators had been unable to find. As was the case with the Dita Beard escapade at the osteopathic hospital in Denver, the mere fact of getting the interview was a bigger story than the content of the interview itself. Crum simply fended off all the charges that had been leveled against him, pleading either innocence or ignorance. But as a result of the PX scandal, General Earl Cole was reduced to the rank of colonel and ordered into early retirement from active duty.

During this period—the early 1970s—I also made two brief trips to Saigon for *60 Minutes*. In September 1971 I went there to do a piece on that fall's presidential election in South Vietnam. Or to be more precise, I tried to explain why, as I put it in my on-air introduction, the forthcoming election was going to be "an embarrassment to the United States and a hollow exercise in democracy for Vietnam." The Nixon administration had hoped that two men, Vice President Nguyen Cao Ky and General Duong Van Minh, would run against the incumbent, Nguyen Van Thieu, to prove that democracy was working in South Vietnam. But when Thieu blatantly rigged the electoral process in his favor, Ky and Minh decided they had no choice but to drop out of the race. This left Thieu as the only candidate and turned the election into a mere referendum, or, as critics of the Thieu government labled it, "a fraud and a farce." I interviewed Ky and Minh in Saigon and concluded my report with the assertion that America's "puny client, Nguyen Van Thieu, has outmaneuvered the powerful United States." And indeed, the cynicism displayed by Thieu and his deputies that fall made it that much more difficult for Nixon and Kissinger to justify their position that the Saigon regime was worthy of continued American support, either on or off the battlefield.

The previous year, I had gone over there to do a much different kind of story, one that we called "Vietnam: Coming and Going." In the spring of 1970, I, a film crew and producer Paul Loewenwater, flew to Saigon aboard a plane that was carrying a fresh contingent of troops to the war. Three days later, we flew back to the States on a plane filled with veterans who were coming home after having spent a year or more in Vietnam. In setting the scene for the in-flight conversations that took place, I noted that in the five years that had passed since the U.S. combat mission began in earnest, more than two million American servicemen had been dispatched to Vietnam; and over forty thousand of them had lost their lives in the war.

On the flight to Vietnam, the mood ranged from wistful to resigned to apprehensive. Some of the young men I talked to openly confessed that they were afraid of what might be in store for them; they spoke not only of their fear of getting killed in combat, but also of their concern about being thrust into situations where they would be expected to kill others. "I think each man has to examine his conscience and ask himself if he could pull that trigger on another man, another living being," one soldier said to me on-camera. "And I've done a lot of soul-searching and I've examined my own conscience, and I find that I couldn't do it." We also learned, from an informal poll we took, that roughly one third of the men aboard that plane were opposed to U.S. participation in the war. And that, as I said at the time, was the "sad reality" that distinguished the Vietnam conflict from past American wars.

On the flight home, the mood was less somber, though hardly jubilant. Those troops who had completed their assignments in Vietnam did not evince pride or joy so much as simple relief that they had survived the experience. In the words of one, they had "lucked out." As a group, the men returning from Vietnam were more supportive of the U.S. military presence there, and what irritated many of them was the dissent, the antiwar protests they knew they would encounter back in the States. One veteran who shared his thoughts with me on that subject had this to say: "I see the right to dissent. The only thing that would really bother me is if someone would say something about myself or fellow soldiers that served in Vietnam. That would lower them in my eyes." He paused and then added: "I'm not really in favor of the war either, but when I looked at the three alternatives of leaving the country or going to prison or going in the Army, I chose going in the Army."

Earlier, on the flight going over, I had talked to a draftee who revealed that he had come close to exercising one of those other options. "At first I was scared," he recalled. "I had all the money and everything to go to Canada. I was going to fly to Montreal. But then I changed my mind and decided, well, some people do come back. I guess I'll take my chances."

But of course there were plenty of young men who, faced with the same decision, had gone to Canada. They were the deserters and draft resisters who had chosen to live in exile rather than run the risk of being sent to Vietnam; and in the fall of 1971, producer Barry Lando and I decided to do a story on them. We were prompted in part by the growing debate over the question of amnesty. President Nixon firmly opposed granting amnesty to those who had fled to Canada and other countries to avoid the war, and while millions of Americans agreed with him, millions of others did not. In fact, hardly anyone was neutral on the question, for it had become a highly emotional issue that cut to the heart of such basic values as patriotism and family loyalty. In November 1971 we went to Canada to discuss the subject with some of the deserters themselves. What we discovered, somewhat to my surprise, was that most of the young exiles we met were in no mood to petition for amnesty and were not even sure that if it were granted, they would return to the States.

During our visit with one large group of refugees (as they preferred to call themselves) at a Thanksgiving dinner in Montreal, I pointed out that amnesty meant a full pardon, forgiveness, wiping the slate clean with no punitive strings attached. Yet even when defined in those generous terms, the response was negative. "We're not going to ask for forgiveness from that government," one of them said. "The only issue of amnesty I think we feel is the issue, do we forgive *them? They* are the criminals, not us." Most of the others in the room supported his statement with loud cheering and applause.

But while that clearly was the sentiment of the majority, it was not unanimous. A young man named Ken Duff was a lonely voice for amnesty at that Thanksgiving dinner. We learned from him that there were thousands of other exiles scattered across Canada who shared his hope that amnesty would be granted so that they could return to their native land. Duff was a nineteen-year-old deserter from the Marine Corps, and at one point we had the following exchange:

WALLACE: Ken, somebody might ask the question "Is it just for Ken Duff to get amnesty? He didn't go to Vietnam. My son did. Maybe I lost my son over there." What about it?

DUFF: Well, it's a hard question, because these people did what they thought was right and what was their duty. But my ideal of what America should be and what America should do as a country is different from theirs, I suppose, because I think in order for there to be a change or in order for that ideal that I have to become real, then I have to live it. And I don't think my ideal includes killing women, children and babies. It's what I was taught and I'm trying to live it.

His pointed reference to "killing women, children and babies" naturally put me in mind of My Lai, and I thought to myself, Ken Duff, meet Paul Meadlo; two young men who, in starkly different ways, had been caught up in the tragedy of Vietnam.

Prior to his exile, home for Ken Duff had been Danielson, Connecticut, and following our encounter with him in Montreal, we visited his parents. Gerald and Gertrude Duff were factory workers and, like thousands of other American parents, they had their own special anguish to bear during this deeply troubled time in our history. That anguish was very much in evidence when I interviewed them at their home in Danielson:

WALLACE: Are you ashamed of what Ken's done? Honestly.

MRS. DUFF: I'm not sure if—no, it's not shame in what he's done. I guess it's a fear that some people might think it shameful. So you lie. People ask you about it and you tell one lie and then pretty soon you tell another lie. Which is very hard to do to someone that don't like to lie.

WALLACE: Mr. Duff, if it came down to Ken's staying in Canada or coming down here, facing two years in prison, what would you advise him to do?

MR. DUFF: Well, I've always preached to them to turn and face the music and take what they had coming to them.

WALLACE: Even if that meant his going to jail for a couple of years? Mrs. Duff?

MRS. DUFF: I wouldn't like that. I would like amnesty because I think he really means it when he says he wants to come home, not that he wants to get away with anything, or, you know, just say, "Well, I did it and I got away with it." I don't—I think he has become, let's say, humble.

WALLACE: What do you say, what is your feeling about the—I suppose the millions of Americans who are saying to themselves at this moment, "Look, they turned their back on their country, they turned their back on their duty. Let them stay up there and rot." Mrs. Duff?

MRS. DUFF: That's a tough question because that's the way I felt, but if nothing else comes of this, I think my son has caused us to open our minds a little bit, which on—I think it was pretty closed on this issue. Red, white and blue, that's me, that's what I've always been . . . But basically, the way our son feels, basically, it's the same as we feel. But it's a whole new different way of looking at things and doing things. Sometimes I look at him and I think he has more moxie than I would ever have had at that age. I know at that age I was—always had dreams. I dreamed of great things, but I never really carried them through. But I think he has a dream, an ideal, and I think he's doing something about it.

WALLACE: And to the mothers and fathers of the kids who fought and some of them were wounded and some of them died, what do you say to them?

MRS. DUFF: Oh, I put myself in their place and it's—

At that point, Mrs. Duff's voice broke and she began to cry. She was, in fact, so distraught that I immediately called a halt to the interview. Nor did I do that only for her benefit, for in

truth my own feelings were edging out of control. I've always
tried to maintain emotional distance from the people I interview.
But that was one time when the normal defense mechanisms
failed me, and I think I know why. After all, I, too, was a
parent, the proud father of one son, Chris, who was twenty-
four then and had recently embarked on his own career in
journalism, and the still grieving father of another, Peter, whose
broken body I had discovered on that desolate mountain path
in Greece nine years earlier. So my heart went out to the Duffs
as they struggled to cope with the moral dilemma of their son's
decision and the bitter resentment it aroused in other parents
who had lost *their* sons in Vietnam.

The producer I worked with on the deserters' story was Barry
Lando, who was a newcomer to the staff of *60 Minutes*. We
were glad to have him, since he had come to us with impressive
credentials in both print and broadcasting. Lando had worked
in South America as a correspondent for *Time* magazine in the
mid-sixties, and later, after he was hired by CBS, he had produced a succession of first-rate pieces for the weekend edition
of the *Evening News*. He was a talented and resourceful reporter. Still, I was not at all receptive when Lando came to me
in the fall of 1971 with a proposal that we do a *60 Minutes*
piece on Lieutenant Colonel Anthony Herbert.

The first and in many ways the most important point to
make about Anthony Herbert is that he was a soldier to the
core and a bona fide war hero. He had enlisted at the age of
seventeen, and the twenty-two medals he won in Korea were
an achievement that speaks for itself. What's more, his performance in combat was more than matched by his military bearing
and manner; indeed, he cut such an impressive figure that the
Army portrayed him as a model of the American fighting man.
He was sent on a promotional world tour and his picture was
displayed on the cover of combat training manuals. After Korea, Herbert continued to serve with distinction in Europe and
the Middle East, and in the late 1960s he was assigned to duty
as a battalion commander in Vietnam, where once again he
demonstrated heroism on the battlefield. In a span of only fifty-
eight days, he won the Silver Star and three Bronze Stars. Then
came a sudden fall from grace. In the spring of 1969, this

dashing war hero was relieved of his command by the same officer who had given it to him—Brigadier General John Barnes. Herbert appealed that decision, taking his case to higher headquarters in Saigon, but following a brief investigation, his appeal was denied.

Soon thereafter, Herbert returned to the States and began a stretch of routine assignments, first at Fort Leavenworth, Kansas, and later at Fort McPherson, Georgia. And that was where he was still stationed in the fall of 1970 when reporters from every major news organization in the country converged on nearby Fort Benning to cover William Calley's My Lai trial. It was then that Herbert first presented a written war crimes report implicating his superiors. Six months later, he went public with charges accusing his superiors, General Barnes and Barnes's deputy commander, Colonel J. Ross Franklin, of covering up war crimes and atrocities he had reported to them in Vietnam. He asserted that it was because of his repeated efforts to have the crimes investigated that the decision was made to take his command away from him. In essence, Colonel Herbert claimed that his military career had been ruined by senior officers who wanted to shut him up.

From the Pentagon's point of view, Herbert's charges could not have come at a worse time. By the spring of 1971, American troops had been bogged down in a full-scale war in Vietnam for six years and there was still no light at the end of the tunnel. And by then, most of the national press and large segments of the public had turned against the war. Moreover, all the grisly details about My Lai that came out during the Calley trial only deepened the sense of dismay and revulsion that so many Americans now felt about Vietnam. Against that background, the U.S. military establishment, already on the defensive, now had to contend with damaging allegations from one of its own—a career officer, an authentic war hero and a man whom the Army itself had cited as a model soldier.

Given those circumstances, it was only natural that the press would take a lively interest in Colonel Herbert and his story. Over the next several months, he was showered with attention from the media. National magazines, influential newspapers and the television networks all did admiring reports on the gallant colonel who, in his pursuit of justice and morality, had

defied his superiors and been martyred for his efforts. None
was more glowing than a long piece that ran in *The New York
Times* Sunday magazine under the title "How a Supersoldier
Was Fired from His Command." The article was written by
James Wooten, then a highly respected reporter for the *Times*
(he later moved on to ABC News), and it led to a lucrative
contract for a book, a Herbert-Wooten collaboration called *Soldier* that was destined to become a best seller. By the fall of
1971, the "Supersoldier" had become a media cult figure, a
celebrity saint. To many Americans, especially those who were
strongly opposed to the war, Tony Herbert was almost too good
to be true.

Among those caught up in the wave of adulation for Colonel
Herbert was Barry Lando. Lando had helped give Herbert and
his story national exposure with a report that appeared on the
July 4, 1971, edition of the *CBS Evening News*. A few months
later, shortly after he had begun working with me on *60 Minutes*, Lando proposed doing another Herbert piece for our
broadcast. But since he had no fresh angle to peg it on, I told
him I wasn't interested. I pointed out that Herbert had been
canonized over and over again in the press, that Lando himself
had contributed to the media benediction, and I was at a loss
to see how adding *my* voice to the chorus of hosannas would
increase the public's knowledge of Herbert. As I recall, that
conversation ended with my rather testy suggestion that Lando
forget about Herbert and other subjects he had done already,
and concentrate instead on generating *new* story ideas for *60
Minutes*.

He took the advice—or at least the last part of it. Over the
next few months, Lando came up with several sound proposals
that we developed into stories, including the Thanksgiving piece
on the deserters and draft resisters in Canada. But at the same
time, he persisted in his efforts to produce another pro-Herbert
story. He was determined to persuade me and Don Hewitt that
the ordeal to which Herbert had been subjected was nothing
less than a parable of the entire U.S. experience in Vietnam,
and that therefore *60 Minutes* almost had a moral obligation to
broadcast a report on it. Hewitt's response was, if anything,
even more negative than mine; he also was loath to devote *60
Minutes*'s precious air time to what he called "monkey-see,

monkey-do" stories that already had been given thorough treatment elsewhere in the press. But Barry didn't want to take no for an answer.

In the meantime, Colonel Herbert announced his retirement from the Army, claiming that the conspiracy to deny him promotion and relegate him to trivial assignments in backwater posts made it pointless for him to remain on active duty. His decision only served to intensify the glow in the halo of martyrdom that had formed around Herbert's public image, and once gain powerful voices in the press rallied to his cause. Now, even more than before, he was portrayed as a modern Dreyfus who had been done in by a sinister military establishment intent on covering up the ugly truths about the U.S. Army's performance in Vietnam.

Lando welcomed this latest development as a fresh opportunity. Herbert had previously told him that once he got out of the Army, he would provide Barry with documents to substantiate his charges. And in March 1972, the recently retired Herbert turned over to Lando a batch of material, including transcripts of taped telephone calls with other soldiers. That seemed to buttress Herbert's position. Herbert also gave him copies of various newspaper articles that had been published over the past year, ever since he first went public with his allegations. Buoyed by this new information, Lando seemed confident that now he had what he needed to induce my commitment to a *60 Minutes* story on Herbert.

Until then, I had not formed a strong opinion about Colonel Herbert, one way or the other. I simply had not given him that much thought. But now, as I looked through the new material Lando had obtained, I began asking myself questions about the timing of Herbert's charges. Why had he waited so long—a year and a half—before blowing the whistle? And in finally speaking out, how much had he been influenced by all the My Lai stories? Had it occurred to Herbert that given the prevailing climate, the surest way to captivate the liberal press and embarrass the Army was to accuse his superiors of covering up war crimes? Perhaps it was nothing more than my natural skepticism coming to the fore, but the more I read, the more I wondered about Herbert. So this time, when Lando asked me what I thought of his favorite colonel, I said: "I'm sorry, Barry, but I don't believe him. I think he may be lying."

That was the last thing Barry wanted to hear, and he blew up: "Jesus Christ, Wallace, you're a goddam reactionary son of a bitch, you know that?"

I responded by telling him what I thought of "knee-jerk, bleeding-heart liberals" who allow themselves to be taken in by a trendy media blitz. This spirited exchange made Lando more determined than ever to prove that he was right and I was wrong about Tony Herbert. He informed me that he had no intention of throwing in the towel on the story. By now I had reached the conclusion that the Herbert case had become such an obsession with Lando that he had to get it out of his system one way or another. So I relented and told him to continue along the lines he proposed. "Go ahead, and try to convince me," I said.

What happened next in the months that followed is a tribute to Barry Lando's journalistic integrity. For the story he eventually produced was not the story he had expected to find, and in the course of tracking it down, he had to admit—to himself and others—that he had been wrong. To borrow from the Dreyfus analogy, it was as if Zola had wound up directing his celebrated *"J'accuse"* at Dreyfus, the martyred scapegoat, rather than at the officers who had conspired against him.

In the course of tracking down Herbert's story, Lando focused on Herbert's widely publicized and most sensational charge, which came to be known as the St. Valentine's Day Massacre. As Herbert told it again and again, on February 14, 1969, while he looked on, unable to stop it, a member of a South Vietnamese detachment slit a young Vietnamese girl's throat as one of her two children clung to her legs screaming; another Vietnamese was suffocating her other child by pushing the child's face into the sand with his foot. Four dead males lay on the ground near her feet. Herbert claimed that he reported these killings that day to Franklin both by radio and in person that evening. Franklin, according to Herbert, refused to believe Herbert or to investigate or report the incident. The Army's rebuttal was that Herbert could not have reported the St. Valentine's Day Massacre to Franklin on February 14 as he claimed, because Franklin was on leave in Hawaii on that date. Since the St.

Valentine's Day Massacre seemed to be one of the few incidents where there was a possibility of proving who was telling the truth without relying on Herbert's word against that of his superiors, the incident became a linchpin in our investigation. By the spring of 1972, both Herbert and the Army knew that Lando would be focusing on the St. Valentine's Day Massacre—and he did. Lando spoke with two officers who said they were in Hawaii with Franklin on February 14, 1969, the date Herbert claimed to have reported the St. Valentine's Day Massacre to Franklin in Vietnam. Two other men whom Herbert had said would substantiate his February 14 report of the incident to Franklin did not do so.

Other men Lando interviewed that spring said that Herbert was not the type of person who would report war crimes—that Herbert himself was capable of brutality. Barry had every reason to believe that one of these men, Bob Stemme, was a staunch ally of Herbert's. For one thing, Herbert himself had mentioned Stemme as someone Lando should interview, and for another, Stemme was active in a protest group called Vietnam Veterans Against the War. This meant that his sympathies were hardly on the side of Herbert's adversaries in the military establishment. And yet Stemme told Lando that he was leery of Herbert's claims, and that, in his opinion, Herbert would not have reported war crimes. Lando encountered similar attitudes in other soldiers he contacted, and when questioned by Lando, one soldier after another was either unable or unwilling to corroborate Herbert's allegations.

In addition, Lando had to wonder about a telephone call he received from a writer named Bob Johnson, who had recently published a book about West Point for which Herbert had written the introduction. Johnson phoned Lando to ask him when the *60 Minutes* report on Herbert was going to be broadcast. He said that Herbert had told him it was being delayed because *60 Minutes* planned to devote its entire hour to the story. This was nonsense. We virtually never give that much air time to a single story, and Barry had said nothing of the kind to Herbert. So here was evidence—unless Bob Johnson was doing a little fishing on his own—of a Herbert claim that Lando knew for certain was untrue.

By this time the Pentagon had met the issue head on. For

several months, the Army had ignored or downplayed Herbert's charges in the apparent belief that the less said in response to them, the sooner they would be forgotten. But by the spring of 1972, the Army, having conducted its own investigation into the case, had issued a thorough, point-by-point rebuttal of Herbert's allegations. In essence, the Pentagon charged that the former war hero and model soldier was lying.

Like so many others who believed Herbert's story, Lando had been inclined to regard the prolonged silence of his military superiors as a tacit admission of some kind of cover-up. But when it finally came, the Army's counterattack along with the unsettling information he was getting from other sources, prompted Barry to reassess his opinion of Herbert.

Then came another revelation that helped undermine Lando's crumbling faith in Tony Herbert. In the late spring of 1972, *Playboy* magazine published a long interview with the colonel, in which, along with his now familiar charges of atrocities and cover-up, he claimed that the man who relieved him in Vietnam, General Barnes, had kept a pet duck and that the soldiers under his command were ordered to salute it. Herbert proceeded to boast that he brought an end to this indignity when he killed the duck, and that Barnes's pet wound up in sandwiches that he and another soldier consumed with relish.

In late June I received another memo from Barry Lando on his favorite subject, but this one differed radically from his previous pro-Herbert pitches. He wrote that even before the *Playboy* article: "I had evidence, strong, that Herbert was not telling the truth." He then directed my attention to the *Playboy* interview, which he described as "wild, particularly the duck bit. I really think the guy is going off the deep end." He pointed out that Herbert's book was due to be published in January or February of 1973 and suggested that would be the ideal time for *60 Minutes* to air its story on the colonel. And in a subsequent memo, Lando added: "Many of the tales Herbert tells and the charges he levels do not bear up to close scrutiny. His book may be as much fiction as fact."

By this time I was getting hooked on the story, and not just because these more recent developments seemed to confirm my earlier suspicion about Herbert. That was part of it, I guess; it's always gratifying to be able to say, "I told you so." But what I found far more intriguing was the dramatic reversal taking place inside Lando. Like some other reporters, he had set out believing in Herbert, but like all *good* reporters, he did not allow his belief to warp his assessment of the information he obtained. A different kind of reporter—an "advocacy journalist," for example—would have been more interested in proving his point and winning the argument than in getting the story and getting it right; and on discovering that his original belief was wrong, such a reporter might well have chosen to take the easy way out and quietly abandon the quest, if only to save face. But that certainly was not the case with Lando. The discovery that he had grossly misjudged Herbert did not dampen his enthusiasm for the assignment; on the contrary, he became, if anything, even more diligent in his pursuit of it.

There was also a more general point to consider. In shifting to a course that challenged his own belief, Lando was moving against the grain of the prevailing bias—and this too appealed to me. The main reason Herbert had been able to get so much mileage out of his charges was because he had raised them at a time when so much of the press was disposed to believe the worst about the U.S. Army and its mission in Vietnam. Now, more than ever, I felt the reports of the Herbert case had cynically exploited the revulsion over My Lai and the antiwar mood that had become so rampant in the early months of 1971 when the Calley trial was dominating the headlines. Hence, I thought if we could put together a *60 Minutes* piece built around evidence that the press had naïvely accepted Herbert's story, it could serve as a healthy reminder that we should all be just as skeptical of those who appeal to our prejudices as of those who regard us as adversaries.

But even though I was eager now to do the Herbert story, I was in no position as yet to give much of my own time and attention to the effort. I was working with other producers on other *60 Minutes* stories that had to be given priority because they were scheduled to be broadcast well before January or February of 1973, the target date we had set for airing the Herbert piece. Nor was that all. Since 1972 was a presidential election year, I also had other commitments. Once again, I had been assigned to work as a floor correspondent at both political conventions that summer, and later I would be doing a few campaign reports for the *Evening News* and preparing for my election-night duties on the East Desk. (In the fall of 1972, as in other years, I reported on the major results in twelve eastern states, from Maine to West Virginia. Other CBS News correspondents focused on other regions—for example, Dan Rather was responsible for the Midwest—while Walter Cronkite provided the national overview from his customary anchor slot.) And since I was no longer plugged into politics the way I had been four years earlier when it had been my regular beat, I had plenty of boning up to do. Thus, in terms of my personal involvement, the Herbert story would have to wait until late fall or early winter.

So it was still up to Lando to mine that lode by himself, at least for the time being. Which he did. Although he continued to work on other assignments during the last six months of 1972, Barry devoted much of his time and attention to the Herbert project. He interviewed scores of people who were connected with the case, and all that reporting only deepened his disenchantment with Herbert.

A highlight of Lando's reporting that summer and fall was his on-camera interview with General Barnes, during which Barnes dismissed the pet duck tale as pure hokum and insisted vehemently that Herbert had never reported any war crimes or atrocities to him. Nor had Herbert been relieved of his command for reporting war crimes. And Barnes offered a laundry list of reasons why he felt compelled to relieve Herbert: Herbert just could not get along with the members of the brigade staff; he was constantly pitting his battalion against the brigade; Herbert frequently changed the description of operations in which his battalion was involved; and his battalion had the highest ratio of enemy killed to weapons captured—which meant to Barnes that innocent civilians were possibly being killed. Barnes summed up his decision this way: "I just didn't have confidence in him. I had lost confidence in him as a commander with the ability to control his people."

These observations were not only intriguing in and of themselves, but they also dovetailed with comments Lando had picked up from others who had served with Herbert in Vietnam. Many soldiers who knew Herbert in Vietnam spoke to Barry

about Herbert's relief. Not one of them thought Herbert had
been relieved, as he had claimed, for reporting war crimes.

During these months Barry kept me posted on all developments, and by December, with the election and other assignments out of the way, I was finally free to concentrate on
the story. Since Barry had filmed the interview with General
Barnes, I turned my attention to Herbert's other principal adversary, Barnes's deputy commander, Colonel J. Ross Franklin.
It was Franklin who had recommended to Barnes that Herbert
be relieved, and when I asked him why, he said that he, too,
had lost confidence in Herbert, especially in his veracity:

> FRANKLIN: Tactically he was the best battalion com-
> mander we had. I counseled Herbert several times and
> once I counseled him on telling the truth or being more
> exact in what he said. I told him at that time that he
> could run circles around all the rest of the battalion com-
> manders if he'd just tell the truth.

> WALLACE: Did Colonel Herbert ever report war crimes
> or atrocities of any nature to you, Colonel Franklin?

> FRANKLIN: No.

> WALLACE: Never?

> FRANKLIN: Never.

> WALLACE: Verbally or in writing?

> FRANKLIN: In no way, neither orally or in writing. This—
> I had many conversations with Colonel Herbert. We dis-
> cussed many things, but never war crimes.

The Pentagon also put us in touch with other officers who were
close to the case and who supported the official position: namely,
that Barnes and Franklin were telling the truth, and Herbert
was not. Yet even as we talked to these men, I could anticipate
what Herbert's reaction would be to their on-the-record statements. He would surely contend that anyone who was still in
uniform could not be trusted to tell the truth in this matter, at
least not in public. Even if they had not been involved in the
original cover-up, they would be induced to go along with it

now to protect their careers. After all (I could hear Herbert saying), they need only look to his own experience for a striking example of what happens to career officers who try to buck the system.

But that argument could not be applied to Ken Rosenblum, the Army lawyer who had headed much of the investigation into Herbert's charges against Barnes and Franklin. At the time he took on that assignment, Rosenblum was serving as a captain in the Judge Advocate General's Corps. Since then, however, he had left the Army and was now working as an assistant district attorney on Long Island in New York. This meant that presumably he was free to speak his own mind, independent of pressures from the Pentagon. I could only assume that Herbert believed that to be the case, for he was the one who had urged us to talk to Rosenblum. Yet Rosenblum's recollection of events was not consistent with what Herbert had told Lando, as I discovered when I interviewed him and brought up Herbert's claim that the Army investigation had been a whitewash:

> ROSENBLUM: It certainly wasn't a whitewash. We traveled all over the country. We took thousands and thousands of pages of transcript. We spoke to witnesses in person and over the telephone. We had access to all the CID files. We were refused nothing and we were permitted to go anywhere that we desired and talk to anyone we desired, in or out of the Army. We had all of the Army's facilities made available to us, and anywhere we wanted to go, we went.

> WALLACE: You were present throughout the whole business of investigating Herbert's charges against General Barnes?

> ROSENBLUM: Yes, I was, sir.

> WALLACE: And you came up with a verdict that the charges just didn't hold water?

> ROSENBLUM: Essentially that's correct. I tried to approach it in a very open-minded way. I have no grudge against the Army, no grudge against Herbert. I knew I was getting out. I was not a career man, and so I had no desire

to protect the Army. Nor did I have a desire to protect
Herbert.

I also questioned Rosenblum about Herbert's alleged report of
the St. Valentine's Day Massacre. Rosenblum insisted that there
was absolutely no evidence—other than Herbert's own assertion—that Herbert had reported it to Franklin or Barnes.

Another damaging challenge to Herbert's credibility came
from another unlikely source: an ardent admirer of Herbert's,
Major Jim Grimshaw, who had served as a company commander under Herbert in Vietnam. Grimshaw had come to our
attention when we read the galley proofs of Herbert's book,
Soldier, which we obtained several weeks before the official
publication. As expected, *Soldier* was for the most part an
elaboration of Herbert's various grievances against the Army.
At one point he told a story about Grimshaw that was designed
to underscore his thesis that his superiors had failed to act in
a responsible manner. He recalled an occasion when Grimshaw
discovered three Viet Cong soldiers hiding in a cave with two
women and a baby, and, at great personal danger to himself,
he crawled into the cave and rescued the baby. According to
Herbert, Grimshaw assumed such decisive command of the
situation that when he emerged from the cave with the baby
in his arms, the women and the soldiers followed docilely
behind. Herbert was so impressed by this valorous act that he
said he put Grimshaw in for the Silver Star, the U.S. Army's
third highest combat decoration. "He more than deserved it,"
Herbert wrote, "but he never received it."

It was a terrific story, and reflected most favorably on Jim
Grimshaw's courage. The only problem was that, according to
Grimshaw, it never happened. As he told Lando and later confirmed to me when I did an on-camera interview with him at
the Pentagon, he never rescued a baby from a Viet Cong cave.
In tearing down the story, Grimshaw said he did so with "dismay and reluctance" because of his admiration for Herbert the
soldier. Expanding on that, he said: "I would stick up for Tony
Herbert for anything. I'd follow him in combat because I don't
think I could keep up with him, he was such a fine combat
leader. However, I feel that as an individual, let alone an Army
officer, a man must have integrity. Therefore, I would not lie

for him or for anybody else."

Not long after I interviewed Grimshaw, Herbert telephoned Lando to report that Grimshaw had called to tell him about our interview and to assure him that the only reason he had contradicted Herbert's story was because the Pentagon had pressured him to do so; his career was on the line and he had no choice in the matter. As soon as I heard this, I phoned Grimshaw and told him what Herbert had said. "Look," I then said, "if you feel this was an interview done under some kind of Pentagon pressure, we don't want to use it."

"Absolutely not," he replied, then he proceeded to spell out his denial on both counts. One, he had said nothing of the kind to Herbert but had called him merely as a courtesy to tell him about our interview. And two, he had been under no pressure from Pentagon officials or anyone else; nor had he been briefed or coached on what to say in the interview. I then asked Grimshaw if he would be willing to repeat these statements to Herbert's face in front of a CBS camera. He said he would be happy to; all we had to do was let him know where and when. So here was an unexpected opportunity for the kind of dramatic encounter we often strive for and always welcome on *60 Minutes*.

Which brings me now, at long last, to the showdown, the *pièce de résistance*—my January 23, 1973, interview with Herbert. I confronted Herbert with what we had learned during our months of investigation: the substantial evidence that Herbert did not report the St. Valentine's Day Massacre to Franklin as he said he had; the failure of anyone who knew Herbert in Vietnam to substantiate that he had been relieved of his command for reporting war crimes; the absence of a single piece of paper to show that Herbert had even rendered a written war crimes report implicating his superiors until seventeen months after his relief; and the absence of any hard evidence to buttress Herbert's claim that the Army investigations into his charges were a whitewash. I also questioned him about the stories we had heard that he himself had either committed or condoned mistreatment of the Vietnamese. None of it seemed to faze him. He clung firmly to the position that all those who disagreed with him were either lying—were, in fact, part of the conspiracy—or were still in the service and under pressure to lie, or were simply mistaken; that is, they just did not remember events as clearly as he did. He stuck to his story with great certitude. I saw him as a kind of modern Luther who, having rebelled against the authority of the Established Church (in this case, the U.S. Army), could no longer accept any faith or truth but his own. His zeal and self-righteousness had carried him to the point where all opposing views were either to be scorned as intentional lies or dismissed as errors in memory. Tony Herbert was, in short, a very tough nut to crack.

I then brought up the subject of Grimshaw, who, unknown to Herbert, was sitting across the hall in a studio wired for sound so that he could listen to our interview. When I mentioned that Grimshaw categorically denied stories that had been written about him in *Soldier*, Herbert again intimated that Grimshaw had been pressured by the Pentagon to bad-mouth him. I then revealed Grimshaw's presence, just across the hall:

HERBERT: Bring him in.

WALLACE: Fine.

HERBERT: Good. And ask him the same questions.

WALLACE: You can ask him whatever questions you want to. Here he is right now.

HERBERT: Hello, Jim.

GRIMSHAW: Hi, how are you doing?

HERBERT: Very fine.

WALLACE: Jim, have you heard what's been going on between the colonel and me?

GRIMSHAW: Yes.

HERBERT: Okay . . .

WALLACE: Have you read the book? Have you read the book?

GRIMSHAW: Yes, I have read the book.

WALLACE: Do you think it's accurate by and large?

GRIMSHAW: Well, the incidents— We have to talk about the incidents that I'm personally involved in.

WALLACE: All right. Sure.

GRIMSHAW: So, now we're talking three incidents, when you get right down to it.

WALLACE: And you've told me—

GRIMSHAW: I'm telling you two thirds, then, are not true.

WALLACE: Were you under any pressure, Jim Grimshaw, to—from the Pentagon or from your commanding officer— to show up at the Pentagon for an interview?

GRIMSHAW: No.

HERBERT: Now, you told me that—

GRIMSHAW: Absolutely not.

HERBERT: You told me that.

GRIMSHAW: And I wasn't briefed.

Later in the interview, Grimshaw told Herbert that he should have checked out his stories with the people he wrote about in his book.

GRIMSHAW: Why didn't you call guys like myself or Hill or some of these guys?

HERBERT: Okay—

GRIMSHAW: You know, you're making us a public figure—

HERBERT: Okay, wait a minute, Jim.

GRIMSHAW: Whether you want— You know, you're trying to do me a very good job and, in a sense, maybe I think it's because of all the problems that occurred and you maybe want to put us in a good light to the American public. But you've made me a public figure. I can't help it. I have to speak out.

The encounter with Grimshaw had its effect. Herbert did not exactly lose his composure—he was far too disciplined for that—but he was visibly shaken, if only for a moment or two. It was evident that Grimshaw's unexpected appearance had scored a palpable hit. After all, here was a man who had no ax to grind—who, indeed, had been portrayed as a hero in Herbert's book—and yet he had taken the trouble to confront his former commander in the midst of a network television interview and declare that what Herbert had written about him was just not true.

Therefore, Herbert had ample reason to be upset, and as soon as we finished the interview, he unleashed his wrath on Barry Lando, who had been with us in the studio from the start. He reminded Lando of the time back in 1971 when he and Barry had discussed the possibility of collaborating on a book about his experience. But instead, once Herbert decided to embark on such a project, he chose to write it with James Wooten of *The New York Times*, and now he accused Lando of waging a vindictive campaign against him because he, Barry, had been rebuffed as the co-author. Barry was livid and I don't blame him, for as he remembered it, his conversation with Herbert about a possible collaboration had been vague and tentative, and he was not at all upset when he learned that Wooten had been entrusted with the assignment. In fact, by then Lando had gone to work for *60 Minutes* and was no longer interested in writing *any* book—with or without Tony Herbert. Moreover, for several months *after* Wooten had been enlisted to work on the book, Barry remained an admirer of Herbert. I can attest to that, because it was during this period that he kept pestering me to do a pro-Herbert story for *60 Minutes*. It wasn't until the spring of 1972—long after Herbert had hooked up with Wooten—that Lando began to suspect Herbert's claims. However, Herbert refused to accept that version of what had happened, and now, in the aftermath of our interview, he and Lando continued to trade insults and accusations. The exchange grew more and more heated until finally Lando, letting his temper get the best of him, blurted out: "I'll get you, Herbert!"

What Lando meant by that was that he had recourse to libel action, but it was, at best, an ill-advised choice of words, and he would have ample occasion to regret having uttered them.

For they would come back to haunt him many times in the years to come.

Our report, which we called "The Selling of Colonel Herbert," was broadcast in early February 1973. In it we gave Herbert his due, tracing his career from the war-hero days in Korea to the prestige he had recently acquired as the media's favorite martyr. Then, getting down to cases, we juxtaposed his charges with the various contradictions we had recorded from other interviews; but we stopped short of drawing any definitive conclusions. The closest we came to an editorial position was in a pair of observations—one by me and the other by Ken Rosenblum—at the end of the report, and the target of those comments was not Herbert or his adversaries, but the national press. Here's what we had to say:

> WALLACE: The deeper we got into this investigation, the more we felt that the way in which the media—including CBS News—reacted to Herbert's allegations was almost as interesting as Herbert's story itself. Several reporters did make an effort to check out Herbert's story, found his case was far from clear-cut and made that obvious in their reports. But many others did not. *The New York Times* did more, probably, to publicize Tony Herbert's story than any other paper. When Herbert passed a lie-detector test on whether or not he had reported war crimes to Franklin, the *Times* gave it a big play. But when the Army said Colonel Franklin—the man Herbert had accused—had also passed a lie-detector test, other papers reported it, but there was not a word about it in the *Times*.
>
> Attorney Ken Rosenblum, the former Army lawyer who investigated many of Herbert's charges, says the attitude of the media towards Herbert was understandable.

> ROSENBLUM: Well, he's highly decorated and a respected soldier, and he makes these charges and he gets a lot of newspaper coverage about it. Because of the temper of the times and what the country wanted to hear, perhaps, or because the media was looking for another hero, they tended to accept these allegations uncritically.

What's more, they continued to accept them uncritically. Although "The Selling of Colonel Herbert" touched off a brief stir, it did little to shake the faith most of the press and public had in Herbert and his charges. As it turned out, our decision to schedule the report to coincide with the publication of *Soldier* worked to Herbert's advantage. He spent the next few weeks appearing on other television programs, as part of his promotional tour for the book; and on one talk show after another, he seized the opportunity to take us to task. Herbert concentrated most of his fire on Lando, continually repeating the charge that Barry had done a hatchet job on him out of spite for having been spurned as Herbert's literary collaborator. He also contended that the rest of us at *60 Minutes* had been motivated by political considerations. Pointing out that CBS News had aired a number of stories about Vietnam and other military matters that had angered the Nixon administration, Herbert claimed that our piece on him had been an attempt to make amends with the White House and the Pentagon. He offered no concrete evidence to back up these accusations, but he voiced them with his usual conviction and, talk shows being what they are, his assertions invariably went unchallenged. It was then that I began to appreciate more keenly than ever the frustration felt by General Barnes and all the others who maintained that Herbert had misrepresented their motives and actions.

The reviews of *Soldier* were, with rare exception, highly favorable. To cite just one example, the reviewer for *The New Republic* wrote such a glowing paean to Herbert and his cause that the magazine's editors felt constrained to insert a reference to our critical look at him on *60 Minutes*. And to no one's surprise, the book became a best seller. It was clear that the questions raised about him in our broadcast did not seriously impair the process we described in the title of our report. No one could deny that "The Selling of Colonel Herbert" was progressing at a brisk pace. (Students of irony were amused by the fact that the publisher of *Soldier*, Holt, Rinehart and Winston, was part of the CBS conglomerate; indeed, the firm was nothing less than the flagship in CBS's large publishing operation. The irony grew deeper and richer, even touching on the absurd, when Herbert sued CBS—in effect taking legal action against his own publisher—and thereby prompting CBS

Under arrest by two of Chicago's finest on the floor of the
Democratic convention in 1968 *(AP Photo)*

Myron Wallace graduates from Brookline High School, Brookline, Massachusetts, 1935.

Mike and Buff, CBS, 1952 *(CBS News)*

Ensign Wallace (far right, standing) aboard the submarine's tender U.S.S. *Anthedon* in Subic Bay, the Philippines, 1944

Night Beat, December 4, 1956, Channel 5, New York

Ted Yates, producer, Al Ramus, researcher, Mike Wallace, interviewer: Just before a *Night Beat* episode in December 1956

Top, Philip Wylie talks of "Mom" on *Mike Wallace Interviews,*
ABC, Mother's Day, 1957. *(ABC, 1957).* Bottom, Sammy Davis sits for
a *Night Beat* interview, 1957, on Channel 5, New York.

Mickey Cohen gets himself—and us—in trouble on
ABC television, May 1957. *(ABC, 1957)*

Lorraine in front of the Bolshoi Theater, Moscow, November 1958

The late Peter Wallace and his younger brother, Chris, who is now White House correspondent for NBC News, in 1961

1968, New Hampshire before the primary. The candidate keeps the press in line.
(CBS News, Irving Haberman)

Coming home from Vietnam—with some young survivors—for
60 Minutes, June 1970 *(CBS News)*

While the U.S. Senate seeks him in vain, we spend a morning with
William J. Crum, "the money king of Vietnam," aboard his
sailboat in Hong Kong Harbor, June 8, 1971. *(CBS News, Bill Brown)*

With Moshe Dayan at Sharm el-Sheikh in 1971, for *60 Minutes*
(CBS News)

Tales of greed by U.S. big oil companies from the Shah of Iran, in
the first of three interviews on *60 Minutes*, March 1974 *(CBS News)*

Bob Haldeman fails to earn the $100,000 fee CBS paid him for his memoirs, in two television conversations on March 23, 1975, and March 30, 1975. *(CBS News)*

It's one in the morning, GOP convention in 1976, the party's over, and four tired floor correspondents, Dean, Wallace, Rather and Mudd, wait to be debriefed by Cronkite in the anchor booth.
(CBS News)

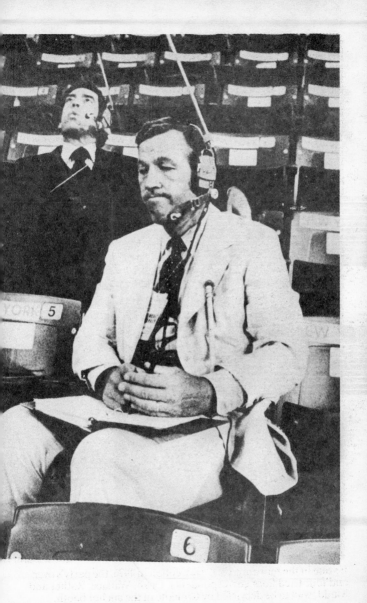

The Maestro, piano virtuoso Vladimir Horowitz, in a singular television interview for *60 Minutes,* on December 26, 1977 *(CBS News)*

Two boys from Brookline, Massachusetts. "Lenny" Bernstein on *60 Minutes,* February 1980 *(CBS News)*

The Wallaces at home in New York, 1982
(Women's Wear Daily)

Pacific Palisades, July 1980. A week before his nomination, the candidate's wife breaks the tension after a tough, on-camera session with him in their living room. The candidate's feet are at lower right. *(CBS News)*

The four of us at play, in 1981, with our faithful assistants. Obscured in the back row, Patti Hassler, now a *60 Minutes* associate producer, Jean Dudasik, to Harry's right, Dawn Akiyama, Bradley's aide, now an actress. And in the front row, Mignette Hollyman, now retired, whose research merits more than I give her here. *(CBS News)*

to respond with a costly legal defense which challenged a story that its own people, at Holt, had purchased, published and promoted. Yes, corporate life in America *is* complicated.)

The libel suit came as a delayed reaction. Nearly a year after we aired the story and shortly before the statute of limitations would have run out, Herbert sued Lando, CBS, *The Atlantic Monthly* (which had published a piece Barry wrote about the broadcast) and me for a total of forty-four million dollars. The main thrust of his suit was that we had committed grave sins of omission. He claimed that we had gathered information, from research and interviews, that would have supported his charges, but that we purposely chose not to include these positive elements in our report. As for motive, he had that part of the script down pat, having rehearsed it so many times on talk shows and other public forums over the past year. Once again, but this time in the formal language of the law, Lando was portrayed as the literary equivalent of a rejected suitor and CBS was accused of defaming Herbert's honor and reputation in order to curry favor with the Pentagon and the Nixon White House, with Wallace serving as CBS's agent in the scheme.

Herbert's suit against us dragged on through the legal process for more than a decade, at a cost of millions of dollars. But partial vindication finally came for us in the fall of 1984 when, in response to our motion for a summary judgment, Federal Judge Charles S. Haight Jr. dismissed eight of the nine libel allegations against CBS. In the aftermath of that decision, all that remained to be resolved was one narrow and debatable claim against one line in the broadcast, and the CBS lawyers were confident that it would not withstand the test of a trial.

In the years leading up to Judge Haight's ruling in our favor, the Herbert case had acquired the stature of a *cause célèbre,* a milestone in the complex field of libel law. It achieved that status largely because of a decision by the U.S. Supreme Court in 1979. In response to a motion filed by Herbert and his lawyers, the Supreme Court ruled, in a six-to-three vote, that a public figure like Herbert has the right to inquire into the thought and editorial processes of anyone who has allegedly defamed him. Many of my colleagues, at CBS News and elsewhere, were and still are deeply disturbed by this decision. They fear that its long-range repercussions may have a chilling and repressive effect on reportorial freedom. I don't share their apprehensions. As long as the libel law requires public figures to prove journalists knew what they broadcast or published was false, or had serious doubts about a story's truth, then it seems to me only reasonable that the plaintiffs be allowed to delve into the area of reporters' thought and editorial processes.

I do know that as far as the Herbert case itself is concerned, my conscience is clear. My opinion of Herbert was shaped by what I read about him, the information Lando gave me, and the interviews that I did. As for Herbert's charges against Lando, I find them particularly ironic. After all, Barry did commence work on the Herbert assignment with a strong belief in the colonel's charges, and it wasn't until he discovered substantial evidence to the contrary that he began to adopt a more skeptical view. And by the time the program was aired, Lando had conducted one of the most thorough and far-reaching investigations I have ever encountered.

As for Tony Herbert, anyone who has spent any time at all with him cannot help but be impressed by his sincerity. And I certainly don't question his bona fides. If he fails to see himself as others see him, well, that hardly makes him unique; most of us suffer from blurred vision in that respect. Thus, I can well understand why Herbert was upset with our *60 Minutes* story on him. But I must also point out that *that* doesn't make him unique either.

"The Selling of Colonel Herbert" was broadcast eight days after a momentous event had taken place in Paris. On January 27, 1973, representatives of the United States, South Vietnam, North Vietnam and the Viet Cong signed a cease-fire agreement. This meant that for the United States at least, the war in Vietnam was finally over. Almost eight years had passed since Lyndon Johnson ordered the huge buildup of American forces that radically changed the scope and complexion of the war; and nearly five years had elapsed since the start of the oft-maligned Paris peace talks. But now, at long last, we had extricated ourselves from the quagmire, and for the next few weeks, we all shared in the joy of those Americans who welcomed home husbands and fathers and sons and brothers, many of whom had languished in prisoner-of-war camps for the past several years.

But the cease-fire accord signed in Paris was so fragile that by the spring of 1973, both the South Vietnamese and the Communists had committed flagrant violations. Heavy fighting resumed in November, and the war continued at a sporadic pace throughout 1974. The occasional lulls in the fighting had less to do with a mutual desire to honor the truce than with internal distractions, as both sides took steps to strengthen their political and economic bases. Then in early January 1975, the North Vietnamese launched what proved to be the decisive offensive of the long war. Within three months, they had seized control of the Central Highlands and were closing in on Saigon. When they captured the capital on April 30, 1975, their victory was complete; and to celebrate it, the Communists renamed Saigon "Ho Chi Minh City."

Like so many others moved to anger and anguish by our participation in that war, I have tried in the years since it ended to put the Vietnam nightmare behind me. It hasn't been easy, especially when I have taken on assignments that dealt directly with the war or its aftermath. For example, in the fall of 1979 I did a follow-up story for *60 Minutes* on three wounded veterans whom I had first met ten years earlier, shortly after they were shipped home from Vietnam without their legs. When I first talked to them—in 1969—they were in the early stages of therapy and rehabilitation. The object of visiting them ten years later was to see how they had coped—and were still coping—with the challenge of going through life severely disabled. At the time of the 1979 update, two powerful and poignant movies about Vietnam veterans, *The Deer Hunter* and *Coming Home,* were playing in theaters around the country, and the message we wanted to emphasize was that the reality of the Vietnam legacy was every bit as wrenching as the fictional stories depicted in those films.

On a much different emotional plane, there was also the ongoing irritation of our protracted litigation with Tony Herbert. Each new development served to remind me (among other things) of the moral ambiguities characteristic of the U.S. involvement in the war. Without putting too fine a point on it, the *60 Minutes* portrait of Herbert as a hero with feet of clay could be viewed as a parable of the overall disillusion we experienced in Vietnam.

For a long time, I assumed that "The Selling of Colonel

Herbert" was to be my last major assignment and my last brush with controversy on a Vietnam-related story. After all, the war was over and with each passing year, it receded more and more into history and away from the province of journalism. But the quarrel with Herbert proved to be a minor flap (at least as far as the general public was concerned) compared with the fire storm that erupted in 1982 when CBS News aired a documentary called "The Uncounted Enemy: A Vietnam Deception." As the correspondent on that *CBS Reports* broadcast, I became embroiled in the furor and libel suit it provoked, and our chief adversary in that dispute was no mere colonel but the man who had served as commander of all U.S. forces in Vietnam, General William C. Westmoreland. However, since the clash with Westmoreland occurred several years later and grew out of circumstances other than those written about in this chapter, we will deal with that episode in its proper context, even at the risk of being accused of saving the best for last.

In the meantime, during the years that *60 Minutes* slowly evolved into a prime-time winner, there were plenty of other trouble spots in the world for us to focus on. As Gay Talese wrote in *The Kingdom and the Power,* his excellent book on *The New York Times:*

> Most journalists are restless voyeurs who see the warts on the world, the imperfections in people and places. The sane scene that is much of life, the great portion of the planet unmarked by madness, does not lure them like riots and raids, crumbling countries and sinking ships, bankers banished to Rio and burning Buddhist nuns—gloom is their game, the spectacle their passion, normality their nemesis.

I agree, and nowhere during those years were the warts on the world more visible than in the Middle East. So, as a "restless voyeur" who was eager to get a first-hand look at the spectacle of people caught up in passions of hatred and terror, I made several visits to that troubled region, so rich in history and so steeped in strife.

CHAPTER

THIRTEEN

EVEN MORE THAN VIETNAM, the Middle East was a sober learning experience for Wallace, for some of the realities he encountered there struck at the core of his ethnic roots. As a Jew growing up in America, he had been taught to believe that the gospel according to Israel was almost as sacred as the Torah itself. Yet the more deeply he delved into the savage desert politics of the Middle East, the more he came to recognize that the Israeli view of the region's past, present and future was not the only defensible position. This shift to a more balanced perception of Israel's historic dispute with its Arab neighbors was gradual and evolved over many years. In the course of that time, Wallace made a dozen or so trips to the Middle East, where he interviewed almost every major political leader, from Golda Meir and Menachem Begin to Anwar Sadat and Yasir Arafat. But no interview on the subject was more important, in terms of its effect on Wallace's own thinking, than one he conducted in New York back in 1957. For that was his first serious encounter with a spokesman for the Palestinian cause and it left an enduring impression on him.

The individual who impressed him so greatly was an Arab scholar named Fayez Sayegh whom Wallace had first met when he was a guest on *Night Beat*. Sayegh's base of operations was the United Nations, even though as a Palestinian he had no formal government to represent; instead, he served as a general counselor to several Arab nations. In those days the forum of American television was rarely made available to any Arab, much less a Palestinian. But Wallace and his producer, Ted Yates, were determined to make waves on *Night Beat,* and their relentless quest for controversial guests and subjects led them to Sayegh. When the program's habitual viewers learned that Wallace had booked an interview with a Palestinian, some no doubt anticipated a stereotype, a scruffy-looking fanatic who, when goaded by Mike's provocative questions, would launch into an anti-Israel tirade and thus provide the verbal fireworks that had become the trademark of *Night Beat* and its host. They were in for a surprise because Sayegh was a refined intellectual who spoke in a rational, low-key manner, but with an intensity of feeling that was far more effective than shrill rhetoric. In other words, as a precursor of future Arab leaders Wallace would meet and interview, Fayez Sayegh was more of an Anwar Sadat than a Yasir Arafat.

Wallace was so impressed and stimulated by Sayegh that he invited him home to dinner the following week, a social courtesy he seldom extended to guests on the program. The two men talked for several hours that night, first over dinner, then over coffee; or to be more accurate, Wallace listened as Sayegh elaborated on the tragic dilemma of the Middle East from a Palestinian point of view. He talked about the home he had lost in Palestine (which had also been his father's and grandfather's home) and about the beautiful orange groves surrounding it, in which he had played as a child. He did not proselytize—at least not in a heavy-handed way—and when Wallace countered with all the arguments he had been trained to deliver on behalf of Israel, Sayegh acknowledged that the Israelis did indeed have a case. The difference, he said, was that the American public had almost no knowledge or appreciation of the fact that the Palestinians also had a case, both historically and morally. That was because the U.S. government and press invariably accepted the Israeli position as the only legitimate one and never bothered to question any of Israel's claims, even those that were clearly dubious.

In later years this would become less true. But in 1957 there was no denying that in terms of official policy and public opinion in America, Israel had everything its own way. Nor was there any doubt where Wallace stood on the issue. Although he was no militant crusader for Zionism, he was staunchly pro-

Israel and in that regard he was completely in step with the vast majority of Americans—Gentiles and Jews. Yet his intellectual curiosity was such that he found Fayez Sayegh fascinating, in much the same way that he later found Malcolm X fascinating. He grew to respect both men because they were fresh and eloquent voices that challenged the conventional American wisdom. Through his contacts with Malcolm, he came to a deeper understanding of blacks and race relations in America, and from Sayegh he gained similar insights into the Palestinians and their historic grievances.

One reason that Wallace was able to respond to someone like Sayegh with a relatively open mind was because he was not locked into an ethnocentric view of the world. Unlike so many of his co-religionists, especially of an earlier generation, he was not inclined to assess every new argument and situation in terms of the question Is this good for the Jews or is this bad for the Jews? He had not been brought up that way. Of course, as the son of Russian-Jewish immigrants, Mike was nurtured on the traditional values of his faith and culture. At the same time, his parents, having found a new home and a new life in America, almost never talked about the old country, the Russia they had left, no doubt because their memories of it brought them little comfort and joy. And when it came to religion, Mike's mother enrolled the family in a Reform temple, where the emphasis was on modern flexibility and a less stringent approach to ritual.

In the years that followed, he continued in that direction. Two of his three marriages were to Gentiles, and his third wife, Lorraine, came from a strong background in another culture and religion. (Her French father had been a priest in his youth. During World War I he had fought as a priest at Verdun, where he was gassed and nearly died. Not long thereafter, he came to the United States to study, and eventually lost his vocation and left the priesthood. Later, he married and wound up in Los Angeles as a professor, teaching French civilization at UCLA. Lorraine was born and raised in Los Angeles, though she always identified more with her father's Gallic spirit and style than with the values and ethos of southern California.) As a young adult, Wallace ceased to be a practicing Jew, at least in the religious sense. He stopped going to temple on a regular basis and, as noted in an earlier chapter, had no qualms about conducting business over lunch on Yom Kippur, the most somber and sacred of Jewish holidays. Indeed, on several occasions over the years, Mike has readily described himself as a "backsliding Jew." And the time would come when fervent Zionists would be so upset by some of Wallace's reporting from the Middle East that they would denounce him as a "self-hating Jew," a traitor to his people and heritage.

But back in 1957 neither Wallace nor anyone else suspected it would ever come to that. For even though he was receptive to Fayez Sayegh's point of view, he did not embrace his point of view any more than he embraced the black-supremacy beliefs Malcolm X preached at Muslim rallies. Backsliding Jew or no, his sympathies and commitment remained solidly on the side of Israel. Still, he made a point of keeping in touch with Sayegh, who proved to be a useful and valuable contact; in the years ahead, he often served as Wallace's entree into the alien Arab world. Just as Malcolm X eventually regarded Mike as one of the few white reporters he felt he could trust, so Sayegh assured his Arab brothers that Wallace was one American Jew who was at least willing to listen to the other side. And given the prevailing climate at the time, they could not ask for more than that.

It was against this background that Wallace made his first trip to the Middle East, a visit to Cairo that could not have been more inauspicious. The year was 1958. By then, he had moved from *Night Beat* to its successor on the ABC television network, *The Mike Wallace Interview.* This was the period when his *bête noire* at ABC, John Daly, was dismissing him with the sneer that he was a "mere interviewer," and Mike was grasping at every opportunity to strengthen his credentials as a journalist. The trip to Cairo was one such grasp.

Egyptian representatives in New York had led Wallace to believe that if he went to Cairo, he would be permitted to interview Gamal Abdel Nasser, then the most powerful and most important figure in the Arab world. So, accompanied by his two closest colleagues at the time, Ted Yates and Al Ramrus, Wallace flew to the Egyptian capital. But even though they explored all the avenues of approach that were open to them,

Mike and his group didn't get anywhere near Nasser. Their various contacts, official and otherwise, counseled them to be patient; they were urged to relax, to take in the pyramids and other tourist sights, and in due course they would be given an appointment with President Nasser. One week went by, then another; by then it was obvious that neither the Egyptians in New York nor the contacts in Cairo had any real influence over Nasser, and that Nasser himself had no intention of granting an interview to this upstart visitor from American television. So Wallace, Yates and Ramrus had to fly back to New York empty-handed. (That fruitless endeavor was similar to a wild-goose chase that Wallace and Yates had embarked on a few months earlier when they flew to Miami and a rendezvous with Cuban exiles who had promised to get them into Cuba for an interview with Fidel Castro, then still a guerrilla leader hiding out in the mountains. On that occasion they had struck out as well. Still, both ventures had been enterprising gambles that were well worth the effort; a television interview with either Nasser or Castro would have been a major coup. But as Wallace and his cohorts took off on the long flight home from Cairo, they were well aware that the Daly faction at ABC would not choose to see it that way.)

Wallace's first trip to Israel came two years later, in 1960, and—in stark contrast to the frustration he experienced in Egypt—it was altogether memorable and rewarding. The event that prompted the visit seemed on the surface to be rather frivolous. The movie version of Leon Uris's novel *Exodus* was being filmed in Israel, and its producer-director, Otto Preminger, invited Mike and other reporters to Israel to help publicize the picture. But this particular trip was different from other Hollywood junkets because as far as the Israelis were concerned, *Exodus* was not a typical Hollywood movie. Since the film depicted the armed struggle to establish the modern state of Israel, its making was viewed as a cause for national celebration, and the country's political leaders were only too happy to bask in the reflected glory. Thus, in addition to the routine chitchat with the stars of the movie (Paul Newman and Eva Marie Saint), Wallace met and interviewed three high-ranking government officials who, in the years to come, would lead Israel through one major crisis after another. There weren't many Hollywood junkets that offered reporters an opportunity to interview the likes of Golda Meir, Moshe Dayan and Abba Eban.

Israel was twelve years old in 1960, and as the young nation approached its thirteenth birthday—a traditional milestone in Jewish law and life—a festive spirit of bar mitzvah was very much in the air. Wallace was deeply impressed by the exuberance and vitality he encountered everywhere he went in Israel during the two weeks he spent there. It was plain that the Israelis, having survived their early years of growth and uncertainty, were now ready to meet the challenge of maturity. As a Jew, Wallace naturally felt a special kind of pride in the triumph of modern Israel. He could identify easily with its people, especially with those who, like his own parents, had fled the ghettos and persecutions of Eastern Europe to seek a better life in a new world; or in the case of Israel, a new country in an old world.

So that first visit to Israel in 1960 was a stirring emotional experience for Wallace, and he returned to New York more convinced than ever that the Zionists were right and their enemies were wrong. He believed not only that Israel had a historic right to exist, but also that Israel's principal ally—the United States—had an obligation to take whatever steps might be necessary to safeguard that existence.

The next time Wallace visited Israel was seven years later, by which time he was firmly established at CBS News. In fact, this was the spring of 1967, and he had just completed his two-month hitch as a war correspondent in Vietnam. On returning to New York, Mike was told that his next assignment was to work on a *CBS Reports* documentary about some of the domestic problems then besetting Israel: soaring unemployment and a disturbingly sharp rise in juvenile delinquency. Israel, it seemed, was going through a troubled adolescence, and the hour-long broadcast would be structured around the question What has happened to the Israeli dream? But before the project could get off the drawing board, the Six-Day War broke out, and it quickly became clear that there was no need to worry about the Israelis and their dream. Instead of singing the blues over a few internal problems, the Israelis and their friends were

raising their voices to hail the conquering heroes. The overwhelming victories over its Arab neighbors greatly strengthened
Israel's geographic position and made its borders more secure
than ever.

Wallace and Charles Collingwood co-anchored the network's coverage of the conflict from the CBS "war room" in
New York. Then, as soon as the fighting stopped, Mike was
dispatched to Tel Aviv to put together an overview report on
the history of the brief war, an "instant special," as it's known
in the trade. He did not embark on the assignment with his
customary zest and energy. For one thing, he was physically
drained from his two months in Vietnam, not to mention the
long hours and heavy strain of co-anchoring all the shifts and
developments in the Six-Day War. Moreover, he was in low
spirits and had been for the past several days, ever since he
received word that Ted Yates, his close friend and colleague
from the *Night Beat* and ABC years, had been killed in Jerusalem while covering the first day of the war for NBC News.
The day Yates died, Mike wrote a eulogy to him that he broadcast on his daily radio program *Personal Close-up*. In the piece
he recalled the years they had worked together, paid tribute to
Yates's courage and journalistic skills, then closed with these
words:

> To hear of Ted Yates's reportorial capacities and exploits,
> one would think he was a big, bluff man's man. He was
> all of that. But he was also one of the gentlest men I ever
> knew—sensitive, incapable of cruelty, fine and honest, a
> dear and devoted friend. His wife, Mary, and his three sons,
> Ted and Eames and Angus, and all the friends who worked
> with him and loved him will miss him very much.

Wallace spent several days in Israel, gathering material for the
instant special broadcast: "How Israel Won the War." Accompanied by the renowned military expert S.L.A. Marshall, Mike
and his camera crew toured all the major battlefields, from the
West Bank to the Golan Heights to the Sinai Peninsula, all the
territories that had belonged, respectively, to Jordan, Syria and
Egypt but which were now under Israeli occupation. From
interviews with Israeli officers and Marshall's perceptive ob-

servations, he was able to recreate the strategy and tactics that produced such swift and decisive victories on three separate fronts. Having just spent two months looking for the light at the end of the tunnel in Vietnam, Wallace was struck by the contrast between the two wars. If Vietnam was for the United States the wrong war in the wrong place at the wrong time (as Mike now believed to be the case), then just the opposite was true of Israel's clash with the Arabs in June 1967. Israel went to war that spring for the best of all possible reasons: Overt acts of aggression that threatened its vital interests had been committed by enemies bent on bringing an end to its existence as a state. Indeed, an Israeli defeat in the war would have been tantamount to national extinction. There was no moral ambiguity in Israel's position, and therefore no need to act with restraint and uncertainty; and instead of getting bogged down in a quagmire, it struck with all the speed and force it could muster and achieved a stunning, clear-cut victory.

In addition to reporting on all that, Wallace also captured on film the spirit of unbridled exultation that engulfed Israel in those first heady days after the war—for this, too, was part of the story. It was a glorious moment for the Israelis, that spring and summer of 1967, and only later would Wallace and others come to look back on it as the high-water mark in the country's brief history. For the truth is that Israel would never again stand quite so tall in the eyes of the world.

In the immediate aftermath of the Six-Day War, Israeli officials kept insisting that they did not want to maintain permanent possession of the Arab territories they had captured and presently occupied. Their avowed plan, or hope, was to use the Sinai, the Golan Heights and the West Bank as bargaining chips in direct peace negotiations with the Arabs. Specifically the Israelis said they were willing to give up all or most of the conquered territories if, in exchange, the Arabs would negotiate a formal peace treaty with them and officially recognize the state of Israel. But the Arab governments would have no part of that proposal; they demanded that Israel must first return all the occupied land, and only then would they consider the question of direct negotiations toward a permanent peace and formal recognition of Israel. As a result, there was no real peace in the Middle East after the Six-Day War, but only a fragile cease-fire that was frequently violated by both sides; and the fighting and killing continued at a sporadic pace over the next several years. In the meantime, the Israeli position hardened. Toward the end of 1967, Israel began moving settlers into the occupied territories, an act that seemed to belie its claim that it had no desire to incorporate them into a Greater Israel. And when Wallace returned to Tel Aviv in January 1969 to do a *60 Minutes* story on the current situation in Israel, he was told by Defense Minister Moshe Dayan—the great hero of the Six-Day War—that Israel had no intention of giving up the conquered territories and going back to its pre-1967 borders. That prompted Mike to ask if Israel would agree to return to the old borders in exchange for "a real peace."

"No," Dayan replied, "not even for a real peace."

The intransigence of the Israeli government could be attributed in large part to its growing arrogance. Even before the Six-Day War, many Israelis evinced a rather haughty attitude toward their Arab neighbors, a clear sense of ethnic and cultural superiority. The 1967 victory, and especially the ease with which it was accomplished, reinforced the notion that the Arabs were confused and pathetic losers who could be treated with disdain, both on and off the battlefield, and many of the Israeli government's statements and actions reflected that sentiment. As a result, after the 1967 war Israel began to suffer its first serious setbacks in the sphere of propaganda and public relations. Even some of its most loyal friends and allies began to criticize the Israeli government for its obdurate political stand and aggressive military actions, which included occasional air raids that struck hospitals and other civilian targets. Contributing to this subtle shift in international opinion was the fact that Egypt, under the leadership of its new president, Anwar Sadat, was moving toward a more flexible diplomatic position—and winning friends in the process. Wallace duly noted this change in the spring of 1971 when he made another trip to Israel for *60 Minutes*. His interview with Dayan on that occasion led to this exchange:

> WALLACE: General, I think there is a feeling developing in the United States right now that Egypt is showing reason about the matter of peace, the recognition of Is-

rael—for the first time—and that Israel is being unreasonable, stiff-necked.

DAYAN: Yes, so I hear, so I hear.

WALLACE: Are you worried about the fact that public opinion in the United States is changing against Israel to some extent?

DAYAN: Yes, yes, I'm worried and I don't like it.

But he was not worried enough to relax his position regarding Israeli occupation of the Sinai. Because Dayan and Israel's prime minister, Golda Meir, viewed their Arab counterparts with a certain condescension, they failed to appreciate that in Sadat, Egypt had a president who was not only more flexible than Nasser but also more formidable. That was demonstrated in 1972 when Sadat expelled all Soviet military experts and advisers from Egypt, thereby strengthening his own authority and independence, and even more so in the fall of the following year when he launched the Yom Kippur War—and dealt another sharp blow to Israel's image.

Not that the Egyptians and Syrians could claim to have won the 1973 war; after sustaining some early losses, Israel seized the initiative and was clearly in command when, after eighteen days of fighting, a United Nations cease-fire resolution was adopted. But the Egyptians fought with an efficiency and élan that they had not displayed previously, and this alone was enough to shatter the aura of invincibility that had surrounded Israel since 1967. Especially was this true in the early stages of the war when the Arabs won several key battles and inflicted heavy casualties on the Israelis. Those casualties were a harsh reminder to Israel that, with its small population, it could ill afford to wage recurring wars of attrition, and therefore could not afford to be quite so cavalier in its attitude toward Arab demands and war threats. For the Egyptians the Yom Kippur War helped exorcise the humiliation they had suffered six years earlier; now that they had recaptured a large measure of their self-esteem, they were more confident of being able to deal with the Israelis on an equal footing. Thus, the stage was set for the bold diplomatic breakthrough that Anwar Sadat initiated in the middle 1970s.

In the meantime, Wallace was becoming acquainted with the disparate and often conflicting forces that made the Arab world such a turmoil of contradictions. From 1970 to 1975, various assignments for *60 Minutes* took him to Egypt, Libya, Saudi Arabia, Lebanon, Jordan and Syria—and he discovered that each country viewed the Middle East dilemma from its own special perspective. His trip to Cairo in March 1970 came just as the Nasser era was drawing to a close. When the volatile Egyptian ruler died of a heart attack later that year, his prestige was at a low ebb. The crushing defeat by Israel in the Six-Day War exposed Nasser as a paper tiger who had failed miserably in his attempt to carry out his bellicose threats, and during the last three years of his life he had to live with the daily humiliation of Israeli occupation troops on Egyptian soil. He remained, to the end, the most prominent figure in the Arab world, but by 1970 his power and influence had greatly diminished. Among the casualties of the 1967 war was Nasser's grandiose dream of becoming "the New Saladin," the architect of a loose but cohesive federation of all Arab peoples, from the Sahara to the Persian Gulf, that would flourish in unity under his leadership.

Wallace had gone to Egypt with producer Palmer Williams to do a story on the general mood of the country three years after the Six-Day War, but he had no more success in getting interviews with Nasser and other high-ranking officials than he had on his first visit to Cairo back in 1958. Having broken off diplomatic relations with Washington in the aftermath of the 1967 war, Nasser was now even less responsive to requests from the American media. But Wallace did catch a glimpse of the man who would soon be succeeding Nasser. He was most unimpressed by what he saw and heard about Anwar Sadat. When Sadat was pointed out to Wallace at a civil-defense rally in Cairo, his eager-to-please smile flashing forth from a face bathed in perspiration projected the image of a very nervous and banal bureaucrat. An obsequious hack, thought Wallace at the time, and in fact, Sadat did have a reputation in those days of being a fawning deputy. The derisive nickname for him in those days was "Nasser's poodle," a sobriquet that Wallace would recall with relish in an interview with Sadat several years later when the Egyptian leader was at the height of his power.

From the land of the pyramids to the shores of Tripoli: In early 1972, Wallace went to Libya with producer Meg Osmer to do a profile of Colonel Muammar Qaddafi, then emerging as a strident new voice in the Middle East. Like his hero, Nasser, Qaddafi preached the need for Arab unity, and—also like Nasser—he envisioned himself as the Man of Destiny who would ultimately lead the Arab forces in their crusade to purge the region of what he called "the filth of Zionism."

For the time being, however, Qaddafi was content to rule his desert country with a puritanical zeal that would have warmed the hearts of those earnest souls who founded the Women's Christian Temperance Union and the Anti-Saloon League. Shortly after he assumed power, he imposed a strict ban on the sale and consumption of all alcoholic beverages. By 1972 it was impossible to get an alcoholic drink of any kind anywhere in Libya, and needless to say that drab state of affairs struck most visiting American journalists as inhospitable in the extreme. But there was no fighting City Hall, for the rigidly enforced prohibition was in keeping with Qaddafi's fervent Muslim beliefs. At one point, while he was being interviewed by Wallace, Qaddafi suddenly stood up, walked over to a corner of the room, spread out a rug on the floor, kneeled down toward Mecca and—as the CBS camera continued to roll—began to pray. A few moments later, having completed his communion with Allah, Qaddafi stood up, returned to his chair opposite Wallace and proclaimed that he was ready to resume the interview. (It's entirely possible that resorting to prayer in such an ostentatious manner is a tactic or diversion that has crossed the minds of other harried Wallace interviewees over the years, but Qaddafi is the only one who ever acted on that impulse.) In that interview Qaddafi explained that his sole guide on matters of faith and morals was the Koran, and the Koran strictly forbids the drinking of all alcoholic beverages, even wine. But as Mike wryly pointed out in his *60 Minutes* piece of Qaddafi, the holy book of Islam is not so severe in its attitude toward other forms of relaxation. "On the subject of wives," he noted, "the Koran generously allows four."

•   •   •

Qaddafi was one of the first Arab leaders to recognize the potential of oil as a weapon to be used against the supporters of Israel. In 1973 he seized control of all the foreign oil companies in Libya and imposed an embargo on all petroleum shipments from his country to the United States. "The time has come," he said, "for us to deal America a strong slap on its cool, arrogant face." Far more worrisome to Washington and other Western capitals, however, were the actions taken that year by the powerful oil cartel OPEC (Organization of Petroleum Exporting Countries). Its decision to cut back on oil production and drastically raise the price of its exports sent a shock wave of inflation through the U.S. and other Western economies. The strongest voice in the OPEC cartel was that of Sheik Ahmed Zaki Yamani, the oil minister of Saudi Arabia. As the world's largest exporter of petroleum, Saudi Arabia was the richest of all the oil-rich Arab states; and it was also the most traditional and stable country in the Arab world.

On the surface Saudi Arabia was every bit as straitlaced and abstemious as Libya under Qaddafi. There, too, the consumption of liquor and other Western vices—such as women appearing in public without veils—were strictly forbidden by law. But beneath the surface there were sybaritic diversions to be found in Saudi Arabia, as Wallace happily discovered when he went there with producer Bill McClure in early 1974 to do a story on Zaki Yamani. As the dominant figure within the OPEC cartel, Yamani was then perhaps the most influential force in the vast and complex world of international commerce. Like all Saudis, he had been reared as an orthodox Muslim, but he also had been educated at Harvard University, where he had acquired a taste for certain pleasures peculiar to Western culture. And it was that side of Yamani, the Western sophisticate, who welcomed Wallace to Saudi Arabia in 1974.

Mike had been told in advance that when he arrived in Riyadh, the Saudi capital, he would be met at the airport and escorted to Yamani's maisonette in the Hotel Al-Yamama, where a dinner party was to be held in his honor. This alone was an unexpected courtesy (American journalists were rarely accorded the red-carpet treatment in Arab countries), but the big surprise was the party itself. When he arrived at Yamani's home, Mike was greeted by the following scene: a live jazz quartet in full swing, playing with all the verve of a Harlem jam session . . . a bevy of extremely attractive Saudi women, unveiled and dressed to the nines in the latest European fashions . . . his host, Sheik Yamani, lounging on the floor and caressing his Pomeranian dog . . . and (the stern edict of the Koran notwithstanding) all varieties of liquor in great abundance. Wallace and the other guests were treated then to a splendid gourmet dinner, which Mike washed down with enough vodka to give him a paralyzing hangover the next morning. It was, in short, a festive night, but it was also the kind of party that could only have been held within the confines of a private and highly privileged home. That point was made crystal clear when it came time to leave and all the women in their Paris originals donned black veils, which they were still required by Saudi law and tradition to wear in public.

The next evening, after he slept off his jet lag and hangover, Wallace did a long interview with Yamani at the oil minister's office. Then, once again, he was invited to dine with Yamani and his friends, and this time, when he arrived at the sheik's home, he found a small group of Saudis watching television and filling the air with laughter. Mike glanced at the television set and saw a face so familiar—yet so completely out of context—that he had to smile. It had taken him twenty hours to fly to this remote and insular country—this land of Mecca, this seat of Islam—and now he was watching—on cassette— *The Dean Martin Show* in a setting reminiscent of a New York dinner party. Yamani arrived a few minutes later, and soon thereafter another superb meal was served. After they finished eating, Mike turned to the sheik and said: "That's simply wonderful food. Who's your cook?"

"Promise not to tell anybody?"

"Okay, sure."

"My mother." Then with a chuckle, Yamani added: "You could almost say my Jewish mother."

"What do you mean, your *Jewish* mother?"

"My mother lives over in Medina, which is seven hundred miles away. But three times a week she cooks my dinner and has it flown here on Saudia Airlines. I then arrange to have it picked up at the airport and warmed in my oven. So I guess you could say that three times a week, I get to eat Mama's chicken soup."

Wallace was entertained by Yamani's seductive charm and good humor, though he suspected that much of what he had seen and enjoyed during his stay in Riyadh had been set up for his benefit. He knew that jazz and free-flowing booze and droll remarks about Jewish mothers and chicken soup were not at all characteristic of King Faisal's conservative and autocratic regime, then ruling Saudi Arabia. Yet he also recognized that the Saudis were going through a dramatic transition. For centuries the desert kingdom had been a stagnant and feudal society, a repressive and theocratic monarchy that viewed all progressive elements in other cultures with suspicion, if not downright hostility. But now, because of their enormous wealth, the Saudis had to deal more and more directly with the outside world, the modern world, and such constant exposure was having an effect on attitudes and behavior within their country. By the early 1970s, the Old Guard, with its rigid adherence to the letter of Islamic law, was steadily losing ground to bright young technocrats like Yamani who, having been educated in the West, had learned to appreciate the value of pragmatism and flexibility.

Nevertheless, the change was gradual; Saudi society was still more traditional and its government far more conservative than those of most of its Arab neighbors. Indeed, much of King Faisal's enmity toward the state of Israel stemmed from his morbid belief that Zionism was a form of Communism, and therefore a potential threat to autocratic regimes like his own. But as a citadel of wealth and stability in a turbulent region, Saudi Arabia had a heavy stake in the establishment of order in the Middle East, and for that reason Faisal chose to pursue a course of moderation toward an eventual peaceful solution of the longstanding Arab-Israeli feud. That policy, in turn, brought the Saudis into conflict with more militant Arab leaders, such as Libya's Colonel Qaddafi, Syria's President Assad and, above all, the radical Palestinians who by this time were waging a war of terrorism against Israel and its allies.

In May 1973, *60 Minutes* broadcast a story titled "Palestine: A Nation in Exile." Mike Wallace was the correspondent who, with producer Bill McClure, put together that report, which he began as follows:

> This month, while three million Israelis celebrate their nation's twenty-fifth anniversary, three million Palestinians—stateless, scattered throughout the countries of the Middle East—look to Jerusalem and Tel Aviv with bitterness and longing. They are the new Diaspora: refugees, exiles from Palestine.
>
> Many of them have lived out the years of Israel's nationhood in the squalor of the camps of Jordan and Syria, Gaza and Lebanon. Out of the misery of their sad quarter century, the Palestinians have developed a nationhood in exile, a politics of frustration. They are fueled by anger at the Israelis, and disillusioned by those Arab brothers who, they fear, would abandon them to secure a settlement with Israel.
>
> It was these Palestinians, after the Arab rout in the Six-Day War, who picked up the fallen Arab banner. They vowed vengeance. While the armies of Egypt, Syria and Jordan reeled from their humiliation by the Israelis, the Palestinians began to train again, became the vanguard of a slowly reawakened Arab pride, folk heroes in the Arab world.

Then he traced the evolution of that resistance movement, from the birth of the Palestine Liberation Organization (PLO), the one official guerrilla force the Arab governments established in 1964, to the outbreak of terrorist activities in the early seventies, most of which were carried out by an ultra-radical splinter group that called itself "Black September." That faction took its name from the results of a spectacular incident that occurred in 1970. In September of that year, Palestinian terrorists hijacked three New York-bound airliners in Europe—one from TWA, one from BOAC and one from Swissair—and diverted them to a desert airstrip in Jordan, where they blew them up.

Until that time, Palestinian guerrillas had been using Jordan as their main sanctuary and training base, and King Hussein had given his tacit blessing to that arrangement. But Hussein professed to be outraged by the Black September hijacking. Moreover, he was alarmed because he had come across evidence that at least one commando group was plotting to overthrow his government; so he ordered the Jordanian Army into action against the Palestinian guerrillas. Ten days of fierce fighting ensued, with heavy casualties on both sides, but by the end of September, Hussein's superior forces had succeeded in driving the guerrillas out of Jordan.

They eventually regrouped in Lebanon, where their presence triggered a bitter civil war, and afterward, a state of political and military chaos persisted until Israel launched its controversial invasion of Lebanon in 1982. (As it turned out, this invasion did little to resolve the chaos in Lebanon. In the aftermath of Israel's attack on Arab strongholds, U.S. marines and troops from three other countries, Britain, France and Italy, were sent to Lebanon as a peacekeeping force, and were soon caught up in the bloodshed of the civil war. In October 1983, 241 American marines were killed in a terrorist assault on their compound at the Beirut airport; it was the worst disaster to befall the U.S. military since the war in Vietnam.) But back in the early seventies, when Arab terrorism was just emerging as a tactic in the Middle East conflict, the big story was the killing of nine Israeli athletes at the 1972 Olympic Games in Munich.

This tragedy was still fresh in everyone's mind when Wallace went to the Middle East in the spring of 1973 to gather material for his story on the Palestinians. One of the questions he sought to answer was whether Black September was directly connected to the official guerrilla force, the Palestine Liberation Organization. By then, a Jerusalem-born engineer named Yasir Arafat had emerged as the leader of the PLO. In those days, however, Arafat was still an elusive figure who as a rule did not make himself available to American reporters. So when Wallace visited the PLO headquarters in Beirut, he had to settle for an interview with one of Arafat's top aides, Kamal Nasser, who was then known as the poet laureate of the Palestine movement.

As a poet and propagandist Kamal Nasser (no relation to the late Egyptian president) preferred to wage war with words rather than guns. Yet he still thought of himself as a guerrilla, a committed soldier in the struggle to liberate Palestine. When

Wallace interviewed him in his tiny, heavily guarded apartment that was not even visible from the street, Nasser flatly denied that Black September's actions had been sanctioned by the PLO.

Moreover, he was eager to get this message across to the viewers of *60 Minutes*. "Mr. Wallace," he said at one point, "I want you to know and I want the rest of the American public opinion to know that if we were Black September, if we had anything to do with it, be sure that we are not scared of anybody to announce this fact to the whole world. Had we been Black September, had we understood the revolution in terms of Black September, we would just tell the whole world. But we are not." Nasser also contended that the Palestinians were "more advanced politically, intellectually, than many of the Arab regimes." And he insisted that despite his hatred of Zionism, he remained an admirer of the Jewish people, whom he remembered fondly from the days "when they were living with us in Palestine." That led to his striking declaration that the ultimate goal of the PLO was to save both "the Palestinians and the Jews from Zionism."

In listening to Nasser, Wallace could hear echoes of conversations he had had with Fayez Sayegh back in New York. The two men were similar in many respects. They were both intellectuals who in a happier time would have concentrated their talents on more contemplative pursuits, such as writing books and teaching at a university. And although they were impassioned believers in the cause they shared, they were rational men who, given their strong sense of history, were able to define the issues and identify their enemies in clear and precise terms. For example, they both went out of their way to draw a distinction between anti-Zionism and anti-Semitism. (In fact, Sayegh often took pleasure in pointing out that the Arabs themselves were Semites.) But the image of Palestinian resistance then being transmitted to the rest of the world was not that of men like Fayez Sayegh and Kamal Nasser. When it came to getting attention, their mere words of protest could not compete with the savage acts of violence being committed by Black September and other terrorists.

Israeli intelligence officials did not accept Nasser's assertion that Black September was acting independently of the PLO and Yasir Arafat. They claimed to have evidence linking the two groups, which meant that in their eyes Nasser was a terrorist and therefore a menace to Israel. What's more, they did not hesitate to act on that premise. Three days after Wallace interviewed Nasser, an Israeli commando unit penetrated into the heart of Beirut, found Nasser in his bed and shot him in cold blood. When the news of the deed reached Wallace, he had already left Lebanon, but he had every reason to believe he was the last Western journalist to have seen Kamal Nasser alive.

From Beirut, Mike and his camera crew flew to Jordan, where they filmed some of the Palestinian refugee camps that had spawned the terrorists of Black September. In his report he observed that the congestion and squalor of those camps made them a natural breeding ground for the kind of bitterness and despair that finds expression in acts of terror, which he described as "the weapon of the desperate and the weak." The CBS News team then drove across the Allenby Bridge into Israel, and on arriving in Tel Aviv, one of the first persons Wallace interviewed was Aharon Yaariv, the former head of Israeli intelligence. It was from Yaariv that he heard the details of the raid in Beirut and the dispatch of Kamal Nasser. In a tone that Wallace found offensive in a man he rather liked, Yaariv said: "Of course, we didn't kill him immediately because he was in bed with two women. First, we let the women go, and *then* we killed him."

Later, after he had returned to the States, Wallace learned from sources within the Arab community that some members of the PLO were blaming him for Nasser's death. He stood accused of having fingered the location of Nasser's apartment to the Israelis. Through its own intelligence network, the PLO had traced Wallace's movements from Lebanon to Jordan and thence to Tel Aviv, where one of the first persons he talked to was the former head of Israeli intelligence. Mike was warned that he should not return to Lebanon as long as the PLO maintained its headquarters there. He had no way of knowing how serious that threat was, but he wasn't about to take any reckless chances. Although Wallace made several more trips to the Middle East over the next few years, he did not set foot again on Lebanese soil until 1979, when he went to interview Yasir Arafat himself. And as we shall see, that visit did not exactly put him in good odor with the PLO either.

• • •

Each of these experiences—from the *Night Beat* interview with Fayez Sayegh and the initial visits to Egypt and Israel in the fifties and sixties to the various pieces he did on the Middle East during the early years of *60 Minutes*—was part of the learning process. Together, they deepened his awareness of the complex issues and simmering passions that made the region such a fascinating and yet dangerous place. Moreover, they served as a kind of initiation, a prelude to the strong and perceptive reporting Wallace did on the Middle East during the middle and late 1970s, a body of work that stands out as one of the major accomplishments of his career.

Some of those assignments also plunged him into fresh waters of controversy. For it was during this period that he was flayed with the charge of betraying his Jewish heritage. This accusation grew out of a 1975 story he did on Syria, which may have the distinction of being the most explosive report ever aired on *60 Minutes*—a large claim, to be sure, but one that cannot easily be dismissed. The furor the report ignited was so intense that its repercussions were felt throughout the CBS hierarchy, even reaching William S. Paley, the imperious chairman of CBS, who presided over the vast corporation he had built from scratch. Like Wallace, Paley was the son of Russian-Jewish immigrants, and he was deeply disturbed by the fact that a program that had aired on *his* network had aroused the wrath of the Jewish lobby and other friends of Israel.

A year or so later, after the storm had subsided, a reporter was interviewing Paley on a variety of matters, and when he casually brought up the Syrian story and the ruckus it had caused, Paley's face clouded over. "A painful experience," he intoned, "a very difficult time for us. All I really care to say about that is thank God we were right, and thank God our correspondent on that story was Mike Wallace." Then in a confidential tone, as though he were revealing a secret known only within the privileged confines of the CBS family, he explained: "Because, you see, Wallace himself is Jewish."

Paley didn't bother to spell it out; in fact, he rather quickly changed the subject. But there was no mistaking his implication that the response to the Syrian story would have been even more hostile if it had been reported by Cronkite or Rather or one of the other non-Jews in the CBS News stable of correspondents. Yet at the time, when all the fur was flying, it's unlikely that he or anyone else would have been able to convince Wallace of that.

I'm sure that the Assad government was aware of the horror stories that had been bandied about in American Jewish circles, and was therefore eager that we see for ourselves how inaccurate they were. For I must say that what we saw bore little resemblance to what I had heard existed, for we found Jews living not just in the Jewish quarter, but outside as well, side by side with Muslims and Christians. We observed schools where Jewish students were allowed to learn at least some of their lessons in Hebrew. A government spokesman told us there were fourteen synagogues in Damascus alone, and when we visited one of them we ran into a young man named Maurice Nusseri. He told us that his father had a flourishing business making objets d'art in copper and brass. I asked him if we could visit his home and talk to his family, and, with only slight hesitation, he proffered an invitation. Arrangements were made and two days later—on Saturday, the Jewish Sabbath—we visited the Nusseri home.

We did not go alone. We were accompanied by three government agents, a circumstance that I took care to point out in our broadcast. In itself this was no big deal because wherever we went in Syria, at least one government official, usually from the Ministry of Information, came along. (Indeed, that kind of escort service is standard operating procedure whenever Western reporters go snooping around in nondemocratic countries.) It turned out that when we arrived at the Nusseri home, Maurice was not there waiting for us, as he had indicated he would be. My suspicions aroused, I immediately asked why he wasn't there.

"Because," said his brother, Albert, "he's gone out to pick up his car."

"His car? But we were under the impression that Jews in Syria were not allowed to drive cars, that they're not permitted to have licenses."

Albert Nusseri gave me a puzzled look, as though he were at a loss to understand where I could have acquired such a strange notion. He replied: "Of course we have licenses. Of course we drive cars."

Since Maurice was not at home, I decided to interview his brother, a pharmacist by trade. Albert actually lived elsewhere with his wife and children, but since it was the Sabbath, they

were visiting his parents. (It's also possible that they wanted
to get a gander at us, the intruders from American television.)
After the camera was set up and we had chatted a bit, I brought
up the question of allegiance:

> WALLACE: Mr. Nusseri, in the case of a war between
> Syria and Israel, would your loyalty go to—would there
> be any division of loyalty between Israel and Syria?
>
> NUSSERI: No. Our loyalty is to Syrian authority. I mean,
> it's not divided . . . I am a Syrian citizen, and that's all.
>
> WALLACE: Of course, your sons aren't old enough, but
> if they were, they could not go into the Syrian Army?
>
> NUSSERI: Now, no, they can't. But I hope that one day
> they will—they will go into the Syrian Army.
>
> WALLACE: Even to fight against Israel, if necessary?
>
> NUSSERI: Of course. Why not?

Later, elaborating on that, he asked me a rhetorical question:
"Wouldn't you feel the same if war came between the United
States and Israel?"

Even as I sat there talking to Nusseri and his family, it
occurred to me that we had been set up. For all McClure and
I knew, the Nusseris were a propaganda tool of the Assad
regime, or to be less sinister about it, they might have been
intimidated by the presence of the three government officials.
I gave that thought plenty of consideration, but in the end I
came away satisfied that the Nusseri family was on the level.
I think I've spent enough time in Jewish households in my life
to know the difference between genuine warmth and a false
front assumed to mislead visitors. And with the Nusseris I
detected no sign of underlying strain or apprehension. Instead,
they gave every indication of being what they claimed to be:
a close, well-to-do Jewish family that was reasonably content
with its lot in life. (I heard later from Jewish organizations in
New York that the Nusseris had been reluctant to receive us,
but felt it was discreet to cooperate with our hosts, the Syrian
authorities. However, when I visited Damascus again nine years

later, in January 1984, that was not what I heard privately from
Maurice Nusseri.)

I also interviewed other Jews in Damascus, notably a teacher
in one of the two schools in the Jewish quarter. She confirmed
that the Jews in Syria were allowed to study Hebrew, attend
synagogue and observe other traditions of their faith and culture. Then I mentioned all the stories I had heard about how
badly the Jews were treated in Syria, and when I asked her
where she thought they came from, she replied in an almost
malevolent tone: "I think that it's Zionist propaganda." That
kind of talk from a Jewish schoolteacher, entrusted with the
development of young Jewish minds, was almost beyond my
comprehension, and I remember thinking, as her answer echoed
in my ears, My God, wait until the folks back home hear *this!*

There was, to be sure, a darker side to Jewish life in Syria
that we did not overlook in our broadcast. Jews could not serve
in the Syrian Army and were rarely allowed to hold a government job of any kind, in large part because they were deemed
to be poor security risks, potential fifth columnists who could
not be trusted in a showdown with Israel. I noted also that they
were not permitted to emigrate or even travel freely within
Syria itself, and that they all had to carry cards which identified
them as Jews. In short, there was no denying that the Jewish
community was kept under close surveillance and that it had
to abide by certain restrictions. But then again that fate was
shared, at least to some degree, by the entire Syrian populace.
Although Syria billed itself as a socialist republic, the Assad
government was a brutally repressive regime, a veritable police
state, and it did not pretend to be in sympathy with democratic
principles.

At the urging of Syrian officials, we traveled to the ancient
city of Quneitra, located near the Syrian-Israeli border. Until
1967 Quneitra had been one of Syria's major agricultural centers, with a population of about fifty thousand. But during the
Six-Day War, Israel seized control of Quneitra and proceeded
to occupy it over the next several years. Then came the 1973
war, and once again Quneitra was transformed into a fierce
battleground. When the UN cease-fire brought an end to that
conflict, Israel still had control of the city, but in the ensuing
negotiations, the Assad government demanded the return of

Quneitra as the price Israel would have to pay to get its prisoners of war back from Syria, and the Israelis reluctantly agreed. However, when the time came to evacuate, the Israelis destroyed most of what was left of the ancient city, reducing it to virtual rubble. That, at least, was the Syrian version of what had happened. The Israelis claimed that all the damage to Quneitra had been done during the war itself.

When we visited Quneitra, we found sufficient evidence to support the Syrian version. Anyone who has ever fought in or covered a war knows that when buildings are shelled by gunfire, they become permanently scarred with pockmarks. But as I walked through the ruins of Quneitra, I noticed that many of the destroyed buildings had not been damaged that way. Instead, they had simply been demolished, razed to the ground, and in front of some of them, we found bulldozer tracks. Moreover, when we talked to members of the UN peacekeeping force stationed there, they corroborated the Syrian allegation. They told us that the Israelis had, in effect, said to the Syrians: You want Quneitra back? Okay, you can have it—decimated. So that, too, went into our broadcast. I reported that the city of Quneitra had been mainly destroyed not by shellfire and war but by bulldozer and dynamite.

By the time McClure and I left Syria, we knew we had a difficult story on our hands, one that was bound to upset those viewers who had been conditioned to regard the complex Middle East conflict in black-and-white terms as a struggle between the Forces of Light (Israel) and the Forces of Darkness (the Syrians and their ilk). Even so, I was not prepared for the firestorm that erupted when we broadcast "Israel's Toughest Enemy" on *60 Minutes* in February 1975. I was hardly a stranger to controversy, but never before had I been swamped by such a deluge of intense and negative reaction. The main thrust of the criticism was that I in particular and CBS News in general had become "dupes of the Arabs."

No doubt, many of the calls and letters and telegrams that came flooding into the offices of *60 Minutes* reflected the sincere, independent concern of individuals who were disturbed by our report. But it was also evident that an organized mail campaign had been launched against us. It's easy to spot that sort of thing. Postcards arrive in bunches with the same post-marks and similar wording. Many of them asked the question "Is Mike Wallace trying to deny he's Jewish?" I also learned that a rabbi sent out a newsletter to the members of his congregation, urging them to write us and complain. In case they hadn't seen the program, he wrote, he would be happy to suggest what they should say. It didn't take a genius to figure out what the impetus was behind all this denunciation.

At that time the so-called Jewish lobby was one of the most powerful pressure groups in America. That is no slur but a simple statement of fact. It was organized, well-financed and extremely savvy, especially when it came to dealing with the media. According to *The Power Peddlers,* a book published in 1977 about the effect of lobbying activities in the United States, "The Israeli lobby is unique among lobby groups with its 'clout' with the press. [No other lobby] has ever succeeded in making reporters look over their shoulders as much as the Israeli lobby."

We were not the first journalists to be raked over the coals for reporting that Jewish life in Syria was not as wretched as it was widely assumed to be. In April 1974 the *National Geographic* published an article in which it made an assertion similar to ours. The writer did not state the case as categorically as we did, but his observations were heretical enough to incur the wrath of the militant American Jewish Congress. Members of the AJC picketed the National Geographic Society's head-quarters in Washington, and applied other forms of pressure to induce a retraction. And they got what they wanted. In November the magazine published a note saying that it had reviewed the evidence germane to the story and had "concluded that our critics were right." It was the first time in the long and estimable history of the *National Geographic* that it had printed that kind of public confession. When we aired our report three months later, the American Jewish Congress, emboldened by its success in getting the *National Geographic* to retract, decided that now it was our turn to be publicly chastised for having strayed from the path of journalistic virtue.

A few days after the broadcast, I received a copy of a letter of complaint that Naomi Levine, the executive director of the AJC, had sent to the Federal Communications Commission.

Then she called me, and requested a meeting with us. Our general policy is to turn down such requests. In almost any story on *60 Minutes*, somebody's ox may be gored, and if we held postmortems with everyone who objected to our reporting, this would take so much time that we wouldn't be able to get any work done on new assignments. That's why we provide a "letters section" at the end of each broadcast as a forum for viewers to air their grievances, and I should have told Levine to avail herself of that service. But the AJC's executive director did a number on me. When she called, she came on all sweetness and light. "This is ridiculous for *Sixty Minutes* and the American Jewish Congress to be fighting," she said. "Couldn't we just sit down and talk this whole thing out? You can listen to what we have to say, and we'll listen to what you have to say. Why do we have to be enemies?" Against my better judgment, I invited Levine into our shop to talk things over, and I persuaded Don Hewitt to host the meeting in his office.

I had extended the invitation to Naomi Levine—to her alone and not to the entire hierarchy of the American Jewish Congress. Yet when she arrived at Hewitt's office, she was accompanied by three other top officials from the AJC—its president, Rabbi Arthur Hertzberg, and two associate directors, Sol Baum and Richard Cohen. I knew what kind of meeting it was going to be when, after the introductions and handshakes, Rabbi Hertzberg turned to my boss and said: "Hewitt? Hewitt? I imagine there's a Horowitz under there somewhere."

Hewitt happens to be Jewish and, in fact, Rabbi Hertzberg's presumption struck close to the mark. As a young man back in the early 1900s, Don's grandfather had changed his name from Hurwitz to Hewitt. Don certainly did not regard it as a shameful secret, a dark blot on his family tree, but he also did not think it was any of Rabbi Hertzberg's business. The remark had absolutely nothing to do with the subject in question—our story on Syria—and he resented the rabbi's suggestion that *he* had anglicized his name to give the impression that he was not Jewish.

The tone having been set by Rabbi Hertzberg's gratuitous remark, what followed in Hewitt's office was a heated exchange of views that resolved nothing. The delegation from the AJC attacked our integrity as journalists, made a few more snide allusions to our moral defects as Jews, and exhorted us to do a follow-up story based on interviews with Syrian Jews who were now living in the United States, all of whom would naturally be furnished to us by the American Jewish Congress. We insisted that our report was based on solid evidence and that we considered it to be fair and objective. We pointed out that we had dealt with the question of Jewish life in Syria in proper perspective, as part of a larger story. (This was true. When we edited "Israel's Toughest Enemy" for broadcast, we began with observations on Assad's obsession with getting back the Golan Heights, the rich Syrian farmland that had been occupied by Israel since 1967, and his regime's close relationship with the Soviet Union. It wasn't until we were six or seven minutes into the piece that we turned our attention to Syria's Jewish community.) But our visitors were in no mood to be placated, and after they left, I had to contend with Hewitt, who was understandably irked at me for having talked him into such an unpleasant encounter.

We soon learned that the American Jewish Congress had just begun to fight. The meeting in Hewitt's office was a courtesy on our part, which we had granted with the understanding that the discussion would take place in an informal, off-the-record atmosphere. But a member of the AJC delegation must have brought a hidden tape recorder into the meeting, or had somehow managed to take copious notes surreptitiously. I say that because a few days later, there arrived in my office a fourteen-page summary transcript of our meeting, along with a letter from Rabbi Hertzberg reiterating all the AJC's objections to our report. "Our differences, although now clarified, are not yet resolved," he wrote. "We remain troubled by what we continue to regard as excessive, inaccurate and distorted representations on your part—none of which has been corrected."

A threatening tone ran through the letter. Rabbi Hertzberg decided it was his duty to remind me that "CBS and its agents are the stewards of an important communications medium which ultimately they hold and operate on behalf of the people." And he closed with the warning that he would be "sharing this letter with others" because "members of the public are not obliged to accept silently and without complaint statements which they believe to be spurious and deceptive, but which are massively disseminated throughout the country." Therefore, it came as no great surprise that the American Jewish Congress called a news conference, at which it released copies of the transcript and letter to the press. In the meantime, it took action on another front, filing a complaint against us with the National News Council.

On most occasions, when we broadcast a piece that provokes a stormy reaction, the tempest lasts only a few days, a week or so at the most. Left to their own inclinations, most people have more pressing concerns in their lives than the programming and editorial decisions of *60 Minutes,* and once they get their gripes off their chests, they put the matter behind them. But the Jewish lobby was determined to keep the pot boiling on the Syrian story, and its well-organized campaign against us continued without letup through the rest of that winter and deep into the spring. Nor was there any relief in sight, for by the end of May we were preparing to rebroadcast the report, and in a way that was not going to mollify our critics.

Ever since the early years of *60 Minutes,* it has been our policy to broadcast fresh stories every week during the regular television season, which runs from mid-September until late May. Then during the late spring and summer months, when we all take time off to recharge our batteries and get pieces ready for the next season, we present repeats of various stories that aired over the previous nine months. In May 1975 Hewitt and I realized that "Israel's Toughest Enemy" would have to be included in that summer's schedule of repeats. We knew that if we chose *not* to rebroadcast it, we would leave ourselves wide open to the charge that we were purposely keeping it off the air because we did not have confidence in its accuracy and fairness. In all likelihood, such an omission would have been construed as a tacit admission that our critics were right. Hence, to make sure that everyone got the message, we made a point of announcing publicly that the Syrian story would be repeated on *60 Minutes* on the second Sunday in June.

We understood that by putting it on the air again we were inviting a fresh barrage of criticism. At the same time, we were by then more convinced than ever that we were on solid ground. In preparing to answer the list of grievances the American

Jewish Congress had filed against us with the National News Council, we had accumulated plenty of new evidence in support of our position. (The National News Council, now defunct, was an organization that judges the validity of complaints of unfairness or inaccuracy in the news media. It had no judicial authority, no concrete power of any kind, but it did wield influence in the sensitive area of public relations. So we decided to respond to the AJC's charges in that forum.)

It is no exaggeration to say that we did more research on the Syrian story *after* it was first broadcast than before we put it on the air. From February until the repeat in June, we interviewed members of the diplomatic community in Washington and at the United Nations, and we also talked to other journalists who had spent quite a bit of time in Syria; they all corroborated the impressions that we had formed during our visit there and reported on *60 Minutes*. Many told us that all the grim stories about the persecution of Jews in Syria were, in fact, fairly accurate accounts of conditions prior to 1970, the year Assad came to power; since then, however, there had been a gradual and palpable change for the better. No one was able to say for certain why that was so, or whether it would last, but a couple of opinions were offered. A few of our sources suggested that Assad wanted to improve Syrian-American relations in the hope of getting some much-needed economic aid from Washington, and that it was with this goal in mind that he adopted a more tolerant policy toward the Jewish community. Others contended that it had nothing to do with that, that Assad simply was willing to accept Syrian Jews as fellow citizens (but with certain restrictions imposed on them) as long as they voiced and demonstrated sufficient loyalty to his regime.

We assembled all this information into an eighteen-point refutation of the AJC's accusations and presented it to the National News Council. Moreover, some of the fresh data we had gathered since February, notably the credit our sources had given Assad for the improved treatment of Jews in Syria, went into an on-camera summation I wrote for the rebroadcast in June. In my closing remarks, I responded to the charges that had been leveled against us and explained how our story had evolved from what we found in Syria. What I said, in essence, was that after a careful examination of the allegations and our own evidence, 60 Minutes had decided to stand by its story.

Of course, this did not endear us to the watchdogs from the American Jewish Congress. I learned later that when they heard that we were planning to rerun "Israel's Toughest Enemy," some of them assumed that we were caving in to their pressure, that they were going to get from us the kind of *mea culpa* that they had wrung out of the *National Geographic*. Instead, what they saw was a repeat of our original report from start to finish, with no deletions and no corrections. The only new material was my on-air rebuttal of their allegations. So, their reaction was predictable and by then all too familiar.

What's more, we still were not entirely out of the woods; in our zeal to be fair and thorough, we committed ourselves to a course of action that made it impossible to put the story behind us. At the conclusion of the rebroadcast, I informed our audience that "our request for permission to go back to Syria to take another, more detailed look at the status of the Syrian Jewish community has been granted." I announced then that "we plan to go back in the coming months." At the time the decision was made to arrange a second visit to Syria I agreed with it. But now, after we had publicly declared our intent to return, I began to have misgivings. I felt that even if everything we found there confirmed our original judgment and we reported that, it would smack of overkill. Just because our critics had overreacted, there was no reason why we should respond in kind. Besides, by this time I had no more appetite for the story; frankly I was sick of it and all the uproar it had caused. Hence, the last thing I wanted to do was return to Syria and dig into it all over again. But we had promised our viewers that we would go back and take another look, and I knew that we could not renege on that.

As it turned out, we did not get back to Syria until February 1976, more than a year after our first visit. When Bill McClure and I returned to Damascus, our government contacts there did not exactly welcome us with open arms, but they were a lot more cordial than they had been the last time we were there. (President Assad and other officials knew all about our broadcast, and were apparently astounded that we had put such a report on the air. Like most Arab governments at that time, the Assad regime believed that the entire American press was a servile tool of the Zionists.) They also were more trusting. Most of the time, when we took our cameras into the Jewish quarter of Damascus, we were accompanied, as before, by an agent from the Ministry of Information, but on this second visit we were occasionally allowed to move about unescorted. Our interviews this time were far more extensive and thorough. I talked to doctors and dentists, teachers and lawyers and merchants, including two tradesmen who are such an integral part of Jewish life in any city, the kosher butcher and the meticulous tailor. They all assured me that their clientele included many Arabs as well as Jews. One doctor I talked to named Nissim Hasbani claimed that he saw as many as sixty patients a day, and when I asked him why he had such a thriving practice, he said: "Because I am Jewish, they come to me more, because I am intelligent, you know." I had to laugh at this version of the cliché (my *Syrian* son, the doctor) and could not resist pursuing it further:

WALLACE: You mean, they like—they like a good Jewish doctor?

HASBANI: Yes. It is Jewish, it is intelligent.

WALLACE: Well, why do we in the United States hear all of these tales of horror about how the Syrian Jews are treated, that it's very difficult for a Jew to get a driver's license, for a Jew to get a telephone? We hear that there is a—

HASBANI: You see, I have a telephone, and I have a car, and I have a house. If anyone want a car, he can have. Anyone want a telephone, he can have. Anyone want to buy a house, he can have. And I'm sure of that . . .

WALLACE: Dr. Hasbani, if all the Jews of Syria were told they could leave the country, go to the United States or Mexico or Israel or wherever, how many of them would go?

HASBANI: I think that not more than five percent go to Israel. And perhaps if they want to leave to the United

States, to Brazil, to other country, perhaps the number
is twenty or thirty percent.

WALLACE: So about one out of three would leave. But
before Assad, how many would have left?

HASBANI: Before Assad, I think that ninety percent leave.

So there it was again: the assertion that life in the Jewish
community had improved dramatically in recent years, ever
since Hafez Assad assumed control of the government. During
our first visit to Syria, we were denied access to President
Assad. Mistrustful of the Western press, he turned down our
request for an interview. But when we returned in 1976, he
agreed to be interviewed, yet another sign that one person at
least had been favorably impressed by the *60 Minutes* report
on Syria. Not only that, but he wound up giving us five hours
of his time. We discussed a great many subjects in the long
interview, including the one that had brought McClure and me
back to Damascus:

WALLACE: Do you worry about the loyalty of your Jewish
citizens here?

ASSAD: No. I think that the Syrian Jews love their country,
and they are satisfied with their way of life. The instructions to our ministers is to treat Jews like all other Syrian
citizens. If there are individual cases, they will be treated
as would similar cases of non-Jews. But this does not
change the general rule, which is: Jews are citizens of
this country.

I should add that back in New York, as part of our reporting
for the updated version of "Israel's Toughest Enemy," I interviewed a Syrian Jew who had managed to escape to the States.
He had been furnished to us by the American Jewish Committee—a more moderate group than the American Jewish
Congress—and for the most part, he did indeed paint a bleak
picture of Jewish life in Syria. He said the secret police kept
the Jewish community under extremely close surveillance, and
he himself had been arrested for "absolutely no reason" and

had to spend three days in jail. So, after listening to his litany of grievances, I asked him: "President Assad of Syria—good man, bad man?"

"He is a good man," replied this young exile, speaking from the freedom of his new life in America. "He is the best one, and not only for the Jews. He is, in general, for all the population."

But finally, let me say that I had no illusions about the overall quality of life in Syria. As I pointed out in all three broadcasts—the first one, the repeat and the update—the Assad regime was a police state and the average per-capita income for *all* Syrians was less than ten dollars a week. I also quoted a remark I heard from a Syrian Arab. "Life for Jews here is no paradise," he told me. Then he quickly added: "But it is not much better for us."

Compared to the furor that greeted our first broadcast on Syria, the reaction to the update was mild and insignificant. For most of our viewers, I'm sure, the shock value had worn off and they were now bored with the story. I could hardly blame them. Even Rabbi Hertzberg and his associates at the American Jewish Congress pulled in their horns a bit. They quietly withdrew the complaint they had filed against us with the National News Council, which was actually a moot concession on their part inasmuch as the NNC already had rejected their charges as "unwarranted." And in the next issue of their publication, *Near East Report,* they grudgingly observed that "it is, of course, entirely possible that Syrian Jews have made some recent gains under Assad's rule." However, in the same editorial they resorted to the cheapest shot of the entire dispute. Drawing an analogy that I found obscene, they compared our broadcasts to "films in which Goebbels portrayed the clean and tidy barracks in the idyllic concentration camps." At its absolute worst, Jewish life in Syria did not approach the black psychosis of the Third Reich, and, in my opinion, even to suggest such a parallel was to dishonor the memory of the millions who suffered and died in the Holocaust.

The first time I interviewed Menachem Begin for *60 Minutes* was in 1973, four years before he became prime minister of Israel. Although at that time Begin was a member of the Knesset—the Israeli parliament—and a leader of the opposition party, he was primarily regarded as a strident voice from the past, a man whose style and exploits belonged to an earlier period in Israel's history. Back in the 1940s, during the years leading up to Israel's war of independence, Begin had been commander of the Irgun Zvai Leumi, a radical guerrilla group committed to the violent overthrow of British rule in Palestine. Under his leadership, the Irgun conducted raids on Arab villages, British troop trains and other targets throughout the region that would later become Israel. But its most daring assault took place in the heart of Jerusalem itself. There, in July 1946, Irgun commandos blew up the south wing of the King David Hotel, the civil and military headquarters of the British government in Palestine. Ninety persons—Britons, Arabs and Jews—were killed and more than a hundred others were injured. The reaction in London, Washington and other world capitals was a cry of outrage. Such prominent Jews as Albert Einstein and Hannah Arendt denounced Begin and his "gang of desperadoes," as they were characterized by one Jewish organization. But Menachem Begin also had his admirers, and in their eyes he was a heroic figure, a freedom fighter who (as it was later said of him) had "helped dynamite the state of Israel into existence."

A quarter century later, Black September and other terrorist groups launched their campaign to dynamite Palestine back into existence, and when I went to the Middle East in the spring of 1973, it was to do a *60 Minutes* story on their guerrilla movement. In putting together that report, I tried to probe into the mentality, the rationale of terrorism. In addition to interviewing Kamal Nasser and other Palestinians, I also talked to Begin and other veterans of the Stern Gang and the Irgun who had carried out commando attacks against the British in the forties. One of them was Nathan Yalin-Mor, who had been in the top leadership of the Stern Gang and who had since earned a reputation as a political writer in Israel. I asked him the question that was preying on my mind.

WALLACE: Was not the state of Israel founded in part on the use of terror by the Stern Gang, by Irgun?

YALIN-MOR: Of course, I admit—

CLOSE ENCOUNTERS

WALLACE: And so?

YALIN-MOR: It's—but you see, I'm not against terror in itself. But I'm against *undiscriminated* terror, against hitting, against killing innocent, uninvolved people.

WALLACE: Do you think Black September has a case?

YALIN-MOR: Of course! I admit they have a case. I admit that they fight for their own independence, as we fought in the 1940s.

WALLACE: But your own prime minister, Golda Meir, says there is no such thing as a Palestinian.

YALIN-MOR: Well, in 1942 I would be able to quote you many speeches in the House of Lords, arguing that there was no Jewish people and no Jewish nation. As they were wrong, Golda Meir is wrong, because the best identification for people existing is the youth fighting, the organization fighting for its cause.

WALLACE: So you, a former member of the Stern Gang, respect the fighters of Black September?

YALIN-MOR: Of course I respect them! I know that— excuse me, I wouldn't like to use the same method as they use, because they do it differently than we did. We killed many British of the British constables here . . . but we didn't kill innocent, uninvolved people.

But Menachem Begin certainly did not respect the fighters of Black September. When I confronted him with the question I had put to Yalin-Mor, he bristled and said: "I don't want any comparison, even by dissimilarity, between us and the Black September. Completely different stories of a fight—either in the aim or in the method or in the intention—and let us not repeat that sacrilege, Mr. Wallace!"

We included both Yalin-Mor's remarks and Begin's disclaimer in our story "Palestine: A Nation in Exile," and once we had it ready for broadcast, I turned my attention to other matters. (Since this was the spring of 1973, I was soon up to my neck in Watergate, preparing for my long interview with John Ehrlichman.) I had no reason to believe then that I would

ever have occasion to see Begin again. True, he was a leader
of the opposition party in the Knesset, but that faction was so
weak, so lacking in popular support that it had never even come
close to winning a national election. The ruling Labor party—
the party of David Ben-Gurion, Levi Eshkol and Golda Meir
—had been in control of Israel's government since the country
was founded in 1948, and its solid hold on the electorate seemed
certain to continue for many years to come. But in politics, of
course, there are no safe bets. In late 1976 a series of domestic
scandals plunged Israel into a parliamentary crisis; and in the
national election the following spring, the Labor party was
swept out of power for the first time, and Menachem Begin,
piecing together a center-right coalition, was able to form a
new government under his leadership.

And so it came to pass that in the fall of 1977, I found
myself flying to Jerusalem to interview Israel's new prime
minister for *60 Minutes*. We covered a wide range of topics in
that interview, and during most of it Begin seemed to be enjoying himself. He displayed a knack for artful evasion and I
was impressed—even amused—by the deft way he parried
some of my questions. At one point, for example, I brought
up Israel's close relationship with the racist government of
South Africa (a sensitive subject for many Israelis and other
supporters), and that led to this exchange:

WALLACE: How much of Israel's enriched uranium for
nuclear weapons comes from South Africa?

BEGIN: I don't know anything about nuclear weapons,
and you ask me about uranium. By profession, I am a
lawyer. I have no idea about nuclear weapons, as you
put it.

WALLACE: But what light can you or will you shed on
those stories of Israel's obtaining enriched uranium from
plants in the United States?

BEGIN: From time to time I read in the press the most
fantastic stories. How everywhere Israel snatches away
uranium from America and from Europe and via Italy.
It belongs to the James Bond stories.

WALLACE: Not so?

BEGIN: I don't pay attention to them.

From a careful reading of the above, one can appreciate Begin's
subtly evasive mode of reply. To dismiss reports as being "fantastic" and "James Bond stories" is not quite the same as flatly
denying that they are true. Then, when I pressed him to confirm
that they were "not so," he adroitly sidestepped that question
as well. A man might choose not to "pay any attention" to
rumors that he's cheating on his wife, but that doesn't necessarily mean he's going straight home from work every night.
In any event, we eventually got around to the most sensitive
subject of all—the Palestinian question. Recalling Begin's testy
response four years earlier to my suggestion that his Irgun
guerrilla movement in the 1940s could have served as a model
for the Palestinian terrorists ("Let us not repeat that sacrilege,
Mr. Wallace!"), I was curious to see how he would react to
that query now that he was prime minister:

> WALLACE: Do you—forgive me—see no similarity of
> purpose between the Menachem Begin of thirty years
> ago and the Yasir Arafat of today?
>
> BEGIN: And who?
>
> WALLACE: Yasir Arafat.

At first, he simply glared at me through his thick glasses,
which, even when he wasn't upset, gave him a stern and owlish
appearance. When finally he did speak, his first words utterly
contradicted his tone and manner. "I will not get angry," he
said. Then, in a long and rambling sermon, Begin upbraided
me for having dared to draw a comparison between his Irgun
commandos, who had fought "for the survival of our people,"
and "the man called Arafat . . . who sends his henchmen to kill
men, women and children" because he "wants to destroy the
Jewish state."

For obvious reasons, the interview soon came to an end,
and after we turned off the camera and microphone, Begin,
still furious, turned to me and said: "Now, I suppose you'll use

your scissors, Mr. Wallace, and clip here and clip there and do what you want."

Now it was my turn to get sore. "Mr. Prime Minister," I asked, "are you calling me dishonest?"

With an exaggerated shrug of innocence, he replied: "Did I use the word dishonest?"

Yet it was plainly clear that he *was* questioning my good faith and I didn't want to leave him on that sour note. So I told Begin that as the son of Jewish immigrants, I had been raised to believe in Zionism, and in all the years since then I had never once wavered in my commitment to the existence of Israel as an independent state. I said that my wife and I had trees planted in Israel—one in memory of my father and another in memory of hers—and that in a variety of other private ways, I had contributed my efforts to raising money and support for Israeli causes. But I pointed out that I could not allow that personal commitment to distort my work as a reporter. Then I reminded Begin that others before me (including some of his fellow Israelis) had made the connection between the Jewish freedom fighters of the forties and the Palestinian guerrillas of the seventies. Thus, I maintained, it was a perfectly proper and legitimate question. But Begin was convinced that I was trying to dishonor his reputation, which meant to him that I was an American Jew who was no friend of Israel or at least no admirer of Menachem Begin, which in his eyes were one and the same.

As we continued to debate the matter, the door to Begin's office suddenly flew open and in walked Israel's defense minister, Ezer Weizman. Flashing a mischievous grin, he said: "I understand that the prime minister is having a fist fight with a reporter." That broke the tension and I took an instant liking to Weizman, whom I had never met before. Having thus intervened, Weizman went a step further. He sensed, correctly, that I had no stomach for continuing the squabble, so he suggested that he and I repair to my hotel for a drink. "You're on," I said, "but I think I'll have *two* drinks."

When we arrived at the bar in the Jerusalem Hilton, we ran into a couple of Israeli reporters, and in the spirit of journalistic fellowship, I told them all about my encounter with Begin. I probably shot my mouth off more than I should have, but I was still keyed up. In any case, a few days later one of Israel's weekly magazines came out with a cover story on the incident, which was highlighted by a full-page photograph of me on one side and Begin on the other in a classic pose of confrontation. I had already left Israel by then, but I heard later that the article, replete with spicy quotes from me, got Begin riled up all over again. And a few days later, when we aired the Begin interview on *60 Minutes,* we naturally included my question about the Arafat comparison and his angry response to it.

There was a brief flurry of reaction to the broadcast, but we were spared a heavy barrage of criticism, in part no doubt because everyone who cared about the future of the Middle East was soon caught up in a large and much more important drama. Indeed, in November of that year the eyes of the entire world were fastened on Jerusalem, where a historic event of far-reaching significance was taking place: the first visit to Israel by an Arab head of state.

The Begin interview was aired on November 6, 1977, and three days later, in Cairo, Anwar Sadat dropped a diplomatic bombshell. In an address to the Egyptian parliament, he said that his desire for a permanent peace in the Middle East was so strong that he "would go even to the home of the Israelis, to the Knesset, to discuss peace with them." It was a bold and imaginative overture, a dramatic break with precedent; nothing like it or even close to it had ever before been proposed by an Arab head of state. The next move was up to Menachem Begin and, to his everlasting credit, he was quick to respond. Two days later he told visiting French officials that he planned to invite Sadat to Israel to discuss a lasting peace. Now the problem was how to go about bringing that mutual desire to fruition. Because Egypt and Israel were still officially at war with each other (and had been since 1948), there was no way for the two governments to communicate directly with one another through normal diplomatic channels.

It was at this critical moment that America's premier television correspondent, my colleague at CBS News, Walter Cronkite, stepped in and played a decisive role. On November 14 Cronkite and his staff in New York exploited the technology of modern television to arrange a live, simultaneous interview with Sadat in Cairo and Begin in Jerusalem. Even though the two men were separated by hundreds of miles of disputed territory, their faces appeared on the television screen side by side; and, with Cronkite serving as an electronic intermediary, now they had the novel opportunity to put their wishes to the test in each other's "presence," so to speak. Having achieved the stunning coup of bringing Sadat and Begin "together," Walter proceeded to make the most of it. He pressed Sadat to specify when he would be ready to visit Israel. The Egyptian president replied, "Within a week." Walter than asked Begin if he was prepared to receive Sadat in Jerusalem on such short notice. Begin answered: "Yes, any time, any day." Thus, in that brief moment on the *CBS Evening News,* Walter Cronkite turned an enterprising journalistic ploy into a diplomatic triumph. Henry Kissinger himself could not have pulled it off with more finesse.

Through other intermediaries, the final details were worked out, and on November 19, 1977, President Anwar Sadat of Egypt stepped off a plane in Jerusalem, the capital of Israel. That visit was the first link in the most promising chain of events to take place in the Middle East in our time. One month later Begin visited Sadat in Cairo, and in September of the following year, they both joined President Jimmy Carter at Camp David, where, after twelve days of difficult and hair-splitting negotiations, they agreed on the series of accords providing the framework for an official peace treaty between their two countries.

Recalling the old Chinese proverb that "a journey of a thousand miles must begin with a single step," one could say that Sadat's first step on the long road to peace was paradoxically an act of war. When he launched the Yom Kippur War in 1973, his ultimate aim no doubt was a clear-cut victory and the expulsion of Israeli troops from Egyptian territory. But he also went to war to give Egypt back its manhood, to exorcise the shame and humiliation that had afflicted the country since its crushing defeat in the 1967 war; and if nothing else, he did accomplish that objective. The Egyptians fought bravely and well in the 1973 conflict, especially during the first few days when they inflicted heavy losses on the reputedly invincible Israeli Army. Sadat had risked everything to recapture Egypt's self-esteem and, having won the gamble, he resolved that never

again would Egyptian blood be spilled in a war against Israel.
Over the next five years, from the end of the Yom Kippur War
to the signing of the accords at Camp David, Anwar Sadat
made the pursuit of an enduring peace the overriding mission,
the central crusade, of his life.

During the latter part of this period, I did three interviews with
Sadat for *60 Minutes*. When I first sat down with him in March
1977—eight months before his trip to Israel—I told him that
someone who knew and admired him had described him as a
man "somewhere between impatient and desperate for peace."
He acknowledged that was an accurate perception of his state
of mind. One reason Sadat was so desperate for peace was
because Egypt's economy was in terrible shape, and he needed
to concentrate all his resources on the severe problems of poverty and overpopulation that were threatening to tear his country
apart. And nowhere were those problems more manifest than
in Cairo itself. In the felicitous words of my *60 Minutes* colleague, Morley Safer, Cairo had become "the Calcutta of Africa," a city overflowing with people—an estimated one hundred
thousand persons per square mile—many of them homeless
souls who had to eke out a wretched existence in the teeming
streets of the capital. Later that year, when I returned to Cairo
to do a story on the country's economic woes (which we called
"Sadat's Troubled Egypt"), I talked to former government officials who had served under Nasser and had become increasingly critical of Sadat's leadership. When I interviewed Sadat
on that occasion, I said to him: "You know what they say about
you? They say you're a politician, but you're no economist.
You're a first-rate foreign minister, but a bad chancellor of the
exchequer."

He fielded that question with his customary grace, but then,
with a concern that bordered on alarm, he conceded that "we
are really suffering from a very acute economic problem. This
is a fact." It was obvious that no one in Sadat's troubled Egypt
was more troubled by the state of affairs than Sadat himself,
and I ended that report with this observation:

It is to forestall an explosion from inside his country or
from outside that Sadat labors so mightily these days for

peace. He understands the impatience of his fellow Egyptians, their envy of the oil wealth of their Arab brothers. He knows his countrymen look to him to bring them better times. So he courts the Americans because he believes the Americans can pressure Israel to make peace. The peace he needs to give his country's economy a chance to flourish. The peace he may just need, in fact, to keep his job.

We broadcast that story in August 1977, and three months later, when Sadat returned to Cairo from his historic visit to Jerusalem, crowds welcomed him home with the kind of cheering that had not been heard in Egypt since the 1952 revolution when Gamal Nasser and his coterie of young army officers (a group that included Anwar Sadat) overthrew the decadent regime of King Farouk. Although most of his Arab allies had branded his trip the act of a traitor, Sadat's daring peace initiative had clearly won the hearts of his countrymen. After all, it was the Egyptians who had borne the brunt of all the wars with Israel, and it was evident that the vast majority shared their president's urgent desire for a formal peace treaty which, among other things, would return the occupied Sinai Peninsula to Egyptian control.

In February 1978 I flew to Cairo to do another story on Sadat. Not only was he bigger news than ever, but his autobiography, *In Search of Identity,* was about to be published in the United States. I read the book in galley proofs and found it a surprisingly candid account of Sadat's life and career. In fact, some of the things revealed in *In Search of Identity* emboldened me to bring up matters in our next interview that otherwise I would not have dared mention. For example, during the years when he served as Nasser's chief deputy, he had a reputation in certain Egyptian circles of being a spineless bureaucrat who did nothing except carry out his master's orders. I wanted our viewers to know about that, so I reminded him of those days when he was known as "Nasser's poodle, Nasser's Mr. Yes-Yes."

Sadat's response was to puff furiously on his pipe, then smile painfully and acknowledge, "Yes, yes, I know it." I then referred to the prevailing attitude in Cairo at the time of Nasser's

death: "No one expected you to survive . . . Everybody said,
Nasser's poodle will last six weeks."

"Four to six weeks," he corrected with a merry laugh.

I must confess that by this time I had become an unabashed
admirer of Anwar Sadat. I respected him as a statesman, a
leader of his people, and in my personal dealings with him
(and this was our third interview in less than a year), he came
across as an honest and sensitive man who was endowed with
considerable charm and a fine sense of humor. On this day in
1978, he seemed to be in especially good spirits, and since I
was feeling rather chipper myself, I decided to have a little fun
at the expense of my producer.

Bill McClure was no longer the producer I worked with on
stories in that part of the world. Barry Lando, my comrade-
in-strife from the Colonel Herbert campaign and other battles,
had recently transferred from Washington to Paris, and he was
responsible now for producing the pieces I did in Europe and
the Middle East. Lando did not have McClure's solid background in the Middle East; he was new to the territory. He also
was Jewish, and I could tell that he was a bit nervous about
this Sadat assignment, his first in an Arab country. But as usual,
he had done a thorough job of research and advance reporting
on the story. In going through the galleys of *In Search of
Identity,* Lando was struck by something he read about Egypt's
returning the bodies of Israeli soldiers to Israel after the Yom
Kippur War. "Applying the Jewish principle of putting a price
on everything," Sadat wrote, "Israelis began to negotiate the
price they expected to pay to recover their dead." Lando showed
the passage to me, and later, when he drew up his list of
suggested questions for the interview, he included the quote
and after it this question: "anti-Semitic?" When I interviewed
Sadat, I asked every other question on Barry's list and mine,
but I purposely skipped the one about the bodies of Israeli
soldiers; then, when the time came to wrap up the interview,
I turned to Lando and said: "Anything else? Something I should
ask that we haven't covered?"

He walked over to me, directed my attention to his list, and
pointed to the sentence from Sadat's book that had aroused his
curiosity. Then I also pointed to the same excerpt and said in

a tone of mock alarm: *"This* question, Barry? *This* is the question you want me to ask? You're sure, Barry, you're absolutely sure that you want me to ask *this* question?" Lando gave me a stricken, how-could-you-do-this-to-me? look and went slinking back to his post outside of camera range. Turning back to Sadat, I read him the quote from his book and said: "When one reads 'Applying the Jewish principle of putting a price on everything,' one says 'Aha, Anwar Sadat! He is anti-Semitic, anti-Jewish!"

Several of Sadat's deputies and aides were in the room with us, and I could almost hear their necks snap as they jerked their heads in the direction of Lando, at whom they directed glares of barely suppressed fury. At the moment poor Barry was probably cursing himself for ever having agreed to team up with me. But as I had fully anticipated, Sadat realized that I was putting on an act, doing a number on my producer, and his response promptly broke the tension. With a hearty laugh and a reassuring glance over at Lando, he said: "Anti-Semite, this is something that has been invented to blackmail anyone and to scare anyone. No. I myself am a Semite. How could I be anti-Semite? They are my cousins."

As it turned out, Lando and I were not the only American "cousins" in Cairo at that time. A delegation of rabbis from the Synagogue Council of America had accepted Sadat's invitation to visit Egypt. Like Lando, the rabbis had come to Cairo with some misgivings, not knowing what to expect, but during an hour-long meeting in the presidential palace, Sadat made a profoundly positive impression on them. In fact, Rabbi Wolfe Kelman of the Jewish Theological Seminary in New York told Sadat that what Pope John XXIII had done to bring Catholics and Jews together, he, Sadat, was now doing for Muslims and Jews.

At the time, however, Sadat was starting to lose patience with another "cousin," the prime minister of Israel. In the early months of 1978, it began to look as though his peace initiative was not going to lead to any tangible result. By the spring, all the euphoria of the previous November, when Sadat made his trip to Jerusalem, had dissipated as Israel remained adamant in its refusal to give up any of the territories it had captured in the Six-Day War. In addition, the Begin government exac-

erbated the situation by continuing its policy of building set-
tlements on the occupied land. In June an utterly frustrated
Sadat publicly warned that Egypt might be forced once again
to wage war against Israel. Begin promptly rejoined that such
a threat was hardly compatible with the "no more war" pledge
Sadat had made in his speech before the Knesset seven months
earlier. Matters continued to deteriorate over the summer until
finally in August, Jimmy Carter stepped in and rescued the
peace effort from the diplomatic doldrums. Both Begin and
Sadat accepted Carter's invitation to join him at Camp David
and commence direct negotiations with each other under the
aegis of Carter's mediation. Those intimate, face-to-face talks
began on September 5, and twelve days later, they produced
the "Framework for the Conclusion of a Peace Treaty Between
Egypt and Israel."

For all three men, Sadat, Begin and Carter, the Camp David
accords were nothing less than the crowning achievement of
their respective public careers. Had any of them been less
flexible, less patient or less determined to see the negotiations
through to a positive result, the Camp David summit meeting
would have ended in failure. Each had to make major concessions. Going into the talks, Sadat and Carter had insisted on a
comprehensive peace plan that would embrace the entire region;
but in order to take the vital first step toward that goal, they
settled for the more narrow Egyptian-Israeli peace. As for Begin, he yielded significant ground on the territorial question
when he agreed to return the Sinai Peninsula to Egyptian control. What made this critical concession feasible was the fact
that of the five disputed territories Israel had occupied since
1967—the Sinai, the Gaza Strip, the West Bank, East Jerusalem and the Golan Heights—the area that mattered the most
to Egypt mattered the least to Israel. Unlike the others, the
Sinai Desert did not constitute part of ancient Israel, the Biblical
homeland; it was after all merely the wilderness in which the
Jews wandered for forty years before they reached the Promised
Land. Moreover, the Israelis regarded the Sinai as the least
important territory in terms of their main strategic concern,
national defense, and therefore the one they could most easily
afford to relinquish.

Left unresolved were the far more complex disputes over

the other territories and the biggest stumbling block of all—
the Palestinian question. In addition to the document covering the Egyptian-Israeli accords, the parties at Camp David
drew up the more general "A Framework for Peace in the
Middle East," which dealt primarily with the East Bank and
Gaza. But although vague guidelines toward eventual autonomy
were set down, no agreement was reached on the ultimate
sovereignty over those areas. Sadat's willingness to defer those
other questions to future negotiations only deepened the rift
between him and his more militant Arab allies. If they regarded
Sadat's visit to Jerusalem as a double cross, a stab in the back,
that was nothing compared to their feelings of outrage and
betrayal when they learned about the independent deal he made
with Begin at Camp David. In the months after the summit
meeting, as the Egyptian and Israeli governments labored over
the fine tuning of the accords, Sadat had to contend with the
open hostility of Arab leaders from Syria, Libya and the PLO.
Nevertheless, he stuck to his course courageously and in late
March 1979, the peace treaty between Egypt and Israel was
formally signed. And as that fateful day in March drew near,
I flew to Lebanon to interview Sadat's most virulent critic—Yasir
Arafat.

It was my second encounter with the flamboyant leader of the
PLO who, over the past decade, had been swaggering around
the Middle East like a Bedouin version of Fidel Castro, the
prototype of romantic revolutionaries in the Cold War era. I
often marveled at the way Arafat always effected the scruffy,
unkempt appearance of a man who had gone two or three days
without a shave. His facial foliage never quite reached the status
of a full-grown beard, à la Castro, yet there was never any
evidence of a razor having just made a clean sweep of things.
He seemed to be endowed with abnormal follicles.

However, when I first met Arafat in the flesh, it was his
eyes that caught my attention. They were unusually warm and
expressive, the kind of eyes one might expect to find in a poet
or a man of religion, but *not* in a world-famous guerrilla leader
who preached violence and revolution.

Our first meeting took place in Cairo in March 1977. Bill
McClure and I had gone there to do a story on Sadat, and when

we learned that Arafat was in town for a meeting of the Palestinian National Council, we made an earnest pitch in his
direction. Over the years Arafat's general policy had been to
avoid direct contact with the U.S. media. Given his constituency, it suited his purpose to adopt the position that most American reporters were propagandists for Zionism, and thus not to
be trusted. But by 1977 he had begun to appreciate the public-
relations points that other Arab leaders (notably Sadat) had
scored by making themselves accessible to the Western press.
So, after considerable haggling with his advisers over the ground
rules, we were able to persuade them that an interview on *60
Minutes* was in the best interests of Arafat and the PLO.

Their decision to grant our request was no doubt influenced
by recent and dramatic news from the States. Jimmy Carter
had been inaugurated just a few weeks earlier, and in one of
his first foreign policy speeches, he called for the creation of
a Palestinian "homeland," thereby becoming the first American
President to endorse that position publicly. Since the proposal
seemed to signal a major shift in the United States' approach
to the Middle East dilemma, most of that 1977 interview inevitably dealt with Carter's speech, which Arafat welcomed as
"a progressive step because for the first time, the President of
America put his hand on the core of the whole crisis in the
Middle East—the Palestinians."

But as subsequent qualifications made clear, what Carter
had in mind was a Palestinian homeland under the effective
control of Arafat's chief Arab rival, King Hussein of Jordan;
furthermore, the terms of the ultimate solution would have to
be acceptable to Israel. In other words, from Arafat's point of
view there was no real, substantive change in U.S. policy, and
as time went on, he came to regard Carter with dismay as yet
another American President who had fallen captive to the Jewish lobby. The Carter-arranged Camp David accords only confirmed Arafat's disillusion. Thus, he was in a bitter mood when
I interviewed him at the PLO headquarters in Beirut, just a few
days before the formal signing of the Egyptian-Israeli peace
treaty in March 1979. This time, the warm, sensitive eyes were
full of fire and the atmosphere throughout the interview was
extremely tense. Most of Arafat's fury was aimed at Sadat,
whom he denounced as "a quisling, a traitor," but his charges

of betrayal also extended to President Carter and the United States. At one point, I pressed him to elaborate on this grievance:

> WALLACE: Why would Jimmy Carter want to betray the Palestinians, because that's what you've said—?
>
> ARAFAT: I think he is a—he's looking for the votes.
>
> WALLACE: So, he's just doing this for votes?
>
> ARAFAT: I am sorry to say.
>
> WALLACE: He—he will betray the Palestinians—
>
> ARAFAT: I am sorry to say that what he is doing is only for some votes, for the new election.
>
> WALLACE: And you—by "some votes," you mean Jewish votes in the next election.
>
> ARAFAT: Maybe. Votes—the Jewish votes or other—other votes.
>
> WALLACE: Well, then, other votes?
>
> ARAFAT: But mainly it is Jewish votes.
>
> WALLACE: I see.
>
> ARAFAT: I am sorry to say it.
>
> WALLACE: Purely political move.
>
> ARAFAT: Nothing—not more.

He then proceeded to make a few sneering references to Carter's avowed commitment to human rights, and when he turned the attack into a question, it prompted me to suggest that the PLO's own performance in that area was less than exemplary:

> ARAFAT: Where is this human rights when he is betraying the Palestinians?
>
> WALLACE: Tell me something. We hear that there are Palestinians fighting alongside President Idi Amin in Uganda. Is that true?

ARAFAT: For training mission. It is a training mission, and not more. It was from five years to now we have this mission.

WALLACE: Why, if you have such a feeling for human rights, why would you have a Palestinian training mission with Idi Amin?

ARAFAT: It is a—it is to help him for training his army.

WALLACE: The butcher Amin you help, and you talk about human rights?

ARAFAT: I am not helping him as—

WALLACE: You are helping to train his people. You admit it.

ARAFAT: I am helping the—the Ugandan people. Idi Amin is not interfering in any other country.

WALLACE: Is he a man you respect, admire?

ARAFAT: At least he is beside the Palestinians.

WALLACE: So you'll take help from wherever it comes?

ARAFAT: He is not aggressor—aggressive.

WALLACE: He is not aggressive against his own people?

ARAFAT: Against the Palestinians.

WALLACE: You are proud of your relationship with Idi Amin?

ARAFAT: Yes.

I then shifted the conversation to a less provocative subject, and soon thereafter the interview came to an end. Actually it was my first visit to Beirut since I had interviewed Kamal Nasser in 1973, just three days before he was killed by Israeli commandos, and I knew that some members of the PLO still suspected me of having fingered the secret location of Nasser's living quarters to the Israelis. I have to admit that badgering Yasir Arafat with questions about the PLO's alliance with Idi Amin was not the best way to go about removing the cloud of suspicion that still hovered over me, and sure enough, as I learned later, some individuals in the PLO chose to regard my "rudeness to Chairman Arafat" as additional proof that I was an "agent of Zionism."

A lot of Zionists would have been surprised to hear that. What irritates me is the double standard some of my fellow Jews have applied to my reporting from the Middle East. They believe that it is perfectly all right for me to remind Anwar Sadat of the days when he was scorned as "Nasser's poodle, Nasser's Mr. Yes-Yes," and altogether fitting to ask Yasir Arafat to justify his relationship with "the butcher Amin." But to confront Menachem Begin with questions about his past as an Irgun guerrilla or to suggest that some Syrian Jews profess loyalty to the Assad government even when it comes into conflict with the state of Israel, well, that's something else again. I am accused of being an anti-Zionist, a self-hating Jew. Until now I have generally refrained from responding to those charges in public. For one thing, I have never known quite how to deal with the self-hating-Jew calumny. To dignify it with a reply is to give the accusation a legitimacy it does not deserve. Nonetheless, let me try to set things straight, once and for all.

It's true that I am not a deeply religious person. (This, by the way, is a spiritual condition I share with millions of other Jews, not to mention nominal Christians.) Yet I have never felt anything but pride in my background and heritage. I had the privilege of being reared in a happy Jewish home by loving parents, and all my life I have treasured the values they instilled in me during those formative years. At the same time, it's true that as an adult, I have followed a secular path away from the strict and regular practice of Judaism. I am, as they say, assimilated. However, I was brought up to believe that that was a large part of the American ideal, the blending of disparate cultures into a sense of national community. Finally—and here's the main point—none of this has anything at all to do with my professional responsibilities as a reporter.

Toward the end of my first interview with Yasir Arafat, in Cairo in 1977, I had brought up the delicate question of assassination. In light of what had happened to one of his top aides, Kamal Nasser, one could assume that Arafat himself ranked high on Israel's hit list. And when I asked him about that, he acknowledged that he lived in constant peril. "For me, my life is nonsense," Arafat said. "The life of my people, the existence of my people, is the main and the major concern and aim of my life. *My* life is nonsense."

When I interviewed him two years later in Beirut, the subject of assassination came up again but in a much different context. On that occasion, the likely target in our discussion was not Arafat, but the man who had become his number one enemy within the Arab world. His bitter assertion that Anwar Sadat was "a quisling, a traitor" conveyed ominous implications.

> WALLACE: In many countries, the penalty for treason is death. So, if necessary, kill Sadat?
>
> ARAFAT: I—it—it is up to them.
>
> WALLACE: In other words, the Palestinians are not going to kill Sadat, but if the Egyptians want to kill Sadat for being a traitor, you say okay.
>
> ARAFAT: Yes.

Of course, that is what happened. Over the next few years, Moslem extremists and other opposition groups inside Egypt began to rebel against Sadat's policies of moderation toward Israel and friendly relations with Washington. The atmosphere in Cairo grew increasingly hostile, and the denouement came in October 1981 when Sadat was slain while reviewing the annual military parade commemorating Egypt's valor in the 1973 war against Israel. Thus, in a sudden burst of gunfire, the world lost the most enlightened Arab leader of modern times.

The assassination of Sadat was merely the latest outrage committed by Muslim extremists, who by the late 1970s had replaced Black September as the chief agents of anarchy and terrorism in the Middle East. In killing Sadat, they had hoped to trigger a full-scale revolution that would topple the modern government in Cairo and eventually convert Egypt into an Islamic theocracy. Once in power, the Islamic fundamentalists would take steps to stamp out all the Western influences that,

in their view, had been corrupting the soul of Egypt and other
Muslim countries. In essence, the Muslim fanatics were re-
belling against the progressive forces of the modern world, and
their ultimate goal was to turn the clock back ten centuries or
so to what they recalled, through the prism of race memory,
as having been an idyllic epoch, a period when the supreme
authority of Allah in that part of the world had not yet been
challenged by political and social intrusions from the West.
There was a time, several years prior to the death of Sadat,
when such a reactionary movement would have been dismissed
as the lunatic dream of religious visionaries who were not in
touch with reality. And in fact, the Islamic uprising did not get
off the ground in Egypt; gunning down Sadat did not spark a
widespread revolution in the country and, with the assassins
quickly brought to justice, the Muslim extremists were thoroughly crushed. Still, by 1981 no one dared to take such a
religious crusade lightly. For by then, we were all painfully
aware of what Islamic revolutionaries had accomplished on the
other side of the Persian Gulf—in Iran.

In the years leading up to the cataclysmic events of 1979—
the overthrow of Shah Mohammed Reza Pahlavi and the seizure
of the U.S. Embassy in Teheran—I had ample occasion to
become acquainted with Iran and its problems. But I must
confess that for me, as for so many others, it was a slow
awakening. Indeed, when I first went to Iran for *60 Minutes*
in 1973, Bill McClure and I were so charmed by the subject
of our story—Empress Farah—that the piece we did on her
turned into a valentine, an exercise in puffery. Here is an example of how I portrayed the First Lady of Iran to our viewers
(over pictures of her limousine being pelted with flowers), in
the summer of 1973:

> In the thirteen years she has been their queen, Farah has
> little by little captured the Iranians. Wherever she goes now,
> whatever the security precautions, she is assaulted with af-
> fection. The most underprivileged among her countrymen
> revere her not just as the holy wife of their godlike sover-
> eign, they worship her as the champion of the oppressed—
> their voice in the exalted and remote regions of the palace.

This description, which came in the opening moments of our broadcast, set the tone for the entire profile. And at the time, we received hardly any complaints challenging our rose-colored picture of Empress Farah and the government she represented. The voices of protest, which were to erupt with so much fury a few years later, were still being stifled to such an extent that they did not reach my ears or the ears of most American reporters who visited Iran in the early seventies. The prevailing view was that the Shah's regime, though autocratic, was stable and, in the context of the Middle East, relatively progressive and enlightened. There was sufficient evidence to back up the Shah's claim that he was making an earnest effort to modernize Iran, to fulfill his promise to transform it into "the most sophisticated country in western Asia." More to the point, his militant anti-Communism put him squarely on our side in the Cold War. The Shah was viewed as our pillar of security in the Persian Gulf.

There was no doubt that I brought some of that bias with me on my first trip to Iran in 1973, and the Empress herself took it from there. As for that part of it, I make no apology. Farah Diba Pahlavi was by any standard a warm, intelligent and appealing woman.

Whatever else it accomplished, the *60 Minutes* profile of Empress Farah struck a blow for American-Iranian relations. No one appreciated our valentine to Farah more than the man who had first claim on her affections. After viewing the profile, the Shah decreed that it be translated and shown in movie theaters throughout Iran, and he even had copies of it shipped to Iranian embassies around the world. Hence, it came as no surprise that when McClure and I returned to Teheran in early 1974, this time to do a story on the Shah himself, we were accorded a royal welcome.

Up to a point, that is, because warm and appealing are hardly words one would use to describe the Shah. Unlike his consort, he was austere and aloof in manner and very much a monarch. When I interviewed him in 1974 and on subsequent occasions, strict forms of protocol were observed. McClure and I and the members of our camera crew had to line up, in an appropriate pecking order, and pay our respects to His Majesty, as though we were newly arrived diplomats presenting our credentials to the Peacock Throne. I could not help noticing that all other Iranians were required to stand, and remain standing, whenever they found themselves in the Imperial Presence.

I first met the Shah in 1973 when we were putting together our story on Farah. At one point, I was invited to have lunch at the Niavaran Palace with the royal family, and while the Shah and I were waiting for the Empress to join us, we began talking in a very formal way about the big story in America that summer—the Watergate scandal. He told me how much he admired Nixon and he expressed concern about the President's political future. I tried to explain that Nixon would have to face the music if he was indeed guilty of an impeachable offense, but it was obvious that the Shah felt no sympathy toward a constitutional system that required a head of state to obey the law. Interrupting my little speech on American civics, he bluntly asserted that the United States had become too soft and permissive for its own good and the good of its allies.

The Shah was "good copy." Indeed, one of his more attractive qualities was his on-camera frankness. Once he agreed to be interviewed, there were no ground rules or restrictive conditions imposed in advance. As long as I minded my manners and took care, periodically, to address him as "Your Majesty," I could ask him just about anything. In fact, he seemed to welcome the vigorous give-and-take of a candid interview. And although he never relaxed his imperious manner, the Shah did evince at times a rather brusque sense of humor, and if he saw an opening to put me down or score a debating point at my expense, he seized the opportunity. What's more, he knew exactly what he was doing. He had a keen appreciation of *60 Minutes* as a forum by which he could communicate directly to the American people, and he recognized that to be drawn into a spirited exchange with me was good television. So I would have to say that as an interviewee, he was my kind of Shah.

One time, a question I put to him upset another world leader more than it did the Shah himself. At the end of one of our interviews, I asked him about the period, in the early years of his reign, when he was "known as 'The Playboy King,' addicted to fleshly pleasures." He seemed to be amused by the question, which he answered by saying that those days were well behind

him and now he had become "a very serious man." Several
years later, there was an allusion to that interview in the Israeli
Knesset, of all places, during a debate between Menachem
Begin and his former defense minister, Ezer Weizman. By then,
three years had passed since my little altercation with Begin
in his office, but the memory of that squabble, and Weizman's
intercession on my behalf, apparently still rankled the prime
minister. As the debate in the Knesset grew more heated, he
resorted to the hoary ploy of implying guilt by association. In
a voice trembling with moral indignation, Begin recalled that
Weizman had befriended "Mike Wallace, this man who dared
ask the Shah of Iran if he was a playboy!" When I heard about
that, it was my turn to be amused.

The first time I interviewed the Shah, in February 1974, the
big story in the news was the sudden use of oil as a weapon
against the United States and other countries that had supported
Israel in the Yom Kippur War. The Organization of Petroleum
Exporting Countries had drastically increased the price of its
oil shipments to the West, and, in addition, the Arab members
of the cartel had imposed an embargo on those shipments.
Anyone who was driving a car in those days does not have to
be reminded of the bleak conditions that prevailed during the
winter of 1973–1974. Long lines at the filling stations were a
daily occurrence from Maine to California, and, even worse,
there were days when it was all but impossible to find a station
that had gas to sell at any price. Next to Saudi Arabia, Iran
was the largest exporter of petroleum in the world and thus an
influential voice within OPEC. Yet the Shah insisted that the
cartel was not the culprit responsible for all the inconvenience
that had been inflicted on American motorists. He claimed that
the United States was still importing as much oil as it did before
OPEC adopted its punitive measures. He was obviously leading
up to something and I encouraged him to spell it out:

> WALLACE: What you seem to be saying is that there is
> some fraud involved, or that there is something going
> on that doesn't meet the eye.
>
> SHAH: Oh, something is going on, for sure.

WALLACE: And who is being enriched by it?

SHAH: The oil companies.

WALLACE: The oil companies?

SHAH: You know that one oil company has made sixty-seven percent increase this year, and another one even more.

WALLACE: Well, the president of ARAMCO acknowledges—

SHAH: Yes.

WALLACE: Not the president, the chairman of the board of ARAMCO acknowledged to us that their profits—the parent company—will go up by four hundred percent next year, just as Iran's profits will go up by four hundred percent.

SHAH: Yes, but this is our wealth, our natural wealth. For them, it's only a question of manipulation.

I had flown to Iran directly from Saudi Arabia and a conversation with that country's oil minister, Sheik Ahmed Yamani. He had charged that the Shah had been the chief motivating force behind OPEC's decision to drive up the price of oil. The Shah flatly denied this, but he also made it clear in the interview that he didn't want to talk about it. At one point, when I tried for the second or third time to bring the subject up, he chose— as a diversionary tactic—to give me a little lesson in geography:

WALLACE: As you know, I have been across the gulf, the gulf that you call Persian and they call Arabian—

SHAH: Why do you call—call it that? You have been to school, haven't you?

WALLACE: Yes.

SHAH: What was the name that you have read during your school days?

WALLACE: Persian Gulf.

SHAH: All right. That's—

WALLACE: (laughing): But they do call it the Arabian Gulf.

SHAH: Well, *they* can do many things.

Shifting to another tack, I suggested that in pushing for a big jump in oil prices, the Shah may have been motivated by a desire to get even with the United States and Western Europe. I reminded him of an old grievance, one that he had chosen to phrase in ethnic or genetic terms:

> WALLACE: You have said that the blue-eyed Europeans, the blue-eyed people of the United States have plundered your country. Do you really believe that?
>
> SHAH: I do, because just only take this oil thing, among others. For fifty years they were taking the oil and flaring the gas.
>
> WALLACE: That is, burning it?
>
> SHAH: Just burning it. What name could you give to this action?
>
> WALLACE: Well, it was uneconomical, they said.
>
> SHAH: Obviously, because they didn't care. It was much less costly to take that oil and without reinjecting the gas into the oil well . . .
>
> WALLACE: And you do believe that we in the United States and the European nations—the blue-eyed ones—in a sense discriminated against brown-eyed oil?
>
> SHAH: So far, yes.

Then I asked the Shah about his autocratic, one-man rule of Iran, which he cited with customary arrogance as the main reason for the rapid economic progress his country had made in recent years. He seemed to take the position that Iran could not have prospered under a democratic government, and when I called him on that, he promptly accepted the challenge. The next thing I knew, we were debating some fine points of political science:

> SHAH: Well, what is a democracy, anyway?
>
> WALLACE: Democracy?
>
> SHAH: Yes.
>
> WALLACE: How do *you* define democracy? Don't we have democracy in the United States?
>
> SHAH: Well, not according to what the Greeks used to say in the public places.
>
> WALLACE: Well, we elect our leaders. You are not elected.
>
> SHAH: Yes, but how do you elect your leaders? According to Watergate, it's a special kind.
>
> WALLACE: You will acknowledge that the United States is a much more democratic society than your own—than Iran.
>
> SHAH: Yes, but what do you mean by democracy, again?
>
> WALLACE: I mean freedom of thought. I mean freedom of expression. I mean freedom of the press.
>
> SHAH: To what extent? To what extent?
>
> WALLACE: I mean electing leaders. I mean opposition—
>
> SHAH: To what extent?
>
> WALLACE: Well, to what extent—
>
> SHAH: Yes, to what extent? If it is a self-destructive masochist kind of thing that will permit you all kind of fraud and corruption, you have it.
>
> WALLACE: Is that really the way you look at the United States?
>
> SHAH: Not—I mean the kind—If you talk about that kind of democracy, I will come back with the same answer— the permissive democracy, regardless of who has it.

WALLACE: What you're saying, Your Majesty, is that "Father knows best." What if you got a leader here who does not have your wisdom, your compassion?

SHAH: Then the relationship between that leader and his people will not be the one existing between me and my people. He will become another leader as we have many in our country, who was kicked out by— Well, my father kicked out the former king here because he had no contact with his people.

Viewed from a post-1979 perspective, the above observation takes on a rich and heavy irony. Yet at the time, the Shah betrayed no sign of concern that he might be tempting fate or indulging in hubris. Then at the height of his power, he would have dismissed as utterly absurd the prediction that in just five years, he, too, would be "kicked out" because he had lost "contact with his people."

Our next interview, one year later, took place in St. Moritz, where the Shah and the Empress and their large entourage had gone on a skiing vacation. On that occasion, I brought up the subject that I had been warned by other Iranians never to mention in the Shah's presence:

WALLACE: Your Majesty, you have a police force, a secret police, called the SAVAK, reportedly as efficient and occasionally as brutal as any in the world. The London *Sunday Times,* which is a first-rate newspaper, investigated SAVAK's activities for over a year—you smile as I bring this subject up—and they published a piece a couple of weeks ago called "Torture in Iran." They wrote that SAVAK brutality ranges from mere fingernail pulling to shoving bottles up rectums to raping women in front of their husbands.

SHAH: Broken—broken bottles.

WALLACE: Why should the police arm of Imperial Iran need to use such methods against their own fellow citizens?

SHAH: Well, first of all, this is so ridiculous that I'm not going to really answer a question like this. It's not true. I'm even astonished why this—why you have really asked this question, not just because the *Sunday Times* has said so or written so.

WALLACE: Well, there have been stories in the United States—

SHAH: There have been stories, and again I say why should they torture people we don't need to? Before we interrogate anyone, we have enough evidence. When he is put in front of those evidences, he just collapses and say everything. We don't have to use these old methods. You said they are as sophisticated as any other police force in the world.

WALLACE: As efficient.

SHAH: They will be as sophisticated as your own services. They will employ the same methods as your own, or the British, or the French, or the Germans.

WALLACE: And you categorically deny the allegations in the London *Sunday Times?*

SHAH: Well, some of those obviously, some of those. It's ridiculous to say about the question of the bottle or raping the woman in front of her husband. This is disgusting.

WALLACE: Your Majesty, you—

SHAH: Not that I accept the fingernails, the pulling of the fingernails, but the others are really disgusting. I don't like it at all.

WALLACE: Well, why do you need a SAVAK at all? Why do you need this secret police?

SHAH: Why? Everybody has. Who hasn't got a secret police?

I let it go at that for the time being, but I was determined to question the Shah further about SAVAK in our next interview.

The opportunity came in the fall of 1976 when Bill McClure and I returned to Teheran to do yet another story on the Iranian monarch. By that time, his appearances on *60 Minutes* seemed on the verge of becoming an annual event. The 1976 visit was my third to Iran in four years, and I must say that my impressions of the country were as ambivalent as those I had formed about the man who ruled it. Iran was a police state—no question of that—but it was unlike any other police state I had ever seen. For example, the Soviet Union and its satellites in Eastern Europe are drab and sterile places where one can almost feel the suffocating presence of the bureaucracies that control every aspect of daily life. There is a sense of being under constant surveillance, and the overall mood in those countries is severe and forbidding.

But Iran did not feel like that. It seemed to be bursting with life and the kind of spontaneous hustle and bustle that one associates with the happy disorder of people who enjoy at least some degree of freedom. The benign climate no doubt helped to create this impression; when it's sunny and warm much of the time, people feel better physically, and that affects their general disposition. Then, too, the presence of so many foreigners—including at that time thirty thousand Americans, many of whom were involved in Iran's fast-growing industrial complex—contributed to the aura of an open and cosmopolitan society. Yet all that was misleading. For the Shah's regime was, in reality, about as repressive as any police state in the Communist bloc, and it was SAVAK that had been assigned the frequently brutal task of keeping everyone in line. On my 1976 visit to Iran, I talked to a man who told me (off-camera, of course) that his brother had been tortured by SAVAK just a few weeks earlier; when I related that to the Shah, his only defense was that it could not have happened so recently. In response, I referred to a report that had been put together by an outside, presumably impartial agency:

WALLACE: Now, when an outfit like the International Commission of Jurists comes here, and then comes out with a report saying that in spite of what you say, Your Majesty, torture continues?

SHAH: How do they know? Well, they can't continue saying this. But you are—they have even accused Great Britain of acting against human rights.

WALLACE: We're talking for the moment about your country.

SHAH: They are putting us in the same category.

WALLACE: In other words, you're saying you do what every country does?

SHAH: Sure. Why not?

WALLACE: If torture is necessary, you torture?

SHAH: Not the torture in the old sense of torturing people, twisting their arms and doing this and that. But there are intelligent ways of questioning now.

WALLACE: Well, they talk about psychological and physical torture.

SHAH: Physical I don't believe. Not anymore. Maybe in the old days. Maybe!

We also talked about the Jewish lobby in the United States. The Shah was as forthright on that subject as he was on most others, and at one point he declared that American Presidents were, in effect, under the thumb of that pressure group:

WALLACE: Why, if this is true, why would the President of the United States pay attention to that lobby?

SHAH: They are strong.

WALLACE: Strong in what sense?

SHAH: They are controlling many things.

WALLACE: Controlling what?

SHAH: Newspapers, media—

WALLACE: Your Majesty!

SHAH: Banks, finances. And I'm going to stop there.

WALLACE: Well, now, just a second! You really believe that the Jewish community in the United States is that powerful? They make the media reflect their view of foreign policy?

SHAH: Hmm. Yes.

WALLACE: They do not report— *We* do not report honestly?

SHAH: Don't mix things, please! I don't say the media. I say *in* the media they have people, not the *entire* media. Some newspapers will only reflect their views, yes.

WALLACE: Well, *The New York Times,* for instance, is owned by the Sulzberger family, who are Jewish. Are you suggesting that *The New York Times* is biased in its treatment of the question of Zionism, Israel's existence, the United States' relationship with the Arab world?

SHAH: I will have to put all the articles of *The New York Times* written on this subject and draw the conclusion. You can put this through the computer and it will answer you.

WALLACE: What you're saying is that, yes, you do believe.

SHAH: Well, let's wait for the answer of the computer.

WALLACE: *The Washington Post?*

SHAH: The same.

WALLACE: The networks?

SHAH: Less.

We then turned our attention to the Palestinians, about whom he was no less outspoken. He accused them of trying to "bully the world" with their "terrorism and blackmailing." Moreover, he contended that other Arab leaders, such as Sadat and Hussein and even Syria's Assad, shared his disgust with the Palestinian tactics. This led to my next question:

WALLACE: And what about the Arab leader who supports the Palestinians, the terrorists, with his oil money, Muammar Qaddafi of Libya?

SHAH: He's crazy.

WALLACE: You really believe that?

SHAH: Oh yes! No doubt. The man is absolutely irresponsible and crazy.

His trenchant diagnosis of Qaddafi's mental condition gave me the opening I needed to probe into another delicate area.

WALLACE: Are you aware of a CIA psychological profile about you, sir?

SHAH: No. I must admit that that's the first time I hear that.

WALLACE: Truly?

SHAH: Yes. What is it?

WALLACE: Would you be interested in hearing what the CIA had to say?

SHAH: Yes, why not?

WALLACE: Really?

SHAH: Yes, why not?

WALLACE: I have your permission?

SHAH: Yes, sure.

WALLACE: You won't send me to the SAVAK if I ask?

SHAH: No, I would spare you this terrible ordeal of going through torture.

WALLACE: This secret study portrays the Shah as a brilliant but dangerous megalomaniac who is likely to pursue his own aims in disregard of U.S. interests.

SHAH: So how could I be your man, your agent?

WALLACE: How do you mean?

SHAH: Safeguarding your interests?

WALLACE: Well, it says that the Shah is an uncertain ally. His dreams of glory apparently—

SHAH: Oh! Ah! I know. So you would like me to be your stooge?

WALLACE: Do you want me to go on, or shall I forget about this, Your Majesty?

SHAH: Well, there are some funny points. Why not?

So I proceeded to quote to him from the CIA profile. His dreams of glory, it said, apparently exceeded his ability to finance them. And the CIA warned that when his oil revenues ran out in an estimated two decades, he might use his new military power to seize some neighboring oil fields. When I asked the Shah what he thought of this assessment of his character, he dismissed it as so much nonsense, which was hardly surprising. But he didn't seem to take offense at my bringing it up, and at the end of the 1976 interview, I raised the question that had intrigued me ever since my first encounter with him two years earlier:

WALLACE: I confess I'm curious. Why are you willing to sit and answer these questions?

SHAH: Because I like this kind of provocations. It gives me the opportunity of clearing or clarifying things that unfortunately are said and not always answered.

But that turned out to be the last time I provoked him. In fact, I never laid eyes on the Shah again, in person, for he turned down all my further requests for interviews.

In response to one of my questions that fall, the Shah acknowledged that SAVAK agents were operating in the United States. Their mission, he said, was to keep a close eye on people and organizations that were "hostile to my country." Actually, much of the agents' attention was focused on Iranian students, who were not hostile to their country as such but were vehemently opposed to the Shah and his regime. By the fall of 1976, "Down with the Shah!" and "The Shah is a fascist butcher!" had become frequently heard battle cries on American campuses, where sizable contingents of Iranian students were enrolled. Those demonstrations were an early portent of the upheaval that would soon bring an end to the Shah's long reign.

When we broadcast that last interview with the Shah in October of 1976, his disclosure of a clandestine SAVAK operation in the States drew an immediate reaction from officials in Washington who, at the time, were doing their best to downplay both the opposition to the Shah and the actions of his secret police. Not long thereafter, the State Department announced that it had investigated and found no evidence that Iranian agents in America were involved in activities which could be deemed "illegal or improper." But by then, Barry Lando and I had begun our own investigation into SAVAK's overseas operations, and we found people who insisted that there was a lot more going on than mere surveillance. Various sources told us that SAVAK was engaged in a systematic campaign of intimidation and terror against Iranian dissidents abroad, and that it had even dispatched assassination squads to the United States and Europe. The most fascinating story, especially in light of later developments, was one we came across in Paris, where a number of anti-Shah Iranians were living in exile. We found a man—a self-described soldier of fortune—who told us that SAVAK had tried to induce him, through a complicated blackmailing scheme, to assassinate several Iranian dissidents. He claimed that a set of pistols had been turned over to him for that purpose. This designated assassin said the number one target on the hit list given to him by SAVAK was an anti-Shah Iranian named Sadegh Ghotbzadeh, but that instead of carrying out the plot, he alerted Ghotbzadeh to the danger that he and other Iranian exiles were in.

We aired the SAVAK story in March 1977, and once again the State Department was quick to respond, this time with even more irritation. Accusing *60 Minutes* of sensationalism, our critics in the U.S. government pointed out that (a) neither Ghotbzadeh nor any of his cohorts had in fact been assassinated, and (b) we had presented no hard evidence to back up the lurid charge that SAVAK, in the Mafia argot, had taken out contracts on enemies of the Shah. That was true enough, as we had taken care to report in our broadcast. But as subsequent events would reveal, the Shah had a strong and urgent motive for wanting to get rid of Sadegh Ghotbzadeh. As a member of the opposition in exile, he was closely allied to its leader, the Ayatollah Ruhoollah Khomeini, and although this did not mean much to most outsiders at the time, the Shah must have known what a threat those two men were to his regime. Nor was it long before the rest of us got the message. Once the Shah was deposed, Khomeini took over as the spiritual head of the Islamic revolutionary government in Iran, and Ghotbzadeh became its foreign minister. And during the hostage crisis that followed, the names and faces of both men became all too familiar to millions of angry Americans.

In the meantime, I did not get back to Iran until November 1978, and by then it was all but over for the Shah. My assignment was to do a story on the protests and riots that were about to escalate into a full-scale revolution. As I stood in the midst of an anti-Shah demonstration in the streets of Teheran that fall, I felt almost overwhelmed by the intensity of the rage that came pouring forth from the mobs. This time, as I said, the Shah turned down my request for an interview. I could hardly blame him. He was no longer in a position to indulge in the luxury of "this kind of provocations," for clearly there were more pressing matters that required his attention. By the end of that year, the Peacock Throne was doomed. The Shah's authority in Iran was on the verge of total collapse, and his paramount concern had to be personal survival—himself and his family. And when the full force of the revolution struck in January 1979, the Shah and the Empress and their children fled Iran for good.

The royal family went first to Egypt, but eventually found refuge in Mexico, where the Shah was able to live, as before, in a manner befitting one of the richest men in the world. His continued survival and extravagant life-style infuriated the Muslim revolutionaries who had driven him out of power. Many of them felt that without the Shah's scalp and vast resources in their possession, their victory was less than complete. Then in October 1979, when the Shah was admitted into the United States to receive medical treatment for his terminal cancer,

Washington and President Carter became the targets of all the wrath and frustration that had been building up in Iran for so many years. As the ugly mood in Teheran grew more rancorous, it led in early November to the assault on the U.S. Embassy and the seizure of its diplomatic corps. Thus began the long nightmare of fifty-two American citizens held hostage in a country that had become consumed by the corrosive hatred of religious fanaticism. As in the French Revolution two centuries earlier, the overthrow of the ancien régime in Iran was followed by a reign of terror.

Almost from the moment the Shah was deposed, Barry Lando and I began a concerted effort to get into Iran to interview the austere mystic who had emerged as the spiritual leader of the revolution. From Lando's base in Paris and mine in New York, we called every source we could think of who could conceivably help us gain access to the Ayatollah Khomeini. Our best contact was Sadegh Ghotbzadeh, whom we had interviewed in Paris two years earlier when we did our report on SAVAK's alleged plot to assassinate him and other anti-Shah Iranian exiles. Since that time, Ghotbzadeh had become a voice of authority in Iran. As one of Khomeini's most loyal and trusted supporters during the long years of exile, he was rewarded with the post of foreign minister in the revolutionary government. Back in 1977 when we tracked him down in Paris, Ghotbzadeh had been only too happy to cooperate with *60 Minutes*. For obvious reasons he welcomed our investigation into SAVAK's sinister activities. Yet now that he was a leading figure in the new government, it was another story; in early 1979 when Lando telephoned him from Paris, Ghotbzadeh gave him the cold shoulder. Striving for a vivid metaphor, he told Barry that *60 Minutes* was as "welcome in Iran as bacon in a synagogue."

But Lando was nothing if not persistent, and in the early days of the hostage crisis, he called Ghotbzadeh again and urged him to reconsider. Barry pointed out that the American people were enraged by the seizure of their embassy in Teheran and the detention of U.S. citizens. Yet in spite of that, he said, *60 Minutes* was willing to give the revolutionaries in Iran an opportunity to "tell your story to millions of Americans."

Ghotbzadeh told Lando that he would think it over and get back to him.

In the meantime, I was working the phones on my end, placing calls to Iranian contacts in New York and Washington. But as always, I had other stories to worry about, and therefore I happened to be in California on another assignment when I received word from Lando that Ghotbzadeh had persuaded Khomeini to grant us an interview. All of a sudden, *60 Minutes* had become kosher in that synagogue, but Ghotbzadeh emphasized that we had to come "right away—instantly!" He said he could not keep the invitation open for very long. I promptly dropped everything else and caught a flight from San Francisco to London. Since I didn't have my passport with me, I called my secretary in New York, Marikay Mead, to arrange for her to fly to London with the passport and other necessary research material and credentials. When I arrived at Heathrow Airport, Marikay was waiting there with the documents; later that day, I flew on to Teheran, where I hooked up with Lando and our camera crew. The next morning we went on to the holy city of Qum, Khomeini's power base in Iran, where, on November 18, 1979—fourteen days after the hostages were seized— we were ushered into the Ayatollah's presence, as promised. It was the first interview to be given to an American reporter since the start of the hostage crisis.

As an interviewee, the Ayatollah Khomeini was no Shah. When we arrived in Qum, we were informed that our questions had to be submitted to Khomeini's people in advance, and in the preinterview haggling, several of them were rejected as unacceptable. Yet even under those rigorous ground rules, Khomeini did not fulfill his end of the bargain. He did not really answer the questions that his people had approved; he simply used us as a pulpit for his propaganda. Most of his replies were little more than the slogans and demands we had been hearing from the street mobs in Teheran since the assault on the U.S. Embassy two weeks earlier. For example: "The Shah is a criminal . . . Carter must return the Shah . . . Unless he is returned, the hostages will not be freed . . . The Americans are safe and healthy . . . Islam protects the prisoners . . . Islam is humane . . ." And so on.

Khomeini uttered these pronouncements in a remote and toneless voice, and throughout the interview, his impassive eyes hardly moved as he stared straight ahead, looking at no one, almost as though he were speaking by rote. I talked *at* him (not *to* him) for more than an hour, and not more than two or three times did he glance in my direction or in any other way acknowledge my presence. I simply could not engage his attention on a human or personal level. Although in some respects, it was an unsatisfactory interview, it did give our viewers a glimpse of the strange and implacable foe we were up against now in Iran.

During those first few weeks of the crisis, many Americans, in and out of government, expressed the hope that the hostages would be released in time to be home with their families for Christmas. They were referring, of course, to the Christmas of 1979. No one envisioned then that the ordeal would extend through all of 1980, and that the hostages would wind up spending *two* Christmas seasons in captivity. Most of us were utterly stunned by what had happened in Teheran; we could not understand the bitterness and hatred that had impelled the Iranian revolutionaries to do something so drastic and hostile that it could have been construed as nothing less than an act of war. The prevailing mood on the home front was not only anger and mounting frustration, but bewilderment, too. Why had this outrage taken place? What were the forces that had brought us to this dreadful dilemma?

In the early weeks of 1980, Barry Lando and I set out to answer some of those questions. As we gathered information for our long background report on the deepening crisis, we began to understand why the explosive events in Iran caught so many Americans by surprise. For we came across evidence that once again, as had been the case in Vietnam, U.S. government officials had not leveled with the citizens they represented.

A large part of that story, which we called "The Iran File," focused on the heavy role the Central Intelligence Agency had played in the internal affairs of the Shah's regime, dating back to 1953 when the CIA helped restore the exiled Shah to power in Iran. This fact had never been denied, but over the years it had been largely ignored or forgotten. However, that turned out to be the least of it. Lando and I got our hands on a classified Senate Foreign Relations Committee report which revealed that the CIA had helped the Shah set up SAVAK by providing money and training. Moreover, the report disclosed, officials in the CIA and other U.S. agencies were fully aware that SAVAK had inflicted torture of the most brutal kind on thousands of Iranian citizens, and that some of those officials had cooperated with the Shah in his efforts to keep that information from reaching the American press and public. We also learned from the Senate report that the U.S. government not only was aware of SAVAK's activities outside of Iran, but that the CIA and the FBI had even assisted SAVAK in gathering evidence about Iranian dissidents abroad, which, once acquired, could be used against them in cruel interrogations back in Iran. (So much for the State Department's 1976 investigation of SAVAK and its pious contention that the Shah's agents were doing nothing "illegal or improper" in the United States.)

It was not a pretty story, but we felt that it had to be told. Before we put "The Iran File" on the air, however, CBS News received several calls from high-ranking officials in the Carter administration who urged us not to broadcast it. They argued that to air such disclosures on *60 Minutes* would only exacerbate the crisis and might even have a detrimental effect on the delicate negotiations to secure the release of the hostages. We took that risk into consideration, but in the end decided that our viewers had a right to know that the actions taken by the Iranian revolutionaries—though deplorable and unjustified in themselves—were at least prompted by legitimate grievances against the U.S. government. So we went ahead and broadcast "The Iran File" in early March 1980.

In our report we did not entirely overlook the other side of the story. We pointed out that during most of his long reign, the Shah had indeed been a loyal ally and a stable presence in the Persian Gulf, and that our government felt it had a vital stake in keeping his regime in power, regardless of the violent excesses committed by his secret police. For the broadcast I interviewed several people who defended Washington's pro-Shah policy, including Joseph Sisco, who had been a top official in the State Department during the Nixon and Ford administrations. Taking the long view, the historical perspective, Sisco said to me: "Mike, six Presidents and six secretaries of state just can't be totally wrong." Perhaps not, but when the then current President and secretary of state—Jimmy Carter and Cyrus Vance—made the decision to permit the ailing Shah to enter the United States, they brought down a terrible fury on themselves and their country. The next thing we knew, the skies over Iran were filled with the spectacle of chickens coming home to roost. And in political terms, the Carter administration never recovered from that act of revenge.

There is no doubt that the hostage crisis brought Jimmy Carter's presidency to its knees, in much the same way that the war in Vietnam forced Lyndon Johnson out of the White House and the Watergate scandal drove Richard Nixon into permanent political exile. I'm not suggesting that it alone cost Carter the 1980 election, for he was already in deep trouble on other fronts. Soaring inflation and other economic woes, along with a growing disenchantment over the big-spending policies of the federal government, were probably enough to make it a Republican year. But the events in Teheran certainly helped seal Carter's doom. Even before that crisis, Carter had seldom acted with decisive authority, and many of his critics charged that he was, in effect, intimidated by the vast powers of the presidency. His cautious response to the Iranian revolutionaries only reinforced this perception, and the longer the hostages remained in captivity, the sharper the criticisms of his strength and leadership. (On the other hand, some people argued that by responding with restraint and patience, Carter saved the lives of the hostages. According to this view, a more aggressive, retaliatory reaction almost surely would have triggered a war of some kind, the first casualties of which would have been the hostages.)

Even the calendar seemed to be part of a conspiracy to thwart Carter's reelection in 1980. The voters went to the polls that November on the first anniversary of the seizure in Iran, and, with the hostages still at the mercy of their captors, the observance of that sad milestone was a telling reminder of Carter's prolonged failure to secure their release. In itself this may have been enough to turn a fairly close presidential race into a Ronald Reagan landslide. What's more, the ordeal was destined to torment the Carter White House until the very last moments of his presidency. When the hostages were finally released on the day Reagan was inaugurated, it was the new administration of the man who defeated Carter that stood to benefit from the mood of relief and elation that swept the country.

In the meantime, the reign of terror continued in Teheran. Like so many of its illustrious forebears—the French and the Russian come instantly to mind—the revolution in Iran soon began to devour its own. My last visit to Iran was in December 1980, a few weeks before the hostages were released, and I interviewed the president of the revolutionary government, Abolhassan Bani-Sadr. By then, Bani-Sadr had become openly critical of the Islamic hard-liners who, he felt, were betraying the original purpose of the revolution. When I interviewed him, he admitted reluctantly that instead of striving to build a democratic government, the Muslim extremists were creating their own police state, complete with torture and other forms of repression reminiscent of the Shah's regime at its worst. And in a private, off-camera conversation, Bani-Sadr told me that even though he had been elected earlier that year by 75 percent of the vote, he himself was now in a perilous position. Six months later, after barely escaping the firing squad, Bani-Sadr fled to a life of exile in Paris.

Many others were not so fortunate, including Sadegh Ghotbzadeh. Like Danton in France almost two centuries earlier, Ghotbzadeh was an early leader of the revolution who went on to become one of its most celebrated victims. He was arrested in April 1982 on charges of plotting to kill his former mentor, the Ayatollah Khomeini, and of trying to subvert the revolution with his efforts to establish a secular government. At his trial that summer, Ghotbzadeh acknowledged his desire to create "a real republic" in Iran, but he denied vigorously that he had been part of a conspiracy to kill Khomeini. Convicted on both counts, he was put to death by a firing squad in September of 1982. By then, hundreds of other Iranians, many of whom were early supporters of the revolution, had been similarly executed. Several years before the upheaval in Iran, the Oxford historian A.J.P. Taylor wrote: "Idealists make revolutions; practical men come afterwards and clear up the mess." In early 1984, as Iran observed the fifth anniversary of its revolution, the country was still steeped in carnage and most of its leaders who had been practical men were either dead or in exile. Hence, there was no way of knowing when, if ever, the effort would be made to clear up the mess there.

Nor was the ultimate fate of their revolution the only problem the Iranians had to confront. The country was still bogged down in its war with Iraq, which began in 1980 when Iraqi forces, seeking to exploit all the turmoil in Teheran, launched a surprise attack on Iran. (As some observers noted at the time, the Baghdad government would never have dared to wage war against Iran if the Shah and his strong military apparatus had still been in power.) In addition, the unstable revolutionary government in Teheran had to keep a wary eye on its formidable neighbor to the north—the Soviet Union. After all, since late 1979 the Red Army had been fighting in Afghanistan, just across Iran's eastern border, and there were many who feared that if Iran continued to flounder in chaos, the Russians might be tempted to regard its rich oil fields and access to the Persian Gulf as ripe for the plucking. (There were others, however, who made the convincing point that the fierce resistance of the Afghans in the conflict was bound to have an inhibiting effect on Soviet considerations of similar adventures in the future.)

By the summer of 1982, there were no less than three wars raging in the Middle East: in Afghanistan, along the Iranian-Iraqi border and in Lebanon, where Israeli troops were on the march. It's possible that two of those wars, and perhaps all three, would never have broken out had Anwar Sadat and the Shah of Iran been alive and in command of their respective governments. But by that time, both were in their graves, and, largely because of their demise, the future of the Middle East appeared to be more troubled and uncertain than ever before.

CHAPTER

FIFTEEN

DURING THE 1970s, as *60 Minutes* gradually evolved into the most successful program in the history of broadcast journalism, Wallace spent more time in the Middle East than in any other overseas theater of operations. The reason, of course: that's where the action was. From the Yom Kippur War to Sadat's visit to Jerusalem, and from OPEC's oil embargo to the revolution in Iran, the Middle East was the center stage of events that altered the course of history. As a frequent visitor who could pick and choose his spots, Wallace observed the drama in the area, interviewed its principal players and reported his findings to the millions of Americans who had become habitual viewers of *60 Minutes*.

However, he also found time to cover stories in other parts of the world. He had periodic assignments in Europe, even though that continent was no longer the attraction that it had been to an earlier generation of American reporters. Long gone were the days when Paris was a movable feast and foreign correspondents were romantic figures who wore trench coats and encountered intrigue on the Orient Express. By the 1970s Paris had fallen prey to the ravages of tourism (fast-food shops, à la McDonald's, could be found on both sides of the Seine), the Orient Express had become just another tedious train ride, and even though some correspondents still wore trench coats, they ran little risk of getting them soiled in the line of duty. Instead of covering revolution in Spain or espionage in the

Balkans, they now filed routine dispatches on economic conferences and orderly elections. But if Europe had become relatively placid and predictable, it was not entirely devoid of stories that aroused the interest of Wallace and his producers.

In 1971 he and Bill McClure did a piece on Jewish life in Romania. In presenting this report, Wallace pointed out that in most Iron Curtain countries, "the Jew is an object of suspicion," not only because Eastern Europe had a tradition of anti-Semitism, but even more so because the pro-Arab Soviet Union and its satellites regarded Israel (and therefore all Zionists) as an enemy. Romania was a happy exception. In open defiance of the guidelines set down by Moscow, the Bucharest government had adopted a policy of treating its Jewish citizens with fairness and some respect.

Then in 1972 Wallace went to Greece with McClure to report on the Papadopoulos government, which he described as "the only military dictatorship inside NATO." He was drawn to the story in part by the fact that the current Greek leadership had become an issue in that year's U.S. presidential campaign. (George McGovern vowed that if elected, he would cut off all military aid to the Papadopoulos regime, NATO ally or no.) Beyond that, a great deal of negative interest in the subject had been stirred up by the movie *Z*, a highly popular and provocative indictment of the colonels who staged the 1967 coup that brought Papadopoulos to power. There was also a melancholy aspect to the trip that had nothing to do with his assignment for *60 Minutes*. For that was Mike's first visit to Greece since he had gone there ten years earlier to search for his missing son, Peter, whose body he found on the mountain path near the Gulf of Corinth.

Of all his European stories, none was more positive and upbeat than the 1975 piece he and producer Harry Moses did on Norway, which they called "The Little Country That Works." At a time when the United States and other Western countries were beset by severe economic problems and social unrest, Wallace observed that Norway has "managed to escape the anxieties of the seventies to a remarkable degree." Then he got down to specifics:

There is no poverty in Norway, no slums, no unemployment. Norwegians live longer than anyone else in the world, and their infant mortality rate is the world's lowest. Their health care system is a model of its kind, and every Norwegian can look forward to a comfortable old age because he'll wind up with a pension that'll take good care of him until the day he dies. Perhaps all that is why Norwegians seem to be a gentler people than the rest of us. At least they kill each other less. Their murder rate is the lowest in the world. And they live together, man and wife, longer than just about anyone: their divorce rate is four times lower than our own . . . One religion—Lutheran. One school system—nationwide. Few immigrants. No race problems.

Then, after revealing through interviews and pictures how all this was possible (a sparse population, geographic isolation, a homogeneous culture, and a huge income from oil) Mike ended the report on a wistful note: "This visitor left Norway reluctantly to go back to the real world."

The next year he was in Bologna with McClure taking a look at "Communism, Italian Style." The main point of this story was that peaceful coexistence, an empty phrase that had no concrete reality in most countries conditioned by the Cold War, had become a way of life in Bologna, where freely elected Communists had been in power for many years. Moreover, by the mid-seventies, Communist candidates had captured control of local governments in several other large Italian cities, where the voters apparently decided that what was good enough for Bologna was good enough for them. Some of the Communists Wallace interviewed in Italy were also practicing Catholics and strong believers in the democratic process, and they saw no contradictions. Needless to say, their attitude did not sit well with such ideologically rigid institutions as the Papacy, the Kremlin and the White House. But then, as Mike noted, the Italians have a proud history of flouting orthodoxies of one kind or another.

In addition to Wallace's work in Europe during those years, he had assignments that took him to Asia and Latin America— all, of course, on top of his regular commuting run to the Middle East. (From 1969 through 1980, he did at least one story a year in the Middle East, and in some years, he made two or three trips to the region.) Nor was he the only member of the team who carried a heavily stamped passport. Over the years, all the correspondents on *60 Minutes* have been constantly on the go, flying over oceans and through time zones to get to a story. In fact, this has been a large part of their, and the program's, appeal, a circumstance no one appreciated more than the man who, having created the act, rejoiced in his reign as the ringmaster of the show. In 1982 Don Hewitt told an interviewer: *"Sixty Minutes is a broadcast on which four reporters take the audience along with them on a story, almost a sharing of their notes with the audience. Newspapers and magazines have overseas bureaus now, and their correspondents don't have to travel anywhere. There are no Floyd Gibbonses or Lowell Thomases or Richard Harding Davises left on earth—except my tigers."*

The pace was especially taxing during the early years when Hewitt had only two tigers on the prowl. It wasn't *too* bad during the first two of those years when Wallace and Harry Reasoner were lunging about, because *60 Minutes* was a biweekly broadcast, which gave Hewitt's predators a chance to catch their breath before moving out again in search of fresh prey. But not long after Reasoner gave up the hunt to take on a sedentary life in captivity—as an anchorman at ABC News—and Morley Safer came aboard as his replacement, the program was switched to a new time slot, 6:00 P.M. on Sunday, and then it went on the air every week. The shift occurred in the fall of 1971, and for the next four years, Wallace and Safer were so peripatetic that their working schedules resembled those grueling itineraries that sadistic travel agents put together for naïve tourists: If this is Tuesday, it must be Rangoon.

At one point during this period, Wallace did a story on a condition to which he needed no introduction—jet lag. In the summer of 1973, he accompanied a TWA pilot on a flight from Boston to Hong Kong, a journey of fifteen thousand miles over three continents and through thirteen time zones. To be sure, there were twenty-four-hour rest stops along the way—in Paris, Tel Aviv and Bombay—but after another one-day layover in Hong Kong, the pilot and his crew had to cover the same distance all over again on the return flight to the States. The *60 Minutes* crew made the return trip, too, and in one of his on-camera comments, Mike noted that going through all those rapid changes in time plays havoc with one's body chemistry, or "body clock," as it's known to students of jet lag. In reporting on the adverse effects of jet lag—the mental stress and physical fatigue caused by the inevitable disruption of normal eating and sleeping habits—he was merely confirming the message his own body clock had sent him, not only on that trip but on other occasions when he had flown halfway around the world under the deadline pressure to get a certain story as quickly as possible and then hustle off to his next assignment on some other continent. When the 60 Minutes season was in full swing, it was not unusual for Wallace to go two or three weeks at a stretch with his system out of synch with local time; sometimes during those periods he would doze off at eleven in the morning or skip dinner because he wasn't hungry at the appropriate hour. Then invariably his body clock would wake him up in the middle of the night to tell him it was time to eat, not an easy desire to satisfy if he happened to be on the road and in a hotel that didn't offer room service to victims of jet lag.

It was hardly the best way to live or work, and as time went on Wallace began to complain: The constant travel and hectic pace were taking their toll, and he and Safer could not be expected to keep it up year in and year out. In more than one conversation with Hewitt, he strongly urged that a third cor- respondent be brought in to share the burden. At first, Hewitt didn't think much of the idea; his main concern was the overall look of the broadcast and he did not want to run the risk of disturbing a winning format. For he recognized, as did others, that Wallace and Safer had evolved into a highly compatible on-air duo. Although off-camera, they did not always see eye to eye—indeed, that part of their working relationship was marred by a certain degree of strain and friction—it was their on-air performance that mattered. So what the viewers saw every week were two reporters whose respective talents and personalities complemented each other in a way that gave the show an appealing balance in tone and style. Whereas Wallace's general approach to a story was blunt, assertive and devoid of frills, Safer, cut from a British mold, relied more on finesse and understated irony to get his points across. Like a shortstop and second baseman who have played together for years, they had blended their skills to form a smooth and impressive dou- ble-play combination: Wallace was adept at fielding the hard smashes, while Safer's strong suit was executing the fancy pivots.

Hewitt appreciated what he had going for him on *60 Minutes,* and he feared that the presence of a third correspondent might disrupt the rhythm and throw everything off stride. Yet he gradually came to the realization that Wallace was right: The need for another correspondent to share the heavy work load outweighed his concern that a third cook might spoil the broth, and in the fall of 1975 Hewitt agreed to make the change. After seven years of being structured around a duet, a journalistic version of "Tea for Two," *60 Minutes* was about to introduce its viewers to *"The Third Man* Theme."

There was another reason why Hewitt felt the time had come to take on a third correspondent. Not long after the new television season began that fall, the CBS brass made the decision to give *60 Minutes* a second chance to play in prime time. Hewitt was told that in December the broadcast would be moved up an hour to 7:00 P.M. on Sunday.

The program had earned that second chance, no question about it. From the very beginning *60 Minutes* had been a critical hit, but during the first three years of its existence, it was nothing more than a prestige show that bombed in the ratings. This is why it was banished from the prime-time schedule in 1971 and consigned to the far less demanding time slot of 6:00 P.M. on Sunday. There, it caught on. Over the next four years, *60 Minutes* gradually built up a large and loyal audience.

The sharpest increase in regular viewers came during the 1973–1974 season and there were a couple of extraneous factors that helped to spark that boost. First, the Watergate affair, then in full bloom, turned America into a nation of news freaks. Watergate junkies could not get enough of their favorite obsession, and among the beneficiaries of their addiction was *60 Minutes,* especially on those occasions when it aired stories that dealt with the scandal. Wallace's interviews with some of the more notorious dramatis personae—Chuck Colson, Gordon Liddy and, of course, Haldeman and Ehrlichman—were box-office bonanzas, the television equivalent of standing room only. The second boon to the broadcast that season was the Arab oil embargo. The severe gas shortage that struck in late 1973 and lasted through the following spring forced millions of Americans to stay home on Sunday instead of visiting relatives or going for a late-afternoon drive. Desperate for diversion, they turned on their television sets, discovered *60 Minutes* and became hooked. So much so, in fact, that after the crisis ended and viewers regained their freedom of mobility, many began to schedule their Sunday outings earlier in the day in order to be back home in time to catch the ticking stopwatch that signaled the start of "another edition of *Sixty Minutes.*"

Thus, by 1975 the program was well on its way to becoming a national institution, and the decision to move it back into prime time was yet another push in that direction. The switch occurred at a time when the CBS network was taking its lumps in the ratings, an indignity to which it was not accustomed. For twenty years, dating back to the days of *I Love Lucy,* CBS had led the opposition, season after season, in the annual battle for prime-time ratings. But in the 1975–1976 season, a remarkable surge by ABC, for years the weakest of the three networks, enabled it to soar past both its rivals and relegate CBS to the unwonted misery of second place. Drastic afflictions call for drastic cures. So, more or less in desperation (the alarmed and frustrated CBS programmers were willing to try *anything* that year), *60 Minutes* was ordered into the fray.

"I've waited twenty years for this," crowed Dick Salant, then nearing the end of his long reign as president of CBS News. During much of that time, he had had to endure the slights and disdain of the prime-time merchants at CBS, who regarded the news operation as a troublesome misfit that kept stirring up controversy but consistently failed to attract the volume of viewers needed to generate big advertising revenues. Over the years Salant's hat-in-hand requests for more money and air time were a constant irritation to the network's programmers, who believed that the prime-time schedule should be filled exclusively with sit-coms and other light entertainment. Now, in the twilight of his CBS career, Salant wallowed in vindication: "I always knew that if I survived in this job long enough, the day would come when those characters would turn to me to help them out with a ratings problem."

Hewitt also welcomed the challenge, but first he had to whip the new format into shape and it was proving to be more difficult than he had anticipated. Once he made up his mind to add a third tiger to his troupe, Hewitt did not waste any time mulling over prospective candidates. He knew right away which correspondent he wanted and promptly extended the offer to Dan Rather, who in recent years had been sharpening his claws on the Nixon White House, a fairly routine diet that suddenly turned into a feast when the seeds planted in that soil produced the rich harvest of Watergate.

Rather was at a critical crossroad in his career in those days, and he almost took a wrong turn. Shortly after Nixon finally threw in the towel in the summer of 1974, Rather relinquished the White House beat, which had been his turf for most of the past decade, and moved to New York to commence a new assignment as the sole correspondent on *CBS Reports*. This program was the network's long-running documentary series, and it evoked memories of the legendary Edward R. Murrow, who, twenty years earlier, had brought his high standards of excellence and integrity to the embryonic craft of TV journalism. In persuading Rather to give up his White House beat and take the job on *CBS Reports*, his superiors made much of the fact that he would become the network's first correspondent since Murrow to be honored with a regular assignment on a prime-time documentary series. It certainly *sounded* impressive, but in truth the documentary form was no longer the dominant force in television news that it had been in Murrow's day. The growth of the evening news shows and the success of other programs, such as *60 Minutes*, had overshadowed the impact that documentaries once had on the viewing public. Indeed, the decision to structure *CBS Reports* around the presence of Dan Rather, who had hit it big during the Nixon years, was prompted by a desire to restore the broadcast to its former status. But as Rather and his colleagues soon discovered, that was easier said than done.

During the year that followed his departure from the White House beat, Rather worked hard on *CBS Reports*, and his full-time commitment to the program did give it a specific and strong identity. But the broadcast only went on the air once a month, and sometimes not even as often as that. Even worse, it was relegated to weak and irregular time slots, and the lack of continuity made it all but impossible for the show to attract a large audience of habitual viewers. Compared with what he had been accustomed to at the White House—where his nightly reports on the Nixon crowd had made him a cult hero in the eyes of Watergate junkies—Rather found himself working from a position of low visibility and minimal impact. Given those circumstances, one would have expected him to jump at the opportunity to become one of Don Hewitt's tigers on *60 Minutes*.

But he didn't. Rather's initial reaction to the offer was cool and equivocal; he seriously doubted it was the right move for him to make at that time. For one thing, he was reluctant to abandon his commitment to *CBS Reports* after only a year. He was not blind to the difficulties he faced in drawing an audience—the erratic scheduling and undesirable time slots—but he believed that with patience and persistence, they could be overcome. To friends who questioned his sanguine view, he pointed out that it had taken *60 Minutes* a long time to make its breakthrough.

Then, too, he was wary of going to work on a broadcast which had already established its own clear identity. He recognized that Wallace and Safer had shaped *60 Minutes* to reflect their personalities, and the last thing he wanted to do was dance on a show which had been choreographed for other performers. He might be willing to play "the third man," but not if the role turned into "odd man out." True, *CBS Reports* had its problems, but at least it was all his own to have and to hold; in that part of the jungle, he was the *only* tiger. He certainly didn't want to give that up to move into a situation where he might be treated as a poor cousin, an unwelcome boarder whose presence in the house is resented by other members of the family. Word had reached Rather that Morley Safer was opposed to bringing in a third correspondent. (That was true, but as Safer told him later, once the decision was made to expand the duo into a trio, he fully agreed that Rather was far and away the best man for the job.) Rather assumed that if Safer felt that way, then Wallace probably did, too; and he was if anything even more concerned about that. He knew Wallace had a reputation for being a jealous guardian of his own turf. He had heard stories of bitter quarrels within the domain of *60 Minutes*, and the picture of Wallace that merged from the gossip was of a demanding and abrasive competitor who, week in and week out, would argue that *his* story was the one that should lead the broadcast. Dan Rather was no shrinking violet—no one had ever accused him of *that*—but he had no stomach for intramural skirmishing, especially since, as the new kid on the block, he would be at a distinct disadvantage. So, with all these reservations, he told Hewitt that he would give the offer a little more consideration, but that, frankly, his preference was to remain in his post at *CBS Reports*.

Hewitt was stunned. Fiercely proud of the way his creation had evolved and fully confident that now it had what it takes to become a winner in the prime-time sweepstakes, Hewitt thought he was offering Rather a big plum and it had never crossed his mind that Dan might turn him down. He quickly enlisted the help of others who shared his belief that Rather was on the verge of making a serious mistake, and at one point that fall, Mike Wallace decided to have a little chat with his younger colleague.

Although by 1975 both Wallace and Rather had been CBS News correspondents for more than a decade, they still did not know each other very well. Wallace had always worked out of New York, and, until recently, Rather had been based in Washington. They had worked together on election-night broadcasts and as floor correspondents at the political conventions, but with these exceptions, their professional paths almost never crossed. Yet as journalists, they were similar in many respects. They were both diligent reporters, aggressive interviewers, and what made them especially effective on television was their knack for grasping a dramatic moment and exploiting it to the fullest. A Dan Rather question at a Nixon news conference often had all the confrontational intensity of a tense encounter between Wallace and an evasive or hostile interviewee. However, because of these similarities, it seemed inevitable that if Rather went to work for *60 Minutes*, he—far more than Safer— would be inclined to pursue the same kind of stories that in general aroused Wallace's interest. This being the case, it occurred to Rather that Wallace probably viewed him as a natural rival, precisely the type of correspondent he would *not* want as a co-star on *60 Minutes*. But when Mike went to talk to him in the fall of 1975, he assured Dan that the truth was otherwise.

First, he told him that he had been pleading for help—a third correspondent—for some time, and that the imminent shift into prime time made the need more pressing than ever. Moreover, he said, Rather was everyone's number one choice for the job. Speaking for himself, Mike said he believed that *60 Minutes* would benefit greatly from Dan's presence, that he had just the right combination of talent, experience and personal appeal to give the broadcast an extra shot in the arm. As for being the new kid on the block, Mike insisted that Rather had no need to worry. He would come aboard as a full and equal partner, and there was more than enough action to keep all three correspondents busy and satisfied. Finally, Wallace said that if Rather did join the team, it would not only help *60 Minutes* but would be an excellent move for him, too, one that could have a significant effect on his future career. In short, Wallace urged Rather in the strongest possible terms to put his reservations aside and sign on.

After thinking it over, Rather decided to take the advice. More than anything else, it was Wallace's pep talk that persuaded him. So Dan Rather went to work for *60 Minutes* that fall and soon realized that he had indeed made the right move. He had no trouble blending into the fabric of the program and stretching his talents to meet the demands of its multisubject format. What's more, the weekly exposure put him back in the forefront of CBS News correspondents who appeared on the air frequently enough to register an impact.

There was yet another, more subtle aspect to the new assignment that worked in Rather's favor. At the time, he was primarily known for his coverage of the Nixon White House, where his strong reporting had made him a divisive and controversial figure. After all, even before Watergate, hardly anyone was neutral on the subject of Richard Nixon, and, as Washington's resident nightclub comic Mark Russell once observed, "Dan Rather is to Nixon what hiccups are to a glassblower." In fact, Rather was never really the anti-Nixon firebrand he was reputed to be, but that was the perception of him that had settled in the minds of many viewers. On *60 Minutes,* however, they became acquainted with a "new" Dan Rather. His stories for that program were not confined to Washington and politics; they extended over a wide range of topics, including features and other back-of-the-book pieces. Thus, as time passed, millions of Americans came to realize that there was much more to Rather than the glowering face of the man

358•   Mike Wallace and Gary Paul Gates

they remembered confronting Nixon with hard questions about criminal acts and the pall of impeachment hovering over his presidency.

This softer, less combative image worked entirely to Rather's advantage, and, as Wallace had predicted, it gave his career a big boost, leading ultimately to his being named to succeed Walter Cronkite as anchorman on the *CBS Evening News*. If that post had opened up in the early or middle seventies, it almost certainly would have been filled by Roger Mudd, who then outranked Rather in the pecking order of CBS News correspondents. Even those network executives who preferred Rather—viewing him as both a better journalist and a more appealing presence—would have been reluctant to recommend that such a controversial correspondent succeed Uncle Walter. What *60 Minutes* did for Rather was to soften the widespread perception of him, while in no way diminishing his stature as an aggressive reporter with plenty of star quality. Hence, by 1980 when the time came to announce Cronkite's successor, the prize went to Rather instead of to Mudd. Even before he was crowned with that honor, Rather had come to appreciate the positive effects of his decision to work for *60 Minutes*. Later he often shuddered at the memory of how close he had come to rejecting Hewitt's offer in 1975. And invariably he made a point of acknowledging his debt to Wallace. "If it hadn't been for Mike," he once told an interviewer, "I probably would have talked myself out of that job, and I would have lived to regret it—that's for damn sure!"

Dan Rather was not the only beneficiary of that decision. Although Morley Safer's first reaction to *"The Third Man"* Theme" was negative, it wasn't long before he came to regard Rather's presence on *60 Minutes* as an unexpected blessing. He had opposed bringing in a third correspondent because he didn't want to add to the heavy pressure he was already feeling from Wallace. Sharing the *60 Minutes* showcase with Mike Wallace wasn't the easiest job in the world, and Safer was aware that many viewers regarded him as "the other guy," the second banana. During his first few years on the program, he suffered a bit from the Lou Gehrig syndrome: No matter how many hits he got on any given day, the fans still bestowed their biggest cheers on The Babe, the Sultan of Swat—in whose shadow

Safer performed on *60 Minutes*. Thus, he was less than enthusiastic about having to make room for a third correspondent,
especially one who like Wallace had demonstrated a shrewd
knack for drawing attention to his work. Safer liked and admired Rather, but he did not relish the prospect of being relegated to the role of *third* banana on *60 Minutes*.

Happily for Safer, adding Rather's bat to the lineup had the
opposite effect. Because they were so similar in style and attitude, Wallace and Rather did spend a lot of time going after
the same kind of hard-hitting, investigative stories, and in contrast, Safer's urbane features and ironic essays were seen in
sharper relief. Wallace and Rather's division of the black-hat
role gave Safer and his low-key style more room to breathe
and flourish. As a result, it was during the years *after* Rather
joined the broadcast that Morley Safer finally began to receive
the critical and popular attention he deserved. By the late 1970s,
numerous articles on him had been published, in which he was
praised as an "elegant craftsman" or—going all out—"the most
gifted writer in broadcast journalism." Wallace and Rather
brought considerable strengths to their work, but neither was
in Safer's class as a writer, a stylist.

One of the fundamental truths of TV journalism, as im-
mutable in its way as a first principle of physics, is that once
a correspondent becomes a major star, his ego inflates to a size
surpassed only by his extravagant salary. Thus, within the domain of *60 Minutes*, every effort was made to sustain the
impression that the three correspondents were full and equal
partners. Each man had his own entourage of producers, researchers and secretaries who were answerable only to him and
his needs. (A member of one such group came up with the
playful suggestion that they all buy sweaters and T-shirts with
the name of their respective leader stitched across the front in
big, bold letters.) When Rather joined *60 Minutes* and new,
spacious offices were constructed to accommodate the three
correspondents, Hewitt brought in tape measures and other
precision instruments to make sure that the cages that housed
his tigers were of identical size and dimension.

However, viewers tend to make up their own minds about
such matters, and to judge from the general response week in
and week out, there was clearly a first among equals—and that
was Wallace. He was the veteran, the senior correspondent who

had been with *60 Minutes* since its inception, and even after Rather came aboard, Wallace's presence continued to dominate the show. He generally took on the biggest and most controversial stories, and the program's most vivid and enduring image, the one that lingered in the mind long after a typical broadcast went off the air, was of Wallace zeroing in on some hapless quarry. But the happy truth was that the reputations of all three correspondents flourished in the new, prime-time format, and the triumph they shared was of epic proportions. For the most remarkable success of all was that of the broadcast itself.

When it was announced that *60 Minutes* was to be given another shot in prime time, most of the know-it-alls in the television industry were quick to predict that it would be lucky to make it through the season in that competitive battleground. Oh, there were a few sanguine souls who dared suggest that it might become a modest hit, the kind of show that scores just well enough in the ratings to retain its slot in the prime-time schedule for two or three seasons. But no one, not even Hewitt, anticipated the phenomenon to come. Over the next two years, *60 Minutes* established itself as one of the ten top-rated programs on the air. By the fall of 1978, it had surged to the head of the pack; and when the season ended the following spring, *60 Minutes* reigned supreme as the number one show on television. Since then, it has been a perennial winner, finishing at or near the top of the ratings every year. In its 7:00 P.M. Sunday slot, Don Hewitt's once-fragile magazine broadcast had evolved into a colossal contradiction in terms: a news program that consistently attracted a larger audience than the most popular entertainment shows, including such long-running blockbusters as *M*A*S*H* and *Dallas*. Nothing like it, or even close to it, had ever happened before in the thirty-year history of network television.

Wallace had hoped that bringing in a third correspondent would alleviate the burden of being constantly on the run, chasing down stories hither and yon, at home and abroad, and often under the pressure of an urgent deadline. However, it didn't work out that way, at least not to the extent that he and others had anticipated. Dan Rather, of course, was quick to pitch in and do his part; indeed, it wasn't long before he, too, found himself living in a frequent state of jet lag. Yet his efforts did little to make life easier for Wallace and Safer. The failure to achieve that part of the desired effect can be attributed in large part to the fact that the shift into prime time imposed even greater demands on everyone.

For one thing, the program went on the air more often. During the years when Wallace and Safer greeted their viewers from the 6:00 P.M. slot, they not only had their annual summer hiatus—when their fans had to make do with reruns—but also there were lulls in the fall and early winter, when professional football games often preempted the broadcast. After they moved into prime time, there were no such respites. At first, when a late game carried over past 7:00 P.M., Hewitt was instructed to air an abbreviated version of *60 Minutes*. But once the show became top-rated, the network's programmers chose to extend the prime-time schedule so that *60 Minutes* could be seen in its entirety. In addition, as the show began to build up a vast audience, the correspondents and producers drove themselves even harder to come up with the kind of stories that would retain all the new viewers they had attracted. In the unlikely event that any of them showed signs of easing up or resting on their laurels, there was always the vigilant Hewitt hovering over them with whip in hand, ready to crack them back into the fast lane. The upshot was that Hewitt found that he frequently had *three* game-weary tigers on the prowl; so, in the spring of 1978, the decision was made to take on yet another correspondent.

Hewitt's first inclination was to appoint a woman or black correspondent to the new post. Ever since its inception, *60 Minutes* had projected the clubby image of an exclusive, white male preserve, and in recent years there had been some grumbling within the CBS ranks. Hewitt was sensitive to that criticism, and more to the point, he honestly believed that such a person, whether a woman or black or both, would bring an appealing new ingredient to the broadcast; provided, of course, that he or she had the talent and experience to play on the same level as the formidable trio of Wallace, Safer and Rather. Hewitt felt that among the leading candidates, the one who had the most to offer was Ed Bradley. Bradley had earned his stripes as a war correspondent in Vietnam, later bolstering his reputation with his excellent coverage of Jimmy Carter's 1976 presidential campaign. As a reward, Bradley had recently been picked to anchor one of the weekend news shows, thus becoming the first black correspondent at CBS News to move up to the anchorman level. And in time he would indeed be invited to join *60 Minutes*, but the offer did not come his way in 1978. At the last minute that year, Hewitt decided that neither Bradley nor any of the other equal-opportunity candidates could match the credentials of another white male, one who shared with Wallace the distinction of having been a charter member of the club. For in the late spring of 1978, a repentant Harry Reasoner returned to the CBS fold.

From 1970 to 1975, Reasoner co-anchored the *ABC Evening News* with Howard K. Smith. Those were his good years at ABC. Largely because of his presence, there was a dramatic improvement in both the quality and ratings of the network's evening news show, which more than justified the big bucks that ABC's executives had shelled out to lure him away from CBS. But then came the fiasco, the union with Barbara Walters, which must rank as the most incongruous anchor pairing in the history of network television, and one that temporarily damaged the reputations of both Reasoner and Walters. An ironclad contract locked Reasoner into that travesty until the spring of 1978, when at last he was free to exercise what he sardonically referred to as "my Barbara Walters escape clause." A wounded and dejected tiger, he went slouching back to CBS, where a forgiving management took him in and nursed him back to health. When Reasoner made his first appearance on a CBS News broadcast in nearly eight years, he radiated such a strong aura of spiritual rebirth that one half-expected him to sign off with a rousing rendition of "Amazing Grace." Then, later, when he was reunited with Wallace and Hewitt on *60 Minutes*, the regeneration was complete. Reasoner rejoiced in his role as a prodigal uncle who, having suffered for his sins, had found his way back to the one, true, holy and apostolic faith.

Reasoner returned to *60 Minutes* just in time to join in the celebration of the program's tenth anniversary. A great deal had happened since that night in September 1968 when the ticking stopwatch was seen and heard for the first time in homes across America, and then Reasoner appeared on the screen, introducing the new show: "Good Evening. This is *Sixty Minutes*. It's a kind of magazine for television, which means it has the flexibility and diversity of a magazine adapted to broadcast journalism." Since that time, Don Hewitt's brainstorm, which had been conceived with Reasoner in mind, had grown into a bustling, high-powered operation that bore almost no resemblance to the modest and struggling "mom-and-pop store" that Harry had left back in 1970. In fact, he went through a difficult period of readjustment. Reasoner's talent and energy had atrophied a bit during the years of frustration at ABC, and for the first year or so after his return to *60 Minutes*, he had trouble keeping up with the brisk pace set by the show's other three correspondents. At one point, there was even talk of pulling him out of the lineup. But Reasoner eventually worked himself back into shape and he was there to share in all the glory when *60 Minutes* began its reign as the number one show on television.

Hewitt now had four reporters roaming the globe (with their producers) in search of stories, and all hands agreed that that was a much better arrangement. Since the broadcast invariably was divided into three main segments, viewers were assured of seeing three of the four correspondents on any given Sunday, and the one who happened to be the odd man out that night would more than likely have a piece on the air the next week. Rotating the star turns gave each correspondent an occasional breather; if he happened to be in town and did not have a story in the show that week, all he had to do was read the letters from viewers at the end of the broadcast.

The next and—as of this writing—last change in the cast of characters occurred in 1981 when Dan Rather left *60 Minutes* to take on a bigger challenge, though not necessarily a higher calling: assuring the loyal viewers of the *CBS Evening News* that he was worthy of the honor bestowed on him. This was no easy task. Over the years Walter Cronkite had become such a towering presence that by 1981, millions of Americans regarded him as nothing less than the apotheosis of broadcast journalism. However, Dan Rather brought his own strong blend of style and authority to what a former colleague, Daniel Schorr, once called "our nightly national seance." And after a shaky start, an uneasy period of transition, he took command of the anchor chair he inherited, and under his leadership CBS continued to lord it over the other two networks in the spirited battle for dinner-hour news ratings.

Moving into the slot vacated by Rather on *60 Minutes* was Ed Bradley who, shortly before making his debut, came up with a clever jape that almost sent Don Hewitt into cardiac arrest. On the surface, Bradley came across as a man of quiet strength and dignity. But beneath that rather formal facade lurked a mischievous sense of humor, as Hewitt discovered one day in the spring of 1981. Not long after Bradley went to work for *60 Minutes,* he typed up a memo to the CBS News personnel department, in which he disclosed that he had recently converted to the Muslim faith; and like Lew Alcindor and Cassius Clay before him, he had changed his name. His new name, Bradley revealed, was Shahib Shahab. (This actually was the Muslim name of a jazz saxophonist with whom Bradley was acquainted.) He informed the personnel department that he wanted the new name on his paychecks and other records, and instructed them to make those changes. He did *not* send the memo to Personnel, but he did drop off a copy at Hewitt's office, then went out to partake of a long lunch, which served to keep him away from Hewitt for the next two or three hours.

At first, when he read the memo, Hewitt assumed it was a joke. The more he thought about it, however, the more he began to wonder. If he had received something like that from Wallace or Reasoner or Safer, he would have known for sure that his leg was being pulled. But Bradley was such an earnest young man, so serious and dedicated in his work, that Hewitt had to face the probability that he was being sincere. As he proceeded to contemplate the implications of the memo, there raced through his mind the new version of the standard opening to the broadcast as the faces of the correspondents flashed on the screen: "I'm Mike Wallace. I'm Morley Safer. I'm Harry Reasoner. I'm Shahib Shahab. Those stories and more tonight on *Sixty Minutes.*" This was not exactly what he had in mind when he asked Ed Bradley to join the troupe.

While Bradley was at lunch, Hewitt did some checking around the office. If it was a gag, then he was determined to get to the bottom of it. But Bradley had played it very cool; at that point, he had not yet taken anyone into his confidence, which meant that when Hewitt confronted other members of the *60 Minutes* staff with the news, they reacted with genuine bewilderment and concern. And so, while Bradley chortled his way through a long and leisurely lunch, Hewitt struggled to keep his mounting anxiety under control.

When Bradley finally returned from lunch, the first thing he did was assure other members of the team that the Muslim name change was just a joke that he had dreamed up to play on Hewitt. Then he went to the office of his new boss and asked him if he had read the memo. Hewitt answered that he had indeed read it, and he wanted to discuss it. That was fine with Bradley, but frankly he didn't think there was anything to discuss. "I don't see this as any kind of big deal or serious problem," he said, "and I hope you don't either." Hewitt gave Bradley a long, searching look, then suggested that it would be a good idea to "get a press release out on this right away." Bradley had played enough poker in his life to recognize an adroit bluff when he saw one. Besides, he told himself, even if Hewitt went ahead and took that step, there would be enough time to alert the PR people before they sent out the release to the public. So he replied that if Hewitt thought his new name was important enough to warrant a press release, then he, Shahib Shahab, certainly had no objection. "At that point," Bradley later recalled with a rollicking laugh, "all the color drained out of Don's face."

By the time he left Hewitt's office, word of the hoax had spread through the shop, and after Bradley returned to his own office, various colleagues dropped in to congratulate him and join in the mirth. Hewitt, meanwhile, sat alone at his desk and brooded about the mail that would be coming in that fall after the viewers of *60 Minutes* were introduced to the program's new Muslim correspondent. After twenty minutes or so, he decided to have another go at Bradley—or Shahab—and when he walked into Ed's office, the assembled group erupted in laughter. Hewitt's first impulse was to fire every one of them.

Bradley had a keen appreciation of the fact that by moving into the *60 Minutes* showcase, he was taking on a big challenge. In particular, he was conscious of the standards that had been set by the program's senior correspondent. Shortly after he joined the broadcast, Bradley told a visiting reporter: "Nobody in this business does what Mike does as well as he does it, but I guess I can knock down a door and browbeat somebody if I have to. If I have a strength, it's the ability to get people to talk. I'm a good listener. When you listen well, people tend to talk more. Mike is great at that. A person will give him an incomplete answer, and Mike won't say anything, and the other guy will rush to fill the silence."

Bradley's predecessor on the show was no less an admirer of Wallace's work, but he chose to praise it from a different perspective. One day, a year or so after he left *60 Minutes* to keep his rendezvous with destiny on the *CBS Evening News,* Dan Rather talked about Wallace's influence on other correspondents, including himself. "We've all learned from Mike, no question of that," he said. "But speaking strictly for myself, what I valued the most was not the tough interviews or the hard-news reporting. I wouldn't care to invite any comparisons, but the truth is that even before I went to work for *60 Minutes,* I was fairly active in those areas."

Rather paused for a moment to let the familiar memory of his years in the trenches of the Nixon White House pass silently through the conversation. Then: "No, I would have to say that for me, the most instructive part of Mike's work was his softer interviews with people in the arts and similar fields. What I discovered, mainly from his example, is that you don't interview Lena Horne or Leopold Stokowski the same way you interview politicians and others who make their living off the public payroll. I was accustomed to dealing with *them* in Washington, but that other world—the world of the arts—was new territory for me, and I learned a lot by watching the way Mike worked that side of the street."

That other world was certainly not new territory for Wallace. In 1975, the year Rather joined *60 Minutes* and began doing back-of-the-book features, Wallace could have boasted that he had been interviewing celebrities of one kind or another for the past three decades, dating back to his radio days in Chicago. His very first interview program was something called *Famous Names,* which went on the air in 1946. Wallace's guests then were mostly show-business types who had come to Chicago to plug their latest play or movie or nightclub act. He eventually outgrew talk-show trivia, and starting on *Night Beat,* he branched out to more consequential subjects. Yet throughout his long career, Mike has made a point of keeping up with the latest trends in American culture and entertainment. His long-running radio show on CBS, *Mike Wallace at Large,* was structured almost entirely around interviews with authors and actors and the like. And from time to time on *60 Minutes,* he would turn away from his pursuit of serious and controversial stories to do personality profiles. Wallace welcomed those assignments because they provided a change of pace, a pleasant diversion, an opportunity to put his wrecking tools away for the moment and allow the sunnier side of his own personality to appear on the air.

Several of his personality pieces were on eminent "long-hairs," as classical musicians were often called back in the days before Americans of the hippie generation adopted the shaggy look as their badge of identity. In 1970 the seventieth birthday of composer-conductor Aaron Copland was celebrated on *60 Minutes.* A few years later, Wallace did stories on two of the world's finest sopranos. His profile of Maria Callas ran in 1974 when the Greek primadonna was making a comeback after an eight-year absence from public performances in Europe and the United States. The following year he turned his attention to the gracious diva from Brooklyn, Beverly Sills, shortly after she made her long-overdue debut at New York's Metropolitan Opera. Viewers who preferred ballet to opera could take pleasure in his 1979 profile of Mikhail Baryshnikov, which Wallace began with the assertion that "never before has one extraordinary dancer so captured our imagination." In his 1980 piece on Israeli violinist Itzhak Perlman, Mike introduced the young virtuoso as a man with "an impish sense of humor." And a few moments later, the *60 Minutes* audience was treated to a fine example of it. After reciting the names of some past and present masters—Jascha Heifetz, Yehudi Menuhin, Isaac Stern and Perlman himself—Wallace asked why so many world-class fiddle players happened to be Jewish. With appropriate manual gestures, Perlman replied: "You see, our fingers are circumcised and, you see, which gives it a very good dexterity, you know, particularly in the pinky."

Of all the stories Wallace did in this genre, none was more captivating than his 1977 piece on one of the undisputed giants of twentieth-century music—pianist Vladimir Horowitz. The occasion was the fiftieth anniversary of Horowitz's American

debut, which he was about to celebrate in concert with the New
York Philharmonic. Horowitz was accustomed to being treated
like royalty. In music lovers throughout the world, he inspired
an admiration that bordered on awe. But Wallace brought to
that interview his customary irreverence, which in this case
took the form of a playful, needling kind of inquiry rather than
an aggressive confrontation. For example, when Horowitz, indulging in a sly, art-for-art's sake affectation, insisted that it
didn't bother him if some other pianist received more money
for a concert, Mike was quick to challenge him:

> WALLACE: If somebody gets more money? You tell me
> one other solo performer in classical music who gets
> eighty percent of the gross, which is what Vladimir Ho-
> rowitz gets.
>
> HOROWITZ: Well, I didn't do it my whole life. After fifty
> years of playing I got this.
>
> WALLACE: You get three times as much as any other
> classical performer today, I am told. And you smile when
> I tell you that because you know it's the truth, and you're
> proud.
>
> HOROWITZ: I'm not proud, but this—it is so.

Later in the interview, Wallace brought up an even more sensitive subject: Horowitz's abrupt decision in 1953 to stop playing concerts for a while. At the time he had said he needed a
vacation from the pressures of touring, but the hiatus lasted
twelve years. When Wallace pressed him about that period in
his life, Horowitz protested that he had not been entirely in-
active, that he made several records during those years. Unwilling to let it go, Mike said: "Yes, you keep saying you were
doing the records. The fact is, you did not face the public for
twelve years."

To judge from Wallace's accusatory tone, one would have
thought that Horowitz had been on the lam from 1953 to 1965,
a fugitive from his artistic responsibilities. Being put on the
defensive was obviously a rare experience for Horowitz, but
instead of taking offense he appeared to be stimulated and even
amused by the sharp thrust of Wallace's questions. Like the

Shah of Iran, he seemed to enjoy "this kind of provocations."
Hence, the more Wallace twitted Horowitz, the more he opened
up and revealed flashes of humor and humanity that seldom,
if ever, had been seen before by those who worshiped him as
a musical deity.

But whatever badgering Wallace did in his musical profiles
was always good-natured. He was invariably drawn to such
subjects because he, too, was an ardent admirer of their accomplishments. He took on those assignments with the intention of turning them into valentines, unabashed tributes to men
and women of exceptional artistry. This is why he was irritated
by some of the reaction to his 1980 look at the diverse talents
of composer-conductor Leonard Bernstein. As was the case in
his treatment of Horowitz, Wallace did not hesitate to tease
Bernstein about certain aspects of his professional style, notably
his penchant for unrestrained theatrics on the podium. But he
did not probe deeply into Bernstein's personal life, and he was
later criticized because he didn't confront the composer of *West
Side Story* with questions about his alleged homosexuality.

Wallace's defense was that the subject was simply not germane. What he had set out to do essentially was a story on the
man and his music, and under those circumstances, he saw no
reason to bring up matters that would only embarrass Bernstein's three children, especially since they were still grieving
over the loss of their mother, who had died about a year earlier.
This was one of the rare instances when Wallace was accused
of having been too *soft* on an interviewee. However, he took
the criticism in stride, because in that respect Dan Rather's
observation was right on target. Wallace did indeed believe that
one should not interview Leonard Bernstein the same way one
would interview, say, a militant leader of the Gay Liberation
Movement who had chosen to make his homosexuality a political issue.

Wallace also gave a few literary lions—and lionesses—a chance
to discuss their work on *60 Minutes*. When he did a story on
Gore Vidal in 1975, he focused on the striking difference between the respected author of such historical novels as *Julian*
and *Burr*—works which had moved one critic to praise Vidal
as "a superlative writer whose elegance is unmatched"—and
the sensationalist who wrote *Myra Breckenridge*, for which he

was scorned as "a sly pornographer who squanders his formidable talent." Pornography was also a chief topic of conversation later that year when Mike did a joint interview with Erica Jong and the man she referred to affectionately as "my literary grandfather"—Henry Miller. And with good reason, for Jong's erotic novel, *Fear of Flying*, with its explicit sex scenes and frequent use of four-letter words, had been described as an updated, female version of Miller's *Tropic of Cancer*, which was such a *succès de scandale* back in the 1930s that he was accused, as Wallace noted, of having "opened the floodgates of pornography."

One female writer who never ventured anywhere near those floodgates was Barbara Cartland, whom Wallace interviewed in 1977. The author of some two hundred romantic paperbacks—which she adorned with such titles as *Kiss the Moonlight, The Elusive Earl* and *The Bored Bridegroom*—Cartland filled her fictional world with chaste maidens, dashing swains, damsels in distress and shameless cads. In her books, cheeks blush, breasts heave and nostrils flare, but the payoff for all that swelling passion is never spelled out. Mike had a merry time listening to Cartland, an English dowager in her seventies, extol the sublime virtues of honor, virginity and romantic love.

In a much different vein, he did pieces on two women journalists who had made their reputations in Europe. Paris was the subject of his 1973 interview with Janet Flanner, who, under the pen name of "Genêt," had been writing about life in the French capital for *The New Yorker* magazine for half a century. As Wallace jogged her memory, she reminisced about Ernest Hemingway, F. Scott Fitzgerald, Gertrude Stein and other American expatriates she knew there in the 1920s.

In contrast to Flanner's nostalgic mood, the passions and preoccupations of Oriana Fallaci were firmly rooted in the present, and when Mike did a profile of her in 1976, it was a meeting of kindred spirits. Fallaci, too, was a reporter whose interviews with world leaders were so strong and provocative that the confrontations themselves often made news. What she and Wallace had in common was the gift of being able to draw people out and induce them to reveal things about themselves that they had never before disclosed in public. (For example, it was Fallaci who cajoled Henry Kissinger into admitting that when he served under Richard Nixon, he felt like a modern cowboy, a lone gunslinger defending the Western world against the desperadoes.) In fact, some of the points Wallace made about Fallaci were clearly evocative of his own career and interviewing style. He noted that when she began plying her craft, "it was mainly actors and entertainers, but today she prefers heads of state." He then named a few—Golda Meir, Nguyen Van Thieu and the Shah of Iran—all of whom, co-incidentally, had also been interviewed by Wallace. And, in what easily could have served as a self-appraisal, he contended that Fallaci turns her interviews "into morality dramas. She plays the role of judge. The interviewee is on trial. And few are found innocent." Inevitably, perhaps, during their own encounter the two heavy hitters mixed it up a little—to their mutual amusement:

WALLACE: Power? Do you have power?

FALLACI: Oh no. I have not power. How can you say—?

WALLACE: None whatsoever?

FALLACI: We are not one of those who think that we journalists have power.

WALLACE: No?

FALLACI: Nah! We are like dogs—bow-wow-wow. (Laughing) And nobody listens to us.

WALLACE: You're an entertainer?

FALLACI: I'm an historian.

WALLACE: You're *not* an historian.

FALLACI: Yes, I *am!*

WALLACE: You're a journalist.

FALLACI: No, sir. A journalist *is* an historian.

WALLACE: No. Now, wait!

FALLACI: Listen! A journalist is a person who writes history in the same moment that history happens. And it is the damn best way to write history because I do not know if it is true what they tell me when I go to school. I'm at school, and I read on the things that were written two or three hundred years ago and manipulated a hundred times by others. But I am sure that when you give me a story on TV with a photo, or an article, it is true.

A rather lofty view of the fourth estate, but Wallace didn't challenge it. For he, too, believed (as did most journalists) that there was more than a grain of truth in the argument that an eyewitness account—"I was there, and here's what happened"—is more reliable than a version that has gone through two hundred years of rewrites.

Other writers he talked to on *60 Minutes* made assertions that were far more difficult to support. One of them was an outright lie. That occurred in 1972 when an obscure author named Clifford Irving piously insisted that he had been authorized to write an "as-told-to" autobiography of the reclusive tycoon Howard Hughes. Irving soon proved to be a charlatan, a smooth-talking con artist, and he later went to prison for the hoax he tried to foist on the reading public through McGraw-Hill, the publisher that in all innocence paid a huge advance— $750,000—for the bogus manuscript.

The following year brought another literary storm, one that swirled around the head of an author with far more imposing credentials—Norman Mailer. Mailer was of course no stranger to controversy. For years he had been a flamboyant public figure, a boisterous debunker of conventional mores and attitudes who, in one of his many "advertisements for myself," strutted about as the heavyweight champion of machismo, ever ready to take on any and all challengers. Yet for all his personal excesses in word and deed, no one had ever really questioned Mailer's professional integrity—until 1973, when he wrote a quickie biography of Marilyn Monroe. Dashing it off in a hectic two months, Mailer relied mainly on other sources for his information, such as previously published books about the late actress. He borrowed so heavily from those sources that he was accused of plagiarism, quite a demeaning charge to be leveled at a major novelist who had won the Pulitzer Prize. Even worse, in the final chapter of his book, Mailer resorted to rank sensationalism. Exploiting all the loose gossip about a love affair between Monroe and Bobby Kennedy—and without offering any evidence to back up those rumors—he proceeded to raise the lurid and bizarre suggestion that Marilyn had been murdered by Kennedy-hating conspirators from within the CIA and/or the FBI. Their motive, Mailer speculated, was to dispatch Monroe in such a way that it would look like a suicide committed for unrequited love of Kennedy. Juicy stuff, to say the least; so Wallace decided to have a go at Mailer on *60 Minutes*.

It was not their first encounter. Back in 1957 Mailer appeared as a guest on *Night Beat*. Even in those unenlightened days, when male chauvinism was socially acceptable, he had a knack for pushing himself beyond the canons of propriety. As noted in an earlier chapter, his big complaint at that time was that the country needed "a man for President," and he went on to disparage the five-star general then occupying the White House. "I think President Eisenhower is a bit of a woman," he said.

Wallace interviewed him again three years later when Mailer was flexing his own political biceps. In November 1960, Mailer was on the verge of announcing his candidacy in the upcoming race for mayor of New York. At one point in the interview, Wallace asked him about the problem of teenage violence, and as usual Mailer was quick to offer a novel and imaginative solution. The kids, he said, should not be disarmed because to a male adolescent, "the knife is an instrument of manhood." Then, after praising the hardy spirit of the Middle Ages, he proposed holding modern "jousting tournaments" between teenage gangs in Central Park. Wallace noticed that Mailer himself was sporting a black eye, a real shiner, and when he asked him how he got it, Mailer replied: "Oh, I was in quite a scrape Saturday night."

This was true, but what Wallace did not know was that when Mailer came home from that Saturday-night brawl, he got into an argument with his wife, Adele, and stabbed her with a penknife. The interview with Wallace was taped on Monday, and while Mailer sat there chatting amiably about the knife as "an instrument of manhood," his wife was undergoing intensive care following an emergency operation in a nearby hospital. Shortly after the interview, Mailer turned himself in to the police, and only then did the press—and the public—learn about the incident. Adele recovered, but since being placed under arrest for stabbing one's wife was hardly an upbeat way to launch a political campaign, Mailer had to wait until 1969 to make his colorful, albeit futile run for mayor on New York.

Given this background, Mike Wallace and Norman Mailer did not need to be introduced to each other when they met in the summer of 1973 to discuss the story that *60 Minutes* would later entitle "Monroe, Mailer and the Fast Buck." Early on, Wallace went straight to the heart of the matter:

WALLACE: Why did you write the book?

MAILER: I started to write it as—to do a preface, to pick up a sum of money. It was a book which was a commercial venture for me. I needed the money very badly. And then what happens? I fell in love with the material.

Wallace promptly interjected to make the point that Mailer "never met Monroe. The material he fell in love with was magazine articles and films and other writers' biographies of the lady." Then, after dealing briefly with the charge of plagiarism, he questioned Mailer about the outlandish theory he set forth in the last chapter of the book:

WALLACE: You don't believe she was murdered, though, really. Down bottom.

MAILER: I— Well— No, I don't know. I didn't know her. I—

WALLACE: I say you don't believe it.

MAILER: If you ask me to give a handicapper's estimate of what it was, I'd say it's ten to one that it was an accidental suicide. Ten to one, anyway.

WALLACE: At least.

MAILER: But I would not—I could not ignore the possibility of a murder.

WALLACE: And do you believe that Bobby Kennedy was there, had been with her, that night?

MAILER: It's possible.

WALLACE: I'm asking you again.

MAILER: I don't know.

WALLACE: Handicap it.

MAILER: I'd say it's even money. Because he was the kind of man, I think, who if—

WALLACE: At her house?

MAILER: Well, no.

Mike reminded Mailer that Monroe's housekeeper and others who were close to Marilyn during her final days had categorically denied the Kennedy connection and just about everything else that Mailer wrote in the last chapter of the book. He asked Mailer then why he didn't make the effort to interview those people and record their firm and unwavering conviction that Marilyn Monroe was indeed a victim of accidental suicide. Mailer's answer was:

> MAILER: I told you I had a choice. I was coming down to a deadline. I had something like twenty thousand words to finish in the last week—
>
> WALLACE: But facts, Norman!
>
> MAILER: Now wait a moment, Mike. Let me just—just give you my attitude on it. What I knew was I was sailing into a sea of troubles, and I said, "Fine, that's what we're going to sail into." Because the alternative was this: I did not have the time to do both.

By this time, Mailer was getting a bit testy. He was being made to look like an irresponsible hack, and he was even more furious when the piece was aired. A few days after the broadcast, he was quoted as saying that the next time he ran into Wallace, he was going to work him over. Ever the macho man, Mailer specified that he would concentrate his blows on the stomach area because Wallace's "face is already so ugly that there's no point in doing any damage to it." (A longtime boxing enthusiast, Mailer seemed to be borrowing from the verbal style of Muhammad Ali in the days when the loquacious one liked to taunt Sonny Liston with gibes that he was "just a big ugly bear.") When a reporter told Wallace about Mailer's threat and asked for his reaction, Mike laughed and said: "Ah yes, that sounds like Norman. What would we do without him? The man's a national treasure."

Marilyn Monroe was not the only Hollywood legend to be featured on *60 Minutes* several years after her death. Wallace also did a profile on Judy Garland in 1975, six years after she died from what the coroner called "an incautious overdose of barbiturates." Garland's sad end at the age of forty-seven was all too symptomatic of her troubled life, but when Wallace interviewed her daughters, Liza Minnelli and Lorna Luft, they remembered her as an exceptionally warm and loving mother. At one point, Minnelli, by then a major star in her own right, had this to say about the Judy Garland she knew: "When you'd sit and talk with her, you really felt that nobody could ever love you more and that you never could ever love anybody more."

Five years later, in 1980, Wallace did a story on Bette Davis, a *living* Hollywood legend who was still going strong at the age of seventy-one. In the interim, there were pieces also on Vanessa Redgrave and Walter Matthau and director Robert Altman. But the high point of his sallies into movieland was his 1978 interview with another director—Roman Polanski.

For a long time, Polanski was known only as a first-rate director of films dealing with violence and psychologically disturbed characters. A native of Poland, he had built his reputation in Europe with such pictures as *Knife in the Water* and *Repulsion*. Then in 1968 he directed his first American movie, an adaptation of Ira Levin's gothic novel *Rosemary's Baby*. This film was a big commercial and critical success, and Polanski seemed to have everything going his way, not only in his career but in his personal life as well. For 1968 was also the year that he married the beautiful actress Sharon Tate.

Then all of a sudden, Polanski's life began to imitate his art. *Rosemary's Baby* was the harrowing story of a young woman, played by Mia Farrow, who was forced to give birth to the son of Satan, and that grisly ordeal was still fresh in the minds of those who saw the movie when *real* horror struck the director's own wife in the summer of 1969. On August 9, Sharon Tate, then eight months pregnant with their first child, and four other people were brutally slain at Polanski's rented home in Los Angeles. The murderers were followers of a bizarre cult leader named Charles Manson. In their twisted fascination with evil, Manson and his disciples were every bit as demented as the Satan-worshipers in *Rosemary's Baby*.

Polanski eventually resumed his directing career, but the eerie curse of life imitating art continued to plague him. His most celebrated film in the years that followed was the private-eye thriller *Chinatown*, starring Jack Nicholson and Faye Dunaway. A shocking subplot in that movie was the incestuous relationship between a father and his daughter, which began when the daughter was in her early adolescence. Three years later, in 1977, Polanski pleaded guilty in a Los Angeles court to the charge of having had unlawful sexual intercourse with a thirteen-year-old girl. In February 1978, the night before he was to be sentenced for the crime, Polanski flew to Paris, where he resumed his career, but this time as a fugitive from justice. Later that year, while he was filming his next picture in France— an adaptation of the Thomas Hardy novel *Tess of the D'Urbervilles*—he agreed to let Wallace interview him for *60 Minutes*. Inasmuch as this was the first time that Polanski talked on the record since he fled the United States, Mike had a big exclusive, and it didn't take him long to get around to the central question:

WALLACE: Why did you get involved with a thirteen-year-old?

POLANSKI: Well, since the girl is anonymous, and I hope— hope for *her* sake that she will be—

WALLACE: She will be.

POLANSKI: I would like to describe her to you. She is not a child. She is a young woman. She had—and testified to it—previous sexual experience. She wasn't unschooled in sexual matters. She was consenting and willing. Whatever I did was wrong I think I paid for it. I went through a year of incredible hardship, and I think I paid for it.

A few moments later, Wallace brought up the appalling events of August 1969, which led to this exchange:

WALLACE: You were reported to be willing to pay top dollar to have Charles Manson killed. "I want him dead!" you are reported to have said. Untrue?

POLANSKI: When the whole tragedy happened I was ranting and trying to help the police and doing all kinds of things to find those culprits. There was this irrational anger. If I could have them, I would kill them. But when they were found, I just felt no belligerence towards them. I just felt nothing. I just don't want to have anything to do with them. I don't care what happens to them. It's not going to change anything. She's gone.

WALLACE: It has been said that the victims, the friends who were murdered along with Sharon, were assassinated twice—once by the murderers, a second time by the press.

POLANSKI: Absolutely. The articles that appeared after that tragedy were so abominable.

WALLACE: There were so many stories about—about kinky sex and about drug taking and about self-indulgence and about—what kind of life did you people lead? Was there anything—?

POLANSKI: Well, you—look, Mike, I'm not criticizing you for it. You try to—to put your questions the way that the audience will for a moment stop eating and start listening to you. And what will remain in their mind is this headline that you just said and quoted, and the headline that I have read many, many times, and not what I am going to answer to you. Because if I tell you that we lived quietly, that we had quiet evenings and listened to the music, that—that Sharon was a lovely cook, it will all seem like alibiing, and it will serve no purpose, because the very fact that you have to ask this questions put me—puts me already in a bad light. Because if you ask someone a question, "Is it true that you had intercourse with a zebra in the middle of Trafalgar Square?" it puts him in a bad light, whether he—even if he says, "Are you completely crazy?" or "Are you joking?" Whatever he will say, there will be in the memory of people this question—that he was asked whether he had an intercourse with a zebra.

The metaphorical analogy he conjured up may have been overwrought—it was reminiscent of the gothic excess that permeates his films—but Polanski had a point and Wallace knew it. By referring specifically to some of the rumors that had circulated about the life-style that Polanski and Sharon Tate pursued in their marriage, he was in effect giving them a credence that they did not necessarily deserve. So Polanski's impassioned response struck home, and Mike promptly backed away from the subject of "what kind of life did you people lead?" Moreover, his own mood underwent an abrupt and decisive change. Until then, the questions he put to Polanski had been pungent and forceful, and there was often a trace of hostility in his voice and manner. But now his attitude softened; he became more sympathetic. And what emerged was a far more complex and fascinating portrait of Roman Polanski.

Later, after the piece had aired on *60 Minutes*, Wallace acknowledged that the result was something other than he had anticipated. Confiding to a friend, he said: "When I flew to France to interview him, I assumed the worst. It never occurred to me that I would *like* Polanski or be moved to any positive feelings toward him. But that's what happened. He struck me as a deeply troubled man who is haunted by dark obsessions, and I guess that's what makes him such a gifted artist. Instead of making easy moral judgments, I tried to reach him, to understand him, and I'm glad it turned out that way."

In September 1979, when *60 Minutes* aired an entertaining profile of Johnny Carson—one of the few pieces Wallace has done on a major personality in his own medium—the popular talk-show host couldn't resist the opportunity to get in a dig. Demanding to know why Wallace was doing a story on him,

Carson protested that he did not deserve the dubious honor. "I'm not running a boiler-room operation," he said. "I have no phony real estate scam. I'm not taking any kickbacks. I did steal a ring from Woolworth's once when I was twelve years old, and I think that's why you're here."

Carson was referring, of course, to the kind of stories Wallace did when he was wearing the black hat and striking terror in the hearts of those who *were* taking kickbacks, running boiler-room operations or profiting from phony real estate scams. Like millions of others, Johnny Carson thought of Wallace not so much as the man who had interviewed the Shah of Iran and other heads of state; even less did he associate him with the light personality pieces on luminaries in the arts and show business. For by 1979 Mike had built up such a reputation as an investigative reporter that this had become his principal métier. During the middle and late seventies, it was his exposés of corruption within government agencies and the private sector that whipped up the biggest storms and, in the process, infused *60 Minutes* with a bold new spirit and identity. With Wallace and his team of producers leading the way, the program evolved into a television descendant of the muckrakers, that vigorous breed of reformers who brought a rare combination of courage, diligence and moral passion to the craft of journalism back in the early 1900s. As was true of the original muckrakers, there were times when in their zeal Wallace and his cohorts got carried away in the excitement of the quest and wound up with stories that conveyed more heat than light, more theater than substance. But for the most part, their vigilance and probing served the best interests of the commonweal. So much so, in fact, that many Americans came to regard Wallace as a kind of unofficial ombudsman. As Harry Reasoner put it shortly after he returned to CBS and *60 Minutes* in 1978: "Now, when people have a problem, something strange or suspicious going on in their community, instead of writing their congressman, they write to Mike Wallace and demand that *he* fix it."

CHAPTER

SIXTEEN

WELL, I DON'T KNOW about *that*. What I *do* know is that if I
had interviewed Johnny Carson ten years earlier, when *60 Minutes* was in its infancy, he would not have greeted me with
needling remarks about "kickbacks" and "real estate scams."
In those days, we had not yet begun to assert ourselves in the
area of investigative reporting. As we struggled to find our
character and gain a foothold in the prime-time schedule, we
were guided by a fairly modest goal: to strike a balance between
my hard-news takeouts and interviews with government figures, and Harry Reasoner's casual essays and features, but it
was the latter that gave the program its distinctive tone and
style.

Over the years Don Hewitt has often said that insofar as he
was influenced at all by print journalism, his model for *60
Minutes* was *Life* magazine, and there were some obvious par-
allels. Like *Life*, we were picture-oriented, tightly edited, and
we sent cameras all over the world to cover major events, while
at the same time we kept an eye out for lively features and
human-interest stories; and of course, we were reaching out to
the kind of mass audience that *Life* had attracted in its heyday.
But if that was the print organ we most closely resembled,
there were times when Reasoner brought a deft *New Yorker*
touch to the broadcast with his wry observations on various

fads and trends that surfaced on the American scene. Among
the subjects he examined in his droll way was one of his favorites: the prevailing national taste in whiskey. Since Harry
himself was a sturdy imbiber, that assignment was a labor of
love, as I pointed out in my on-air introduction to his "Essay
on Whiskey" in January 1969:

> I think you can understand that as journalists who cover any
> and everything, there are certain stories that appeal to us
> more than others. Harry Reasoner has been working on a
> story for some time now. I don't believe that in all the years
> I've known Harry, I have ever seen him devote himself to
> a story more completely and with more apparent pleasure.
> Herewith that report.

As for me, I was content to let Reasoner have most of the fun.
I recognized that he had a special flair for offbeat stories, and
that those were the pieces which gave *60 Minutes* an extra and
appealing dimension. Largely because of them, our new series
came across as a refreshing departure, a breaking away from
the relentlessly sober and often stuffy tone of most documentaries and other network news programs. And to provide an
appropriate contrast to Harry's light features, I was cast as the
straight man, the heavy, my work being mainly confined to
conventional front-page stories, including the expected interviews with government leaders and other public figures. At
first, I had no objection. After all, I had made my reputation
as an interviewer—that was *my* acknowledged forte—and I
could easily understand why Hewitt wanted me to concentrate
on assignments that led to one-on-one encounters with Richard
Nixon, Spiro Agnew, John Mitchell and other newsmakers who
were then dominating the headlines.

As time went on, however, I began to yearn for a less
restrictive role, something a little different and more challenging. I certainly didn't want to encroach on Reasoner's turf, not
even after he relinquished it in 1970 to pursue his fortune at
ABC. One reason I welcomed Morley Safer as his replacement
was because I thought he would bring to the broadcast many
of the characteristics Harry had demonstrated, and that's exactly

what happened. Morley quickly settled into Reasoner's urbane role as though it had been created for him. What I wanted to do was chart a separate course into fresh territory. To be candid, I was looking for a way to sharpen and strengthen my own identity on *60 Minutes,* and in the early 1970s that opportunity began to open up for me. There was nothing dramatic about it, no moment of sudden inspiration when I said to myself: "Aha, I will now plunge into the troubled waters of investigative reporting and make some waves there." But there were two events—one internal, the other external—which pushed me in that direction.

The first one, the internal prod, was the presence and influence of Barry Lando, who joined our staff in the fall of 1971. Lando had come to us with strong credentials as a reporter in print and broadcasting, and he was, if anything, even more determined than I to break new ground on *60 Minutes.* Diligent, ambitious and resourceful, Barry wanted to produce stories that required lots of digging, stories that would provoke reaction and controversy. He was, in short, my kind of producer.

I don't want to overstate Lando's role and contribution at that point. It would be misleading to suggest that he had stepped into a vacuum on *60 Minutes.* Even before he joined us, there were other producers who had broken out of the mold of routine interview pieces and taken on controversial assignments requiring hard and perceptive reporting. Paul Loewenwarter had to do plenty of legwork to prepare a searching report on the Black Panthers in early 1970. So did Joe Wershba when he produced a couple of tough prison stories in 1969, one on homosexuality in a Philadelphia jail and the other on brutality in the U.S. Marine brig at Camp Pendleton. Another producer, Bill Brown, was the hero of our 1971 piece on William Crum, for it was his probing in Washington that enabled us to track down "the money king of Vietnam" in his Hong Kong hideaway. Jeff Gralnick also did a first-rate job in putting together our 1969 story on severely wounded casualties who had just been brought home from Vietnam; that report was so poignant that I did two updates on those amputees in the years ahead, long after Gralnick had left our shop and forged a new career for himself as an executive producer at ABC News.

But having acknowledged the value of those early efforts, as well as others I could cite, I would still say that it was Lando more than anyone else who provided the big breakthrough. Almost from the moment he came to us, I felt that Barry had something special to offer. And I was right. For by the summer of 1972, after he had been with *60 Minutes* less than a year, he had drawn me—and the program—into the complex and spirited adventure of the Colonel Herbert story.

Lando's dissection of Tony Herbert and the gullible press coverage of his allegations was as much of a milestone for *60 Minutes* as it later proved to be in the annals of libel law. Never before had one of our producers spent so much time—almost a year—digging into the details of a single story. Never before had a member of our staff gone through the sobering experience of uncovering evidence that contradicted his own strong premise, finally leading him to the point where he felt he had no choice but to repudiate his own previous report, which he had done for the weekend edition of the *CBS Evening News*. And never before had we broadcast a story so critical of our colleagues in the national press; for as I suggested earlier, the target of our exposé was not just the colonel himself but also the media, which, by accepting his claims at face value, had elevated him to the status of a celebrity saint. By any criterion, Lando's work on that assignment stands as a model of investigative reporting, and one of its effects was to push *60 Minutes* into a new and more challenging sphere.

Moreover, the timing of the broadcast could not have been more fortuitous. When "The Selling of Colonel Herbert" was aired in February 1973, the dark edges of the Watergate cover-up story were just starting to unravel, and a side effect was to glorify the gumshoe drudgery of investigative journalism. Suddenly, scores of reporters, having succumbed to the cloak-and-dagger fever spread by the Woodward and Bernstein triumph, were now ready to forsake whatever they had been doing so they might probe the murky depths of clandestine corruption. I and some of my producers were among those who caught the bug; in fact, the Watergate scandal was the other goad, the external force, that propelled us onto the investigative path.

Even without the Watergate impetus, I could understand

why Lando and other producers I worked with were attracted
to investigative stories. Ever since *60 Minutes* first went on
the air, field producers have been an integral part of our reporting process. Indeed, it is no exaggeration to say that the
symbiotic relationship between each correspondent and his team
of producers has been a decisive factor in the program's success. But it's also true that a producer's contribution varies a
great deal from one assignment to the next. For example, when
I do a story that is structured almost entirely around an interview—as with Richard Nixon, the Shah of Iran, or Vladimir
Horowitz—most of the burden falls on me. I prefer to do most
of my own homework in preparing for those encounters. Interviews are my department, and the people who work with
me understand that. Hence, on that kind of assignment, a field
producer may come up with a separate list of questions from
mine. In addition, he'll handle the logistics, and supervise the
camera crews and the editing of the film. But delivering the
essence of the story—the interview itself—is basically my
job.

In constructing long investigative reports, however, I must
rely on my producers to carry the ball most of the way, as
Lando did when he pieced together the various elements that
went into "The Selling of Colonel Herbert." One reason is
simply because they have the time and I don't. During the
regular season, when the *60 Minutes* schedule is in full swing,
I have to go on the air almost every week with a fresh story
of one kind or another. This means that I can't just drop all
other projects and spend several weeks, or even months, doing
the kind of intensive spadework that an investigative piece
requires. But my producers and researchers *do* have that kind
of time, so it's up to them to develop those stories from scratch
and to guide them through the critical stages.

Nor is it just a question of my time and availability. Another
reason for relying on my producers and researchers to take the
initiative is because investigative journalism often requires a
furtive approach. In particular, when he's just starting out on
a story, a reporter may prefer to work on the qt, like an undercover agent, and there's no way I (or any of my on-air
colleagues on *60 Minutes*) can move around incognito and
insinuate myself into a delicate situation. Producers sometimes

complain about their relative obscurity—and it's true that they don't get the public recognition they deserve—but if we didn't have them working that way, as skilled off-camera reporters, we could never get to first base on an investigative story. Once we correspondents come into the picture, with or without a film crew, it's all out in the open.

Yet even during those early stages, when I have to refrain from direct participation in the reporting of an investigative piece, my role is hardly passive. No *60 Minutes* assignment I'm involved with can get off the ground without my enthusiastic approval; and from that point on, even though I'm usually simultaneously engaged in other projects, I try to keep tabs on how the new story is progressing. If a producer is having problems, I offer advice; if I feel he's going off in the wrong direction, I don't hesitate to challenge him. In other words, I try to exert my influence as an editor during the period when such a story is developing and taking shape.

But to reiterate, it's my producers who deserve most of the credit for the investigative reports I've done on *60 Minutes*, and when we finally hit our stride in that area in the mid-1970s, there were three in particular who led the way. One was Barry Lando; having done so much to launch us into that new frontier with "The Selling of Colonel Herbert," he continued to set the pace during the post-Watergate years. So, in taking a look at a few of the investigative stories we did that caused some commotion and swept *60 Minutes* into fresh waters of controversy, let's start with Lando and a piece called "Fake ID," which he produced in the winter of 1975–1976.

Once Lando decided to look into the use of false identification (a story originally suggested to me by Frances Knight, then the head of the U.S. Passport Office), it did not take him long to discover that it had become a national problem of startling proportions. Everyone from heroin smugglers to illegal aliens to renowned fugitives from justice, such as Patty Hearst and James Earl Ray, had made use of the scam, and it was costing the U.S. economy more than ten billion dollars a year. What made the practice so widespread was the relative ease with which one could obtain the documents needed to establish a bogus identity. The challenge was how to get that message across to our viewers in the most effective way. The conventional method would have been to find someone who had profited from the experience and was willing to talk about it on-camera. We could also interview government officials who had to cope with the problem. Actually we did both and included the interviews in our report. But additionally, we came up with a scheme of our own that brought the story to life in a way that was especially striking. Lando and I were able to cajole a researcher on our staff named Lucy Spiegel to set about acquiring a set of phony credentials. Then we followed her, step by step, with a camera crew as she proceeded to construct a false identity. It worked like a charm.

The critical first move in putting together a fake identity is to obtain an official copy of a birth certificate. So Lucy Spiegel launched her treasure hunt at the Birth Records Office in Washington, D.C. Officials there had a record of everyone ever born in the District of Columbia, and there are more than seven thousand similar offices in major cities, county seats and state capitals throughout the country. But although the birth data at these offices were quite thorough and accurate, the system had no way of recording a person's death on his or her birth certificate—and that was the loophole we chose to exploit. When Lucy arrived at the D.C. Birth Records Office, she said she had lost her birth certificate and gave her name as "Miss Diane," someone who had actually died in childhood some twenty years earlier. She submitted a few vital facts we had dug up—the kind of information that appears on birth documents—and in no time at all, she was given a bona fide copy of the dead girl's birth certificate, as her own.

While Lucy's application was being processed, Lando and I showed up at the Birth Records Office with a camera crew and began filming. The man in charge of the proceeding, John Crandall, knew we were doing a story on fake ID, but he did *not* know that Lucy was a *60 Minutes* researcher who had assumed a false identity; and of course, we said or did nothing to let on that we were in any way acquainted with Miss Diane. In fact, at one point, in response to my question, Crandall acknowledged that "we would have no way of knowing" for sure that Miss Diane was not an impostor.

WALLACE: So what you have here is a legal document that this woman can use for whatever purpose.

CRANDALL: For whatever purpose. To claim estates, to inherit money, to get passports, to get unemployment. For almost anything.

WALLACE: And if she were an impostor—I'm sure she's not, but if she were an impostor—she could use it for fraudulent purposes?

CRANDALL: Yes, she certainly could.

Crandall seemed to be amused by my suspicious inquiries, and when the time came to present Miss Diane with her new birth certificate, he asked her in a playful tone: "You're not going to use that for fraudulent purposes, are you?"

Knowing that our camera was rolling, Lucy met the challenge head on. "Of course not!" she replied in a voice that snapped with indignation.

Her phony birth certificate gave Lucy the foundation on which she could easily build a false identity, and over the next few weeks our camera crew tagged along as she made her rounds to various government offices in Washington and the city's Maryland suburbs. By the time she completed her illegal paper chase, Lucy had assembled an impressive dossier. Her bogus credentials included a certified copy of a birth certificate, a Maryland age of majority card, a Social Security card, a state unemployment card, a food stamp card, a Maryland driver's license and—the most precious document of all—a gold-embossed U.S. passport. The next step was to demonstrate, on film, just how great a menace a person can be with that kind of arsenal at her disposal. With her phony credentials, Lucy had no trouble opening a checking account at a Maryland bank with a modest deposit, and once she received her personalized set of checks, we sent her on a shopping spree in Washington. We followed her from store to store as she bought a camera, a Bulova wristwatch and a few clothes, including a lamb's-wool coat that cost $236.25. The total amount of her purchases came to $636.30, and she paid for everything by check, even though she only had about a hundred dollars in her account—and that under a phony name.

Finally, we wanted to illustrate the point that such a person would probably skip town before those checks began to bounce. This led us to Lucy's next target: an Eastern Airlines ticket office in downtown Washington, where she bought a one-way ticket to Mexico City on a flight scheduled to leave that evening. To pay for it, she wrote a check for $161.25, under her assumed name, and backed it up with her false ID. The people at Eastern, like those at most of our other stops, knew we were doing a story on fake ID, but they had no idea that Lucy had any connection with us and therefore had no reason to suspect that she was an impostor. After she received her ticket, I approached the Eastern agent:

> WALLACE: I wonder if I can ask you some questions?
>
> AIRLINE AGENT: Sure.
>
> WALLACE: First of all, forgive me, this young woman could simply go to Mexico and disappear from sight, and Eastern Airlines would be out a hundred and seventy dollars odd.
>
> AIRLINE AGENT: That's right. Well, I'm quite satisfied that she is okay. I mean—
>
> WALLACE: Why?
>
> AIRLINE AGENT: Well, I just have that feeling. After all, I have been in the business twenty-eight years. I should know a little about accepting checks.

When we broadcast "Fake ID" in February 1976, the general reaction was that we had come up with a dramatic and effective way of presenting the story. But a few critics raised some questions about the ethics of the method we employed. One objection was that in doing what she did, Lucy had violated the law. Of course, this was true in a purely technical sense, but needless to say, as I noted at the end of our report, everything that Lucy acquired on that assignment was either paid for or returned to its proper source. And I find it hard to believe that anyone who saw the piece could have believed that she or we were trying to get away with something illegal.

Somewhat more serious was the charge that by concealing her true identity from the various officials and merchants we came into contact with, we had hoodwinked them and subjected them to embarrassment on national television. There is some validity to that perhaps, but my own view is that none of the people we encountered behaved irresponsibly. They simply were doing their jobs in accordance with the policies they had been instructed to follow. As for us, our purpose clearly was not to suggest that the targets of our stratagem had been careless or derelict in their duties, but rather to expose the flaws inherent in the system.

Among those who did approve of our approach were some of the government officials who had to deal with the fraudulent practice. When we rebroadcast "Fake ID" a few months later, we were able to report that our story was being used as a training film for passport officers and U.S. consular personnel. In the meantime, a federal task force had been appointed to look into the problem. One of its recommendations was to close the loophole Lucy had exploited so successfully; that is, it called for a national procedure for cross-indexing births and deaths so that when a person dies, the fact will be indicated on his or her birth certificate. Even so, I wound up our story with the pessimistic observation that "nobody doubts that fake ID will continue to be a multibillion-dollar dilemma." And sure enough, this illicit subterfuge has continued to plague the American economy.

Not long after the "Fake ID" broadcast, we aired a story called "The Clinic on Morse Avenue," also produced by Barry Lando. Our subject was corruption within the Medicaid program. We focused on several clinical laboratories in the Chicago area that were suspected of running lucrative kickback operations. In putting together the report, we worked closely with a nonpartisan reform group in Chicago called the Better Government Association.

One of the trails we followed in our investigation led to a doctor named Herbert Myer, who had a large Medicaid practice on Chicago's South Side, and the tale he told us was all too typical. Dr. Myer said he had recently been approached by a

man from one of the city's clinical laboratories who offered to
pay part of the doctor's overhead if, in return, Myer would
give his Medicaid business to that lab. At our request, Myer
asked the lab representative back to his office for another visit.
To document that visit, we installed a one-way mirror in the
office wall, and on the day of the appointment, we set up a
CBS News cameraman behind the mirror. Under Illinois law
we could film the meeting, but we could not record secretly
what the lab representative said. So, with Dr. Myer's permission, I hid in a closet so that I could overhear their conversation.
I heard the laboratory agent say that whatever profit his associates made on any Medicaid business Dr. Myer sent them,
they would split with the doctor in the form of rent for a portion
of his office. The agent said that, according to his attorney,
such an arrangement was perfectly legal.

As it turned out, that eavesdropping stint in Dr. Myer's
office was merely a test run, a dress rehearsal for a far more
elaborate masquerade we dreamed up. In an effort to discover
how pervasive such practices were in the Chicago area, we
decided to set up our own medical clinic. Joining forces with
the Better Government Association, we rented a storefront on
Morse Avenue on the city's North Side for $450 a month. The
phony clinic was run by two BGA staff members who invited
a number of labs to come in to discuss using their services. In
no way was it suggested that the clinic wanted any kind of
kickback. To document those visits, we installed another one-
way mirror behind the desk at the clinic and stationed our
cameras behind it. Representatives from eleven labs showed
up, and nine made offers similar to the one I had overheard in
Myer's office. Two weeks later, several of the labs were invited
back to the Morse Avenue clinic for further discussions, and
this time I joined the party. Following the procedure we had
initiated in Myer's office, I hid behind a wall in the back room,
from which I could hear everything that was said in the front
office. Once again, because of Illinois law, we did not record
secretly what the lab representatives said. So I waited until the
visitors offered specific kickback deals, then I walked into the
front office and confronted them. I explained that *60 Minutes*
was doing a story on the Medicaid program, informed them

that I had overheard the offers they had made, and warned them that from now on whatever they said in my presence would be recorded.

The first people to arrive at our clinic that day were two men who identified themselves as the owners of North Side Clinical Labs, and they came quickly to the point. They said that if the Medicaid business the clinic sent them amounted to one thousand dollars or more a week, they would return half that money to the clinic by renting a small space in the back. In other words, they offered to lease a few square feet in the rear hallway for at least five hundred dollars a week, which was more than four times the rent of our entire clinic. Nice work if you can get it, and we could have gotten it if our bogus clinic had actually been engaged in a Medicaid practice. After listening from behind the wall for a few minutes, I walked in on the two men and explained what we were doing. Our cameraman also came out into full view, and we began to film, and record, what turned into a fairly frank discussion about kickbacks. Among other things, the lab owners insisted that if they did not bestow kickbacks on clinics and doctors, "We would be out of business tomorrow. It's as simple as that."

Other visits that day produced similar results, although some of the lab representatives were not as candid and cooperative as the first two I confronted. For example, there was the man from D. J. Laboratories. Compared with most of his competitors, he was downright stingy; he offered to give back only 25 percent of the money received from the Medicaid business the clinic sent his lab. When I appeared on the scene, he tried to weasel out of the deal he had proposed a few moments earlier:

> WALLACE: I want to interrupt, if I can. I'm recording this for broadcast, and I just heard you say that you will give back twenty-five percent in a kickback, twenty-five percent in a rebate. Is that correct?

> LAB REPRESENTATIVE: Well— Wait a minute. You look familiar to me.

> WALLACE: Yeah. Tell me something: How much in the way of kickbacks and rebates do you get involved with, and why?

LAB REPRESENTATIVE: I— I don't give— I don't give kickbacks.

WALLACE: You just—I heard you right in here. You offered twenty-five percent in a rebate to these two gentlemen, to this new clinic.

LAB REPRESENTATIVE: Well, I—I didn't mean it that way. I think I better not say anything now.

As we suspected when we set up the phony Morse Avenue clinic, our little closet drama played very well on television. Instead of just interviewing doctors and various government officials investigating corruption in the Medicaid program, we showed the action as it was taking place. Even so, when the piece was aired in February 1976, a few voices were raised in disapproval. Taking a stand that foreshadowed the charges leveled at the ABSCAM "sting" a few years later, our critics accused us of "entrapment." I couldn't disagree more. Deception, yes—no question of that, for we clearly acted under false pretenses—but not entrapment, as I understand the term. Unlike some of the ABSCAM investigators, who lured their targets into criminal acts by offering them unsolicited bribes, we said or did nothing to indicate that we were looking for kickbacks. Every lab representative who compromised himself made the first overture without any prompting from the BGA people who were posing as the operators of our phony clinic. As far as those laboratory agents were concerned, the clinic on Morse Avenue was just another routine stop, business as usual, and that's what we recorded.

At the time, federal and state investigators were starting to move in on Chicago's clinical laboratories. But when I interviewed some of those officials for our report, they acknowledged glumly that the situation in Chicago was not an isolated case, that the problem was indeed a national one. Here's what one of them said to me: "The Medicaid program, Mike, is totally without controls. It is a joint federal-state program, and both are passing the buck to the other. Everybody is supposed to be enforcing the law, but nobody is. And that's the fact of the matter. If you're going to rip off the government, there is no easier way to do it than to go after Medicaid."

However, at least steps were taken to curb the corruption in Chicago. When we did an update on "The Clinic on Morse Avenue" the following year, we could report that "eleven labs have been temporarily suspended from the Medicaid program there, and nine others are completely cut off, terminated." In addition, the U.S. Attorney's office had taken action, with the result that six labs already had pleaded guilty to criminal charges, and more indictments were expected. "And what about the taxpayer?" I asked at the end of that update. "What did he get out of all this? Well, the state tells us that since our report and their investigation, the amount of Medicaid money paid out annually to medical labs there has dropped by almost thirty percent—a savings of three-and-a-half-million dollars a year."

Barry Lando and I returned to Chicago in late 1977 to do a piece on another phase of widespread corruption in that city. Actually, it wasn't really our story per se, but one that we joined in progress. For several weeks that fall, an investigative reporter for the *Chicago Sun-Times* had been gathering evidence on certain city inspectors who were accepting bribes to overlook health-, building- and fire-code violations. To get to the bottom, the reporter, Pam Zekman, also worked closely with the city's Better Government Association. Moreover, Pam and the BGA adopted a tactic similar to the one we had used to get the goods on Chicago's clinical laboratories: They opened their version of a phony clinic, except in this instance the bogus establishment was a neighborhood bar called, appropriately, the Mirage Tavern.

The new proprietors of the Mirage Tavern identified themselves as "Mr. and Mrs. Ray Patterson," but in reality they were Pam Zekman and an investigator for the BGA named Bill Rechtenwald. Working as a married couple, they tended bar and generally ran the place. When Pam and Bill opened the tavern for business, they purposely left many glaring code violations uncorrected, and to document the sting operation they were planning, room was made, behind a fake ventilation outlet, for a *Sun-Times* photographer. Then later, when *60 Minutes* was invited into the story, our cameraman joined the photographer at his concealed post, which gave them a bird's-eye view of the action.

A key figure, a middleman in the setup, was a business broker and accountant named Philip Barasch. He helped Pam and Bill find the tavern, but that was the least of the services he provided for his new clients, whom he knew as Mr. and Mrs. Patterson. Acting on his own initiative, Barasch gave them step-by-step instructions in how to pay off various city inspectors. He said that he personally would telephone the inspectors and tell them when to come to the Mirage Tavern; then he told Pam and Bill what to do when the inspectors arrived. Specifically, he instructed them to put money in an envelope with his business card and tell each inspector: "This is from Philip Barasch, my accountant." Pam and Bill followed the advice, and the payoffs proceeded like clockwork. One by one over the next few days, the fire, building, health and plumbing inspectors arrived at the tavern on schedule, and, after making a cursory check of the place—during which they ignored the numerous code violations—each accepted his envelope and left. What the inspectors did not know, of course, was that their visits were being photographed secretly. Recalling the criticism directed at *60 Minutes* when we broadcast "The Clinic on Morse Avenue," I put the question to Pam Zekman:

> WALLACE: You're a newspaper reporter, a Pulitzer Prize winner. Is there entrapment involved here?
>
> ZEKMAN: None whatsoever. We are opening a business just like hundreds of thousands of people in this city open businesses every year.
>
> WALLACE: And?
>
> ZEKMAN: And we are letting whatever comes through the door come through the door.
>
> WALLACE: In other words, you're not advertising in any sense that there are kickbacks available or—
>
> ZEKMAN: We're avoiding that at all possible costs.

Among the services that Phil Barasch offered the proprietors of the Mirage Tavern was advice on how to reduce their tax bite by shaving 40 percent off their income reports. He instructed Pam and Bill to keep two sets of books, one with the legitimate figures, and the other, with the 40 percent sliced off, was to be sent to him. Then, if any government accountants or auditors came snooping around, Pam and Bill were told to direct them to Barasch and not show them the legitimate books. Nor was Barasch the only one who provided this kind of counsel. Five other accountants were hired to handle the tavern's finances, and they, too, gave Pam and Bill detailed instructions on how to conceal part of their income and thereby reduce their tax liability.

To flesh out the part of the story that we were doing for *60 Minutes*, Lando and I set up an on-camera interview with Phil Barasch in a hotel suite we had rented. Unbeknownst to Barasch, Pam Zekman and Bill Rechtenwald were standing by in an adjoining room. After asking him a few leading questions, which he parried, I told Barasch that his Mirage Tavern clients, Mr. and Mrs. Ray Patterson, were there and I invited them to join us. Confronted with this face-to-face situation, Barasch reluctantly acknowledged that he had given the Pattersons advice on how to pay off the various city inspectors. But when we moved on to the matter of falsifying income reports, and Bill Rechtenwald recalled that Barasch "sat in our place and showed us how to cut back the gross figures by forty percent," Barasch stiffened and began to stonewall:

BARASCH: I don't believe that.

WALLACE: What do you mean, you don't believe it? They're sitting here.

BARASCH: Let them sit there. I just don't believe that. The average person that I have does their own cutting, and we take the figures as they have them.

RECHTENWALD: And you don't know anything about the cutting? You don't know that they cut?

BARASCH: I do not.

But Rechtenwald had come to the interview armed with records that clearly implicated Barasch, and the two men were soon engaged in a spirited argument over what had occurred in their business dealings with each other. At the heart of Barasch's resentment was the feeling that he had been singled out as a scapegoat. So I tried to disabuse him of that notion. I interrupted the squabble to say that the Pattersons had contacted several other accountants, and all had offered similar advice on how to hide part of their income. In fact, I continued, it was my understanding that Barasch himself had told them that shaving the gross figures was a routine practice in small, cash-oriented business concerns like the Mirage Tavern. In a sense, I was now playing "good cop" to Bill Rechtenwald's "bad cop," and since I seemed to be expressing some sympathy for Barasch's position, he relaxed a bit. I should mention also that even though the CBS News camera was quietly rolling, we were conversing in a private hotel suite and there was a strong sense of being alone, cut off from the rest of the world—all of which helps to explain what happened next. When Barasch averred that the widespread practice of tax fraud was "common knowledge," I took that as my cue and moved in for the clincher:

> WALLACE: I know it's common knowledge, and apparently you are among the people who do it. That's all that we're trying to— I mean, look, *between you and me*—
>
> BARASCH: Yeah.
>
> WALLACE: —you do it, everybody does it.
>
> BARASCH: I presume everybody does it to an extent.

Between you and me! Poor Phil Barasch momentarily forgot that he was being interviewed on camera for *60 Minutes*, and when we aired the story a few weeks later, his admission that "everybody does it" (including himself) was made "between you and me" and the millions of viewers who were watching that night. In the meantime, having induced him to open up on the subject, I pressed him to elaborate:

> WALLACE: You mean, if they wanted to put every tax accountant in jail who did that kind of thing—
>
> BARASCH: They'd all be in.

WALLACE: They'd all be in?

BARASCH: That's right . . .

WALLACE: There are tough penalties, you know. For tax evasion, it's criminal fraud: up to a ten thousand dollar fine, up to a year in jail on each count.

BARASCH: Yeah, in jail. That's right.

WALLACE: These people—you, and you've got four hundred businesses. You could go to jail for four hundred years!

BARASCH (laughing): I'm not going to live that long.

WALLACE: You're really not very worried about it?

BARASCH: At this stage of the game, I'm not very worried about it.

But when it came to the next stage of the game, Phil Barasch had ample reason to worry. For in the aftermath of the *Sun-Times* exposé and our auxiliary report, there were these developments: A federal grand jury subpoenaed Barasch's records and those of the other five accountants who had been hired by the Mirage Tavern. A random audit of fifty-four small businesses by state revenue inspectors revealed that all were underreporting their income. The various inspectors caught on-camera in the Mirage were either suspended or dismissed from their jobs, and the departments they represented were given a thorough housecleaning. As for the tavern itself, Pam and Bill turned it over to new owners who did not hesitate to exploit the bar's brush with notoriety. In addition to offering their customers food and drink, the new proprietors did a brisk business selling novelty T-shirts, on each of which was inscribed this cynical boast: *I Inspected the Mirage.*

As I mentioned earlier, Barry Lando was just one of three producers I worked with during the middle and late seventies who seized the initiative in the investigative sphere. Another was Marion Goldin, an intense, capable and determined reporter who had come up through the ranks in our Washington bureau. For several years Goldin had worked as the chief researcher for Eric Sevareid, and in meeting that daily challenge she became thoroughly conversant with the intricacies of politics and government. She joined *60 Minutes* as my Washington producer in late 1972, and a few months later, when the Watergate scandal broke, Goldin concentrated almost all her energies on piecing together the complex elements of that story. Thus, when I finally turned my attention to Watergate in the spring of 1973, I relied heavily on Marion's depth of knowledge and sound judgment. She was the one who briefed me, step by step, through many of the fascinating intrigues and innuendoes as we prepared for the long, one-on-one interviews I did with John Ehrlichman and others who were caught in the web of deceit that inflicted, in John Dean's phrase, "a cancer" on the American presidency. The Watergate storm eventually blew itself out, and like so many other reporters who had been engrossed in the story, Goldin had some trouble adjusting to the placid climate of the Ford and early Carter years. The occasional sparks of controversy that flared up in Washington after Watergate were as nothing compared to the high drama of events that had forced a President to resign in disgrace. Hence, even though Goldin continued to produce first-rate Washington stories during this period, she began to look elsewhere, beyond the Potomac, for suitable targets to probe. One that she zeroed in on was a health spa in California called Murrieta Hot Springs. The result of her foray was one of our best and most dramatic investigative efforts.

We first learned about Murrieta from some viewers who wrote to complain about unhappy experiences they had had there. Over the years the mail has been a rich source of stories for *60 Minutes*. By the mid-1970s, after our move into prime time, we were receiving more than a thousand letters a week, many of which sought to alert us to crimes and other misdeeds that the letter writers deemed worthy of our attention. Such was the case with the clinic at Murrieta and the promise of "miracle cures" it made to victims of cancer and other serious diseases. After reading through the correspondence, Marion Goldin did some checking and discovered that Murrieta's "miracles" had also aroused the suspicions of California's medical authorities. In addition, she was told that the people who ran Murrieta went out of their way to court wealthy patients who, once enrolled in the cure program, were pressured into making large financial contributions to the clinic.

With that as an impetus, we decided to take a closer look. This entailed another deception on our part, one that in its way was just as elaborate as the phony clinic we had set up on Morse Avenue in Chicago. Goldin and two other members of the *60 Minutes* team—cameraman Greg Cook and soundman James Camery—enrolled at Murrieta under false pretenses. Camery identified himself as a wealthy, semiretired investment counselor who had just been told that he had leukemia. Cook, asserting he was a traveling photographer by trade (thus justifying the camera equipment he brought with him), said he was Camery's concerned nephew, and Goldin claimed to be the ailing man's longtime secretary. To make the bait even more enticing, they arrived at the clinic in a rented Rolls-Royce.

During their weeklong stay at Murrieta, Camery was examined just once by a doctor, who assured him that he did not have leukemia. However, he wasn't given a clean bill of health, because the doctor diagnosed Camery's illness as a leaky lung, which he said required treatment. The essence of this treatment was a three-day fast, consisting only of lemon juice and distilled water. Later we learned that this regimen—the three-day fast, followed by a light vegetable diet—was imposed on all the patients at Murrieta, whether they suffered from cancer or constipation, arthritis or acne. The other big event in the cure program was a series of urine tests. Twice a day, Camery had to hand a sample of his urine over to various "counselors" (none of whom was a doctor, or even a nurse) who, after testing it, came up with a set of mysterious numbers that supposedly reflected the state of his improving health.

But Camery only pretended to go along with the drill. During his three-day fast, Goldin and Cook were able to smuggle breakfast and lunch to him in his room; in fact, the supervision was so lax that they had no trouble sneaking him out to dinner every night. And to test the validity of the program even further, there were occasions when Cook's urine or Goldin's was presented to the unsuspecting counselor as Camery's latest offering. Yet even then he was given the cheerful news that his urine number revealed he was making marvelous progress toward a full recovery. So much for Murrieta's "miracle cures."

In the meantime, my colleagues had ample opportunity to become acquainted with other patients, most of whom were older women. One of them, who was suffering from painful arthritis, said she was told to go off her medication because it wasn't doing her any good. Even more disturbing was the experience of two diabetics, who were urged by the counselors to cut down and eventually eliminate their insulin; had they followed that advice, they would have imperiled their health and even their lives. Most of the patients our group came into contact with brought up the subject of money and the efforts to pry financial donations out of them. Camery knew exactly what they were talking about. On his first day at the clinic, when he was told that he had a leaky lung, the rented Rolls-Royce caught the eye of his examining physician, who, after giving it a long and admiring look, said to Camery: "You should go down and see Doctor Rudd. Maybe you'll want to invest in this place. We can always use a few million."

"Doctor" Rudd was R. J. Rudd, the promoter of the Murrieta clinic. Claiming to be a Baptist minister, Rudd preached every Sunday at the Murrieta chapel. But when the *60 Minutes* team met with him one afternoon, Rudd did not dwell on spiritual matters, or even health care. All he wanted to talk about was money, contributions to the cure program, and in his pitch to put the arm on Camery, he extolled the virtues of various tax shelters that could be exploited for that purpose. Using a hidden camera and microphone, my colleagues were able to film and record their conversation with Rudd, as well as other high points of their stay at Murrieta; and after a few days of gathering evidence, they felt they had enough to move on to the next phase of our assignment. The time had come for me to get into the act. So I showed up at Murrieta with another film crew and indicated I was there to do a routine, conventional story on the clinic for *60 Minutes*. At first, I did not let on that I was acquainted in any way with one of the patients currently enrolled in the program.

Taking the position that he had nothing to hide, R. J. Rudd agreed to be interviewed. I began with questions about his background. He acknowledged that he had no training in medicine, but he was quick to cite other academic credentials—one Ph.D. in economics and another in philosophy—and he even showed me the diplomas to back up his claims. One diploma was from Christian Tennessee University and the other from Trinity Christian College in Florida, two schools I had never heard of, and with good reason. For when we checked with education officials in Tennessee and Florida, we were told that the diplomas were nothing more than mail-order degrees from nonexistent universities. As for Rudd's religious vocation, Baptist Church officials assured us that he had never been ordained a minister. In short, Rudd was a complete charlatan, and the entire operation at Murrieta was an accurate reflection of the man's shady character.

Then we discovered that the rip-offs at Murietta were not confined to the "miracle cures" and the large donations being wheedled out of wealthy patients. Rudd and his associates also ran a health food store where sundry products were sold that had little to recommend them except their exotic names. For example, there was something called Formula-X, which we took to an outside chemist. After testing it, he told us that it consisted almost entirely of rubbing alcohol, which could be purchased at a local drugstore for about nineteen cents a quart. The Murrieta store was charging twelve dollars for a three-ounce bottle of Formula-X. We also had the chemist test a product called Mivita, which turned out to be plain water with a very small amount of bland material added to give it coloring. Yet Mivita—which sold for six dollars a quart—was being promoted as a remedy for all kinds of ailments and disorders. So when I interviewed Horace Gibson, the Murrieta doctor who examined James Camery and discovered his leaky lung, I asked him about that particular panacea:

WALLACE: Do you recommend Mivita?

GIBSON: For certain uses.

WALLACE: What uses?

GIBSON: Well, it's good for wounds, wounds externally.

WALLACE: Well, wait a minute. I've taken a look at that bottle of Mivita and it says, drink it.

GIBSON: You can drink it.

WALLACE: You can drink it. You can use it for a douche. You can use it for an enema. It's good for hemorrhoids. All those things?

GIBSON (nodding): Hm-hmm.

I eventually got around to telling Rudd and his associates that we had enacted our own version of *To Catch a Thief*. And in disclosing who Camery and his entourage really were, I gave an account of the steps that had been taken to test the validity of Murrieta's cure program: the violations of the three-day fast and the phony urine samples that were given to the counselors. I also mentioned some of the complaints about the money and treatment that we had heard from other patients at the clinic. But even when my queries took on an accusatory tone, Rudd continued to insist that his intentions were honorable:

WALLACE: The question is, are you preying on human frailty? Preying on the elderly? On the abandoned? Taking money from people who can't afford to give that money in order to try to build yourself some kind of a small empire.

RUDD: I don't believe that's true.

WALLACE: Many who disagree with you would say there's a kind of a con-game operation going on at Murrieta Springs right now. They're not delivering what people are paying for.

RUDD: Well, I still feel this is not a con game. I feel it's a sincere effort by a lot of good people who are giving some of the best years of their lives to—to build a retreat program where people can come and get nutritional assistance.

The more deeply we probed into Rudd's murky past, the more we realized that Murrieta was merely the latest in a series of land promotions, health food schemes and other dubious enterprises he had been engaged in over the years. In fact, Rudd was currently facing charges in Florida, stemming from a case in which an elderly leukemia victim lost $25,000 in a land-investment scheme. The victim's name was Golden Zimmerly, and when we tracked her down, she told us that she had turned her savings over to Rudd because she trusted him. "I never thought a Baptist minister or any kind of minister would cheat you out of your money," she said. "I didn't know they were that crooked, but I found out that they are. That is, if he is a minister."

We included Zimmerly's story in our report "This Year at Murrieta," which we broadcast in January 1978. In summing up the man and his works, I put a question to law-enforcement officials: "The more we learned about R. J. Rudd, the more we wondered how he had been able to evade the law all these years. Only federal and state authorities can answer that."

Their answer was not long in coming. When we aired an update on the story a few months later, we reported that Rudd had been convicted of defrauding Golden Zimmerly out of $25,000; he was sentenced to five years in jail and ordered to pay a $5,000 fine. What's more, his other legal problems were starting to catch up with him. We reported that charges were pending against him in Virginia and California, and that the Justice Department's organized-crime strike force had launched an investigation into his activities. As for the Murrieta Hot Springs health spa, it had been declared bankrupt with liabilities of nearly thirty-seven million dollars.

"This Year at Murrieta" provoked a flood of letters, many of them dealing with the mail-order Ph.D. degrees that R. J. Rudd received from nonexistent universities. In that respect at least, Rudd had plenty of company, for one viewer after another had a tale to tell about people who had acquired phony diplomas that they were using to advance their careers or, in some cases, merely putting on display to impress their friends and acquaintances. Our curiosity aroused, Marion Goldin and I decided to do a piece on this wave of academic fraud. The result was a report called "A Matter of Degrees." Thus, the lode we mined at Murrieta not only proved to be a rich vein in its own right, but it put us squarely on the trail of another good story.

Goldin soon discovered how easy it was to obtain mail-order degrees. Responding to advertisements in several magazines (including such respected journals as *The Atlantic Monthly* and *Saturday Review*), she began to receive catalogs of schools with official-sounding names, like Roosevelt University and John Quincy Adams College. In reality, these colleges were no more than mail drops, but that didn't make any difference. In a fairly short time, Marion received, through the mail, Ph.D. degrees in engineering, science, psychology and nursing, even though she had no background whatever in any of those subjects.

California had the embarrassing distinction of being the nation's leader in the granting of mail-order degrees. When I asked a state education official why California was so active in that field, he replied in a way that suggested he was less than enthralled by the trendy enthusiasms and popular culture of his native state. "We have Disneyland," he lamented, "we have Hollywood, we have all the religious sects, and we have diploma mills." But there was another, more serious reason, and that was the state's permissive legal standards. All the California law demanded was proof of $50,000 in assets and a statement of educational purpose. These alone gave one the right to open a "university" and commence selling degrees. Nothing else was required—no faculty, no classrooms and no irritating final exams.

We decided to focus our attention on a diploma mill in Hollywood called California Pacifica University. It was more than a mail drop, for the president of California Pacifica, Ernest Sinclair, maintained a suite of offices and employed a clerical staff. Still, it was a far cry from Harvard, although one would not have thought so from Sinclair's description of the place. In promotional brochures, he characterized the school as "the custodian of the intellectual capital of mankind." That was enough to whet our interest, so we sent two members of the *60 Minutes* staff—production assistant Gail Reiter and cameraman Wade Bingham—to California Pacifica to find out what they had to do to earn advanced degrees from that academic citadel.

Reiter, who was twenty-four, had had less than a year of college. Yet in her first meeting with Sinclair, he promised her both a bachelor's degree and a master's degree; he also offered her a job as registrar of the university. Bingham, in his early fifties, had attended college as a young man for just one year. But Sinclair assured him that his thirty years of experience as a cameraman were all the credentials he needed for a degree. Bingham paid $2,150 for tuition, and although he never went to class, never read a textbook and never took an exam, he received a master's degree in business administration from California Pacifica.

Not long after Wade Bingham's "graduation," a film crew and I visited the California Pacifica "campus," which was located in a Hollywood building just above a wig shop. When we walked into Sinclair's office, he was on the telephone. But he interrupted his conversation to acknowledge our arrival:

> SINCLAIR (on phone): Hey, wait a minute. Hey, *Sixty Minutes* is in here. Can you believe it?
>
> WALLACE: How are you?
>
> SINCLAIR: *Sixty Minutes* here. Hold the phone.
>
> WALLACE: Nice to see you.
>
> SINCLAIR (still on phone): I'm trying to tell you his name. Let's see, there's Dan. No, this—hey, this is my favorite. Gosh! What's your—what's your last name?
>
> WALLACE: Wallace. Mike Wallace.
>
> SINCLAIR: Mike Wallace!

As his exuberant greeting indicated, Ernest Sinclair was a man of high spirits. Indeed, he happened to be one of the most engaging rogues I had met in some time. His flaky charm made him easy to like, even though one could hardly approve of his business ethics. When I questioned him, Sinclair cheerfully admitted that selling phony college degrees was a lucrative line of work. "I want to reach the white-collar man that has the money—that's number one," he told me, and he had reached enough of them in the past three months to take in more than $100,000 in "tuition fees." I noted that the brochure for California Pacifica, which contained a number of misleading inducements, featured an impressive-looking display of faculty members. So I asked Sinclair about some of them, starting with Mario Ugarte, who was identified as the dean of the college of education:

> WALLACE: Is he here now?
>
> SINCLAIR: He's not here.
>
> WALLACE: Rosalba Riano, the administrative assistant?
>
> SINCLAIR: Right. We did make communication with her by telephone, and she is alive and well, and she's in New York in the garment district.
>
> WALLACE: But she's no longer your administrative assistant?
>
> SINCLAIR: No. I know I'm—no, she never did come to our school.
>
> WALLACE: Terrell Harvey, is he still dean of your college of law?
>
> SINCLAIR: I could—I could probably say yes, and I could probably say no.

Sinclair finally confessed that California Pacifica had no faculty. But he still insisted that he was running a legitimate operation, that in selling those bogus degrees he was committing no crime. Nevertheless, he did not deny that in years past he had been in trouble with the law—plenty of trouble, too, as we found out when we checked into his background. We discovered that Ernest Sinclair was an ex-con who had served time in three states, California, Georgia and Alabama. All his convictions were for mail fraud and similar offenses. Yet even when I confronted him with his criminal record, Sinclair continued, in his disarming way, to justify his diploma mill. Why, to hear him tell it, he was a good Samaritan who served the needs of those who had become victims of society:

> SINCLAIR: We had a person not too long ago with an aircraft company right here in town. He came to me shaking all over. He said, "Mr. Sinclair, I've been with them seventeen years. I don't have a degree. And my supervisor came and told me, 'We're having a cutback,' and said, 'If—if you have a degree, we will consider keeping you.'" So society has gone mad.
>
> WALLACE: And you're simply taking advantage of this market that society has established, this appetite of—for degrees?
>
> SINCLAIR: I'm just like Oral Roberts, Bishop Sheen, Billy Graham and all the rest of them. I consider that we're helping humanity . . . They need a degree because society demands it. I don't put the demands there.

But U.S. postal authorities took a less indulgent view of Sinclair's activities. A few days after I interviewed him, he was arrested once again on charges of mail fraud. (Ingratiating to the end, Sinclair wrote later from prison to inform me that he intended, finally, to go straight and to thank me for helping him see the light.) That took care of California Pacifica University, which promptly went out of business. But there were still plenty of other diploma mills to be found in California and elsewhere, and many were enrolling enough students to make the legal risk worthwhile. As I observed at the end of the report, which we broadcast in April 1978, one could not feel much sympathy for the people who purchased the phony degrees, for they knew precisely what they were buying. In most cases, they were only too willing to be part of the fraud. The real victims were the people who unwittingly hired teachers, retained lawyers or placed their faith in doctors whose credentials, in academic terms, were not worth the paper they were printed on.

• • •

CLOSE ENCOUNTERS 409•

The third producer whose investigative work deserves to be
acknowledged here is Norman Gorin. A longtime member of
the CBS News family (he began in our Washington bureau in
the late 1950s), Gorin joined *60 Minutes* in 1971. Like Barry
Lando and Marion Goldin, he was a persistent and resourceful
reporter who constantly had his eye out for stories that would
have some impact and shake people up. During the years when
60 Minutes was making its big move into investigative journalism and we came to be perceived as a program that blew
the whistle on acts of fraud and corruption, Gorin was in the
forefront of that effort. Yet he was quick to recognize that as
we began to build our reputation, we ran the risk of taking on
a crusade mentality, and Norman's sharp sense of humor
was a healthy antidote. Once, when a friend called him to suggest a story idea, his first response was: "Yes, but is it a national disgrace? It has to be a national disgrace. That's the only
kind of story I'm allowed to work on nowadays."

Along with other shortcomings, I tend to be a compulsive
needler, and the more comfortable I am with someone, the
more I delight in the verbal thrust and parry. I mention this
because during the time we worked together, Gorin and I constantly baited each other, just as over the years Harry Reasoner
and I had seldom passed up an opportunity to zap each other
with jocular insults. On one occasion when Norman was con-
valescing in the hospital, I sent him a cactus, and on the get-
well card I wrote: "From your prickly friend." Even though he
was flat on his back, recovering from major surgery, I figured
he would not take that lying down. And sure enough, a few
days later, he came back with a riposte. "Nice try," his thank-
you note read, "but adding the suffix doesn't change a thing."
It took me a second or two to realize what he was referring to.

In early 1979 Gorin and I had reason to suspect, from certain
letters we received, that the leaders of the Worldwide Church
of God were prime candidates for "national disgrace" attention
on *60 Minutes*. The one hundred thousand members of that
church were pouring about $80 million a year into its coffers—
more money than was being collected by Billy Graham and
Oral Roberts combined—and there was some question as to
how a lot of those tax-exempt dollars were being spent. The
Worldwide Church of God was based in Pasadena, and among

those who were eager to look into its financial affairs was the California attorney general. He was trying to force the church to open its books so he could find out if a large portion of the money donated by the faithful was being siphoned off for personal use. When Gorin and I heard about this, we decided to launch our own investigation.

The head of the Worldwide Church of God was Herbert W. Armstrong, but we were unable to contact him. His chief adviser and spokesman, Stanley Rader, told us that Armstrong was a reclusive man who did not give interviews to the press. But after a generous dinner we bought him and his wife at La Scala in Beverly Hills, Radar himself offered to answer any questions we cared to ask, and since he also happened to be the church's treasurer, the man who controlled the purse strings, we readily accepted his invitation.

Stanley Rader certainly did not pretend to be lacking in worldly possessions or creature comforts. When I interviewed him, he proudly disclosed that the church paid him a salary of more than $200,000 a year, and the perks that came with it would have stirred the envy of any corporation executive. In addition to his plush executive suite in Pasadena, Rader had at his disposal a limousine and chauffeur as well as a multimillion-dollar jet plane to fly him anywhere in the world. Beyond that, he had a lavish expense account; according to his own estimate, Rader had run up more than $250,000 in expenses the previous year. Nor was he the only one who made liberal use of the church's money. Rader also authorized annual, six-figure payments to others to cover the cost of first-class plane tickets and other travel expenses. All that money, he insisted, was spent to spread the gospel. If true, then that was missionary work on a grand scale, a far cry from the road to Damascus, where Saint Paul started. I thought of Paul and his contemporaries when Radar told me, with considerable fervor, that the man he served, Herbert Armstrong, was worthy of being compared to the early disciples who occupy such a hallowed place in Christian belief and history:

> RADER: No question in my mind. He is the most amazing human being that God has ever placed on this earth in two thousand years. No question.

WALLACE: In other words, he is the equivalent of the men who sat with Jesus Christ at the Last Supper?

RADER: In my opinion, yes.

But Rader could no longer count on Armstrong to return the compliment, as Norman Gorin learned from various contacts he had made within the church. For in the preceding months, several members had complained to Armstrong about Rader's misuse of church funds, and in response, Armstrong had begun to put some distance between himself and his treasurer, to whom he had delegated so much authority. He also had become concerned about Rader's own ambitions, the overt moves he was making to put himself in line to succeed or even supplant Armstrong.

This was more than conjecture on our part; we were not merely taking someone's word for it. From one of his contacts, a high-level member of the church who was part of the anti-Rader faction, Gorin obtained the tapes of two telephone conversations with Armstrong that our source had recorded surreptitiously. In the first conversation, Armstrong spoke of his concern that Rader was attempting to take over as leader of the Worldwide Church of God. "He's deliberately trying to put himself there," he told our source. "I don't want to think that anyone has their eyes on fifty, sixty, seventy million dollars a year. But that is quite a magnet." In the second conversation taped by our source, Armstrong read from a draft of a letter he was sending to Stanley Rader: "I have to say candidly, Stan—for we have to face the facts—that very near unanimously, neither the ministry nor the lay members of the church will accept you as their spiritual leader."

When I interviewed Rader, he had no idea that the tapes had been leaked to us. Thus, when I asked him about the recent friction in his relationship with Armstrong, he vigorously denied it. I then told him about the tapes, revealed what Armstrong had said in those recorded conversations, and asked him if he wanted to hear them. He clearly had not expected to be put in that position, but he could hardly refuse to listen to the evidence we had acquired.

Until then, Rader had come across as glib and self-assured,

a man who seemed to welcome the challenge of *60 Minutes*. He was sure that he held the upper hand because he arrogantly assumed that no other member of the church had talked to us. But now, when we played the Armstrong tapes in his presence, Rader lost his composure and launched into a tirade. First, he accused us of having acquired the tapes illegally. Then he threatened to sue us, to "go to any court in any land." Finally he resorted to a personal attack on me and my line of work, which I quote now in fond memory of that lively encounter:

> Mike, look, I think you'd better scrap everything, because you're on my list, okay? You're never going to live it down, Mike, I guarantee it. I'll use it as a springboard to show just what the press is, because you're contemptible ... I'd like you to get out of here, immediately. I hope you got it, and I hope you have the guts to use it.

Needless to say, we did use it, every bit of it. In fact, Rader's temper tantrum was the high point of our *60 Minutes* report, which we called "God and Mammon." When we broadcast it in April 1979, the attempt to build a legal case against the Worldwide Church of God was still up in the air. But even though Rader was having his problems within the hierarchy, he continued to work hard on behalf of the church and his patron, Herbert Armstrong. Partly because of his intense lobbying, the California legislature passed a law that severely limited the power of the state attorney general to probe into the financial affairs of tax-exempt religious organizations, like the one Rader represented. That, in effect, scotched the legal effort to hold the church accountable for the vast resources it had accumulated over the years.

By then, however, Rader's days as a church leader were numbered. A few months after the new law was passed, he was eased quietly out of office, although he continued to receive a six-figure salary as Armstrong's personal adviser. Some disenchanted members of the church were unkind enough to suggest that Rader's salary, after he stepped down as treasurer, was nothing more than hush money. According to this view, Herbert Armstrong had ample reason to keep Rader happy, and in clover. Whatever the case, Stanley Rader was no longer empowered to spread the word of God in an official capacity. But he still had plenty of Mammon, and there was no small comfort in that.

Southern California was also the scene of another investigative piece Gorin had produced a few months earlier. This story came to us "over the transom." One day in July 1978, Don Hewitt received a letter from a man named Jack Fertig who identified himself as the former director of a federal antipoverty program called GLACAA, an acronym for Greater Los Angles Community Action Agency. Fertig had left GLACAA a few years earlier, but in recent months he had heard disturbing stories from some of his former colleagues about the people who were running the agency now. GLACAA, he wrote, had become a hotbed of graft and corruption, and he urged *60 Minutes* to go after the unscrupulous characters who were ripping off the federal government and, in the process, exploiting the victims of poverty they were supposed to be helping.

Fertig's letter arrived just as Hewitt was about to leave on vacation. He was not alone, for July is the quiet month in our shop, the time when most of us get away for a few weeks of R and R. One of the new field producers who happened to be in his office that day was Norman Gorin; so Hewitt promptly turned the letter over to him and took off for his summer home in the Hamptons.

After reading through Jack Fertig's letter, Gorin decided it was a lead worth pursuing, especially since he already was planning a trip to the West Coast, where he had some reporting to do on another story. He placed a call to Fertig, who offered to set up a meeting with the GLACAA employees who had brought their complaints to his attention. When the meeting took place in Los Angeles a week or so later, Gorin heard plenty of allegations, but the people who made them had no solid evidence to back them up. In fact, Norman was struck by the naïveté of the young social workers, most of whom seemed to feel their accusations were enough to justify a report on *60 Minutes*. Gorin explained patiently that he had to have more substance, that he needed documents and other data in order to build a case against the men who were running the antipoverty agency. "Give me something tangible," he said, "and we can proceed from there. But I can't commit *Sixty Minutes* to this story until you come up with some facts, some hard evidence."

Gorin then called for volunteers, and by the time the meeting broke up, he had recruited an eager corps of GLACAA employees to work, in effect, as reporters for *60 Minutes*. The thorough job these social workers did for us on the inside, where they ran the risk of getting caught and summarily fired, gave us all the ammunition we needed, and then some. Over the next several weeks, they managed to smuggle out of the GLACAA office a raft of material—payroll records, telephone bills and the like—and deliver it to Gorin, who usually rendezvoused with his secret agents on a street corner near the Biltmore Hotel in downtown Los Angeles. The leaked documents revealed that the top officials in the agency were misusing federal funds to finance personal trips, pay bills for services that were not rendered and bestow high salaries on "phantom employees" who never came to work. Nor was that all, for the tangle of mismanagement and corruption that permeated GLACAA included numerous other offenses, too.

When I arrived in Los Angeles in September and read the file that Gorin had assembled, I knew we had an explosive story. But there were still a few loose ends to be tied, and I was itching to get into the act. First, I did some on-camera interviews with members of the GLACAA staff who had cooperated in our investigation. One of them was Jim Metz, a middle-level supervisor. I asked him about a young woman named Carolyn Borunda, who, according to the records Gorin had obtained, was paid $1,595 during the month she was on the agency's payroll. Gorin had been told that she was one of those phantom employees he had been hearing so much about, and Metz all but confirmed this. He said that although Miss Borunda was "supposedly working on a project that would be my responsibility, I've never seen her and I've never heard from her."

Gorin and I set out to find Carolyn Borunda, but when we arrived at the home address listed on her job assignment, we discovered that she didn't live there. The older woman who answered the door at that address told me that Carolyn lived with her husband, Fred Perez. What made *that* disclosure so interesting was the fact that Fred Perez was the name of a man who had been fired from GLACAA a few months earlier for alleged corruption. We were unable to find an address for Perez in any of the GLACAA documents that Gorin had accumulated; so I consulted the city telephone directory and eventually located him. This was not the first or the last time in my experience that an ordinary phone book, to which we all have routine access, proved to be a useful source of information on a story. Carolyn Borunda's husband did indeed turn out to be the same Fred Perez who had been kicked out of GLACAA a few months back. He refused to let us talk to his wife, but at least we were able to establish the connection. And this wasn't the only link in the chain that continued to bind Perez to the GLACAA operation. One of his best friends was Victor Mena, the deputy director of the agency and the man who hired Carolyn Borunda. Moreover, Gorin was told by two different sources that Mena wound up with half the $1,595 that GLACAA paid for her illusory services.

Most of the incriminating evidence in Gorin's file pointed to Victor Mena as the chief culprit in the GLACAA scam. Yet for a long time, prior to my arrival in Los Angeles, he had no idea that we were on to him. During the weeks that Gorin was gathering data from his undercover agents, he avoided any direct contact with Mena and the other agency officials who had been implicated. But now, we decided, the time had come to confront Mena cold with a camera crew. So we simply walked into the GLACAA office one morning and requested an interview. I explained to Mena that we were looking into certain allegations that had been made against him, and we wanted to record his side of the story. Taken unawares, he nervously agreed to be interviewed for *60 Minutes*.

I began by asking about Carolyn Borunda and other dubious employees who had been hired at high salaries. Included in that group was the sixteen-year-old son of a friend of Mena's named Matthew Chapa:

> MENA: Matthew Chapa is a young man that I hired for a couple of weeks.
>
> WALLACE: As a systems analyst?

MENA: I—I don't recall, really.

WALLACE: Apparently—

MENA: I've had several people work for me.

WALLACE: Well, a systems analyst, what does that mean?

MENA: It could be several things. It could be a reviewing of procedures, analyzing systems, that type of thing.

WALLACE: A young man like that can review procedures and analyze systems?

MENA: Sure.

WALLACE: For $1,512?

MENA: I don't know that's what we paid him.

WALLACE: That's what it says right here.

I showed him a copy of Matthew Chapa's employment contract, which was one of the many nuggets that Gorin's team of volunteers had dug up for us. As for the rest of the interview, it proceeded in the same vein. I asked Mena about various expenses that seemed suspicious or excessive; not just salaries but legal fees and other services. And most of the time I had the documents in hand to support my contention that federal funds allocated to GLACAA to combat poverty in Los Angeles had been flagrantly misused. In effect, I accused him and his cronies of outright fraud, of stealing the money from Washington that was supposed to go into programs to help the poor, and by the time we finished the interview, Victor Mena knew he was in trouble.

Mena's boss was the director of GLACAA, Martin Samaniego. He had been appointed to that post the previous year, and one of his first official acts was to hire Mena as his deputy. When we told Samaniego about our investigation and all that we had learned about Mena, he professed shock. He had no idea that such things were going on within the agency, he told us, and Gorin and I had to admit that most of the evidence we had acquired did not implicate Samaniego. If he was directly involved in the rip-offs, then he had covered his tracks very well. He had "deniability," as they used to say in the Nixon

White House. But to borrow another line from the Watergate imagery, Martin Samaniego had his own "smoking gun" buried in the data, and once we found it, we knew exactly where to aim it.

At a salary of $51,000 a year, well above the poverty level, Samaniego was paid more than Jerry Brown, then the governor of California, and he lived in a style befitting his income. A visitor to his attractive home could not help noticing the trappings of affluence (a swimming pool, a few horses on the property, for example) except that to do so, one had to go to Mesa, Arizona. Samaniego lived in Arizona, and he spent most of his time there, as Gorin discovered one night when he was sifting through GLACAA's telephone records. He was in effect running the Los Angeles antipoverty program from another state. Clearly the people who hired him—GLACAA's board of directors—and his superiors in Washington would not have condoned absenteeism. Yet they were under the impression that Samaniego lived in suburban Los Angeles, and with good reason. Not long after he took over as director of the agency, Samaniego asked GLACAA to reimburse him to the tune of $2,974.46 for moving his household goods to his new home in California. As proof of this expenditure, he submitted a paid bill and a copy of his personal check in that amount made out to the Valdez Transfer Company in Phoenix, Arizona. But when we contacted the owner of Valdez Transfer, he told us that his company had not moved Samaniego's household possessions to California and that he never received a check for such a service. When I interviewed Samaniego, I asked him about that:

> WALLACE: Did you move your household goods to California?
>
> SAMANIEGO: No, I did not.
>
> WALLACE: Did you ever get the money?
>
> SAMANIEGO: I got the money. Yes, I did.
>
> WALLACE: Did you cash the check?
>
> SAMANIEGO: Yes, I did.

WALLACE: Did you keep the money?

SAMANIEGO: I still have the money, that's correct.

WALLACE: In other words, you in effect stole $2,974.46 from GLACAA.

SAMANIEGO: I don't look at it as—as stealing money from the agency or from GLACAA.

All the information we assembled was turned over eventually to Ira Reiner, the city comptroller in Los Angeles. His office was the official watchdog for the federal funds that were poured into GLACAA, nearly half a billion dollars in tax money over the past decade. Reiner had his own suspicions about the GLA-CAA operation, and when he heard about our investigation, he offered his help and encouragement. In fact, during the weeks when Gorin was exhorting his corps of secret agents to come up with the goods, he often worked in Reiner's outer office. And Reiner did not hesitate to acknowledge his appreciation. At the end of our report, broadcast in October 1978, he appeared on camera and announced: "We have evidence at this time that we're in the process of verifying that was brought to our attention by *Sixty Minutes* with respect to some very clear evidence of fraud. And that's why I'm going to call for a formal federal audit, a fraud audit of GLACAA."

Nor did he let it go at that. A few months later, when a reporter from *Parade* magazine interviewed him about the GLACAA exposé, Reiner said: "I was really impressed with the producer, Norm Gorin. He had this incredible Dick Tracy instinct. He got stuff my auditors didn't get." Gorin also got stuff that no other reporter got, for we were all alone on that story. In a gracious gesture, the *Los Angeles Times* and other California newspapers complimented us for the way we came into their territory and beat them on a major local story.

Then there was the impact on GLACAA itself, for seldom in the history of *60 Minutes* has a story had such swift and devastating repercussions. Even before we went on the air, there were these developments: Victor Mena resigned as deputy director, GLACAA's board of directors paid off Martin Samaniego to terminate his contract, which still had more than a

year left to run. Ira Reiner not only called for a federal fraud
audit, but he also requested the House and Senate committees
which have oversight responsibilities for poverty programs to
commence an inquiry into GLACAA. (This, in turn, swelled
into a full-scale investigation by the FBI, which eventually led
to indictments against Mena and some of his accomplices,
including Fred Perez and the agency's lawyer, Raoul Severo.
All three men were later convicted, and two of them, Mena
and Severo, were sentenced to five years in prison.) Finally,
two days before we broadcast "GLACAA," we received a call
from the White House informing us that President Carter had
heard about the *60 Minutes* investigation, and, having confirmed our results, had ordered GLACAA to shut down its
operation at the end of the year.

Yet even as we were putting the wood to the people who
ran GLACAA, I had to wonder how many other antipoverty
agencies had fallen into the clutches of corrupt operators. Ira
Reiner, for one, was convinced that GLACAA was not an
isolated case. When he was interviewed for our broadcast,
Reiner said, "It's these hustlers that take over these programs
that use the poor as a shield. The poor get the hole in the
doughnut, and these hustlers get the doughnut."

The stories I've described, from "Fake ID" to "GLACAA,"
are just a sampling of the investigative pieces that my producers
and I put together in the middle and late seventies. I could
easily have altered or expanded the selections to include more
recent examples, reports done in the early eighties. But I have
focused on the 1975–1979 period because those were the years
when we firmly established our credentials in the investigative
area.

I should mention also that for every assignment we were
able to develop into a report solid enough to put on the air,
there were plenty of others that did not pan out. Like most
journalists who toil in the investigative field, we had our share
of frustrations, times when we followed trails that didn't lead
to anything. "Where there's smoke, there's fire" is an adage
that impels all good reporters to take up the quest, but it doesn't
always work out that way. On some occasions, the smoke turns
out to be a false alarm. In short, investigative journalism is a

gamble, a high-risk pursuit. No matter how diligent or enterprising a reporter, inevitably there are many times he's going to come up empty. And when that happens, all he can do is swallow his disappointment and hope that the next opportunity will lead to pay dirt.

By the end of the seventies, we had struck pay dirt often enough to make it all worthwhile, and in the process we took on a new and stronger identity. During this period, the general perception of *60 Minutes* underwent a decisive change. I had a clear sense of that change when, in traveling around the country on different assignments, I ran into people who were eager to identify themselves as loyal viewers of the broadcast. In earlier years when such encounters took place, in airports and hotel lobbies, the questions and comments tossed my way generally dealt with a recent interview with some government leader or a celebrity in the arts. But by the late 1970s, most of the viewers who greeted me in public preferred to talk about the investigative work. And not only about pieces I had already done, but frequently about stories they wanted me to explore. I kept bumping into people who jumped at the chance to alert me to some scandal or outrage that was ripe for exposure on *60 Minutes*. They would give me vivid accounts of foul deeds and the culprits perpetrating them, and urge me to take appropriate action: "You really should look into this, Mike. It's right up your alley."

And I would listen carefully. Some of that attention was mere courtesy, for if there were regular viewers who chose to regard *60 Minutes* as a kind of unofficial ombudsman, then the least I could do was listen to them. But beyond that, there was always the possibility that such tips might actually lead to something, and in fact some of our best stories have come from the most unlikely sources.

It's also true that the more closely *60 Minutes* came to be identified with investigative journalism, the more criticism it aroused. Many who were entrusted (by themselves or others) to pass judgment on television news programs professed to be disturbed by some of the deceptions we employed to get to the heart of a story. To be fair, even some of our thoughtful colleagues—fellow reporters and editors—were expressing con-

cern about the zeal with which we and others who had caught
the investigative bug were going about our business. By the
early 1980s, it had reached the point where almost every time
we aired an investigative piece, our tactics were called into
question. In a sense, we were drawing almost as much attention
to ourselves, to our *modus operandi*, as we were to the corrupt
practices we were trying to expose. Once it reached that point,
we decided we could no longer ignore the criticism that was
being leveled against us. Specifically, it was Marion Goldin
who came up with the proposal to give our detractors their due
by inviting some of them to appear on a special edition of
60 Minutes. After Don Hewitt and I gave our okay to the project, Marion proceeded to make all the arrangements, and in
September 1981 we opened the new season with a broadcast
entirely devoted to the subject of our alleged transgressions.
Somewhat self-consciously, we called it "Looking at *60 Minutes.*"

The format we chose was an old-fashioned panel discussion,
and we invited the following people to take part: Eugene Patterson, a veteran newspaper editor known to be an outspoken
foe of some of the flashier aspects of investigative journalism;
Bob Greene of *Newsday,* who had won a Pulitzer Prize for his
own work as an investigative reporter; Ellen Goodman, the
syndicated columnist; and Herb Schmertz, a vice-president of
Mobil Oil who in recent years had been making a career out
of knocking the media for what he considered their liberal bias
and unfair coverage of large corporations such as his. In one
of his rare on-camera appearances, Hewitt sat in on behalf of
60 Minutes, and so did I. Finally, we asked media critic Jeff
Greenfield to moderate the exchange of views. Or as I put it
in my on-air introduction: "We brought in Jeff so that someone
perhaps more dispassionate than I would steer the discussion."

To prepare for the colloquium, we showed the panel excerpts
from some of the more flamboyant investigative pieces we had
done recently, including "Fake ID," "This Year at Murrieta"
and "The Clinic on Morse Avenue." Then, after the group had
viewed each excerpt, the debate began. For example, from
"Fake ID" we showed the scene in which one of our researchers,

Lucy Spiegel, assumed a false identity in order to obtain a birth certificate in that name. Jeff Greenfield then asked the panel: "Is that fair game to send somebody that you know is an impostor out to prove that you can get false documents that easily?"

Ellen Goodman didn't think so. She accused us of taking the position "that in the pursuit of deceit, deceit is okay, that as journalists, we have the right to use untruths because we are going for a greater truth." Eugene Patterson was even more critical. "You're talking about breaking the law here," he said. "There are other ways to have covered this story. The Passport Office probably had case history after case history that *Sixty Minutes* could have followed up on."

But Bob Greene took issue with Patterson: "You raise the point about breaking the law. While this may be a technical violation of the law in what you're doing ... the point is that *Sixty Minutes* here was using this device as a very dramatic way of going to the American people and saying this is going on and it's bad." To no one's surprise, Hewitt and I agreed with Greene.

Turning our attention to "This Year at Murrieta," we showed the scene in which three members of the *60 Minutes* team enrolled at the cancer clinic—in a rented Rolls-Royce—under the guise of a wealthy leukemia victim and his entourage. Once again, Greenfield opened the discussion, this time with a question directed at Eugene Patterson.

> GREENFIELD: All right, Gene, that's clearly deception on an ambitious scale—renting Rolls-Royces and all that—but if you assume that this clinic was endangering the health of people who came there, how else could you conclusively demonstrate that without putting someone through that clinic, knowing that if you said you were a CBS investigative reporter, you'd never find out how they treated patients?

> PATTERSON: It's a good story, it's great television, it's terrible journalism. The way you go at that story before you, as a last resort, go phony the way we did here, is to find people who have been victimized by that cancer clinic, which is the way journalism operates.

Hewitt was all revved up to respond, so I was happy to let him have the floor. He pointed out that it was complaints from people who had been victimized by the clinic that led us to Murrieta in the first place, and that we included interviews with some of those patients in our report. But then Patterson asked why we didn't confine ourselves to that, and "make your story out of those people."

"Because," Hewitt replied, "whereas newspaper readers are convinced when they read interviews with people, television viewers, to be convinced, want as much documentation as you can give them. This is the only way that we could document that what we were being told by those people was, in fact, true."

We also took a look at the so-called ambush interview, whereby a reporter with a camera crew surprises his quarry on the street or in his office. As I pointed out, when a reporter resorts to that technique, he usually does so because his request for a formal interview has been turned down or because he has every reason to believe that the request would be rejected. We showed the panel scenes from four *60 Minutes* stories in which, respectively, I, Reasoner, Safer and Rather accosted unwilling interviewees. Whether they approved of the tactic or not, all the panelists agreed that it was peculiar to television news. Then Greenfield asked: "Can a person say, 'No comment' on television with impunity? Doesn't it always look bad?"

"Yes," answered Ellen Goodman, "I think it always looks bad. I think that's a real difference between television and print, between broadcast and print, that whenever somebody says, 'No comment' whenever they don't want to talk to a camera, they automatically look bad. And it makes the camera an inherently unfair weapon if they use that all the time."

Support for Goodman's argument came from an unlikely source—Hewitt. "I'm going to surprise you," he said. "I agree with you. I think this is probably a technique that has been abused, and I have a feeling that we shouldn't be trying to get people to talk to us who obviously don't want to talk. In fact, what you're asking a man to do is to testify against himself on-camera. You shouldn't do that."

I had to smile at that. I found myself thinking of all the times that Hewitt, barking orders from the comfortable haven of his office in New York, had exhorted correspondents and producers in the field to go after a presumed culprit who declined to be interviewed on-camera. On those occasions he took the position that our viewers were entitled to see such a person's reaction to our presence and request instead of merely taking our word for their refusal to talk. Yet now here he was siding with our critics on that point. *Et tu Brute!*

Then there was "The Clinic on Morse Avenue," where we had installed a one-way mirror, stationed a camera behind it, after which I hid behind another wall, so that I could eavesdrop on conversations with visitors from clinical laboratories who came in to offer kickbacks. We showed one of the scenes in which I emerged from behind the wall and confronted two lab representatives with the proposal I had just heard them make to our bogus clinic. After the panel viewed this footage, Greenfield suggested that "on the surface, this is very close to pure entrapment. There is nothing that that medical clinic is doing except trying to entice people in to prove kickbacks." But Bob Greene came rushing to our defense with a strong reply: "I'm troubled, and I'm constantly troubled, by—particularly in our media—the loose use of the word entrapment."

"Hear, hear!" I interjected.

Then Greene said: "That television camera did not show me anybody doing anything that they wouldn't be disposed to do, and it did not show me them saying, 'Will you give us a bribe?'"

Goodman had a slightly different objection. "I think it doesn't reflect well on the journalist who's jumping out of the potted palm," she said. To which I replied: "May I? As the reporter behind the potted palm, I wasn't eavesdropping electronically. I could hear it. I was about as far from the people involved as you are. And all that we were doing was getting pictures ahead of time. Then I came out from behind the partition and said, in effect, you're talking kickback, I heard you talk kickback, we are recording this for broadcast, what do you say?"

At that point, Greenfield, shifting to another tack, raised an ethical consideration that was vaguely reminiscent of the biblical injunction that only "he that is without sin" should cast the first stone. "Excuse me," he said, "if I, as a sometime media critic, hired a camera crew to infiltrate and put a camera in the offices of *60 Minutes* to show how you guys got a story and you found out, I really don't think that you would accept this as an investigative entrepreneurial report. I think you guys would hit the ceiling." Then, fixing his gaze directly on me, he put forth the challenge in more personal terms. "I guess the question is, how would you like it done to you? How would you like somebody to point a camera at you that you didn't know was there, to confront you with embarrassing material, perhaps about a life you once led or something you once did?"

"I wouldn't like it," I admitted, "which is why I lead a life beyond reproach."

The line got a big laugh, which was nice, but in truth there was a heavy irony in Greenfield's question and my cavalier response to it. In recent months I had been involved in two embarrassing incidents, for each of which I was justly reproached. At the time of the first gaffe—an ill-advised conversation with Morley Safer over a story he wanted to do on Haiti—I was the victim of internal leaks, just as the young men in charge of GLACAA had been done in by sources from within their own shop. The second incident, which caused me far greater anguish, was even more insidious. In the course of an interview for a story I was working on in California, I uttered a tasteless and insensitive remark that, wrenched out of context, was construed as a racial slur. And on that occasion I was the victim of a camera crew that had been instructed to record my comments without my knowledge; that is, I was set up in much the same way in which we had set up the lab representatives in our phony clinic on Morse Avenue. In the case of both misadventures, there was no doubt a certain poetic justice at work, but at the time I had a lot of trouble seeing it that way. For I was hurt and angry, at myself and others.

I remember thinking that this was a hell of a time to become embroiled in public disputes over my professional conduct. Here I was in my early sixties, with four decades of broadcasting experience behind me; and although I have never been one to rest on laurels, I felt that I had put together a decent body of work, especially in the years since I've been with *60*

Minutes. Yet now, abruptly, at this late stage of the game, I had to defend myself against attacks on my honor and reputation. Nor was there any comfort in the realization that in both instances, I had no one to blame but myself.

CHAPTER

SEVENTEEN

BACK IN THE SPRING OF 1972, Wallace did a *Sixty Minutes* piece on Haiti, a country which for fourteen years had suffered under the rule of Francois "Papa Doc" Duvalier, one of the most brutal and oppressive dictators of modern times. Duvalier's reign of terror ended in April 1971, but shortly before he died, Papa Doc decreed that his nineteen-year-old son, Jean-Claude—who was inevitably dubbed "Baby Doc"—would succeed him as President for Life. One year later, Wallace and a *60 Minutes* crew flew to Port-au-Prince to film a story on Haiti, past and present, or what it was like to live under the two Docs—Papa and Baby.

It would have been impossible for any honest reporter to do such a story without being critical of Haiti's despotic regimes, and Wallace did not attempt to gloss over what he called the "unlovely" facts of Haitian life. He pointed out that "for 167 years, ever since its revolution dislodged the French in 1804, Haiti had been torn by terror, bloodshed and despair." He reported that "today Haiti is the poorest country in the Western Hemisphere. Most of her five million people live at bare subsistence level, and the average annual income for a Haitian is seventy-five dollars." As for the political climate, he noted that "during the fourteen years that Papa Doc was in the palace in Port-au-Prince, tales of savagery there became a

commonplace. His dread Tontons Macoute—his secret police—imposed a rule as fearful as any in the long and bloody
history of Haiti."

Wallace did manage to find a few silver linings in all that
gloom. "Anyone who travels there," he observed, "must be
enchanted by the gentleness of the Haitian people and by the
brooding beauty of their land." And he suggested in a guarded
way that in the past year, since Baby Doc's regime had replaced
his father's, there had been a few faint signs of change for the
better, notably a decrease in terror and at least some effort to
improve the wretched economic conditions. But for the most
part, the picture he painted was bleak, as any accurate portrayal
of that stricken country had to be.

In choosing to do the story, Wallace was asking for trouble,
not so much in his professional life but in his own family. As
reported in an earlier chapter, Lorraine Wallace lived in Haiti
with her two children for seven years prior to her marriage to
Mike in 1955, and in the years since then, she continued to
have close family ties in that country. Her first cousin, Nancy
Chenet, lived on the island with her Haitian husband and their
three children, and the Chenet family had gone through some
tough times during the years when Papa Doc was in power.
For example, Nancy's father-in-law, Rony Chenet, Sr., spent
almost two years in prison as a political detainee. Given those
circumstances, a hard-hitting *60 Minutes* story on Haiti by Mike
Wallace, the husband of Nancy Chenet's first cousin, would
probably not make life easier for the family. In fact, Mike's
report did not create any serious problems except for a few
murmurs of disapproval from some government officials, but
Nancy was still upset by the piece and she passed the message
on to her cousin in New York. Lorraine, in turn, was sufficiently
distressed to take up the matter with Mike. She begged him to
promise her that he would never do another story on Haiti.
"You have the rest of the world," she said. "Lay off Haiti."

Mike readily agreed; indeed, he felt in retrospect that it had
been rather callous toward the family for him to do a story on
Haiti. As for the future, there was certainly no pressing need
to go back there; after all, Haiti was not like the Middle East
or Southeast Asia or any other trouble spot constantly in the

forefront of international news. It was a backwater, a place
most Americans never thought about, and besides, as Lorraine
pointed out, he still had the rest of the world to pick on. So
he promised his wife that from now on, he would "lay off
Haiti."

That's how matters stood for the next nine years. Then one
day in January 1981, Don Hewitt called Wallace into his office
and informed him that Morley Safer had proposed doing a story
on Haiti. Hewitt was aware of Lorraine's concern (he and
Wallace had discussed it at the time of the 1972 piece), so he
suggested that if she still had strong feelings on the subject,
then perhaps Mike should have a talk with Morley. Wallace
thanked Hewitt for alerting him to the problem, and promptly
walked down the hall to Safer's office, where after spelling out
the situation, he made his pitch: If Safer was all gung ho about
doing the story, then fine; Lorraine and her relatives would just
have to accept that. But he added that Hewitt had led him to
believe that Safer was not yet committed to the assignment, it
was still just an idea he was kicking around, and if this was
the case, then could he see his way clear to back off the Haiti
story? If so, Wallace said, he would consider it a personal
favor.

If Wallace had taken that request to any of his other on-air
colleagues—to Harry Reasoner or Dan Rather or Ed Bradley,
who was about to come aboard as Rather's replacement—the
answer almost surely would have been an uncomplicated yes.
But the personal chemistry between Wallace and Safer was not
good. Safer still harbored resentments from his early years on
60 Minutes when he and Wallace were the show's only correspondents and he chafed in the role of second banana. In
those days he had often felt that Mike and some of his producers
went out of their way to preempt the limelight for Wallace, to
make sure he was assigned to most of the big and important
stories, which served to exploit the prevailing perception that
Wallace was the star of the broadcast and Safer merely "the
other guy," the sidebar man. This was no longer the worry or
problem it once had been. For one thing, the competition between the two men had been diluted by the presence of other
correspondents on the program; and for another, Safer felt far

more secure about his own position and identity on *60 Minutes*.
But he still did not feel close to Wallace, and he certainly didn't
think he owed him any personal favors.

Hence, his first reaction was to tell Mike in a frosty tone
that he did not find his argument very persuasive. But then,
after making the point and allowing it time to sink in, Safer
yielded and said that in order to keep peace in the family, he
would reluctantly agree to stay away from Haiti. Mike thanked
him, and when he went home that night and told Lorraine what
had happened, he urged her to telephone Morley and thank him
as well. She did, but later remarked to Mike that Morley didn't
seem to appreciate her call, and that he had been "very curt"
to her over the phone.

Journalists are inveterate gossips who, if not otherwise occupied, love nothing more than to wallow in shop talk. Thus, it
would have been unrealistic to expect Safer—or Hewitt, for
that matter—to keep such a juicy story to himself, and neither
man did. Lively accounts of Wallace's request were soon making the rounds, first within the domain of *60 Minutes,* then
elsewhere at CBS News, eventually reaching friends and acquaintances outside the organization. Various members of the
staff, especially those who felt no loyalty to Wallace, could
not resist the temptation to dine out on the story of how the
tough and fearless star of *60 Minutes,* the man who sallied
forth every week to slay dragons, had practically begged Morley Safer to dump an assignment because it might upset his
wife and her relatives in Haiti. The grapevine sizzled with that
story, and in time it reached the ears of Les Whitten, an associate of Jack Anderson whose syndicated Washington column
thrived on such tidbits.

A little more than a month after his talk with Morley Safer,
Wallace arrived at the office one morning and was told by Safer
to expect a call from Les Whitten. Morley said that Whitten
had phoned him the day before to ask about the Haiti business,
and that he had refused to discuss it. A few minutes later, when
Whitten called, Wallace filled him in on the background—the
story on Haiti in 1972, Nancy Chenet's reaction and the subsequent promise he had made to Lorraine. He concluded by

saying that his concern about the family was "the sole reason" for his appeal to Safer. Whitten volunteered his opinion that under the circumstances it didn't seem like much of a story, and that he frankly couldn't understand why anyone who cared about the credibility of *60 Minutes* would want to leak that sort of thing to the outside press. When Wallace seized on that as his cue to ask who had leaked the story to him, Whitten naturally declined to reveal his source, but he did specify that he had not gotten it from Safer.

Les Whitten may have thought that it wasn't much of a story, but his boss obviously didn't agree with him. A few days later, on February 27, 1981, Jack Anderson devoted two thirds of his column to the incident, and he cast Wallace in the role of a heavy-handed censor. The column began:

> The television hit *60 Minutes* fully deserves its reputation as a bold investigative show that specializes in the butchery of sacred cows. It has championed the abused against institutionalized greed and violence.
>
> Yet one of the program's superstars, Mike Wallace, killed an exposé of conditions in the poverty-stricken dictatorship of Haiti because he has in-laws living there.

Then, after recounting the background details Wallace had related to Whitten and Mike's version of his meeting with Safer, Anderson wrote:

> Safer would not comment, but it is understood he felt he had been "leaned on very hard" and had been "put in a difficult position" by Wallace. Safer also told friends Wallace seemed concerned about his wife's family's business interests and his own liking for Haiti vacations, saying, "I would never be able to go back" if the show were done.

When Wallace read that, he was livid. It was true, that he and Lorraine had often spent Christmas vacations in Haiti, but he had never discussed that in his meeting with Safer. Nor had there been any mention of his "wife's family's business interests." So, after reading that, he wondered: Was this the tale

Morley himself was spreading around, or had it been embellished by some malicious gossip who had heard it through the grapevine? Whichever the case, Wallace knew that these "friends" of Safer's, whoever they were, were certainly no friends of his.

Jack Anderson's column put the fat squarely in the fire. Over the next several days, one reporter after another called *60 Minutes* to ask about what now became known as "the Haitian Affair." What made the situation even more unsettling was the fact that both Safer and Wallace were out of town on assignment much of the time, Morley doing a story in Colorado and Mike working on one in California. Before Wallace left for California, he did take a call from Tom Jory of the Associated Press, and used the opportunity to set the record straight on one critical point. As Jory wrote in his AP dispatch, which appeared in newspapers throughout the country: "Wallace took issue with Anderson's suggestion that he had 'killed' Safer's planned story. 'I have no authority to kill a *60 Minutes* story,' he said. 'How can I kill a story?'"

Yet other newspaper accounts echoed Anderson's contention that Wallace had done precisely that; and, far worse, in some of those stories, quotes from Safer and Hewitt were used to back up the charge. For example, in putting together a followup report on the imbroglio, Robert McFadden of *The New York Times* placed a call to Safer in Eagle Pass, Colorado, and quoted him as saying: "Mike is willing to talk to anyone who wants to hear him. I'll leave him to be my spokesman on it. It's his affair. He initiated it. It's his claim and I'm not going to comment on it. I don't feel I have to defend my ethics." The clear implication there, of course, was that somebody else—guess who?—had to answer for his ethical conduct. Hewitt also was taking the high road, largely at Wallace's expense, and being less than candid about his own role in the affair. He told McFadden that he had no first-hand knowledge of any approach to Safer by Wallace, but that he would regard such an approach as "inappropriate."

In addition, both Safer and Hewitt were asked by McFadden and other reporters if they planned to go ahead with a *60 Minutes* report on Haiti in spite of Wallace's objections. Safer wisely referred all such questions to Hewitt, who was quoted as saying: "I don't know whether we're going to do this story or not. But I do know that if I do assign it or if I don't assign it, the fact that Mike Wallace has relatives in Haiti has nothing to do with it. It will be judged on its own merits as a news story."

As a news story, the merits of Haiti were marginal, to say the least. Hardly anything had changed there since Wallace did his report in 1972, except that Jean-Claude Duvalier was now twenty-nine and therefore a little old to bear with dignity the sobriquet of Baby Doc. As for his subjects, most continued to live in squalor, for Haiti still had the wretched distinction of being the poorest country in the hemisphere. If he had chosen to be completely honest, Hewitt no doubt would have said that if he did decide to assign a story on Haiti, it would be for the following reason: that he had been badgered into doing so by all the hullabaloo in the press over Wallace's tête-à-tête with Safer.

Bill Leonard, then president of CBS News, actually did say it in so many words a few days later when he and Hewitt formally announced that Haiti would definitely be the subject of a *60 Minutes* report. "I think it has to be done now," Leonard said. "Even the perception that the personal interest of a reporter at CBS could affect whether or not a story is done is unthinkable. If we didn't do it now, it would raise the question about whether the judgment was made for personal reasons, rather than as a pure news judgment."

Wallace agreed with that decision. When a reporter called him in California to get his reaction, he said: "There's only one way to clear the skirts of *Sixty Minutes* and that's to go ahead and do the story. Because of everything that has blown up, I think we'd be derelict if we didn't do the story now." Mike also admitted—for the first time in public—that in asking Safer not to do a story on Haiti, "I obviously made an error."

A posture of contrition was, of course, the appropriate one for Wallace to assume at that point, but it did not reflect his gut feelings. For in truth, he was furious. He felt that he had been betrayed by Safer, which did not surprise him, and even more so by Hewitt, which he had not expected. When Wallace returned to New York from California, he sat down and wrote a memo to Bill Leonard. He recounted—once again—the background details that led up to the two conversations on that fateful day in January, first the one with Hewitt, then the one with Safer. And in summing up everything that had happened, Mike wrote: "The mistakes made in this whole episode are enough to go around." He proceeded then to spell them out:

"Hewitt shouldn't have told Wallace to go see Safer. Wallace shouldn't have made the approach to Safer. Safer should have told Wallace to buzz off, and that he intended to go ahead with the story. Safer shouldn't have retailed the story to persons who were happy to pass it on, and should have made any allegations concerning business ethics and vacations to Wallace personally. Confronted with the story by Whitten, Wallace should have told the truth, as he did, but then acknowledged his error in approaching Safer. And finally, Hewitt shouldn't have told an inaccurate story to *The New York Times*, permitting Wallace, in effect, to twist slowly in the wind. Having said all of this, the initial fault was mine. I don't see the point in belaboring it further, nor in further comments from the participants. It is my understanding from Don that Ed Bradley will be doing the story eventually. I'll butt out."

But for Wallace at that point, butting out was easier said than done. Even after it was announced that *60 Minutes* intended to go ahead and film a story on Haiti, Mike continued to draw fire for his attempt to keep it off the air. And of course, given his reputation, he made a most inviting target. For example, to illustrate a tough piece on the subject by its television columnist, Marvin Kitman, *Newsday* ran a cartoon that depicted a typically aggressive Mike Wallace thrusting a microphone in the face of a stricken transgressor who, in this case, also happened to be Mike Wallace. The question asked in the cartoon was: "Now let me put it to you this way, Mr. Wallace, are you not then guilty of censoring the news?"

In the meantime, Hewitt was having trouble getting a correspondent to do the story on Haiti that he had promised. For understandable reasons, Safer no longer had any stomach for the assignment; so Hewitt pitched it to Ed Bradley, who made it clear that he didn't want anything to do with it either. At the time Bradley was preparing to embark on his first season as a member of the *60 Minutes* team, and he was determined to get off on the right foot. The last thing he needed was to take over a dubious assignment which, because of all the fuss, had become damaged goods, a no-win deal. Fortunately for Hewitt the outside press eventually lost interest in the Haitian Affair, and as time went on, he rarely had to explain why the story was not being done. One year passed, and then another, and still no report on Haiti appeared on *60 Minutes*. The way things were going, Baby Doc Duvalier would be in his dotage by the time *60 Minutes* returned to Haiti to film another story on his regime.

Then one day in the early spring of 1983, Wallace walked into Hewitt's office and dropped a bombshell. He announced that he and Barry Lando wanted to do a story on Haiti. Hewitt was stunned, but before he had a chance to reply, Mike continued, saying that he had discussed the matter at some length with Lorraine, and had managed to persuade her that it was the right thing to do. He said he realized that more than two years had passed since all the commotion over his appeal to Safer, and that as far as the public was concerned, it was a dead issue, safely buried in the past. But he reminded Hewitt that he had promised to assign the story on Haiti, and therefore somebody had to do it. And that somebody, he insisted, should be Wallace. As the news of his decision spread through the offices of *60 Minutes*, it created quite a stir. When the mischievous Norman Gorin heard about it, he said to Wallace: "Hey, Mike, what are you going to call this story—'Likey'?" (As opposed, of course, to "Hatey.")

However, the report that Wallace and Lando put together on Haiti in 1983 was no whitewash. Mike observed that the majority of Haitians lived in such abject poverty that they formed a "fourth-world country," too poor even to be accorded third-world status. And he came up with fresh evidence to support the charge that the people of Haiti were governed by a callous and corrupt regime. Wallace reported that the Duvalier family had $90 million stashed away in U.S. banks alone, and that Duvalier's wife received a salary of $75,000 a *month*. All in all, his follow-up story on Haiti was even stronger and more critical than the one he had done eleven years earlier, and this was the general reaction when it finally appeared on *60 Minutes* on Christmas night, 1983. Thus, by electing to do the story himself, Wallace was able to bring an unseemly episode to an honorable conclusion. However, when it came to dealing with the next controversy he brought on himself—one that came to be known as "the watermelon-and-tacos incident"—he would not be so lucky. For that was a blunder which left him vulnerable to far more serious attacks.

During much of March 1981, when the Haitian Affair was the talk of the media and Wallace was taking his lumps for that, he and a young *60 Minutes* producer named Martin Phillips were busily at work on another story. They were looking into the subject of lien contracts, complicated documents that unwary customers sign when they purchase an air conditioner or carpeting or other major home improvement. The fine print in many of those contracts stipulates that the buyer is putting up his house as collateral, and that if he fails to make his payments, the sales company can not only take away the customer's home improvement, but his entire house as well. Moreover, these nonjudicial foreclosures, as they are called, can be carried out without having to go to court; in recent years thousands of people had lost their homes that way. The problem was especially prevalent in southern California, which was where Wallace and Phillips went to film their story.

They soon discovered that many of the victims of this questionable practice were blacks and Hispanics who, because of deficiencies in education, were unable to read or understand the fine print in the lien contracts. In fact, the story that Mike and his producer put together centered on the plight of a black woman and a Chicano, each of whom faced foreclosures after they signed contracts for expensive air conditioners without realizing that they had put up their homes as collateral. The financing of their purchases was handled by San Diego Federal, a savings and loan association, which sent warning letters to the customers after they failed to make their payments. It came to pass that among the people Wallace interviewed was Dick Carlson, a senior vice-president at San Diego Federal. But Carlson agreed to sit down with Wallace only on the condition that he could hire his own videotape crew to record the interview. This was a perfectly reasonable request, and neither Wallace nor Phillips had any qualms about granting it. After all, a filmed interview is by definition an on-the-record event, and it never occurred to Mike that he could be done in by his own métier. Yet that is precisely what happened.

The interview itself proceeded along a normal and predictable course. Wallace asked Carlson some tough questions about lien contracts and the people who had fallen prey to them. Carlson acknowledged that the practice was abused from time to time with unfortunate results, but in general he defended nonjudicial foreclosures as necessary evils. At one point, in response to a question, he said:

> I think the whole thing comes down to the entire credit system in the United States, that lenders will not make certain kinds of loans unless they have recourse of some kind. They simply won't do it. Maybe the system that we have is wrong and maybe it ought to be changed. I must say, though, that if you eliminate the ability of a lender to ultimately foreclose on a person without having to go through a lengthy judicial process, you will substantially reduce the amount of money that's loaned—particularly in certain parts of town, I'm afraid to say.

That last line was a thinly veiled reference to black and Hispanic neighborhoods. Wallace thought he might pursue that with Carlson, but before he had a chance, the CBS News cameraman ran out of film, and there was a break in the interview while he changed reels. It was Wallace's understanding that when the *60 Minutes* camera stopped rolling, it was an official time out, so to speak, which meant that the cameraman Carlson had hired was supposed to turn off his equipment until the interview resumed. (That was the customary agreement when there were two crews recording an interview.) Wallace usually welcomed such breaks as an opportunity to relax and engage in banter and small talk. And on occasion, this time could be used to disarm the interviewee and lull him into a less wary or defensive frame of mind. In any case, during the break in the filming, Mike began reading from a typical lien contract in a mocking, incredulous tone, and the tangled syntax and arcane legal language came out sounding like gibberish. Reacting to Wallace's performance, Carlson admitted that "these things are hard to read." And in response, Mike uttered the words that would later come back to haunt him. Under the impression that no cameras were rolling, he said: "You bet your ass they're hard to read," and he suggested that they were especially difficult to comprehend "if you're reading them over the watermelon or the tacos."

This remark elicited a small laugh from Carlson and others in the room, and Wallace himself joined in the mirth. But the tasteless joke was on him, and it wasn't funny.

Nearly a month went by before he became aware that he had a problem. First, a telephone call came from Jim Drinkhall, a reporter for *The Wall Street Journal*. Drinkhall said he had received a tip that San Diego Federal had in its possession a videotape of a racial remark made by Wallace during a *60 Minutes* interview with one of its officers. Then and only then did Mike realize that the camera crew hired by Carlson had not observed the ground rules and had continued to shoot during the break in the interview when the CBS News cameraman was *not* rolling. Wallace was furious and more than that, he was apprehensive. He could not remember precisely what he had said during those moments when he thought he was talking off the record, but it was obvious from the accusatory tone of Drinkhall's questions that he had been told or led to believe that Wallace had uttered an offensive racial epithet. At the time—the early spring of 1981—Mike was still nursing his wounds from the Haiti flap; now, on top of that, he had to face the prospect of being branded a racist in the national press.

After telling Drinkhall that he would get back to him, Wallace went to work on the phone. He placed calls to several San Diego Federal executives, including Carlson. When Carlson confirmed that the bank had recorded his offhand remarks on videotape, Wallace exploded and accused him of dirty pool. The normal procedure, he said, was that any comments made when the CBS News camera was not filming were off the record, and therefore the other camera should not have been rolling at that point. But Carlson replied that he had told Wallace at the beginning of the interview that the crew he hired was on hand "to get an uninterrupted record of what's happening here." Still, he and the bank's other officers professed to be concerned about the leak and how to handle it. They, too, had received calls from Jim Drinkhall and had informed him that they would neither release the tape nor disclose any quotes that were on it. That at least was something, and although Wallace was still upset, he thanked them and urged them to continue taking that stand.

But the next day he made another foolish mistake. Convinced that he would never be able to put the matter to rest as long as that telltale tape existed, Wallace called the San Diego Federal executives again, and this time he suggested that they erase those portions of that tape that, ethically, should never have been recorded in the first place. "I know this is not a very good thing to ask in this era of erased tapes," he said, but then added that given the unusual circumstances—the improper taping of an off-the-record conversation—he felt justified in making the request. The bank's officials were wary of his proposal, but they agreed to think about it. In the meantime, Wallace himself did some quick, hard thinking, and soon images of Richard Nixon and the infamous eighteen-and-a-half-minute gap in the White House tapes began to flash through his mind. This was enough to bring him to his senses, so half an hour later, he called the bank's executives again and told them to forget about his earlier request. "You go ahead and keep it," he said. "Don't do a thing. Keep all of it, just as it is."

Soon thereafter, Carlson and his colleagues came up with a solution of their own. They informed Wallace that they were shipping a copy of the tape to him, and that henceforth, all press queries about it that came into San Diego Federal would be referred to his *60 Minutes* office in New York.

Before the copy of the tape arrived in New York, Drinkhall called again, but this time Wallace was ready for him. He realized now that the reporter had no solid facts to go on and that his previous calls had been little more than fishing expeditions. So Wallace told Drinkhall that although he still had neither seen the tape in question nor had read a transcript of it, he had done some checking with others who were present

at the interview, and they confirmed his own recollection that
the so-called racial remark was nothing more than a casual joke
he had uttered off the record when the CBS News camera was
not filming. When Drinkhall asked him to repeat the joke,
Wallace truthfully replied that he could not recall it in so many
words; and besides, he added, it had been said off the record,
and he preferred to keep it off the record. That was apparently
enough to deflate Drinkhall's curiosity; he and *The Wall Street
Journal* soon lost interest in the story. Thus, Wallace succeeded
in dodging that first bullet.

For the next several months, nothing happened. The report that
Wallace and Martin Phillips filmed on lien contracts had been
edited and deposited in the "bank" of *60 Minutes* stories that
were to be broadcast the next season, after the summer reruns.
There was no pressing need to put it on the air because it was
one of those general, timeless stories that was not tied to breaking news or a specific event. In fact, it still had not appeared
on *60 Minutes* in early November 1981 when Wallace received
a call from Robert Lindsey, a reporter for *The New York Times*.
Lindsey said that the *Times* had received an anonymous letter
about a San Diego Federal videotape which apparently showed
Wallace speaking out of line on a sensitive racial subject. So,
there it was again, more than six months after *The Wall Street
Journal* had made its pass at the story.

Choosing his words with care, Wallace told Lindsey exactly
what he had told Drinkhall: that the quote on the tape was
nothing more than a jocular, offhand remark he had made off
the record during a break in the interview. But Lindsey was
pursuing a somewhat different angle. He wanted to know if
the San Diego Federal had used the existence of the tape as a
threat to pressure Wallace into killing the story or diluting its
criticism of the bank. Mike learned later that Lindsey had asked
Dick Carlson the same question—in reverse: in other words,
did Wallace offer to kill the piece or pull his punches in return
for having the tape destroyed? Keenly aware of the charge that
Jack Anderson and others had leveled against Wallace a few
months earlier, Lindsey decided to chase the chimera of another
private deal that smacked of censorship. Once he was satisfied
that there was no pot of dirt at the end of that rainbow, he,

too, lost interest in the story. So, the second bullet whizzed by, a clean miss; but the next one would find its target.

The call from Lindsey convinced Wallace that the best course of action was to get the lien-contract story on the air as soon as possible. He and Phillips agreed that the report would speak for itself, and that once they saw it, the program's viewers would clearly recognize that Wallace's sympathies were all on the side of the minorities who had signed those contracts. They took the matter to Hewitt, who promptly rearranged the show's schedule, and "Goodbye Home Sweet Home," appeared on *60 Minutes* in late November. Once it was aired, Wallace assumed that he was past the danger point and no longer had any cause for concern. He felt that he had met his responsibility, the story was now in the public domain, any fool could see that it did not reflect a racist point of view. But of course, the report that he and Phillips had put on the air was only part of the story; and a week or so after "Goodbye Home Sweet Home" was broadcast, Wallace learned from his contacts in California that a reporter for the *Los Angeles Times* was making a determined effort to come up with the rest of it.

The reporter's name was Nancy Skelton, and when finally she phoned Wallace in late December, he quickly realized that she was not merely calling to check out a rumor or some vague tip that had been tossed in her lap. She had done a thorough job of reporting and had obtained from various sources all the salient facts: notably, the precise wording of the watermelon-and-tacos quote as well as a damaging account of Wallace's clumsy attempt to get that portion of the tape erased. Even so, he still tried to talk her off the story, to persuade her, as he had persuaded Drinkhall and Lindsey, that the remark was a "dumb joke" he had blurted out when he assumed he was talking off the record, and that as such, it was not germane to the piece he had done for *60 Minutes*.

But Nancy Skelton wasn't buying any of that. She had her story and she intended to go with it, and all she wanted from Wallace were answers to a few questions. Thus, Mike now had to make the kind of difficult choice he had inflicted on so many others over the years: He could either hide behind the lame shield of "No comment," or he could try in some way to put the best possible face on a deplorable situation. He chose the latter course. When Skelton asked him why he had tried to get the tape erased, he said he was deeply concerned that "those cold words, taken out of context, would make me look mean, graceless and bigoted, and I'd like to believe that I'm none of these things." Then, in an effort to explain the remark itself, he said: "Look, I happen to have a penchant for obscenity and for jokes. Anybody who knows me, I'm afraid, knows that I do ethnic jokes and I do obscenity from time to time." Having thus portrayed himself as a stand-up comic in the Lenny Bruce tradition, he went on to make the point that when it came to ethnic put-downs, he did not play favorites. "Sometimes I even tell Jewish jokes," he disclosed, "and I'm Jewish."

Those quotes, along with the other incriminating information Skelton had gathered, appeared in her story, which was published on the front page of the *Los Angeles Times* on Sunday, January 10, 1982. Her long narrative treatment of the incident also included lively quotes from some of the officials at San Diego Federal. Dick Carlson, for one, could not resist gloating over the irony that it was Wallace of all people who had fallen prey to a candid camera. "Here's the master of the ambush," he crowed, "the guy who literally represents the public interest in this country, the final arbiter of truth and justice, if you will, and who'd think a small savings and loan company in California would catch Mike Wallace?" When he read that, Wallace wondered if Carlson hadn't been dealing from the bottom of the deck all along.

Through its syndication service, the *Los Angeles Times* was able to place Skelton's scoop in other newspapers across the country, many of which gave the story a big play. And in the days that followed, other reporters, aroused by the scent of blood, rushed in to pick at the leftovers from Skelton's kill. This time, the press really gave Wallace a working over. Even those critics who stopped short of branding him a racist were quick to denounce the remark as the kind of "tasteless and contemptible" joke that would invite the snickering applause of real bigots. What's more, there was little that Wallace could do or say in his own defense, and he knew it. The previous year when he had been embroiled in the Haiti dustup, he was able to argue, with some justification, that although he erred in judgment, his motive was a compassionate one. His wife's anxiety over the welfare of her family in Haiti was genuine, and Mike had responded to that. But this time, he had no such excuse—no excuse at all, really—and the sheer stupidity of what he had done made him sick at heart. In a letter to a friend he recalled the feeling of dread that came over him when he realized that the story was going to come out. "I hated the thought that I was about to be exposed as a racist, a bigot, a real-life Archie Bunker," he wrote. "I cannot tell you how many sleepless nights I suffered through because I'd been nailed out of my own mouth."

The line about suffering through sleepless nights was no exaggeration, for his sense of anguish ran very deep. One of the first things he did after the story broke was to seek out various black co-workers at CBS and apologize to them. And in the weeks that followed, he reached out to longtime friends in the black community for their understanding and support. He felt compelled to remind them and others of all the stories he had done over the years on black issues, stories which, for the most part, were openly sympathetic to the civil rights movement and similar crusades for social justice. Most of his listeners did not need to be told that, because the people who knew Wallace—especially those who knew him well—were fully aware he was no racist. Still, they were touched by his remorse, and he, in turn, needed their reassurance. Several of his colleagues at CBS News commented at the time that they could not remember when they had seen Mike so distraught. They knew that as a rule, Wallace thrived on controversy and welcomed a spirited public scrap. But this was different, for he had no stomach at all for this kind of fight.

Yet even as they rallied to Wallace's defense against the charge of racism, many of his friends and colleagues readily acknowledged that the source of the trouble—the flippant crack about watermelon and tacos—was very much in character. For it was true, as he told Nancy Skelton, that he had a penchant for obscenity and for ethnic jokes. But more than that, he had a knack for blunt putdowns, and his co-workers were often stung by his verbal barbs. For example, he loved to rib overweight colleagues about their waistlines, and to tease feminist friends who, in his view, were excessively earnest about themselves and their cause. Indeed, when Wallace was in that kind

of mood, nothing was sacred, and under the right circumstances
he would not have hesitated to rag Ed Bradley about water-
melons or some other racial stereotype. (For his part, Bradley
understood this roughhouse game and recognized that beneath
the playful verbal aggression, Mike had nothing but respect for
both him and his work. In fact, Bradley was one of the first
to come to Wallace's defense when everything hit the fan in
the early weeks of 1982.) To many of his colleagues, the now-
notorious remark was merely a typical Wallace quip, reminiscent of many others they had heard him utter over the years.

But there was more to it than that, for the culinary one-liner
also reflected his assessment of the man he was interviewing.
One of Wallace's favorite techniques was to feign sympathy
with an interviewee's values or point of view in an effort to
establish rapport and create the impression that he and the target
of his queries were on the same wavelength. For instance, in
conducting an interview with a classical ballet dancer like Mikhail Baryshnikov, he would adopt a manner and tone that differed radically from, say, one he would assume in the presence
of a Mafia hit man. In that respect, Wallace (as well as many
other good interviewers) was not unlike Zelig, the chameleon-
like character in the Woody Allen film of that name who adapts
his psyche and behavior to conform to those of the person he
happens to be with at the time. Thus, the watermelon-and-tacos
remark was to some degree a calculated effort to find out if
Carlson might indulge in a similar indiscretion when the interview resumed. Of course, it also could be argued that such
a tactic was a form of verbal entrapment that in itself was a
breach of ethics; nevertheless, it was a stratagem he had used
many times over the years, and often with success. This time,
however, it didn't work, and Wallace was the one who got
caught in the barbed wire.

Yet even this lamentable episode had a diverting postscript,
a tale that might have inspired Damon Runyon had he been
around to put his distinctive stamp on it. The heroine was Rita
Quinn, who had known Wallace since she went to work for
him on *Night Beat* in 1956. Their friendship had continued
throughout the years, and when Wallace was going through his
watermelon-and-tacos ordeal, Quinn was working as a secretary to the new president of CBS News, Van Gordon Sauter.

Moreover, since many of the complaints about Wallace passed through Sauter's office, Rita was privy to all the flak that Mike was getting and commiserated with his plight.

Rita was also an avid horseplayer, and in the early summer of 1982—some six months after Nancy Skelton's article ignited the controversy—she had a day off and drove down to the racetrack in Monmouth, New Jersey. She had a stretch of bad luck in the early races, and since the long afternoon was drawing to a close, she needed a big score to recoup her losses. As she studied the entries for the final race, a longshot named Little Watermelon caught her eye. There was absolutely nothing in the horse's past-performance chart to recommend an investment, but Quinn, deciding the time had come to play a hunch, made an across-the-board bet on Little Watermelon. A few minutes later, the longshot came thundering home ahead of the field, and Rita had turned her bad day at the track into a triumphant one; she won nearly two hundred dollars on that race alone. As she walked briskly to the cashier's window to collect her bonanza, she smiled and said to herself: "Thank you, Mike."

By then, all the furor about the incident had run its course. Over the winter and spring of 1982, Wallace had managed, through word and deed, to persuade most of his accusers that his tasteless and flippant remark had been nothing more than that; it did not reflect a racist mentality. Yet even though he had succeeded finally in putting the regrettable affair behind him, it did not mean that his professional life returned to normal. For in the early weeks of that summer, Wallace was embroiled in yet another crisis, except this time he was not alone.

A few months earlier, in late January, CBS News had aired a powerful documentary called "The Uncounted Enemy: A Vietnam Deception." Wallace was the correspondent on this *CBS Reports* broadcast, the highlight of which was his interview with General William C. Westmoreland, who stood accused—by some of the officers who had served under him in Vietnam—of having presided over an elaborate deception of enemy troop strength in that war. In May, *TV Guide* published a highly critical piece about the broadcast, which it ran under the provocative title: "Anatomy of a Smear—How CBS News

Broke the Rules and 'Got' Gen. Westmoreland." This article, in turn, prompted CBS News to conduct an investigation into the making of its own documentary, which took place in the late spring and early summer of 1982. Although Wallace was caught up in it, the chief target of both the *TV Guide* article and the network's investigation was not the big-name correspondent who had narrated the report, but the documentary producer who had done most of the work on the story—George Crile.

A former editor at *Harper's* magazine, Crile had been hired by CBS News in 1976 to produce a documentary on the CIA's clandestine military activities in Cuba. That was a challenging assignment, and he turned it into an auspicious debut in a new medium. Dick Salant, then president of CBS News, had been with the network since the Edward R. Murrow era, the reputed golden age of television documentaries; yet as far as he was concerned, "The CIA's Secret Army" was "one of the all-time great documentaries." Crile went on to produce other excellent documentaries, notably "The Battle for South Africa," for which he won a Peabody Award and an Emmy. And in the fall of 1980, he decided to go after a story that had intrigued him for years.

Back in 1975, when he was still at *Harper's*, Crile had edited an article written by Sam Adams, who had been a CIA analyst in Vietnam during the critical months leading up to the Tet offensive in early 1968. During that period the CIA and General Westmoreland's MACV (Military Assistance Command, Vietnam) engaged in a serious dispute over the enemy "order of battle"—the official size and composition of the North Vietnamese and Viet Cong forces in South Vietnam. In writing about this secret quarrel, Adams charged that MACV deliberately underreported the enemy's troop strength; and he contended that because of those doctored estimates, U.S. troops in the field, political leaders in Washington, and the American people were caught unprepared for the size and scope of the attack the enemy launched on Vietnam's Tet holiday in late January 1968. When he wrote the article for *Harper's* in 1975, Sam Adams was the only major figure in the dispute who had dared to go public with the story. But in the fall of 1980, when

Crile visited him at his farmhouse in Virginia, Adams revealed
that other key officials from both the CIA and MACV were
willing to come forward and talk about the deception and their
participation in it.

This was the story that Crile wanted to develop into a *CBS
Reports* documentary. A week or so after he talked to Adams,
he submitted a lengthy proposal to his superiors. A few weeks
later—in early January 1981—he was given the green light to
proceed, but only on a provisional basis. Bill Leonard, then
president of CBS News, said that in order to get a firm commitment to a broadcast, Crile would have to come up with
plenty of solid information—on film. Leonard made it clear
that because of the explosive nature of the story, it could not
be built around unnamed sources who were willing to talk for
background only, outside of camera range. He told Crile that
if there were indeed allegations from other officials besides
Adams, then he would have to get them nailed down, in full
view and on the record. Otherwise, said Leonard, the project
would be scrapped.

In the meantime, Crile had approached Wallace about the
assignment. Aside from the stature and marquee value that
Mike would bring to the broadcast, Crile wanted him because
he knew that one of the most crucial elements in the report
—one that could ultimately determine its success or failure—
would be the interviews with high-level military and civilian
officials who would have to answer for the systematic deception
that had occurred. For example, whoever sat down with General
Westmoreland, an imposing and formidable presence, would
be obliged to ask him some very tough questions, and no one
was better equipped for that difficult task than Mike Wallace.
When Mike heard what Crile had in mind, he said he thought
it was an excellent idea for a documentary, but that given his
60 Minutes obligations, he didn't see how he could commit
himself full time to such an ambitious undertaking. Crile quickly
explained that he would be doing all the spadework and even
most of the interviews, and that Wallace would only be brought
in to interview Westmoreland and a few other heavyweights.
(Crile had done some on-air reporting and interviewing in his
previous documentaries, and in fact, he was trying to bolster

his credentials in that area in the hope of becoming a full-time correspondent who produced his own reports.) Well, said Wallace, if that was going to be the arrangement, then yes, he could do it. Not long thereafter, Mike was officially assigned to the project.

Crile then set out to gather the evidence and information he needed to turn a provocative idea into a concrete story. Working closely with Sam Adams—who was hired by CBS News as a consultant—he tracked down and interviewed scores of officials and other sources who, in one way or another, had been close to the events in question. The results were staggering, for among those who broke fourteen years of silence and gave detailed, on-the-record accounts that supported Adams's main allegations were some of Westmoreland's own top intelligence officers in MACV as well as their counterparts in the CIA. By April 1981 Crile had enough hard evidence on film to persuade Bill Leonard to give his approval to a full-length documentary on the subject. Indeed, the information that Crile was assembling went well beyond Adams's original charges. From his numerous interviews, George was able to piece together a story of deception and cover-up that was carried out in three distinct and vital areas: (1) the false estimates of enemy troops in South Vietnam in 1967; (2) the suppression of reports of heavy infiltration by North Vietnamese soldiers down the Ho Chi Minh Trail, an influx that later (after all the damage was done) would be recognized as a necessary prelude to the Tet offensive; and (3) a post-Tet decision to alter the earlier estimates of enemy troop strength, to conceal the duplicity of those reports—in effect, a cover-up of the cover-up.

This was the ammunition Crile gave Wallace when the time came for him to interview General Westmoreland in May 1981. Although Crile had gone through the topics to be discussed in a long telephone conversation with the general and in a letter he delivered to him the day before the interview, Westmoreland evinced no sense of foreboding. He had nothing but pleasant memories of his first meeting with Wallace back in 1967, when he was running the show in South Vietnam and Mike had arrived in Saigon to commence his brief tour of duty there as

a correspondent. (It was a mere coincidence that he happened
to be in Vietnam just at the time when the intelligence deception
was taking shape; and of course, neither he nor any other
reporter on the scene was aware of that secret decision.) In
those days, Wallace was still a hawk, still a supporter of the
U.S. intervention in Vietnam, and Westmoreland, sensing this,
gave him the red-carpet treatment: a personal, daylong air tour
of firebases, forward positions and field briefings across the
length and breadth of South Vietnam. However, that personal
attention did not achieve the desired result of keeping Wallace
in the fold of true believers, for it was during his two-month
stay in Vietnam that he began his conversion from hawk to
dove; by the time he left Saigon in May 1967, Mike had come
around to the view that the full-scale commitment of American
troops in Vietnam was a mistake.

Even so, he and Westmoreland maintained a cordial, though
distant, relationship through the years that followed. For example, in March 1972, when *60 Minutes* aired an update of
the story Wallace had done a few years earlier on three wounded
veterans who had been shipped home from Vietnam without
their legs, Wallace received a "Dear Mike" letter from Westmoreland. "I just want to tell you that it was a first-class piece
of reporting," the general wrote. "I have never seen better."
So, when Wallace came to interview him in the spring of 1981,
Westmoreland did not seem to expect the grilling to which he
was subjected. Even though George Crile had sent him that
letter spelling out the topics to be discussed in the interview,
Westmoreland seemed not to have prepared himself for the
toughness of the questions that Wallace put to him.

Armed with the information that Crile had obtained from
his various sources, Wallace began with questions about the
CIA's assertion in the early months of 1967 that U.S. troops
were facing a much larger enemy than the official estimates
indicated. As expected, Westmoreland dismissed that CIA claim
as "unreliable." Then Wallace asked him about General Joseph
McChristian, his own intelligence chief at MACV, and Westmoreland, rising to the bait, described McChristian as "a superb
intelligence officer." Then Wallace said:

•   •   •

WALLACE: So when it came to reporting on the enemy, you didn't especially count on the CIA's work on this score. You stood by the work of General McChristian and his staff.

WESTMORELAND: Well, sure. The CIA was very remote. We were on the scene.

Wallace then confronted Westmoreland with the fact that both McChristian and his chief deputy in Vietnam, Colonel Gains Hawkins, had recently told CBS News—in on-camera interviews—that they came up with information in the spring of 1967 which corroborated the CIA's contention. What's more, they said that they presented the information to Westmoreland along with a proposal that MACV's intelligence reports be revised to reflect a dramatic increase in enemy strength estimates—something on the order of 200,000 more Viet Cong. Westmoreland acknowledged that such a meeting did take place, and he admitted further that he rejected the proposal to jack up the estimates. When Wallace asked him why he didn't accept the recommendation of General McChristian, "a man whom you call a superb intelligence chief," Westmoreland replied: "I didn't accept it because of political reasons."

WALLACE: What's the political reason? Why would it have been a political bombshell? That's really—

WESTMORELAND: Because the people in Washington were not sophisticated enough to understand and evaluate this thing, and neither was the media.

That stunning disclosure went directly to the heart of the matter. For by the spring of 1967, Lyndon Johnson knew that the war in Vietnam was threatening to destroy his presidency. Two years had passed since he had ordered the huge buildup of U.S. forces, and now, with the troop levels moving toward half a million Americans committed to the struggle, a growing tide of disenchantment with the war was starting to sweep across the country. Thus, Johnson knew that neither Congress nor the American public would tolerate another major escalation, especially one on a scale necessary to defeat an enemy nearly twice as large as previous intelligence estimates had indicated. Additionally, such an escalation would have fanned the flames of the antiwar movement, which by the spring of 1967 was emerging as a major force of opposition to LBJ's reelection hopes. Such a move also would have given fresh ammunition to the skeptics in the press, many of whom had already begun to question the wisdom of Johnson's decision to transform the conflict in Vietnam into an American war.

Westmoreland had a vivid appreciation of all those factors, as Wallace later noted in the narration for the documentary: "Consider Westmoreland's dilemma. If he accepted his intelligence chief's findings, he would have to take the bad news to the President. If he didn't, well, there was only General McChristian to deal with." Wallace went on to say that "shortly after Westmoreland suppressed his intelligence chief's report, General Joseph McChristian was transferred out of Vietnam. It was at that point, we believe, that MACV began to suppress, and then to alter, critical intelligence reports on the strength of the enemy."

Most of the interview with Westmoreland focused on the step-by-step decisions that were made in 1967 "to suppress and then to alter" those reports. Seldom has a major figure in American history been put so squarely on the spot in a network television interview. As Wallace continued to confront him with the testimony of officers from his own command, all that Westmoreland could do in response was plead ignorance, deny the charges made by his own people, or try to justify some of the decisions that contributed to the alleged cover-up. At one point, as his anger and frustration mounted, he turned on Wallace as though he were a junior officer who had stepped out of line. Mike was asking him about a decision in the summer of 1967 to drop an entire category of the Viet Cong Army—the self-defense militia—from the enemy order of battle. Other sources had told Crile that that bookkeeping maneuver had been dictated by the overall strategy of keeping the total estimate of enemy troops under the acceptable limit of 300,000, and Wallace was pressing Westmoreland to acknowledge it. But instead, the general decided that the time had come to put Wallace in his place with a sharp verbal reprimand. "This is a non-issue, Mike," he said. "I made the decision. I don't regret making it. I stand by it. And the facts prove that I was right. Now let's stop it!"

At first, Wallace appeared to be taken aback by the rebuke. "All right, sir," he said in the timorous voice of a junior officer, in effect apologizing to his commanding general. But a moment later, he resumed his hard questioning:

> WALLACE: Isn't it a possibility that the real reason for suddenly deciding in the summer of 1967 to remove an entire category of the enemy from the order of battle—a category that had been in the order of battle since 1961—was based on political considerations?
>
> WESTMORELAND: No, decidedly not. That—
>
> WALLACE: Didn't you make this clear in your August twentieth cable?
>
> WESTMORELAND: No, no. Yeah. No.
>
> WALLACE: I have a copy of your August twentieth cable—
>
> WESTMORELAND: Well, sure. Okay, okay. All right, all right.
>
> WALLACE: —Spelling out the command position on the self-defense controversy.
>
> WESTMORELAND: Yeah.

At that point Wallace read from an August 1967 cable that had been sent by Westmoreland's top deputy in Vietnam, General Creighton Abrams, with Westmoreland's full approval: "We have been projecting an image of success over the recent months. The self-defense militia must be removed or the newsmen will immediately seize on the point that the enemy force has increased." Faced with that concrete evidence, Westmoreland had no choice but to acknowledge that a major reason for the decision was to throw the press off the scent.

Even by the standards that Wallace himself had set over the years, his interview with General Westmoreland was a forceful and compelling encounter, but it could not have turned out that way if George Crile had not laid the groundwork with his own thorough reporting. During the spring and summer of 1981, Mike conducted three other interviews for the documentary: one with Sam Adams, whose charges and recollections were needed to establish the theme of the broadcast; another with Lieutenant General Daniel Graham, who, according to some of MACV's intelligence officers, was also involved in the deception; and the third with Walt Rostow, one of President Johnson's top foreign policy advisers during the period in question. But the Westmoreland interview was the key element, the *pièce de résistance*, and when the documentary was broadcast several months later, it formed the vital nucleus around which the other players in the extraordinary drama revolved.

Most *CBS Reports* documentaries are one-hour broadcasts, but Crile and Wallace were given ninety minutes of prime time for "The Uncounted Enemy: A Vietnam Deception." This in itself was an acknowledgment that they had come up with something special, and when Crile completed the editing in the fall and his superiors looked at the finished product, they all agreed it was a strong and riveting report. Even those who were cynical about the war—who had long believed that the men in authority at the time had deliberately deceived the American public—were struck by the revelations they heard, and even more so by the visible anguish that came through in some of the interviews. For the officers who chose to speak out in public after all those years of silence did so with reluctance and with heavy hearts. As Wallace later wrote in an internal memo when the documentary was the object of an in-house investigation: "Most whistle-blowers speak out of anger. These men spoke in sorrow, or in shame that some of them had participated in a fraud. There was nothing in it for them to go on the record so long after the fact. It was painful and it showed."

One of the most poignant moments occurred during the interview with General McChristian when Crile asked him to comment on just what it meant for a commanding officer to impose an arbitrary ceiling on intelligence estimates of enemy strength. (This was one of the broadcast's charges against General Westmoreland.)

CRILE: What does that constitute, sir?

McCHRISTIAN: From my point of view, that is falsification of the facts.

CRILE: Are there statutes in the Uniform Code of Military Justice that would speak to that situation?

McCHRISTIAN: Not that I'm aware of. But there's something on a ring that I wear from West Point that the motto is: "Duty, Honor, Country." It's dishonorable.

Among those who assembled in a screening room that fall to view "The Uncounted Enemy" before it went on the air were Bill Leonard, Roger Colloff, vice-president in charge of documentaries, and Howard Stringer, the executive producer of *CBS Reports*. Crile and Wallace were also on hand, along with others who in one way or another had a stake in the program. Everyone grasped the historic importance of the broadcast—Leonard predicted that it would trigger a fresh national debate on the Vietnam ordeal—and in view of the impact it was likely to have, there was some concern about the use of a specific word. In his on-camera introduction, Wallace said:

Tonight, we're going to present evidence of what we have come to believe was a conscious effort—indeed, a conspiracy—at the highest levels of American military intelligence to suppress and alter critical intelligence on the enemy in the year leading up to the Tet offensive.

Dictionaries were consulted, and a thorough discussion of the matter ensued. In another memo written at the time of the in-house investigation, Roger Colloff recalled that "we recognized the use of the word 'conspiracy' was an issue that needed to be discussed, given the strength of the word." But in the end, Colloff wrote, "We agreed that use of the word 'conspiracy,' while tough, was warranted by the facts presented by the broadcast and the underlying research." Subsequently, the CBS News executives authorized the use of "conspiracy"—in big bold letters—in a full-page newspaper ad for the documentary. Nor were Colloff and his colleagues the only ones who recognized "the strength of the word." For when General Westmoreland finally made his legal move—in the form of a $120 million libel suit against CBS—he and his lawyer based their complaint in large measure on the network's assertion that the actions chronicled in the documentary were "indeed a conspiracy."

"The Uncounted Enemy" aired on January 23, 1982. Three days later General Westmoreland held a news conference at the Army-Navy Club in Washington, where he denounced the broadcast as "a preposterous hoax." Joining him in the counterattack were some of his closest associates from the Vietnam days, including the former U.S. ambassador to Saigon, Ellsworth Bunker, and Lieutenant General Daniel Graham, who had been cited in the program as a figure in the cover-up. But despite the supporting cast and the righteous wrath of the leading player, it was not a persuasive performance. Pressed by questions about some of the specific issues raised in the broadcast, Westmoreland often seemed as unsure of his ground as he had been during the interview with Wallace, which he characterized as a "star chamber" inquisition. Moreover, it was obvious, from their expressions, that some of the supporting players did not agree with all of the general's denials and assertions. Most intriguing of all was an unexpected revelation that came near the end of the news conference. In response to a question, Westmoreland disclosed that he had told President Johnson in March 1967 that "the war could go on indefinitely" if the United States did not cut off the flow of reinforcements down the Ho Chi Minh Trail, a step which both Johnson and his successor, Richard Nixon, refused to authorize. In various newspaper accounts of the press conference, reporters noted that Westmoreland never allowed such pessimistic concern to creep into his public statements about the war in 1967. Throughout the months leading up to the Tet offensive, he stoutly averred that the war was being won and that the enemy was being slowly ground into submission.

The initial press reaction to the documentary was overwhelmingly favorable, and it was not confined to the customary reviews by television critics. For example, *The New York Times* ran an editorial praising the broadcast. And in many ways, the most telling and unexpected accolade came from the conser-

vative columnist William F. Buckley, who over the years had
been a staunch defender of the U.S. intervention in Vietnam,
as outspoken on the subject as any hawk in the land. Describing
the program as "a truly extraordinary documentary," Buckley
wrote that it "absolutely establishes that Gen. William Westmoreland, for political reasons, withheld from the President,
probably from the Joint Chiefs, from Congress and from the
American people information about the enemy that was vital
to any sensible reordering of one's thoughts toward the war,
whether one were dove-minded or otherwise." Then, turning
his attention to the centerpiece of the broadcast, the interview
with Westmoreland, Buckley came up with this wry observation: "It is always astonishing to me how Mike Wallace con-
trives to get people to consent to go before a camera to be
questioned on subjects concerning which they should prefer
silence. I am sure that Wallace, using whatever magic it is he
disposes of, would have succeeded in getting Jack the Ripper
to talk to him on the subject of how London's streets were
crowded with unnecessary young ladies."

But the positive reaction of those early days after the broadcast was destined to be overshadowed by the critical article
which ran in *TV Guide* a few months later. The article was
written by two reporters, Don Kowet and Sally Bedell, who
in building their case against "The Uncounted Enemy," received
valuable assistance from a source (or sources) within CBS
News. Kowet and Bedell were able to obtain unedited transcripts of on-camera interviews and other inside material and
information that went into the making of the documentary. In
addition, they interviewed many of the principals in the story,
and from all those elements, they constructed "Anatomy of a
Smear—How CBS News Broke the Rules and 'Got' Gen.
Westmoreland."

Nearly all the charges in the *TV Guide* article dealt with
reporting and editing procedures rather than with the substance
of the documentary, and when Wallace and Crile read them,
they quickly recognized that most of the allegations were specious and could easily be refuted. In fact, many were nothing
more than judgment calls, the kind that all reporters have to
make when faced with the inevitable limitations of time (on
television) or space (in print). For example, Kowet and Bedell

complained that some of the officials interviewed by Wallace
and/or Crile were either given short shrift on the broadcast or
not included at all. Elaborating on this criticism, they charged
that Crile had stacked the deck against Westmoreland by building so much of the documentary around interviews with those
officers who agreed that a large-scale deception had taken place
in Vietnam, while slighting others who would have challenged
that contention.

It's true, of course, that Crile could have included any number of Westmoreland loyalists who would have sided with the
general's claim that there was no conspiracy to deceive Washington and the American public about the real strength of enemy
troops in 1967. That, after all, was the official position, the
party line, and it was hardly news. What *was* news was the
fact that some of the top officers in Westmoreland's own command had decided to end years of silence by making such
dramatic disclosures on national television. That was the crux
of the story. For it was *their* revelations that gave the broadcast
its compelling force and authority, and Crile would not have
been much of a reporter if he had failed to recognize that fact.

Kowet and Bedell also claimed that "The Uncounted Enemy" distorted the views of two of the major intelligence officers from Westmoreland's command: General Joseph
McChristian and his chief deputy, Colonel Gains Hawkins. But
shortly after the article was published, both McChristian and
Hawkins sent letters to CBS affirming their support of the
broadcast and its fairness. When another reporter later asked
Kowet about that, he replied: "Who cares? I don't give a damn
whether *they* think they were fairly represented. That's not the
issue. They're not journalists." From that statement, one can
only conclude that Kowet and Bedell were making some judgment calls of their own.

Yet it should also be noted that interspersed among all the
specious allegations in the *TV Guide* article were a couple of
legitimate, palpable hits that could not be refuted. They had
to do with Crile's treatment of a reluctant whistle-blower, a
former CIA officer named George Allen, who was an expert
on enemy strength in Vietnam.

Allen, Sam Adams's immediate superior in the CIA hierarchy in Saigon, had acknowledged in private conversations

that the CIA had caved in to MACV's demands to lower the numbers, for political reasons. However, when Crile interviewed him on-camera, Allen came across as stiff and halting and rather inarticulate. So Crile asked him to submit to a second interview, to which he agreed. As Crile would be the first to admit, General Westmoreland didn't fare well in his interview either, but he wasn't given a second chance.

The other offense was more egregious. Before he filmed the second interview with Allen, Crile showed him the footage of some revelations made by other officers who had spoken out in public for the first time. Of all the criticisms in the *TV Guide* article, that was the one that Wallace and others at CBS News found most disturbing. And Crile himself later acknowledged that the special screening for Allen was a "stupid" thing to do. "I did it on impulse," he said. "I wanted him to see that he wasn't alone, that the real charges were being made not by him but by Westmoreland's own command." (But neither of these matters affected the substance of the documentary.)

The implicit message running through the article was that the substance of the documentary was wrong, that its thesis and conclusions were seriously flawed. Otherwise, why go to all the trouble of mounting a point-by-point assault on Crile's reporting procedures and editorial judgments? Moreover, why, in deciding on a title for the article, choose a flash word like "smear" and follow it up with the charge that CBS News "got" General Westmoreland? Yet when push came to shove, Kowet and Bedell explicitly denied that implication. At the end of their critique, they wrote: "We do not know whether Crile and his colleagues were right about General Westmoreland and his military intelligence operation." At that point, a dispassionate reader might well have been moved to inquire: "Then what is all the fuss about?"

Yet if the ultimate objective of the two reporters was not to challenge the substance of the broadcast but merely to stir up a fuss over procedures, then the article was a howling success. The greatest impact, of course, was felt within the world of CBS News, where it had a polarizing effect. On one side were those who believed that Crile's reportorial transgressions—especially his treatment of George Allen—served to undermine the integrity of the entire project. This faction took the position that Crile had been entrusted with a precious responsibility, a prime-time documentary of an important and controversial subject, and with his method of reporting, he had violated that trust and given the celebrated CBS eye a nasty shiner. On the other side were those who regarded the *TV Guide* piece as a reprehensible hatchet job; in their view, the word "smear" more accurately described the article Kowet and Bedell had written than it did the broadcast they attacked. Included in this group, of course, were Wallace and Crile, who stood ready to respond to the article with a strong and unequivocal defense of "The Uncounted Enemy." But before they had a chance to draft a public reply, they were beaten to the punch by the management of CBS News. Moreover, the nature of that official response seemed to cast the documentary—along with Wallace and Crile themselves—in a most ambiguous light.

"Anatomy of a Smear" was published in May 1982, and in many ways it could not have come out at a worse time. It hit the newsstands while CBS's annual affiliates meeting was taking place in San Francisco, and within that group the article struck a responsive chord. In years past, many conservative owners and managers of stations in the CBS family had not been happy with the network's coverage of the war in Vietnam, and the portrayal of General Westmoreland in the *CBS Reports* documentary had revived some of those old resentments. And now the piece in *TV Guide* seemed to confirm their worst suspicions about that broadcast. The CBS News executives who were attending the affiliates conference were made uncomfortably aware of the general reaction to the article. "I wouldn't want to ascribe it a number on the Richter scale," Roger Colloff later recalled, "but there was certainly a tremor."

One person who felt that tremor most acutely was the new president of CBS News, Van Gordon Sauter. Although he was new to the job, Sauter was no stranger to the network or its affiliates. In his rapid climb up the corporate ladder, he had held high-level positions at two CBS-owned stations: news director at WBBM in Chicago and general manager at KNXT in Los Angeles. He left KNXT in late 1980 to become head of CBS Sports in New York, and a little more than a year later—in March 1982—he took over as president of the news

division. Along the way Sauter had developed a reputation for
being a savvy and resourceful executive who did not beat around
the bush when it came to making tough decisions. And that
spring in San Francisco, he demonstrated his flair for quick
and decisive action.

After reading and digesting the article in *TV Guide*, Sauter
convened an emergency meeting with his top deputies in his
hotel suite, and made the critical decision. On the third day of
the affiliates conference, in his maiden speech as president of
CBS News, he announced that Bud Benjamin, a senior executive producer with imposing credentials, would conduct an
in-house investigation of all the charges and report on his findings. That was the long and short of it. Conspicuous by its
absence was a statement of support for the documentary.

At the time there were those at CBS News who thought that
Sauter had overreacted to the *TV Guide* piece; and in the months
that followed, as the controversy escalated into a multimillion-
dollar legal battle, this view gathered force and momentum.
Even some of Sauter's associates on the executive level had
the impression that his background in station management had
made him overly sensitive to the concerns and biases of the
affiliates. There also was a widespread rumor that spring that
Sauter had succumbed to pressure from his superiors in the
corporate hierarchy. For his part, Sauter had repeatedly denied
that pressure from above or from the affiliates had anything to
do with his decision to order an official, in-house investigation
and to let the public know, through the forum of the affiliates
meeting, that the documentary was going to be subjected to
formal scrutiny. "Of course, I discussed it with others, but the
decision was mine and mine alone," he reaffirmed in an interview several months later.

Among those who felt that Sauter made the wrong decision
were some longtime members of the CBS News family who
had been around in the sixties and seventies when Dick Salant
was president of the news division. They were quick to recall
how Salant had responded in 1971 when another controversial
CBS Reports documentary, "The Selling of the Pentagon," came
under heavy fire. On that occasion, the network had had to
cope with a far more formidable attack than the one launched
by *TV Guide*, for "The Selling of the Pentagon" became the

target of a highly publicized congressional investigation. But even when faced with that kind of pressure, Salant's only public reaction was to make a strong statement in support of the broadcast. (Unlike Sauter eleven years later, Salant had the advantage of having been at the helm when the earlier documentary was going through its various phases of production, and therefore he was familiar enough with the preparation of the broadcast to be assured of its essential accuracy and fairness.) However, he did not let it go at that. Salant and his deputies also looked into the allegations about reporting and editing procedures. One result of that inquiry was to provide a new list of guidelines to clarify CBS News standards. However, all this took place behind closed doors, beyond the glare of public scrutiny.

Dick Salant was forced to step down as president of CBS News in 1979 when he turned sixty-five, the company's mandatory retirement age; and when the Westmoreland controversy erupted three years later, he did his best to stay out of it. Reporters approaching him with questions about Sauter's decision and how he would relate it to the way he had handled the earlier uproar over "The Selling of the Pentagon," were discouraged from making a comparison. ("The circumstances were entirely different," was his stock answer.) He did not want to put himself in the position of second-guessing a successor; nor did he wish to appear to be setting himself up as a role model. But in private conversations with friends from his years at CBS, Salant was more candid. He believed that Sauter had made a mistake; and moreover, he suspected, from his own experience, that corporate pressure had something to do with the decision to inform the affiliates that an internal investigation had been ordered. Salant also admitted, in private, that if the decision had been his to make, he would have reacted in much the same way he had in 1971. First, he would have taken steps to ascertain that the substance of "The Uncounted Enemy" was valid, and once assured of that, he would have issued a public statement in support of the broadcast. He would not have bothered to comment on the *TV Guide* article's allegations regarding procedures, but if any of them had bothered him, he would have instructed his deputies to look into those areas quietly on an informal basis and strictly under his supervision.

"There would have been no formal report," he confided to one former colleague, "and certainly no public announcement about what we intended to do internally. The important thing in this kind of situation is to keep it from getting out of hand. When you officially assign a report to be done by somebody, you're delegating, and after that, whatever you get, you're stuck with. And if you've made a big deal in public about that report, then you're *really* stuck with it."

That was a lesson that Van Sauter was about to learn the hard way. By making "a big deal in public" about the internal investigation he ordered, Sauter transformed a minor irritation—the *TV Guide* article—into a major *cause célèbre* which, in turn, helped provoke the acrimonious libel suit that followed.

The person who had to shoulder the burden of Sauter's decision was Bud Benjamin, a man of vast experience in television news. Benjamin had been at CBS since 1957, and at various intervals over the years he had served as executive producer of such showcase broadcasts as *The Twentieth Century, CBS Reports* and the *CBS Evening News with Walter Cronkite*. Indeed, his position at the network was so strong that at one point, in the mid-1970s, he was a prime candidate for the presidency of CBS News, and he came within a whisker of succeeding Dick Salant in that post. Also working in Benjamin's favor was his impeccable reputation for integrity and fairness, qualities that were essential prerequisites for the special assignment he was given in May 1982. As another CBS executive said at the time: "With Bud doing the investigating, no one can accuse us of a whitewash."

Over the next few weeks, as spring faded into summer, Benjamin interviewed thirty-two people—twelve of them were CBS employees—and reams through reams of unedited transcripts and other pertinent data. By early July he had assembled his findings in a lengthy document that came to be known as the Benjamin Report. In this report Benjamin acknowledged that some of the allegations in the *TV Guide* article were valid; for example, the special screening and second interview that Crile had granted to George Allen. Most of his criticisms, like those in the article itself, dealt with reporting and editing procedures. On the other hand, Benjamin also came up with some fresh charges of his own, citing flaws in the broadcast that were not spelled out in *TV Guide*. Some of them, however, were so inconsequential that they hardly seemed worthy of mention. For example, in the broadcast, Wallace identified Sam Adams as a CBS News consultant on the story. But Benjamin maintained that Adams should have been identified as a *paid* consultant, a nit-picking clarification that an alert editor no doubt would have deleted on grounds of redundancy. It is commonly understood that consultants, in television and elsewhere, do not work for nothing. At the other extreme, addressing himself to a critical point that subsequently would have legal ramifications, Benjamin contended that a "conspiracy" had not been "proved."

Benjamin also had a few words of reproof for *TV Guide*. After enumerating what he thought was wrong with the documentary, he wrote that "on the other hand, *TV Guide* may have been wise in not challenging the premise of the broadcast. It seems odd, to say the least, for the magazine to launch an attack of this dimension and still say of its investigation: 'Its purpose was not to confirm or deny the existence of the conspiracy that CBS's journalists say existed.'" Then Benjamin commended George Crile (though not by name) for his diligent and thorough reporting in tracking down all the elements that went into the documentary: "To get a group of high-ranking military men and former Central Intelligence Agents to say that this is what happened was an achievement of no small dimension. These were not fringe people but rather prototypical Americans."

But this terse accolade, coming at the end of a long and largely critical treatise, did little to mollify the resentment and dismay that Crile and Wallace felt when they read the Benjamin Report. As far as they were concerned, Benjamin had given far too much credence and legitimacy to the charges in *TV Guide*, most of which, in their view, were specious and easily refutable. It was almost as if Benjamin had chosen to confront the allegations from the standpoint of Don Kowet and Sally Bedell, and to base his investigative report on their terms rather than on the terms set forth in the broadcast. Like Kowet and Bedell, he became so preoccupied with procedural questions that he seemed to lose sight of the central and most important fact: namely, that the substance of "The Uncounted Enemy" was sound and above reproach. Nor were Wallace and Crile alone in thinking that Benjamin had botched the investigation and had issued a report that was a disservice to the documentary in particular and, by extension, to CBS News in general. Others at the network shared their consternation, including several people who could not be accused of having a vested interest in the broadcast. Hence, in July 1982, as copies of the Benjamin Report were reviewed by various people at CBS, it—rather than the broadcast—became the focal point of controversy, and the man caught in the middle of this new and heated internal dispute was Van Gordon Sauter. For now that Benjamin had completed his work and had turned in his report, the ball was back in Van Sauter's court.

Dick Salant was right. "When you officially assign a report to be done by somebody, you're delegating, and after that, whatever you get, you're stuck with." Now Sauter was stuck with a report that was being discredited by some of the most able people in his news organization. Had he been more circumspect about the internal investigation, he could have at least given some thought to keeping the Benjamin Report under wraps. But his open announcement at the affiliates meeting had alerted the outside press to the course of action he had initiated, and thus he had to follow through with some kind of official and public statement. Nor could Sauter seriously consider repudiating the conclusions of an investigation that he himself had ordered. His only realistic option was to try, as best he could, to reconcile the adamant and opposing views that evolved out of the long and stormy meetings with the two factions, and that is precisely what he attempted to do.

The formal statement which Sauter released to the press that summer began with this flat assertion: "CBS News stands by this broadcast." But then, guided by the objections set down in the Benjamin Report, he cited certain flaws in the documentary that, in effect, raised more questions than they answered. The result was a statement of support which could not have been more equivocal and confusing. Sauter himself acknowledged as much when, in summing up CBS News' official position, he wrote: "In reviewing this statement, it may be bewildering to some outside CBS News that within our organization there can be debate regarding editorial decisions. But ours is a collaborative business, and such debates are natural and of great value."

Of great value, perhaps, but certainly bewildering, and hardly the public posture that CBS News should have been projecting at that point. The whole purpose behind Sauter's public call for a formal investigation was to clear the air and resolve the controversy in a definitive manner, one way or the other. But the ambivalent tenor of Sauter's statement, with all its awkward clarifications and seeming contradictions, was almost certain to have the opposite effect. That point was clearly grasped by Tom Shales, the televison critic for *The Washington Post*. In a follow-up column that appeared under the headline "CBS' Lavish Apologia," Shales wrote: "Killing, or at least impugning, the messenger who arrives with bad news is an old tradition, but you don't often find the messenger bopping himself over the head. Instead of dispelling the cloud that had formed over the program, CBS News all but seeded it for rain." And as that storm cloud darkened and grew ready to burst, the next sound to be heard was the thunderclap of a multimillion-dollar libel suit.

General Westmoreland had been contemplating legal action ever since "The Uncounted Enemy" went on the air in January 1982. But the first few lawyers he approached at some of the nation's most prestigious firms were not at all encouraging. Clark Clifford of Clifford and Warnke in Washington, D.C., strongly advised against a libel suit. As did Edward Bennett Williams, and Stanley Resor, a former secretary of the Army and partner in the New York law firm of Debevoise and Plimpton. All three men—and others whom Westmoreland contacted—stressed the difficulty he would face, as a public figure, in building a case for libel. But Westmoreland refused to be dissuaded, and his search for a lawyer eventually led to Dan Burt, president of the Capital Legal Foundation, in Washington D.C., one of the several conservative public-interest firms that have sprung up in recent years. Burt agreed to represent Westmoreland, and in September 1982 the $120 million libel suit was filed. Not only that, but Burt assured the general he would not have to pay a dime of his own money for litigation costs.

The Capitol Legal Foundation, which is heavily supported by contributions from various right-wing groups, would foot the entire bill.

In deciding to take on the case, Burt may well have been influenced by the fact that in the months since the broadcast—and the early favorable reaction to it—the public climate had shifted in Westmoreland's favor. First came the *TV Guide* piece, with its "smear" headline and charge that CBS News "got" Westmoreland. Then came the response of CBS News to that article: the public call for a formal investigation and, once it was completed, Van Sauter's ambiguous statement of support for the broadcast. Among the flaws Sauter cited in his statement was one in particular that was certain to catch the eye of a lawyer who had been solicited to consider Westmoreland's grievance. Taking his cue from what he read in the Benjamin Report, Sauter wrote: "We now feel it would have been a better broadcast if it had not used the word 'conspiracy' . . . Our colleagues involved in the production of this broadcast are convinced that the interviews and events related to this question justify the use of the word 'conspiracy.' The use of the word 'conspiracy' in its application to the facts within this broadcast presented ample evidence of deception but we now believe that a judgmental conclusion of conspiracy was inappropriate."

As Westmoreland's attorney, Burt was quick to seize on that statement and construe it as a big plus for his side. Nor was he the only one to do so. In an incisive and arresting examination of the way CBS handled the controversy, which was later published in *The American Lawyer* magazine, reporter Connie Bruck wrote that Sauter's "memorandum reads like a *mea culpa*." (Incidentally, this Latin phrase also appeared in the title of Bruck's article, "The Mea Culpa Defense—How CBS Brought on the Westmoreland Suit and Sacrificed One of Its Own.")

So, buoyed by the article in *TV Guide* and CBS's official reaction to it, Dan Burt was in a confident and upbeat mood when he launched the litigation against the network in September 1982. And in the months that followed, he kept up the pressure, making legal moves that, if nothing else, resulted in publicity triumphs, clear-cut victories in the arena of public relations. First, Burt filed a motion to gain access to the Benjamin Report, and he won that discovery battle in April 1983 when Federal District Judge Pierre Leval rejected CBS's argument that as an in-house document, the report was privileged. Leval ruled that CBS could not claim confidentiality for an internal inquiry and at the same time issue a press release based on it; in other words, Sauter's public statement had rendered the Benjamin Report discoverable.

The immediate effect of that court decision was to yield the Benjamin Report to the public domain, where the press proceeded to have a field day with it. The fact that most of the allegations in the report were a year old, having appeared in *TV Guide* the previous spring, did not diminish the editorial appetite for giving them a big play, and with good reason— for this was different. The *CBS Reports* documentary was now the target of a multimillion-dollar libel suit, and moreover, *these* criticisms of the broadcast had been formally set down by one of the network's own, an esteemed prince of the CBS church. Hence, in one media forum after another, the network found itself attacked with ammunition that had been supplied by its own internal document. And Dan Burt did his best to advance the notion that he now had CBS on the ropes and was moving in for the kill. Interviewed by *USA Today* shortly after the Benjamin Report was released, Burt proclaimed: "We are about to see the dismantling of a major news network."

Later that spring, still on the offensive, he struck again. In early June of 1983, Burt learned, from a deposition he had taken, that George Crile had taped a telephone conversation with former Secretary of Defense Robert McNamara; he brought this to the attention of his chief adversary—David Boies, a partner in the New York firm of Cravath, Swaine and Moore— who was representing CBS in the litigation. When Crile was asked about it, he acknowledged that he had taped the interview and that he believed the tape either had been lost or erased in the normal course of business so that it could be used again. Burt cried foul and threatened to file a letter with the court, charging that CBS had surreptitiously taped the conversation with McNamara, destroyed the tape and improperly concealed those facts in pretrial proceedings. Incensed by the accusations that he had destroyed the tape and that he and the CBS lawyers were lying, Crile made a thorough search of his home for tapes that he might have overlooked on previous occasions when assembling material pertaining to the broadcast. He found what he was looking for, and then some. His search uncovered a cassette containing part of the conversation with McNamara as well as telephone interviews with George Ball, a former undersecretary of state; Matthew Ridgway, a former Army Chief of Staff; and Arthur Goldberg, a former U.S. ambassador to the United Nations. Crile promptly turned the cassette over to his lawyers.

However, the damage was done, for the confusing sequence of events cast Crile in the worst possible light. In press accounts of this latest development, the suspicion was raised that Crile had purposely concealed the tapes from the CBS lawyers. Moreover, it turned out that the interviews on the newly discovered cassette had been recorded without the permission of the interviewees, and that in McNamara's case, the conversation had been off the record. Since surreptitious taping was a violation of the CBS News guidelines, this latest disclosure brought Crile into direct conflict with his employer—and codefendant. Like many other producers and correspondents at CBS News, Crile had nothing more than a cursory knowledge of the company's guidelines; thus he didn't realize that the surreptitious taping—which, he insisted, was done only for the purpose of accuracy—constituted a violation of those standards. But his superiors were not about to accept ignorance of the rules as a legitimate excuse.

When Sauter learned of this new development, he was furious. Despite his lukewarm and highly qualified support for "The Uncounted Enemy" the previous summer, Sauter had emerged in recent months as one of Crile's strongest defenders, in large part because he was more convinced than ever that the substance of the broadcast—based on Crile's reporting—was thoroughly sound. In fact, he even had approved Crile's request for a challenging new assignment: to produce a documentary on the political and military strife in Nicaragua. Several of his colleagues on the executive level had vigorously opposed this decision, but Sauter took the position that it was better for all concerned to have Crile go to work on a new project. Now,

however, Sauter felt betrayed, so he resorted to disciplinary
action. Five days after Burt first raised the question about the
McNamara tape, Crile was suspended, with full pay, from all
editorial duties at CBS News. As Sauter explained later: "I had
just reached my tipover factor on Crile."

In terms of public perception, suspending Crile was hardly
beneficial to CBS and its litigation in the Westmoreland case.
By taking that action, the management of CBS News seemed
to be saying that it had lost confidence in the man who had
produced "The Uncounted Enemy." Thus, the suspension of
George Crile in June 1983 was perceived as a heavy negative
for both Crile and CBS, and it was at that point that the network's position in its legal battle with General Westmoreland
appeared to hit its lowest point.

In truth, however, surface impressions were misleading. For
during the months when Dan Burt was chalking up flashy,
public-relations victories in the press, his adversary, David
Boies, was quietly scoring critical points on the legal front,
where the contest ultimately would be won or lost. Early on,
he won a change-of-venue motion, moving the case from
Greenville, South Carolina, to New York City. What made this
a crucial victory was not only the fact that South Carolina is
Westmoreland's home state, where he is revered by many as a
hero, but also because certain technicalities in its libel law
make it one of the few states in which lawyers generally concede that the advantage lies with the plaintiff.

But the main reason Boies had become so confident about
the outcome of the litigation is because of the depositions he
had taken. "They could not be stronger," he told a reporter in
the summer of 1983 as he approached the end of his first year
on the case. Among those which he cited with special satisfaction was Westmoreland's deposition, taken in June of that
year, at around the time Burt was celebrating his press coup
over the McNamara tape and Crile's suspension. "Westmoreland said he couldn't remember anything the broadcast said
about him that was unfavorable, except for the word conspiracy," Boies disclosed. "He testified, too, that until the program
he was wholly unaware that people in his command were making charges that numbers had been suppressed, and that he

talked to these people afterwards but didn't ask them about the charges to see if they were true or not."

Actually, ever since the litigation began, some lawyers contended that Westmoreland had no legitimate right to sue for libel. They based their argument on what is known in legal circles as the seditious libel theory: Westmoreland could not sue for criticism of his official conduct, since as a high government official he was one with the government; thus, his suit would be tantamount to the government suing for criticism. According to Boies, no high government official had ever filed such a libel suit before, and he, too, was of the opinion that "Westmoreland is libel-proof."

Still, Boies did not count on dismissal of the suit on that narrow point. Instead, he built his legal fortress on the solid ground of a truth defense, based on the cumulative evidence gleaned from all the depositions he had taken—or what he called "the enormous, unambiguous support for the program." For by the end of 1983, Boies had compiled an imposing dossier of sworn testimony that not only corroborated the documentary's main thesis, but also confirmed most of the fine points and specific details scattered throughout the broadcast. Needless to say, some of the witnesses were men who had already broken their silence and were interviewed, on-camera, for the broadcast. But many others were high-ranking military and civilian intelligence officers who had not appeared on the program. In other words, the case that Boies was building in defense of "The Uncounted Enemy" was substantially stronger than the one that had been presented in the documentary itself.

In early 1984, David Boies was so pleased with the way the litigation was going that he decided to share the good news. Accordingly, he put together a sampling from his treasury of depositions and affidavits, and sent copies to Wallace, Crile, Sauter and other interested parties at CBS so that they would have a clear appreciation of the arsenal they would have on their side when the case finally came to trial. In introducing the excerpts of sworn testimony he had obtained from key witnesses, Boies wrote that "at the heart of this controversy is a simple question: Was there a systematic deception or not? Was the country misled by the intelligence reports issued by

General Westmoreland's command?"

The first witness he quoted was Colonel Gains Hawkins. The colonel was Westmoreland's order-of-battle chief in 1967, which meant he was the officer with primary responsibility for estimating the size of the enemy. In his sworn testimony, Hawkins described his problems in reporting enemy strength:

> I briefed General Westmoreland on our new figures. General Westmoreland would not accept the revised estimates... He voiced concern that the new figures would lead Congress and the American public to think that we had made no progress in the Vietnam war.

Nor did Hawkins shirk his own share of the blame for what happened:

> I certainly believe that I participated in a cover-up. I took figures out of these new estimates and I reduced figures arbitrarily, and I consider this to have been a cover-up. This is what fits my understanding of the word cover-up.

At the same time, he left no doubt who, in his opinion, should bear the ultimate responsibility for the "cover-up":

> Who initiated it? Always you've got to go back up to the top. When the figures were not—when the new figures were not approved by General Westmoreland, he's the man—he's the officer that has to approve this for it to become official, and it was my understanding that this was his wish, that the figure would not exceed the already established levels of enemy strength. So, if you take it from that standpoint, I guess it has to go back to the top man, who was General Westmoreland.

Boies then introduced George Allen, formerly the CIA's most experienced analyst in Vietnam. Allen had been a reluctant whistle-blower, the source whom George Crile decided to interview a second time. And Allen alluded to his reluctance in his sworn testimony:

I feel some sense of guilt on it, yes . . . and that was why I initially was reluctant to get involved in the CBS documentary because of my sense of guilt at having participated in or contributed to or having been an accessory to what in essence was a conspiracy to manipulate the numbers in order to mislead the public on the war in Vietnam.

Allen and Hawkins had been heard from before; both men had been principal players in the CBS broadcast. But then Boies turned to the sworn testimony of high-ranking officials who had not appeared on the program. The first witness he quoted was Colonel J. Barrie Williams, who was the main Vietnam enemy strength analyst for the Joint Chiefs of Staff and a former intelligence chief for the Army's Rapid Deployment Force. Actually Williams had been one of Crile's prime confidential sources during the period when he was gathering information for "The Uncounted Enemy." But he declined to be interviewed for the record, on-camera, mainly because he was still deeply involved in military intelligence. In fact, when Boies took his deposition, Colonel Williams was on active duty as commander of one of the most sensitive intelligence operations in the U.S. military. In his sworn testimony, Williams discussed the "numbers game," which he described as "the machinations that we went through to keep our [enemy] estimates within a given end strength." He elaborated:

My personal belief is I think the policy-makers were misled by the numbers game and I think the American people were misled by the numbers game. Unfortunately, there may have been those of us within our own organizations, and I speak of the defense establishment, who started to believe what we were saying and thereby misled ourselves.

In the course of giving his testimony, Colonel Williams recounted his warning to a fellow officer, who had asked Williams if he would participate in a lawsuit on Westmoreland's behalf:

One of the first calls I got [following the broadcast] was from a Colonel Chuck Thoman, who used to be my boss

at DIA [Defense Intelligence Agency] . . . He wanted to know
if I could refute or would attempt to refute anything that
was said on the show, and I told him, no, that I thought
basically that the show was very accurate and was painting
a picture of what had happened on the numbers as I knew
in my involvement. His comment was, "Well, Danny [Lieu-
tenant General Daniel O. Graham] and I are working with
General Westmoreland and we are thinking of bringing a
class-action suit on this."

My comment, to my recollection, to Chuck at that time
was, "Chuck, you ought to drop this thing because you are
ultimately—you know the substance is true—and you are
merely going to perpetrate something that will be an embarrassment to General Westmoreland and the United States
Army."

Another new voice included in Boies's sampling was that of
Colonel Donald W. Blascak, a career U.S. Army intelligence
officer who had two tours of duty in Vietnam. From 1966
through 1968, he was detailed to work for the CIA in the office
of the Special Assistant for Vietnamese Affairs. When he submitted his affidavit, Colonel Blascak was serving as the chief
intelligence officer for two U.S. Army divisions and an armored
cavalry regiment in West Germany. In his sworn testimony,
Blascak said:

I believe that MACV's deliberate understatement of enemy
strength figures in 1967 and the imposition of a ceiling on
the total enemy strength figure—in which the CIA and the
rest of the intelligence community ultimately acquiesced—
can accurately be characterized as a "conspiracy." A number
of officers, military and civilian, worked consciously and
in concert to present a misleadingly low figure for the total
strength of the enemy forces. Of the officers directly involved in these events, Sam Adams stands alone in having
preserved his values, his objectivity as an intelligence officer
and his integrity intact throughout the process.

Then turning to the question of motivation, Colonel Blascak
sought to explain why the effort was made "to present a misleadingly low figure for the total strength of enemy forces":

I am convinced that the military officers—from the Commander to the intelligence staff officers—who imposed this ceiling and made it stick rationalized the imposition of a ceiling on the enemy strength figures as a means of justifying the continuance of our war effort in Vietnam to a public growing weary of the war and skeptical of our progress in it. Nonetheless, as a career professional intelligence officer, it is disturbing to me that this well-intentioned quest for a successful outcome in the war resulted in a conscious and wrongful distortion of intelligence—for when intelligence officers lose their objectivity and shape their conclusions to support particular policies, the result is not intelligence but propaganda.

A similar point was made by John T. Moore, who had been a CIA intelligence analyst in Saigon from December 1965 to July 1967. His responsibilities in that post included reviewing military reports, captured enemy documents and POW interrogation reports to detect trends in enemy activity. In his sworn testimony, Moore offered this observation:

Based on my experience as a CIA analyst, I have become convinced that there was a conspiracy or cover-up among various elements of the intelligence community, including persons from MACV, CIA and DIA, to distort and to suppress intelligence information during the months prior to the Tet offensive so that the American public would have the impression that we were winning the war.

However, of all the excerpts Boies quoted, none was more compelling, in strictly personal terms, than the sworn testimony of Richard Kovar, who had been on the executive staff of the CIA's Deputy Director for Intelligence (DDI) from 1962 until January 1968. His principal assignment on the DDI staff was to monitor all cables, memoranda and analytical products relating to Vietnam. At the time he submitted his affidavit to Boies, Kovar occupied a sensitive post at the White House. His assignment was to write President Reagan's daily intelligence report. In his testimony Kovar addressed himself to the significance of the broadcast:

I watched the CBS Special Report entitled "The Uncounted Enemy: A Vietnam Deception" when it was broadcast on January 23, 1982. As I watched the story unfold, I found myself cheering aloud much of the time and wanting to weep the rest of the time. For the very first time, I realized with painful clarity that what we had all been involved in was not some abstract academic process but a train of truth versus falsehood that led directly to the debacle of the Tet offensive. Sam Adams had been right, and I and Mr. Helms and Paul Walsh had been wrong. It was not just the CIA versus the Army, but ultimately a matter of truth or consequences, and the consequences had been military and political defeat and death and maiming for untold numbers of Americans and Vietnamese.

Further on in his affidavit, Kovar stated:

I believe that CBS should rebroadcast the documentary in prime time on each anniversary of the Tet offensive so that no one intelligence analyst, soldier or citizen who watches it will ever let anything like this happen again.

All the above excerpts deal with the central question, the one which, in Boies's words, lies "at the heart of the controversy." Was there a systematic deception, a conscious effort to mislead Washington and the American people about the reality of enemy troop strength in Vietnam?

In his sampling Boies also included sworn testimony that pertained to some of the more detailed charges in the broadcast—the specific ways in which the deception or cover-up was carried out. Those quoted statements were grouped under various headings: "The 300,000 Ceiling," "Arbitrary Reduction of Enemy Strength Figures" and "The Suppression of Higher Infiltration Estimates." In these areas too, the testimony was impressively unequivocal in support of the documentary. Then, after summing up the evidence, Boies wrote in conclusion:

"So far as we know, this now constitutes an unprecedented case study of a troublesome phenomenon that has plagued the formulation of American foreign policy in recent years. Put simply, it is that whenever controversial policies are implemented, political pressures tend to be placed on intelligence organizations to come up with reports that justify those policies. It should be remembered that none of the witnesses cited in this document had anything other than honorable records as professional intelligence officers. All wanted to win the war, none were eager to participate in the documentary. They all have come forward, we would submit, in the hopes that by bearing witness to what happened in the past, it would not happen again."

The case of General Westmoreland versus CBS went to trial in October 1984 and, as the battle lines hardened that fall, legal buffs were touting it as the most celebrated case involving a former high-ranking official in the U.S. government since the Alger Hiss perjury trial in 1949. But it hardly lived up to that billing, in large part because the eventual outcome was seldom in doubt (which was certainly not true in the Hiss case), and when it came, the abrupt denouement was almost anticlimactic.

If there was a high point for the prosecution, it came in November during the nine days that Westmoreland was on the stand. At the age of seventy, the general still cut an imposing figure and, to go along with his erect military bearing, he projected all the virtues—patriotism, sincerity, firm resolve—of a West Point man who had devoted most of his life to serving his country in uniform. All of that gave weight to his repeated denials of the charges that had been leveled against him in the CBS documentary and to his countercharge that the media had to bear much of the blame for the failures in Vietnam. There were a few spirited moments during cross-examination when David Boies roughed Westmoreland up a bit, catching him in some telling discrepancies, but even then, Boies had to proceed with care and restraint. If he went too far and appeared to be bullying the retired four-star general, that would not sit well with the jurors, most of whom clearly liked and admired West- moreland.

In an effort to contrast the positive impression Westmoreland made on the jury with a strong, negative impression, Dan Burt called George Crile to the stand as a "hostile" witness. After all, one of the central issues in the dispute was Crile's own character and integrity, and Burt knew that if he could score a few solid points in that area it would certainly help his case. But Crile was ready to take on that challenge. During the nine days of grilling that Burt put him through, George came across as a responsible journalist who was in full command of all the pertinent facts in the case. In his defense of the documentary— and the various decisions that were made in putting it to- gether—Crile was calm, lucid and thorough to a fault. In fact, on a couple of occasions, the presiding judge, Pierre Leval, felt obliged to rebuke him for his lengthy responses, for elab- orating on matters in a way that, at times, went beyond the scope of the questions that were put to him. But even that tendency reflected a zeal that, to some observers, only made Crile a more persuasive witness.

But Crile was, if anything, even more persuasive a few weeks later when he returned to the stand as a witness for the defense. It was then that the trial reached its moment of high drama. To make the most of Crile's testimony, Boies chose to show the entire documentary, from start to finish, stopping the tape at key intervals along the way to have George explain precisely why this or that had been done in a certain way, or why such-and-such had been used at that particular point in the narrative. It was during this long and detailed presentation that the jury saw George Crile at his best, and by the time he finished his testimony, predictions began to circulate, in and around the courtroom, that CBS was likely to win its case on the firm rock of a truth defense.

Then came the icing on the cake: the testimony of General Joseph McChristian and Colonel Gains Hawkins, the two, high- ranking, intelligence officers from Westmoreland's own com- mand, whose revelations had been so compelling when they appeared on "The Uncounted Enemy." Now, in the fourth month of the trial, they came forward to reiterate, under oath, all that they had said on the broadcast—and then some. For in their court testimony, the two officers went into even more detail about the deception that was carried out under General West- moreland's command.

The testimony of McChristian and Hawkins had a devas- tating effect on Westmoreland who, in preparing for the trial, had managed to persuade himself that he would be spared that ordeal. Despite what McChristian and Hawkins had said on the broadcast and in pretrial depositions, Westmoreland and his lawyer still clung to the belief that when push came to shove, the two officers would not go on the stand at the trial and point the finger of blame at their former commander. And when they did precisely that, it took all the fight out of Westmoreland. More than anything else, it was their testimony that prompted the general to throw in the towel.

On February 17, 1985—just two days before Mike Wallace was to make his first appearance on the stand and only one week before the case was to go to the jury—Westmoreland suddenly withdrew his $120 million libel suit against CBS. And just like that, it was all over. When Westmoreland's decision was made public, many of his conservative supporters reacted with shock and dismay. They had been pulling for him to win "revenge" against the network, and now some of them felt that the general had wilted under pressure and had deserted the cause. But Westmoreland knew what he was doing. He realized that the trial was going solidly against him and thus there was no point in drawing it out to its formal and official verdict. Westmoreland's big mistake was not withdrawing when he did, but rather his decision to initiate the costly libel suit in the first place. And in that respect, his legal action stands as a parable of the U.S. involvement in Vietnam. The mistake was not pulling out of Vietnam when we did, the tragedy was that we ever allowed ourselves to get caught up in that quagmire.

There is an old Chinese curse that, to less subtle Western ears, sounds more like a benediction: "May you live in interesting times." But accepting the way this proverb is understood in China, there is no doubt that for Mike Wallace, the early 1980s were "interesting times," a period during which he was caught up in one dilemma after another: first, the flap over Haiti, then the watermelon-and-tacos incident, and, following swiftly on the heels of that episode, the controversy over the West-moreland broadcast that escalated into a multimillion-dollar libel suit. Thus, at a stage in his career when, by all rights, he should have been able to glide along serenely on his reputation and the laurels he had earned, Wallace had to defend himself against charges of misconduct, both on and off the air.

Yet it would be misleading to suggest that those difficulties were anything more than distractions, bumps on the road which had no adverse effect on the rest of his work. For in all other respects, his professional life as the premier correspondent on *60 Minutes* continued to flourish. And, as had been his wont since the early years of the broadcast, Wallace still covered stories and people on a wide variety of fronts, from politics to the arts, and from trouble spots abroad to investigative subjects at home.

He continued to keep an eye on Washington, although events there did not engage his attention the way they had a decade earlier when the Watergate scandal was driving a stake through the heart of Richard Nixon's presidency. In the fall of 1981, he did a piece on what had become that year's number one social issue—the antiabortion or right-to-life movement—and the man who was leading that crusade in Congress, Representative Henry Hyde. A few weeks later, as Nancy Reagan neared the end of her first year in the White House, Mike interviewed the First Lady, his old friend from his early radio days in Chicago, whom he had known longer than her husband had. And soon thereafter, he did a story on another woman who had emerged as a strong and influential voice in the Reagan Administration: the outspoken ambassador to the United Nations, Jeane Kirkpatrick. Then in the fall of 1983, as American voters braced themselves for the onslaught of another presidential campaign, Wallace interviewed the man who was about to carry the banner of black power into the mainstream of national politics—the Reverend Jesse Jackson. In fact, it was on that *60 Minutes* broadcast that Jackson publicly announced his candidacy for the Democratic presidential nomination.

Wallace also continued to seek diversion in lighter personality pieces, profiles of celebrities in the arts and other back-of-the-book fields. Most of his more recent stories in this genre were about women. In the spring of 1981, he did a piece on Dr. Mary Calderone, the controversial sex counselor (it was called "Dirty Old Woman"), and another the following year on the reigning queen of tennis, Martina Navratilova. Then during the 1983–1984 season, he took a close look at two of the country's most prominent actresses: Helen Hayes, the *grande dame* of the American theater, and Shirley MacLaine, whose stunning performance in the film *Terms of Endearment*—and the Oscar she won for it—gave her career a dramatic boost. There also was a rare, two-part profile of a much different kind of celebrity, a man who, though a household name in certain circles, had lived for years behind a thick veil of secrecy and had never before consented to be interviewed on television. The fascinating subject of that one was the longtime Mafia chieftain, Joseph Bonanno, whose "real-life" story bore a striking resemblance to the dark fictional world portrayed in *The Godfather*.

In the meantime, Wallace's heavily stamped passport continued to take a beating at airport counters around the world. As one would expect, he made several more trips to his favorite overseas stamping ground—the Middle East. In the fall of 1981, he flew to Beirut, where on his two previous visits he had aroused the displeasure of some members of Yasir Arafat's Palestine Liberation Organization. Wallace was drawn to the Lebanese capital that fall by the promise of an exclusive interview with Frank Terpil, the former CIA agent who in recent years had been an adviser to Uganda's Idi Amin and Libya's Muammar Qaddafi. In that interview Terpil talked for the first time in public about his relationships with Amin and Qaddafi, the world of international arms sales, and charges of bribery and corruption in the U.S. intelligence community. At the time, Terpil was wanted back in the States, from where he had fled after being convicted and sentenced to fifty-three years for illegal possession of weapons he intended to sell to terrorists. Mike also made two trips to Israel in the early 1980s. The high point of one of them was an interview with Jacobo Timmerman, the Argentine writer and ardent Zionist who, after emigrating to Tel Aviv, wrote a highly critical book about Israel's invasion of Lebanon in the summer of 1982. On the other visit, he did a story on what day-to-day life was like for Arabs then living in Israel, a sort of companion piece to the controversial Jews-in-Syria broadcast a few years earlier. And in Janaury 1984, after the U.S. Marine peacekeeping force had been drawn into the civil war in Lebanon, Wallace returned to Damascus to film a report on the Lebanese conflict from Syria's point of view—a story that provoked a fresh round of criticism from pro-Israeli factions.

Also during this period, he traveled to the two major powers in the Communist world. He returned from China in 1981 with two stories, both of which focused on that country's enormous population. One of them was called "One Billion Consumers," and the other was entitled "The Largest Army in the World." Then in early 1984 he flew to Moscow to do a story on *Pravda*, the Communist party newspaper and the Soviet Union's answer to a free press.

Finally, he returned to Vietnam in 1982, his first visit to that forlorn country since the end of the war seven years earlier. That journey also resulted in two separate stories on *60 Minutes*. One—"Vietnam Revisited"—was a general look at life under Communist rule in Hanoi and Ho Chi Minh City, formerly known as Saigon. The other one was a human-interest piece on the children who had been fathered by American GIs and who, along with their Vietnamese mothers, had been left behind in Vietnam. Called "Honor Thy Children," that broadcast caused quite a stir, and one of its aftereffects was to ease the red-tape restrictions that had been thwarting the earnest efforts of those men who were yearning to be reunited in America with their Vietnamese wives and children. Moreover, Wallace and the producer, Barry Lando, won an Alfred I. Du Pont Columbia Award for "Honor Thy Children."

Actually that was one of two *60 Minutes* stories Wallace did that year which received a Du Pont Award. The other one, produced by Ira Rosen, was an exposé of drug trafficking and cover-up in the Chicago police force. Called "Good Cop, Bad Cop," it was just one of many investigative pieces broadcast in the early eighties as Wallace and his team of producers continued to mine the vein that, a few years earlier, had done so much to change the tone and complexion of *60 Minutes*. They did a report on a Hughes Aircraft employee who had sold secret company plans to a Polish Communist agent. They did one on Nazi infiltrators who had managed to slip into the United States after World War II and, in the years since then, had enjoyed the blessings of life in America. They investigated charges that employers at the I. Magnin department store were guilty of practicing age discrimination, and that chemicals had turned the Niagara River into an "industrial sewer." They looked into allegations of toxic waste at a Long Island dump site, and of fraud and waste in the U.S. Navy's shipbuilding program. There also were investigative pieces that dealt directly with consumer concerns. Included in this category were reports on the adverse side effects of such products as Selacryn, a new drug for high blood pressure; Oraflex, a new drug for arthritis; and chlordane, a pesticide used as protection against termites.

In putting together those and other stories in the investigative sphere, Wallace and his production team adhered to the pattern that had been established in the early and middle 1970s. His field producers would do most of the research and preliminary legwork; then, when the time came to confront the alleged transgressors, Mike would arrive on the scene and take over the interviews. By the early 1980s, many business executives had become so apprehensive about a face-to-face encounter with Wallace or some other aggressive television interviewer that they enrolled in special courses set up to help them cope with that ordeal. For by that time, newly formed firms, such as the Executive Television Workshop, were offering training programs in how to respond to the probing questions of investigative reporters on television. Thanks in large part to *60 Minutes*, this service proved to be an enterprising idea whose time had come, and the men who ran those programs—some of whom, incidentally, were refugees from the television news business—soon found themselves presiding over thriving concerns. For his part, Wallace—who was used or cited as the ultimate model, the *bête noire* in many of the mock interrogations—became so intrigued by the success of the workshops that in 1983, he and producer Grace Diekhaus decided to do a story on them. The results of their efforts was a rather amusing *60 Minutes* piece called "Camera Shy." That's what appeared on the air, but within the shop, everyone called it something else. In fact, the working title for that story when it was being put together was "Mike Fright."

Two men who chose to meet the challenge of "Mike Fright" head-on were Joe and Bill Coors, the proprietors of Coors beer. In 1982, Wallace and producer Allan Maraynes set out to do an investigative story on that Colorado brewery. They were drawn to the subject by a raft of allegations that the Coors brothers were antiblack, antiwoman and antihomosexual in their hiring practices, and that they treated their employees unfairly—at times even inhumanely. When they began to work on this assignment, Wallace and Maraynes suspected that at least some of the charges were true, and that the report would be critical of the way the Coors brothers ran their company. Yet in the course of their investigation, they discovered that just the opposite was true: that Coors was not discriminatory in its hiring practices. Almost without exception, the workers they interviewed at the brewery were happy in their jobs and regarded the Coors family as benevolent employers. In fact, the more deeply they delved into the story, the more Wallace and Maraynes came to realize that Coors had been a victim of a systematic campaign that, for the most part, had been orchestrated by labor-union leaders who were furious at the Coors brothers because they had managed to persuade most of their employees to work without a union. Thus, it was the critics of Coors rather than the brewery that came under heavy fire on *60 Minutes*. This was yet another example of a reporting team starting out with a certain premise and then being led, by the facts encountered along the way, toward an altogether different conclusion.

The Coors piece was called "Trouble Brewing," and it ran on *60 Minutes* in the fall of 1982. The following spring, when the program began airing reruns of its best stories from the previous season, "Trouble Brewing" was one of the first to be rebroadcast. And a few days after that rerun, Joe Coors placed an advertisement in several leading newspapers across the country. As newspaper ads go, it was a striking departure from the norm. It began with a large and dramatic headline that proclaimed: "The four most dreaded words in the English language: MIKE WALLACE IS HERE." Then, after hooking the reader with that grabber, Joe Coors proceeded to recall what happened:

When Mike Wallace and the *60 Minutes* crew showed up and said they wanted to do a story on Coors, I figured I had just two choices:

     1. Tell them to go away (knowing they'd probably do a story on us anyway).

2. Throw open the entire brewery to them (and see what happened).

I chose the second course of action. I told Mike that he was free to go anywhere in our brewery and talk to anybody about anything.

If you saw the *60 Minutes* rerun last Sunday, you saw what happened.

He then gave a brief synopsis of the *60 Minutes* story on Coors and concluded the ad with these words:

We didn't sponsor it. We had no say in what they said about us. But we think what Mike and his people found out about Coors is of interest to anyone who likes good beer.
And the truth.

In the meantime, the CBS management had taken steps to make sure that "Mike Wallace is here" continued to be recognized as "the four most dreaded words in the English language." A few weeks before the Coors ad appeared, Wallace turned sixty-five. And as he passed that milestone, a new contract went into effect that would keep him on *60 Minutes* for the next five years, although it did give him the option of cutting down and slackening his pace a bit if he so desired. Wallace had not anticipated that turn of events, and with good reason. For the new contract he signed was a matter of no small significance, since it constituted a sharp break with company tradition.

CBS had a long-standing policy of mandatory retirement at the age of sixty-five, and it had been rigorously enforced over the years, even when it concerned the network's top correspondents. For example, both Eric Sevareid and Charles Collingwood, two stalwarts from the Murrow years who had helped to establish CBS as the perennial leader in broadcast journalism, were obliged to retire when they reached sixty-five. And it was no coincidence that Walter Cronkite was approaching his sixty-fifth birthday when he stepped down as anchorman on the *CBS Evening News,* although in his case, the decision was largely voluntary. (Moreover, after relinquishing that anchor chair to Dan Rather, Cronkite moved into the role of Special Correspondent and continued to appear on CBS News broadcasts, albeit not on a regular basis.) So Wallace was the happy recipient of an unprecedented honor. When he signed the new contract in 1983 he became the first correspondent in the history of CBS News who was authorized to remain on duty, in a competitive and fully active role, past the age of sixty-five.

The decision to keep him working on *60 Minutes* had nothing to do with sentiment or with personal affection for Wallace. Instead, it had everything to do with economics. Ever since the broadcast made its big breakthrough in the mid-1970s, the executives in charge of prime-time programming at CBS had been more than a little puzzled by the extraordinary success of *60 Minutes*. In their restless search for popular shows that would score well in the ratings, they were accustomed, by years of ingrained habit, to think in terms of entertainment vehicles, not news programs. But even though they did not entirely understand what made *60 Minutes* tick so well, year in and year out, they were savvy enough to recognize that Wallace's presence on the program had a great deal to do with its enduring success. Thus, when the moment of truth came in 1983 and they had to make a choice between tradition and revenues, the executives at CBS were not about to retire the goose that kept delivering such golden eggs.

CHAPTER

EIGHTEEN

THE POPULARITY of our broadcast *has* baffled many people, both within and outside the television industry, and so I might as well begin this summing up with an attempt to answer the question that has been asked so often in recent years: Why has *60 Minutes* captured such a large and loyal audience? I've read a couple of college theses on the subject and I've heard it debated over coffee at dinner parties; in addition, many of the people who write about television for a living haven't hesitated to give us the benefit of their expertise, as well as to caution us not to let success go to our collective head. And I'm sure you won't be surprised to learn that within our own shop, we've batted the question around in office bull sessions. So here, for whatever it's worth, is my opinion.

First of all, we were blessed by a happy combination of timing and circumstance. As you read in an earlier chapter, back in the winter of 1973–1974, when the Arabs were imposing their oil embargo, millions of Americans were forced to stay home on Sundays simply because they didn't have enough gas to justify casual outings or social visits to the homes of friends and relatives. Desperate for diversion after they finished reading the Sunday papers, they began to fiddle around with the television dial—and there we were. Yet just as important was the fact that we were now ready to be discovered by them. That was our sixth season on the air, and by then we had ironed out most of the kinks that had plagued us in the early going. Thus, when the time came for *60 Minutes* to take on the challenge of holding on to that large wave of new viewers, we more or less had our act together.

What we had to offer those who stumbled on us by accident, as they turned to television to relieve their boredom, was a different kind of news program. Yes, it was serious, and yes, it dealt with important issues. But it was also more personal because we chose to focus on people rather than on events and issues, and that, I believe, helped to make our stories more engrossing. This emphasis on personality also extended to the correspondents. It was just Morley and me in those days, and we began to sense a change in the perception of the broadcast as many viewers gradually came to identify with us, to see the stories we were reporting through our eyes.

There was yet another phenomenon, peculiar to that winter of 1973–1974, which clearly worked to our advantage. The wind of Watergate had been blowing out of Washington since the previous spring, and had stimulated a fresh appetite for news in general and, even more so, for the kind of stories we were doing. For by then, we had ventured into the combat zone of investigative reporting, and at a time when so many Americans were caught up in the Watergate obsession, it certainly didn't hurt to be perceived as muckrakers or ombudsmen who were blowing the whistle on other acts of fraud and corruption. Still, there was much more to our repertoire than muckraking and investigative pieces, which was something our growing audience understood and appreciated. Indeed, we heard from viewers who let us know that they didn't give a hoot about kickback schemes or phony health clinics. But they continued to tune us in because they wanted to see our reports and interviews from foreign capitals, or our profiles of actors and musicians, or Morley's urbane essays on the sundry human foibles he discovered in his travels at home and abroad. All that enabled us to strike a responsive chord in living rooms across America, and as word-of-mouth and a lot more attention in the press came into play, we proceeded to build a new and sturdy base of viewers. So much so that two years later, when we were tossed into the pressure cooker of prime time, we had the momentum we needed to take that perilous leap in stride.

Yet having said all this, I confess that there are times when I still find it hard to believe. Anyone who has been in television as long as I have (and I go back to the beginning, to the period that David Brinkley, another old-timer, once referred to as "the mists of the forties") knows only too well that the prime-time merchants in our business have almost always viewed news programs with undisguised disdain. They resented the existence of documentaries and the like because they were the traditional loss leader, the soft underbelly in an otherwise lucrative prime-time schedule. Among other things, the enduring success of *60 Minutes* has jabbed a thumb in the eye of that conventional wisdom. Yet even though I've lived through it and been a part of it, I really never expected to see the day when a news broadcast would consistently challenge the most popular entertainment shows in the weekly ratings. However, that is what happened and I think it will continue to happen. After all, unlike *Dallas* and *The A-Team,* we don't have to worry about running out of plots or exhausting our story line. The nature of news and the kind of features we do provide the regenerative tonic that keeps *60 Minutes* going; it's a large and diverse world out there, and there is always plenty of new material. So, as long as we, as a group, maintain our competitive edge and our enthusiasm for going after fresh and provocative stories, I'm confident that *60 Minutes* will survive—and flourish—long after I have shuffled off into the sunset and the retirement that some critics seem to feel is long overdue.

Ah yes, the critics. Actually, we have little reason to complain about the press coverage we've received over the years. Most of it has been favorable, and some of it enlightening. But inevitably, as we grew more popular and evolved into an established hit, reviewers began to cast a more baleful eye in our direction. As soon as we were perceived as big shots, we became inviting targets for potshots. I'm not going to respond to all the brickbats that have come our way, but there are three in particular that have recurred often in recent years. Since they seem to be the main objections to *60 Minutes* (and since you may have read or heard them, too) let me address myself to them.

(1) *Show Biz:* A common criticism is that we are in show

business, not journalism. Some of that frankly smacks of journalistic elitism, the kind of attitude that frowns on any story that is not important with a capital I and serious with a capital S. To those who think that way, every time we do a celebrity profile or some other soft, back-of-the-book feature, we are being "trivial" and are "wasting" the precious air time that has been granted to *60 Minutes*. Nonsense. We are, after all, a magazine broadcast that is committed to a multisubject format, and we have never pretended to be anything else.

Yet even some critics who concede that point accuse us of being trivial in our treatment of serious subjects because of the way we "dramatize" or "sensationalize" them. This gets back to what I wrote earlier about the effort we make to focus on people rather than issues or events. There's no denying that we go after the most articulate, the most persuasive, the most villainous and the most effective way to deal with complex subjects—like chemical warfare, the insanity plea, new economic theories or the question of safety in nuclear power plants— is to place them in the context of graphic and compelling stories, stories told engrossingly by the participants, the people who have first-hand knowledge of the tale we're telling. If that's show biz, then so be it.

(2) *Ambush Interviews:* A notion has taken root in certain quarters that whenever we do an investigative story, invariably a point comes when a *60 Minutes* reporting team can be found lurking outside someone's home or office, eager to pounce on our "quarry" with sadistic glee in order to satisfy the lust of our viewers for public humiliation. Such a view of what we do is a trifle overdrawn, to say the least. Don't get me wrong: I plead guilty to having done my share of so-called ambush or "confrontation" interviews over the years, and I have not hesitated to defend that tactic when I thought it was warranted. If nothing else, it has served as a graphic demonstration of the lengths to which some miscreants will go to avoid being asked, on-camera, about their transgressions. And at other times, it has been more than that. For example, when we walked into that Hollywood diploma mill and confronted the proprietor with the evidence of his illegal activities, it was not only good television, it was also enterprising reportage. Taken unawares, he blurted out the truth about his operation and eventually went

to jail. We achieved similar results with the shady character who ran that phony cancer clinic in California, and with the young hustler from GLACAA who was ripping off federal funds that had been allocated for the poverty program in Los Angeles.

But the notoriety we gained from those stories (which inspired the not-so-funny joke that "you know it's going to be a blue Monday when you arrive at your office and find a *60 Minutes* crew there waiting for you") has had its effect. We no longer have the element of surprise going for us, and, in adjusting to that, we discovered that we can do our reporting just as effectively without resorting to the dramatic ploy of an unexpected confrontation. Forsaking the ambush interview has not impaired our ability to turn out solid investigative reports. And I trust that one of these days our print brethren, the critics who watch over us, will take the trouble to acknowledge that we haven't "ambushed" anyone in several years.

(3) *Tendentious Editing:* There is no doubt that any story, in either print or broadcast journalism, can be edited to conform to a certain point of view, or that any of the interviews within a story can be cut and manipulated to reflect that bias. But if a correspondent, producer or film editor on *60 Minutes*—or even all three working in tandem—were to try to impose his or her political, social or economic bias on a story, it wouldn't stand a chance of succeeding because of the "fail-safe" procedure that governs every piece put on the air. Here's how it works: After a correspondent and producer have returned from the field with all the raw film of a given story, a "rough cut" (a long and tentative version of the piece) is shown to Executive Producer Don Hewitt and Senior Producer Phil Scheffler. Since they have not been involved in the reporting, Hewitt and Scheffler bring fresh eyes to that footage, and they specifically look for signs of bias or unfairness or imbalance. If they spot any, they point them out and issue the appropriate warning. Then later, a "fine cut" is screened not only by Hewitt and Scheffler, but also by the CBS News vice-president in charge of our operation, who at that stage brings another pair of fresh eyes to the story. (Five executives have occupied that position over the years, starting with Bill Leonard when we first went on the air; the latest man to be entrusted with the responsibility is Eric

Ober, who was appointed to the post in early 1984.) Therefore, in order for an overtly biased report to appear on *60 Minutes*, everyone from the executive level down would have to be in on the fix—and this simply doesn't happen.

I don't mean to suggest that errors or misrepresentations don't slip into our stories from time to time, but when they do, almost always they're the result of omission, carelessness or poor judgment—but not calculation. We're far from perfect in the way we go about our business. You certainly know by now that I have not always behaved wisely or properly and some of the blunders I've committed have been beauts. And I'm not alone. You can be sure that a warts-and-all portrayal of anyone who has labored long in this craft would include at least a few blemishes.

Not long ago, my former CBS News colleague, Dan Schorr (who in recent years has been working for the Cable News Network), came up with the observation that "we aren't the good guys anymore." Dan seemed to be yearning for the "good old days" of the Watergate period (he did a lot of reporting on that story) when there was a widespread perception of the press as the noble posse that went after the outlaws and brought them to bay. Well, speaking strictly for myself, I don't think it's accurate, nor does it serve our best interest to be perceived as the good guys, the all-virtuous knights in shining armor, for the inescapable truth is that we can get carried away with our own sense of self-importance. At our worst, we who work as journalists (especially those of us who report for powerful institutions like CBS News) can be arrogant and self-righteous, too willing to assume that we are always on the side of angels and too ready to suspect the motives of those we scrutinize.

At the same time, we have to guard against tilting the other way. Indeed, some of our detractors contend that once *60 Minutes* became entrenched as a perennial hit, we began to lose our edge and play it safe. According to this view, we have become so complacent that we have allowed ourselves to be drawn inside the tent, to become part of the establishment, in league with the status quo. I don't buy that. Again, speaking only for myself, I don't think I've lost any enthusiasm for the chase, for going after the kind of stories that fly in the face of conventional wisdom. Nor have I lost the healthy skepticism that I try to bring to every story I cover. But I'd hate to see that skepticism curdle into cynicism. Maintaining the delicate balance between the two is not easy, and that's one reason why I genuinely welcome criticism, as long as it is well meant. Since we make such a big fuss about our role as watchdogs in a free and open society, we would be hypocrites if we resented those who take us to task when we step out of line.

But there are times, unfortunately, when the criticism is clearly not constructive. Like the rest of my colleagues, I was dismayed by the largely inaccurate broadsides launched against Dan Rather and *60 Minutes* during the Dr. Carl Galloway libel trial in the spring of 1983. It was as though many of our peers (especially in the print media) had decided that we had become too big for our britches. So, instead of concentrating on the merits of the case, they seemed to take delight in the fact that *60 Minutes* had been drawn into a highly publicized legal fight. Well, we won that case; in fact, so far we have prevailed in every libel action that has been brought against us over the years, and there have been more than a hundred such actions. Most of them have been nothing more than nuisance suits that were easily dispensed with out of court, and the others were decided in our favor by juries or withdrawn by the plaintiff during trial.

That, in effect, is what happened with General Westmoreland. To everyone's surprise, he withdrew his suit just two days before I was scheduled to testify and a week before the jury was scheduled to begin its deliberations. Why did he withdraw? The only plausible explanation I can think of is that he had come to understand that the jurors would decide against him on truth, and that would have caused him extraordinary pain. They had heard his fellow West Pointer, General Joseph McChristian, label as "improper" Westmoreland's 1967 actions with respect to enemy-strength estimates. They had heard his Order of Battle Chief, Colonel Gains Hawkins, tell them that he had followed command instructions he knew to be "dishonest." Beyond that, Westmoreland's lead lawyer, Dan Burt, had read the language Judge Pierre Leval planned to use in his charge to the jury, language that, in view of the testimony of our defense witnesses, made it apparent that CBS would win. The general, in my opinion, simply decided to cut his losses and get out.

Strangely, during the four months we spent in that cold and drafty courtroom in New York, I came to have a certain sympathy for the general. Despite the pain and difficulty he had triggered with his law suit, I began to feel—as the months went by—that he was simply the captive of bad advice from Dan Burt who, along with the wealthy aficionados of the right wing who funded the libel action, was "using" Westmoreland as a stick with which to beat the news media in general and CBS News in particular.

The general's wife, Kitsy, attended court every day, knitting her way through hours and hours of complicated testimony. She is a warm and delightful woman and we became friends of a sort. When the trauma of the trial plus a bout with the flu put me in the hospital for ten days with what was labeled "nervous exhaustion," she and the general sent me flowers. By that time we three had become companions in misery, daily spectators at the live autopsy that a libel trial can become.

By the time the proceedings were aborted and the jury was discharged, we'd even gotten to the point of planning for a dinner some months down the road, to—in Westmoreland's words—"let it all hang out." By the time this book is published, I've no doubt the general and I will have broken bread together and exchanged candid views on the imprecision of military intelligence and fairness in the media, plus sundry, related subjects.

On that score, let me return now to the critics of *60 Minutes* who contend that we are guided by ulterior or even dishonest motives in the stories we do and the way we edit them. It simply is not true that we approach a story—any story—with an ideological ax to grind. Perhaps I should say that any reporter who *does* bring that kind of baggage into his work has no chance of lasting very long. I don't know anyone in our business who doesn't recognize that our most precious commodity is our credibility, and every time we slip up and jeopardize that, we do so at our peril. As for the charge of bias that has been leveled specifically at *60 Minutes*, Don Hewitt has responded with his customary vigor. In an article published in the "My

Turn" column in *Newsweek* in the summer of 1983, Hewitt
wrote:

> We are nobody's darling. If you don't believe it, ask the
> World Jewish Congress and the PLO, both of which have
> at various times held us in contempt. Ask the Pentagon,
> which refuses to speak to us, or the Gay Rights people, who
> can't make up their minds whether to mount an attack against
> us or give us an award. Ask the National Council of Churches
> and the National Rifle Association, both of which think we
> are in league with the devil. Ask the Irish Republican Army,
> which thinks we are Fascists, and the South African gov-
> ernment, which thinks we are Marxists. Ask Henry Kissin-
> ger or Muammar Qaddafi. For that matter, ask Menachem
> Begin what he thinks, and then ask Yasir Arafat the same
> question. You could have done the same with the Shah and
> the Ayatollah. On that score, how it must confound the
> critics that Joe Coors, I. F. Stone, Jeane Kirkpatrick and
> George Kennan all thought they were treated fairly by *60
> Minutes*.

As you may have noticed, this is not the first time I have
brought Hewitt's voice into this narrative to buttress a point or
clear the air about something or other. After all, he's been
chirping in my ear in his exuberant way day in and day out for
the past sixteen years, and I can't pretend that he hasn't had
some influence on my work or, for that matter, on how I have
chosen to view that work. As the founding father of *60 Minutes*,
as well as the steadfast defender of the faith and keeper of the
flame, Hewitt's vital and various contributions to the broadcast
have been well documented in this book. Beyond that, I would
like to say that he is one of three men—all of them producers—
who came into my life at critical points and formed strong
working relationships with me that were not only productive
at the time, but also had positive and lasting effects on much
that followed. The other two are Ted Yates and Av Westin.

If Yates had not been at Channel 5 back in 1956, it's almost
certain that *Night Beat*—which was his idea—would not have
come into existence. And of course it was in those interviews
on *Night Beat* that I found the tone and style which, for better

or worse, have been my trademarks ever since. Then later, in 1963, when I came to work for CBS News with a suspect reputation—as the man who had appeared in cigarette commercials and on dubious entertainment shows—I was given a chance to prove myself as anchorman on a new broadcast, the *CBS Morning News*. The executive producer of that program was Westin, and the solid partnership we formed was perhaps the main reason why the *Morning News* was a success. This success enabled me to win acceptance from those new colleagues who, a few months earlier, had greeted my arrival in their midst with skepticism and disdain. And in 1968, it was Hewitt who badgered me into giving up full-time political reporting and going to work for the new magazine broadcast he was preparing to put on the air, a project that I thought at the time had little chance of even getting off the drawing board. I must say that I find it hard to believe that seventeen years have passed since that day in the spring of 1968 when Don descended on me, his eyes ablaze, and launched into his sales pitch: "You and Reasoner will be just great together. Harry will be the white hat and you'll wear the black hat."

Yet he remains today what he was then: the driving force and spirit behind *60 Minutes*, the engine that keeps it—and us—running in high gear. To me, Hewitt's most endearing trait is his almost naïve tendency to believe the best about most of the people who work on the broadcast. However, because he truly does believe in their talent and commitment, he is able to draw the very best out of them; at times, he even induces them to outdo themselves, to demonstrate that they are better than they thought they were. Don hates meetings or any kind of formal atmosphere. His rich and irreverent humor sets the tone in our shop and serves as a constant reminder to the rest of us that there is no place in it for pompous prima donnas who take themselves too seriously. Most remarkable of all, he still brings to his work, even after all these years, an unabashed, even childlike enthusiasm. During a television career that dates back to 1948, Hewitt has had to look at miles upon miles of film footage, and yet on any given day he will come bounding out of a screening room in high flush, eager to proclaim to everyone within earshot that he has just viewed another gem, another small classic that will add more luster to the reputation of *60 Minutes*. Sometimes he's right, but even when he's not, it's nice to know that we have that kind of spirit and support behind us.

As for my on-air colleagues, I have little to add to what you've already read. When I joined CBS News in 1963, no one was more openly scornful of my presence there than Harry Reasoner. But he also was one of the first to admit that he had misjudged me, and once we got all that settled, we became friends—and have been good friends ever since. When Harry left us in 1970 to pursue his lot at ABC, I was truly sorry to see him go, in large part because I knew I would miss his companionship, but also because I was more than a little concerned about the effect his departure would have on the broadcast. One reason we were able to sustain the loss of Reasoner so well was because of the way Morley Safer moved into his slot and put his distinctive stamp on the program.

It is common knowledge in our shop that Morley and I have had our differences over the years, tensions that grew out of competition for stories, for producers and for turf within the domain of *60 Minutes*. But I'm happy to say that in the past couple of years, those frictions have diminished to the point where they scarcely exist anymore, largely because neither of us feels he has as much to prove as he did when we first began to work together. We both have left indelible marks on the broadcast, and we know it. And by the way, those fights we used to have were never over the question of professional competence. Morley knows full well that even when we were quarreling or barely speaking to each other, I always had the utmost respect and admiration for the quality of his work.

Back in 1975, when I finally persuaded Don Hewitt that Morley and I needed help—another correspondent to share the load—we all agreed that the one we wanted was Dan Rather. I never really understood why Dan was at first so reluctant to accept the offer, but I'm certainly glad that he eventually decided to cast his lot with us. Dan brought a strong new voice and presence to the broadcast and helped to take us to the promised land when we made the shift back into prime time in 1976. Working on *60 Minutes* during the middle and late seventies didn't exactly hurt him either. As it turned out, Rather's sojourn with us was the last leg in his long journey up the mountain at CBS News. He reached the summit in 1981 when he was chosen to succeed Walter Cronkite as anchorman on the *CBS Evening News*. And nowadays, if we crane our necks, we can catch glimpses of him up there, reigning serenely over all he surveys. I'm told that it's lonely at the top, but Dan seems to be bearing up well.

By the time Rather left us, Reasoner had returned to *60 Minutes;* and so, to fill the vacant slot in our quartet, we brought in Ed Bradley. Ed had lobbied for the job, but he did so gracefully, which didn't surprise me because I knew him to be a graceful man. He has other impressive qualities, too: a quiet strength and authority as well as, when the occasion suits him, a mischievous sense of humor. As you've read, Ed demonstrated that shortly after he came to work for us in 1981 when he hoodwinked Hewitt into believing that he had become a Muslim and had changed his name to Shahib Shahab. And now, of course, Diane Sawyer has joined us. During the years we'd been on the air without a female comrade, we had yearned for one. We had been asked dozens of times why, in these years of the belated accession of women to all manner of jobs, had *60 Minutes* remained virgin. The fact is that early on—three or four years after we first went on the air—a remarkably capable woman was set to join Morley and me as a correspondent on the program. Her name was Michelle Clark and she had earned the nod through her savvy, determined and knowledgeable reporting, especially on politics. But tragically, her life was cut short in a plane crash in Chicago.

After that, somehow, events conspired to deny us a woman—until Diane. Her versatility, her background in politics (she served in the press office of the Nixon White House), her stint covering the State Department for CBS News, and her "iron fist in a velvet glove" made her an ideal choice for us. In Diane's first season on *60 Minutes*, she reported from locales as varied as the parched deserts of Mali to the posh, Southampton premises of Gloria Vanderbilt. Diane travels well in all kinds of stories.

So now there are the five of us—Morley, Harry, Ed, Diane and me—and I think that "mix" is about as varied and interesting as it can get. We do differ from each other, but mainly in style, not substance. We are all generalists who can cover every kind of story, from hard news and investigative pieces to profiles and other features. The proof of *that* is the fact that the five of us *do* take on all kinds of stories, varying our diet from one dish to the next as we move through a long season of broadcasts.

I say the five of us, but in reality there are six. Indeed, to hear Andy Rooney tell it, the rest of us are mere scene-setters, preliminary acts sent out to warm up the audience for the main event: those "few minutes" of wry diversion that Rooney provides at the end of the broadcast.

Andy has been kicking around television almost as long as I have, though during most of those years he worked behind the scenes as a writer. He wrote for Arthur Godfrey back in the fifties and for Harry Reasoner during the sixties. (He obviously had the kind of talent that was suited to performers who specialized in the folksy and the quaint.) Then in the early seventies, Andy began to venture forth from behind his typewriter and deliver his own stuff on the air. Once he became convinced that the camera was not going to bite him, he began to relax, and a few years later, when Hewitt finally decided that Rooney had an appealing on-air presence, he brought him onto *60 Minutes*. Right from the start, Andy's deceptively simple commentaries struck a responsive chord in our audience, and now this professional curmudgeon is insisting that *he's* the main reason for the show's success.

Rooney and the rest of us whose mugs appear on the screen all the time are only the most prominent members of the *60 Minutes* family. And in reading through this reminiscence, I realize, with regret and dismay, how many others I've overlooked.

First, Palmer Williams. For a long time Palmer was, next to Hewitt, the mainstay of our operation. His early background was in newsreels, the visual precursor of TV journalism, and later, in the 1950s, he worked with Ed Murrow and Fred Friendly on those great *See It Now* documentaries at CBS. In 1968, when Hewitt put together the original staff for *60 Minutes,* he had the good sense to make this wise old pro his second-in-command.

As the senior producer of the broadcast, Palmer had strengths in certain areas where Hewitt was not at his best. Given his mercurial temperament, Don does not have much patience for details. So, Palmer soon evolved into our nuts-and-bolts man, the one who kept the house in order. He took charge of budgets and schedules, and made sure that correspondents, producers and camera crews converged on a given destination at the right time. But he was also in many ways the conscience of *60 Minutes*, especially during the early years when we were groping to find our identity. His sharp and experienced eye was an invaluable asset in the screening room; over the years it was Palmer, more than anyone else, who was likely to catch a small but critical error or weakness in a story we were preparing. And because Hewitt had no stomach for unpleasant confrontations, Palmer often had to shoulder the burden of resolving the internal disputes that flared up from time to time. Surrounded by fragile and outsized egos, he was adept at cooling passions and putting things back in perspective. When he retired a couple of years ago, his title and responsibilities passed into the able hands of Phil Scheffler, another veteran who has been working in television news since the early 1950s.

The importance of field producers on *60 Minutes* has been spelled out in an early chapter, and I hope that I have given them their due, if not all by name, then at least as a group. However, when a producer and I take to the road in pursuit of a story, we work with camera crews. They, too, are part of the collaborative process, and until now I have barely mentioned them. The key figure in any film crew is, of course, the cameraman. It is his eye, his attention to detail and movement that can deepen and enrich any story. The best of them are also good reporters; they help us keep the story in focus and remind us of questions we've forgotten to ask. In addition, the good ones are skilled at putting the people we talk to at ease; and this alone on occasion can transform a nervous encounter into a productive interview.

Good cameramen are not easy to find, so when we come across one, we do our best to hang on to him. (Or her; although it's a male-dominated field, there are some first-rate camerawomen, too.) Bob Clemens on the East Coast and Wade Bingham, who works out of Los Angeles, have been with us since *60 Minutes* first went on the air. Both men are now in their fifties and I can't think of a part of the world they haven't seen through their lenses. When you have either Bob or Wade on a shoot, no matter how adverse conditions are in the field, you know when you get back to the editing room in New York, the film you'll see will be exactly what you had hoped to see. Beyond this, their warm companionship over the years has often made my life on the road a lot more pleasant than it otherwise would have been. Invariably, after I've finished an assignment with Bob or Wade (or other good cameramen), I've felt that I haven't thanked them enough because they seldom get the credit they deserve. On *60 Minutes* and most other news programs, the cameramen are the unsung heroes behind the stories we see on the television screen.

What Bob Clemens and Wade Bingham are to their craft, Ken Dalglish is to his—film editing. In strictly technical terms, a film editor's job is to follow the instructions of a producer during the laborious and often tedious process of editing the raw footage of a story down first to a rough cut, and then to a fine cut that can be put on the air. But good film editors—and Dalglish is one of the best—bring far more to their work than mere technical skills. For when a producer returns to the editing room in New York with some twenty thousand feet of film, out of which he must shape a finished piece that will measure perhaps six hundred or eight hundred feet, he welcomes the fresh eyes of an editor in making those critical judgments. If he's working with a wise and resourceful film editor who has sound journalistic instincts of his own, then the chances of putting together a strong and affecting story are immeasurably enhanced. That's where someone with the experience and clear judgment of a Ken Dalglish can be invaluable. Now in his early sixties, Ken has done it all, and he knows what works and what doesn't work. Moreover, he has the good sense to realize when to offer advice and when to sit back and follow the producer's lead. Altogether, there are about twenty film editors who work on *60 Minutes,* and all are solid professionals who bring that extra dimension to the editing process. I've singled out Ken for special mention because, like Clemens and Bingham, he has been with us since the beginning of *60 Minutes,* and his work over the years has been consistently superior.

Last but far from least, there is Merri Lieberthal, who has been with me since the days before *60 Minutes* went on the air. Back in 1966, when I hired her as my secretary, she was a chubby, good-natured and mildly competent young woman, who much to my dismay, was given to crying jags on some of those infrequent occasions when I found fault with her work. However, she came with me when *60 Minutes* started up; and not long thereafter, she began taking on assignments that entailed more responsibility. Today, Merri is the program coordinator of *60 Minutes*, which means that her duties range from fiscal to editorial, and—in a less official sense—from sister confessor to scoutmistress. She is the one who makes the final tape edit that viewers see on Sunday night; she integrates the commercials, times the broadcast and, in the process, soothes the savage passions that erupt in the control room and the tape room every time we go on the air. I take special pride in her accomplishments, for the plain fact is that none of us on *60 Minutes* would get along very well without the calm professionalism she displays, often in the midst of wild disorder. Oh yes, I should also add that Merri hasn't cried in years, at least not in *my* presence, and having lost that baby fat, she is now fashion-model slim. (Not incidentally, the chores Merri used to perform for me have been carried out with similar virtuosity the past few years by my good and valued friend and assistant, Barbara Dury, a young woman whose composure under fire— mine—never ceases to amaze me.)

There are others, so many others, who should be mentioned, but I'm sure you get the picture that ours is a happy shop, as well as a productive one, and this, I think, is one of the reasons why *60 Minutes* has flourished. When this improbable adventure began in 1968, I was fifty years old, an age when many people in our business, though by no means past their prime, have some of their best years behind them. But my years on *60 Minutes* have been without question the most gratifying of my professional life; and not long ago, as I approached what I assumed would be the day of reckoning, my sixty-fifth birthday, I began to dread the prospect of having to give it all up. Oh, I tried to put the best face on it, to persuade myself that after forty-four years of banging around in radio and television, it was time to make a graceful exit. But when I was given the unexpected opportunity to elude retirement and stay with the broadcast for a few more years, I found I couldn't turn it down; the gravitational pull of the program and the people who work on it, with whom I've shared so much over so many years, was too strong to resist.

One person who would have been content had my decision gone the other way was my wife. As you've read, Lorraine has been a loyal and devoted friend and love over the years, and never more so than during the difficult fall and winter of 1962–1963 when, in the desolate days following the death of my son Peter, I struggled to reorder my priorities and move my career in another direction. But, being the supportive wife of a reporter who is compulsive about his job—a certified workaholic—has taken its toll, especially during the wander-lust years on *60 Minutes*. The sad fact is that Lorraine has had to suffer through too many nights alone, waiting for laggard telephone calls from Omaha or Managua or Beirut.

Based not only on my own experience but also on wistful conversations I have had with other reporters who have shared their private concerns with me, I know what a heavy strain all that time on the road puts on a marriage. I'm not talking about infidelity. That's not what robs this kind of marriage of its special intimacy. Instead, it happens because two separate lives are being lived under one name and ostensibly one roof, but without any consistent pattern that can be reliably determined in advance. It becomes impossible to establish the stable routine that provides the day-to-day foundation of most traditional marriages. Mainly because of all the traveling, so much that is consuming and engrossing in a reporter's life takes place outside the orbit of the home, beyond the ken of one's wife. No matter how much the stay-at-home mate tries to keep abreast of that "other half" of her husband's life, she can't help but feel that she's not really a part of it. Thus, slowly but inevitably, they grow apart, and without really meaning to do so. For Lorraine and me, it finally came to legal separation, with divorce con-templated, a sad ending to thirty years together. It's a stiff price to pay, and this is a point I try to stress when I talk to young people who, in their innocence, find themselves attracted to the "glamour" of a career in journalism.

Yet even with the example he had before him in his own family, my son Chris (Peter's younger brother) chose to earn his keep as a reporter. Following his graduation from Harvard, he got himself a job with the *Boston Globe*. From there, Chris moved into television news, first in Chicago, then in New York, then with NBC News in Washington, where, in recent years, he has been covering the Reagan White House. I am naturally proud of all he has accomplished in such a short time, but I have purposely refrained from making a big deal of his success in this book, and here's why: Chris is very much his own man with his own clear identity, and he never needed his father's name or notoriety to advance his career. He's done it on his own.

When Chris and his wife, Elizabeth, began to raise a family, they resolved that their children, Peter and Megan, would not be brought up in a home from which their father was gone much of the time. Having watched his old man lapse into the life of an ambitious, driven itinerant, Chris was determined to avoid that fate. And so, to his everlasting credit, he has made career concessions that keep him in Washington most of the time, close to Elizabeth and their children. As a result, he is plainly a more attentive husband and father than I ever was, and I respect him for it.

On the other hand, I haven't been completely derelict in that area, and among the paternal joys I've treasured over the years is one I inherited. When Lorraine and I were married in 1955, her daughter, Pauline, was seven, a sunny, outgoing youngster who didn't quite know what to make of this stranger who had come into her life. A few years went by during which we continued to eye each other a trifle warily. But in early 1963, when I went to work for CBS News, she was in high school and just starting to become aware of such exotic matters as politics and civil rights. Those were subjects I was covering as a reporter in those days, and the fact that I could talk about them with some presumed authority opened up a line of communication between us; the close and loving relationship we formed then has endured to this day. Pauline is now a successful businesswoman (she's the top executive at CONRANS U.S.A.), and her political views have undergone a drastic change over the years. Back in 1963 when she first began to ask me questions about current events, she was infatuated with the Kennedys, who were then in power; but she eventually got that out of her system, and nowadays she's the family conservative. I claim no credit for this conversion. Like Chris, Pauline has found her way on her own.

A few months ago, I was interviewed by a young reporter. (Young reporters seem to get a kick out of interviewing me. More often than not, they arrive at my office with an unmistakable gleam in their eye, as if to say, "Okay, buster, now it's *your* turn!") In the course of this interview, I was asked what I would choose for my epitaph. Since I had just recently dodged the bullet of imminent retirement, I made a point of reminding the reporter (she was depressingly young) that I was still working at my trade and was still maintaining a regular pulse beat, and therefore I hadn't given much thought to what may or may not be said about me when I'm gone. All the same, given the realities as an insurance actuary would no doubt be inclined to view them, I decided it was a legitimate question; so, after mulling it over, I came up with a three-word epitaph: "Tough—but fair." That may seem minimal, but to me that says it all, for I can think of no finer tribute to the kind of work I've tried to do. Tough—but fair.

In the meantime, happily, life—and its voyage of discovery—goes on, which means that you can be absolutely sure of one thing: Come hell or high water, we'll be back next week with another edition of *60 Minutes*.

INDEX

INDEX

Bestselling Thrillers — action-packed for a great read